CATHEDRAL WINDOW QUILTS

LYNNE
EDWARDS

THE CLASSIC FOLDED TECHNIQUE AND A WEALTH OF VARIATIONS

www.mycraftivity.com

A DAVID & CHARLES BOOK

David & Charles is an F+W Media Inc. company
4700 East Galbraith Road, Cincinnati, OH 45236

First published in the UK and USA in 2008
First UK paperback edition 2009

A catalogue record for this book is available from the British Library.

ISBN-13: 978-0-7153-2712-8 hardback
ISBN-10: 0-7153-2712-7 hardback

ISBN-13: 978-0-7153-2713-5 paperback
ISBN-10: 0-7153-2713-5 paperback

Printed in the USA by CJK
for David & Charles
Brunel House Newton Abbot Devon

Commissioning Editor: Jane Trollope
Desk Editors: Demelza Hookway and Bethany Dymond
Project Editor: Lin Clements
Art Editor: Sarah Clark
Layout: Sue Cleave
Production Controller: Ros Napper
Photographers: Simon Whitmore and Karl Adamson

Visit our website at www.davidandcharles.co.uk

David & Charles books are available from all good bookshops;
alternatively you can contact our Orderline on 0870 9908222
or write to us at FREEPOST EX2 110, D&C Direct, Newton
Abbot, TQ12 4ZZ (no stamp required UK only); US
customers call 800-289-0963 and Canadian customers
call 800-840-5220.

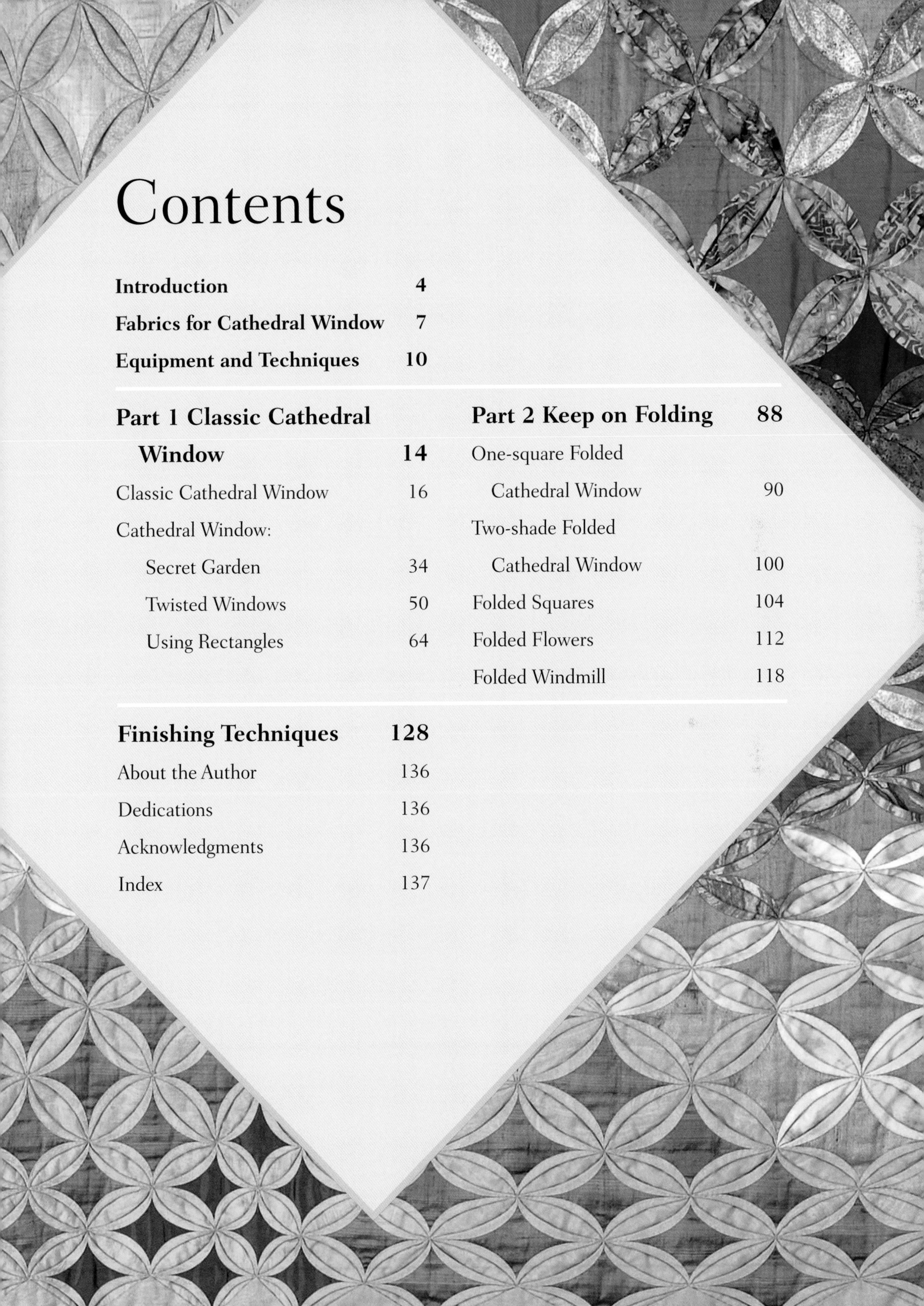

Contents

Introduction

Cathedral Window is a traditional patchwork technique, usually interpreted in old quilts as rows of folded squares of cream calico with a random arrangement of patterned fabric squares in the windows. It uses about four times its area in the folded squares, so is very greedy of fabric and makes a heavy quilt. Because I use a variety of fabrics and colours for both the folded squares and the overlying windows, I tend to make smaller pieces such as wall hangings, where the subtlety of the designs can be best appreciated.

The first documented evidence of the Cathedral Window design used in a quilt appeared at the Chicago World's Fair in the United States in 1933. Possibly its subsequent popularity in the US was partly due to the fact that it needed no backing or borders, and during those Depression years the only fabric most quilters had was a pile of plain cream-coloured corn sacks, which could make the folded squares and a few scraps of coloured fabric which made the windows.

Evidence of Cathedral Window patchwork has been seen more recently in China and Korea, where the design seems to go back several centuries. Aware of my interest in Cathedral Windows, many people have sent me samples and information. Anne Roberts from Sussex has a modern baby carrier that she bought in China which was made using the Cathedral Window design. She also found illustrations in a book on Chinese costume that showed the pattern. Known as the 'coin' pattern, it was a symbol of prosperity and was believed to ward off evil.

Opposite: Mandy Lovick started this quilt in 2003 while on holiday. After leaving London for Devon in 2004, their belongings were put into storage, including Mandy's sewing machine and fabric stash, so the Cathedral Windows work was re-started while they lived with friends and house hunted. The new home took up much of Mandy's time, so she carried on Cathedral-windowing, and one day realized she had enough for a single quilt – and here it is.

Left: A piece of traditional Cathedral Window from the United States made around 1960, given to me by Susan Harvey from Jersey.

Angela Chisholm from Edinburgh sent me extracts from a catalogue that accompanied a 1990 exhibition of Korean wrapping cloths. These are decorative cloths called *potaji*, used in Korea since the 15th century, which are used for wrapping, carrying or covering many objects. The cloths often include patchwork and a technique called *ciatamani*, which is what we know as Cathedral Window. A photograph in the catalogue shows a detail of one of these cloths, where the method of stitching back the curve – the spaced backstitch – is the same one that I use. With these two examples of a long tradition of the technique in the East, I wonder whether returning missionaries could have brought it back to the United States or England early in the 20th century. Most people's idea of Cathedral Window is this traditional one, as can be seen in the little block from Susan Harvey shown on page 4. It is also used wonderfully in Mandy Lovick's bed quilt (see previous page), where a whole collection of scraps begged from friends has been used for the windows and the design framed with a strong blue border strip.

A detail from my Candyfloss wall hanging (see page 74), a colourful combination of square and rectangular Cathedral Window blocks in gorgeous batik fabrics.

Using cream calico and scraps is just one approach to this technique. When I made my first Cathedral Window blocks years ago I had never seen a Cathedral Window quilt, so I launched straight into stronger colours and interesting textures. There were no quilt shops in those days offering specialist cotton fabrics, so I used patterned dress fabrics like Liberty Lawns, and for the plain colours went to the polished cotton fabric found in furnishing shops produced specifically as curtain lining. It was pure cotton, very cheap and came in a very wide range of shades. My aim was to use a collection of closely related shades so that I could combine blocks of all of these to creep the colour gently across the quilt rather than have strong contrast and those polished cottons fitted the bill nicely.

Now it's a different story. Quilt shops abound with a huge selection of exciting textures, batiks, marbled fabrics, exquisite prints and all in a multitude of colours and tones. How could we limit ourselves to cream calico with all these goodies to choose from?

Using This Book

- See pages 10–13 for useful information on the basic equipment you will need for Cathedral Window patchwork, plus the marking and cutting techniques required.
- The first section, Classic Cathedral Windows, describes in easy steps how to make a classic Cathedral Window block and I would suggest you begin here to familiarize yourself with the technique.
- This classic Cathedral Windows section is followed by chapters describing variations on that block, such as Secret Garden, Twisted Windows and windows using rectangles. The quilts in these chapters often use blocks based on all these techniques and refer back to earlier sections, to avoid repetition.
- The second part of the book, Keep on Folding, describes techniques similar to Cathedral Window in their appearance but not in their construction. They have the advantage of having raw edges, so they can be used in designs with other more conventional forms of patchwork if desired. They are intriguing and fun to do and if you want to dip into one of these areas rather than tackling Cathedral Window techniques first, that's fine.
- The majority of quilters use the imperial measuring system but metric equivalents have also been given throughout.
- On diagrams, the right side of the fabric is abbreviated to RS and the wrong side to WS.
- All seam allowances are ¼in (6mm) unless otherwise stated.

Fabrics for Cathedral Window

All my quilts start with stroking a collection of fabric, so this is for me an important aspect of any technique. I know Cathedral Window is very wasteful of fabric, but all the more excuse to buy some more, especially when the results are so gorgeous. In Cathedral Window designs there are two layers of fabrics to consider – the folded background layer plus the top layer of windows, so the choosing takes me even longer than usual.

Using the Right Fabric

Fabric for the background folded squares for Cathedral Window has to be folded into four layers and the bias folded edges pulled back into a curve, so medium-weight or even fine cotton is the best choice.

Test your fabric, in case you have one which, when pressed with a steam iron, will shrink in one direction but not the other – this happens with more fabric than you would expect. When in doubt, wash all your chosen fabric before use. I advocate this but seldom do it myself, I'm afraid. I just iron the piece of fabric before cutting it with as much steam as I can get from my iron, working on the principle that any shrinking will occur at that stage.

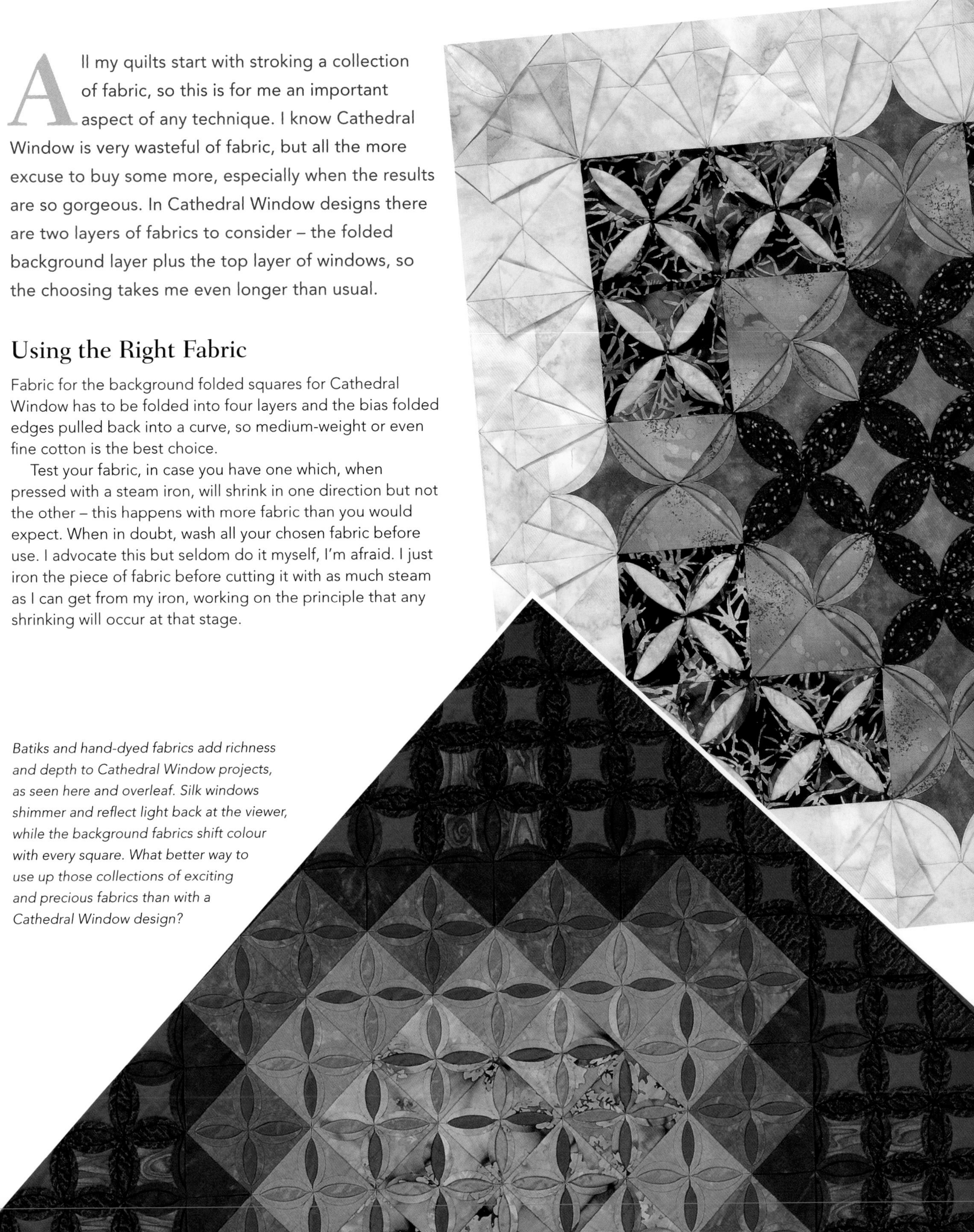

Batiks and hand-dyed fabrics add richness and depth to Cathedral Window projects, as seen here and overleaf. Silk windows shimmer and reflect light back at the viewer, while the background fabrics shift colour with every square. What better way to use up those collections of exciting and precious fabrics than with a Cathedral Window design?

If you need to use a fabric that is floppy or loosely woven, spray starch it thoroughly before cutting out the squares. Once the squares are cut it is too late to starch them, as the wet fabric will distort when it is ironed dry and will no longer be an accurate square, and accuracy is important here. Spray starch firms up the fabric beautifully, making it easier to cut and prepare it for stitching. As you begin to stitch and handle the fabric, it softens again.

Window Fabrics

The fabric appearing in the 'windows' can be made of virtually any fabric you wish to use. Stabilize flimsy or soft fabrics by backing them with a fusible (iron-on) interfacing before cutting out the windows. You can treat silky fabrics that fray badly in the same way to prevent the edges unravelling while you work. The window is placed on top of folded squares of the chosen background fabric, so you don't have to worry about the weights being equal or the fabrics being of the same type. Consider using silk or any kind of glitzy fabric as well as cottons. Thick velvets can be hard to handle with this technique, but if you don't mind struggling a bit, go for it. The windows need not even be made from a single fabric. For example, try foundation-piecing some miniature crazy patchwork for a window, or embellish with beads and decorative thread.

The back of my wall hanging, Winter Solstice, showing how I used different blacks and greys for the folded background squares.

What wonderful fabrics we have now to use in our quilts: pure cottons that fold well and are as complex and organic as a painted surface; batiks and marbled fabrics in all the shades we could desire. Perfect for Cathedral Window!

Making Colour Choices

I always take some time 'cooking' the fabrics for my pieces, arranging them on a surface, moving them around and generally getting the feel of the colour mixes.

Think of your design as two layers – the background folded shapes makes one design layer and the overlying windows makes the second, top layer. So, rather than having just one fabric for the background, find two or three that are closely related and use them for the folded layer to make a richer design. The back of my Winter Solstice quilt (below left) shows all the different blacks and greys that were used for the folded background squares in that design.

Similarly for the window design, use several shades that combine well and will look good lying on top of the background fabrics. These may be a stunning contrast like the gold windows used in Winter Solstice or a much more subtle colouring that blends in with the background layer, as in Fronds, shown right.

Start with your favourite fabric that you are aching to use and then study some of the pieces shown in the book to see which effects please you most. Add to your starting fabric with several others in the same team and once you have a good selection that will combine for the background layer, audition the second team for the overlying windows. You will have hours of harmless fun doing what we quilters really like to do best – arranging fabric, sighing over it and stroking it…

The front view of Fronds, showing the different shaped windows in various shades of silk, which flow across the background folded layer.

The front of Winter Solstice, showing the gold window fabrics, which glow brightly when teamed with the folded background squares.

Different textures and fabrics like cottons, silks and linen weaves can all be used in Cathedral Window designs, either in the folded background areas or for the overlying windows.

Equipment and Techniques

This section describes some of the basic equipment you will need for successful Cathedral Window patchwork. Much of this is equipment used for most patchwork techniques, but some may be new to you and one should never assume that everybody knows everything. There may well be a piece of equipment described here that will become your favourite tool in all your future projects – you just never knew about it before.

Cutting fabric accurately is important, for Cathedral Window blocks as well as other patchwork blocks, so cutting techniques are also described in some detail. In particular I deal with cutting squares rather than strips or small pieces as this seems to be an area that quilters are a little shaky on. They come up to me in workshops or at shows and say, 'I bought this square ruler because I know it's really useful but I can't remember why'…Hopefully these instructions will help guide you through, because those rulers really *are* useful.

Equipment

The following guidance on the equipment you will need to create the wonderful effects possible with Cathedral Window quilting should be useful, especially for those new to the technique.

Marking Pencils

A marking pencil is needed to draw round templates for odd shapes and windows. I use a fine wind-up lead pencil or a sharp watercolour pencil in white or blue if it shows better on the fabric. I also use watercolour pencils to mark any quilting that I might do in a border. These are also known as aquarelle pencils and are available from art shops in dozens of shades. For quilting I choose a shade similar to the fabric but dark enough to be seen clearly. The line wears off the fabric as it is stitched and can be lightly sponged to remove final traces.

Needles and Threads

Cathedral Window is one technique where I like to use a thread that matches as closely as possible the fabric, even for the initial machine stitching of the folded shapes. If you do have to ease the shapes to fit with the steam iron, there is nothing worse than seeing a line of tiny stitches showing up as if in neon along a seam. Using matching thread will prevent this from happening. A shade darker is better than lighter – the best test is to lay a thread across the fabric to see if it virtually disappears. I use cotton thread wherever possible, although if the shade that I need is only available in a polyester thread, then I will use that.

For the hand-stitched windows I sometimes use the very fine silk thread much favoured by appliqué enthusiasts, provided the colour of the thread suits my fabric. It is the near invisibility of the stitches that I am most concerned about.

I use 'sharps' or milliner's needles for the hand stitching in a size 10. The needle has to be strong enough to get through four layers of fabric, or even more at times, which means that the finer needles bend too easily. Sadly, I have to resort now to a needle threader at all times, which means the small eye is not a problem. Try the table-top needle threader – it's wonderful!

Pins

I could probably write a book on choosing the right pin for the right job. For all general pinning I use silk pins, which are fine and longer than the usual pins but still strong enough to stand up to pinning through several layers and even machining over them. For pinning the windows I use the shorter, fine appliqué pins so that the pins don't extend beyond the centre area. I find that thicker pins cannot get through the layers without distorting the fabric, and glass-headed pins drive me mad as I keep getting the thread wound round the heads as I stitch. However, these may be your absolute favourite, so do use whatever you find most comfortable and efficient.

Cutting Techniques

When I first started making Cathedral Window designs there was no rotary cutting equipment or even decent rulers – yes, I am that old… I used cardboard squares as templates, drew around them, then cut out the shapes with sharp scissors. Now we are all so used to short-cutting the tedious processes with easy-to-use, high-tech equipment that it would be very hard to go back to these early methods.

Cutting Out

I use rotary cutting cutters and rulers to cut all the squares I need for the background folded shapes. Odd shapes like the rectangles are not so easy and generally templates must be used, but this is only when there is no alternative. For the most frequently used rectangle size (folded rectangle 4in × 6in/10.2cm × 15.2cm see page 66), I've designed a specialist ruler that can be used with a rotary cutter to cut the starting shape more efficiently (see Creative Grids, page 136).

TIP

A sharp blade in your rotary cutter will help preserve your board as well as cutting layers of fabric more effficiently. You will be amazed at how much difference it makes!

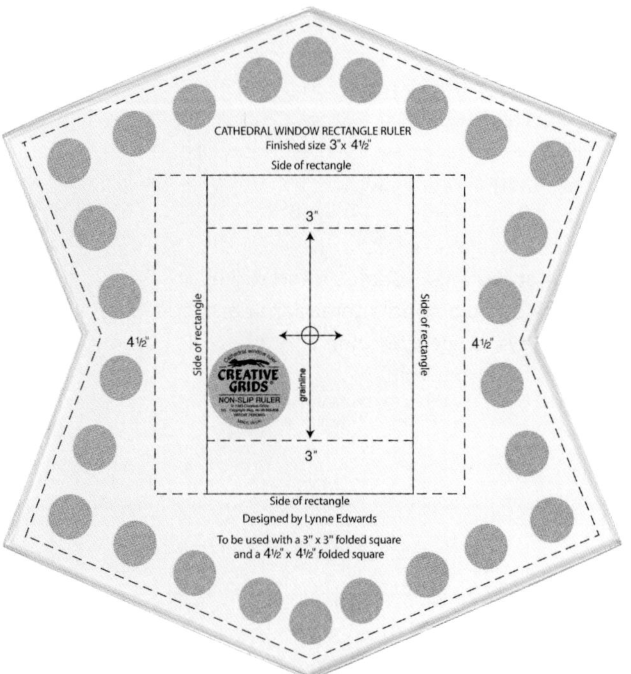

This Cathedral Window ruler will help you to cut out the odd shape speedily and accurately with a rotary cutter and board. Details of the size of squares that link with the rectangle are printed on the ruler so all information is at hand.

Cutting Squares

If you are an ace with all rotary cutting equipment you can give a sigh of quiet pride and ignore this section. If, however, you possess one of those square rulers that you bought because it's really useful but now you can't remember how or why, this may be helpful. If you want to buy just one square ruler for all general uses I would recommend the 12½in (31.8cm) square as it covers most projects.

Cutting Squares in Bulk

1 To cut a number of squares all the same size e.g., 8in × 8in (20.3cm × 20.3cm), cut a strip from the fabric as long as possible and in a width to match the chosen measurement of the squares (e.g., 8in/20.3cm). Straighten one end of the cut strip.

2 Place the strip horizontally on a cutting board so that the straightened end is on the left (Fig 1). Left-handers should place the cut end to the right and work from that end of the fabric. Stack several layers of fabric to save time if you wish.

Fig 1

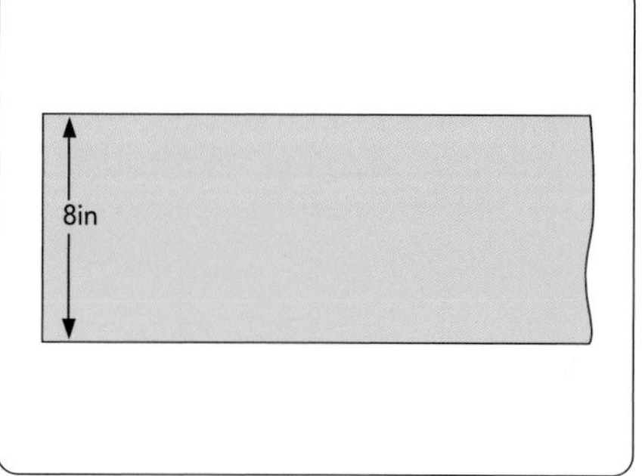

3 Place the square ruler on the fabric with the diagonal marking running from top right to bottom left. Move it across the fabric until the straightened end of the fabric and the bottom edge of the fabric strip are lying underneath the chosen measurement (e.g., 8in /20.3cm) on the square ruler (Fig 2). Left-handers should position the ruler with the diagonal marking running from top left to bottom right on the trimmed end of the fabric before moving it over the fabric to the correct marking. The fabric you see trapped under the square ruler is the square that you want.

Fig 2

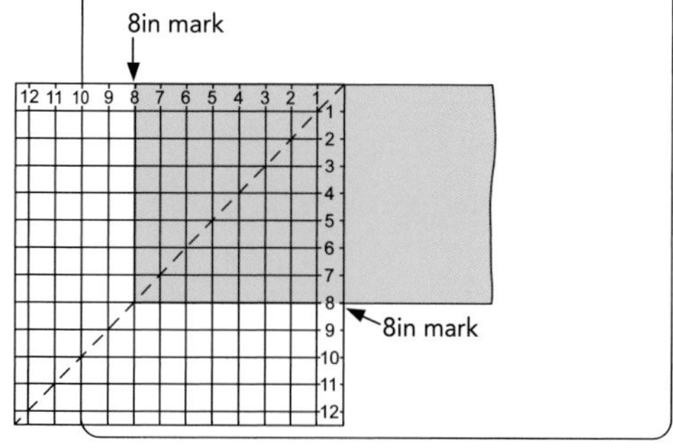

4 Cut along the right side of the ruler to make the square. Remove it from the board before repositioning the ruler on the fabric and cutting the next square.

TIP

If the squares you are cutting are not in a whole inch measurement e.g. 6½in × 6½in (16.5cm × 16.5cm), look closely at your square ruler. Many of them have an extra ½in (1.3cm) added on two sides (Fig 3). To make the ½in (1.3cm) markings as easy to see and use as the whole inch markings, just turn the ruler round through 180°. The extra ½in (1.3cm) strip will be along the top and down the right side. Left-handers should turn the square ruler until the diagonal marking runs from bottom right to top left with the extra strip along the top and down the left side. Move the ruler over the fabric until the trimmed end of the fabric and its bottom edge line up with the chosen measurement (e.g., 6½in/16.5cm) marked on the square ruler (Fig 4). Cut along the right side of the ruler to make the square.

Fig 3

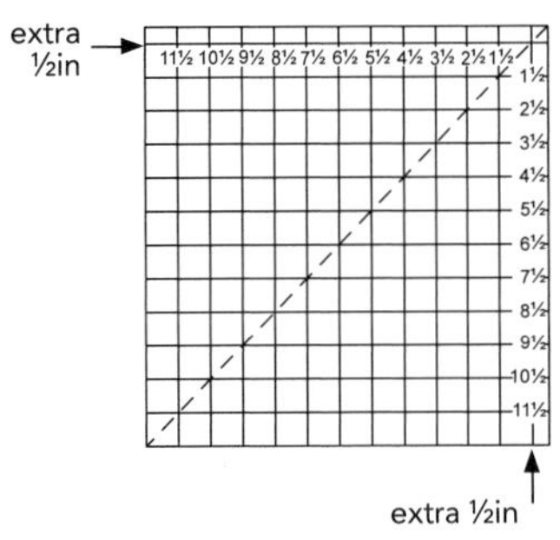

Fig 4

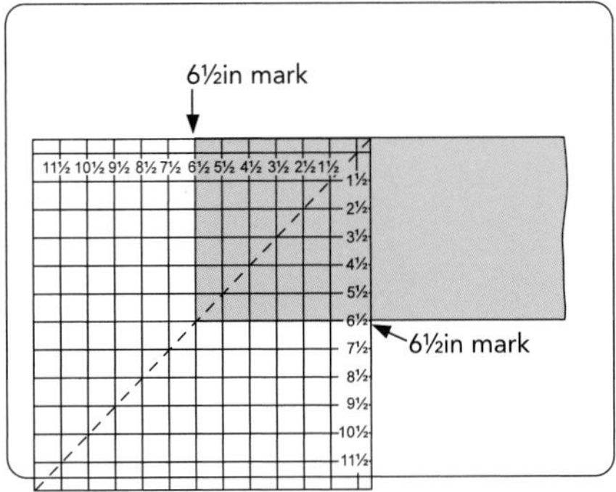

TIP

Many rotary cutters have retractable devices to make them extra safe, but I prefer the older models that have a guard which pushes on and off manually. Get into the habit of always pushing the guard up to protect the blade as you finish cutting every time and never ever lay the cutter down without the guard in position.

Cutting Just One Square

1 Place a corner of the fabric on the cutting mat and position the square ruler on it so that about ¼in (6mm) of fabric extends beyond it on two sides (Fig 5). Match the grain or weave of the fabric with the top and side of the square ruler.

Fig 5

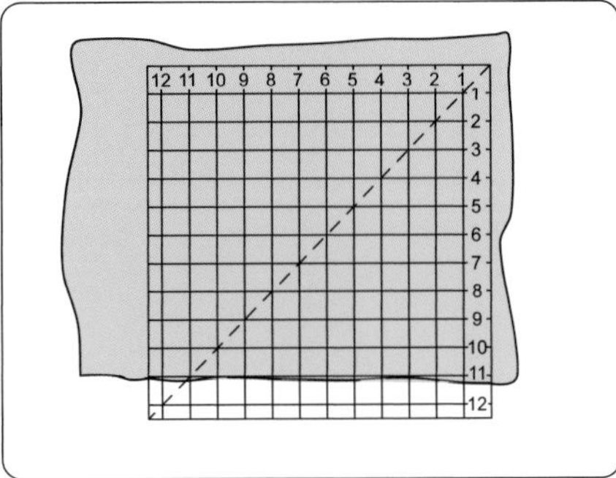

2 Trim these two edges by cutting along each length with a rotary cutter (Fig 6). Left-handers should work from the left side of the fabric.

Fig 6

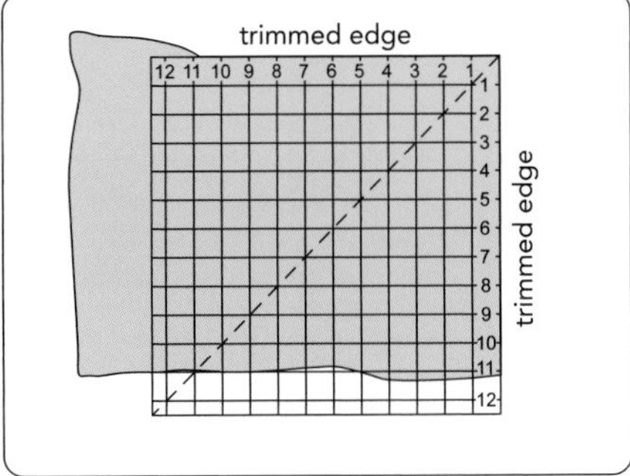

3 Turn the fabric through 180°, so that the two cut edges are at the bottom left corner. To cut an 8in (20.3cm) square, place the square ruler on the fabric with the diagonal marking running from top right to bottom left. Move it across the fabric until the two trimmed fabric edges are lying underneath the 8in (20.3cm) lines on the square ruler (Fig 7). Left-handers should position the ruler with the diagonal marking running from top left to bottom right on the trimmed corner of fabric before moving it over the fabric to the correct marking. The fabric you see trapped under the square ruler is the square that you want.

Fig 7

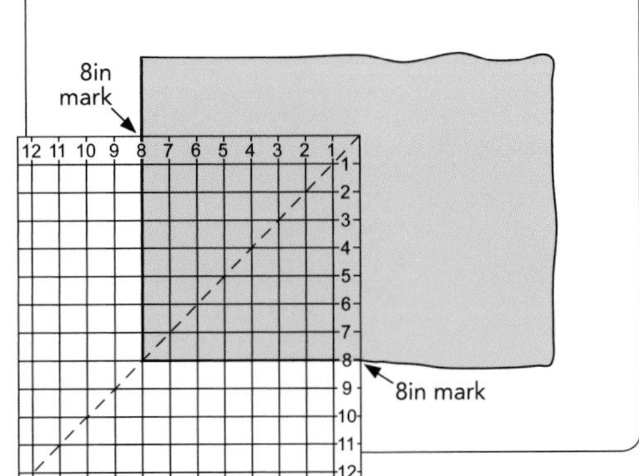

4 Cut along the remaining two sides of fabric to complete the 8in (20.3cm) square.

TIP

If a ½in (1.3cm) measurement such as 6½in (16.5cm) is needed and your square ruler has the extra ½in (1.3cm) feature, first trim two sides as before. Then turn the ruler round so that the diagonal line is running from bottom left to top right with the extra ½in (1.3cm) strip along the top and down the right side (Fig 8). Left-handers should turn the ruler until the diagonal marking runs from bottom right to top left with the extra strip along the top and down the left side. Move the ruler over the fabric until the two trimmed edges of fabric line up with the 6½in (16.5cm) markings on the square ruler. Cut along the remaining two sides of fabric to complete the square.

Fig 8

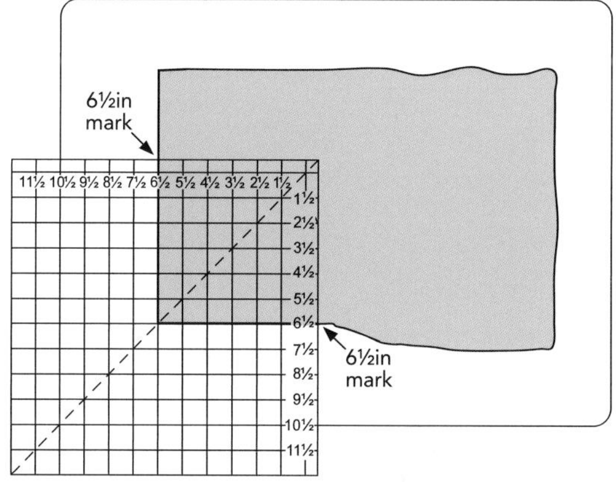

TIP

If you run over a pin with your rotary cutter, the blade will be damaged and will never cut completely cleanly again, and rotary cutter blades can be expensive. So before laying the fabric in place on the cutting board, sweep your hand over the surface of the board to move aside any rogue pins that may be lying in wait there. If you use a smaller size rotary cutter, which will easily cut two or three layers at a time, the replacement blades are half the price of the larger version!

Making Templates

For the overlying square windows I use rotary cutting equipment to cut as many as I need speedily and efficiently. If I want to cut a specific section of fabric such as a flower or star, I make a template for the window shape from template plastic so that I can place it exactly in position on the design and draw round it. I still use a rotary cutter and ruler rather than scissors to cut the window out, but you use any method that suits you. Oddly shaped windows that occur in some of the complex designs must be made as templates and drawn around individually in the usual way.

When making a template from those printed in this book, trace the desired shape on to good quality tracing paper, including the arrow that shows the direction of the grain or weave of the fabric. Cut out the traced shape roughly, keeping about ¼in (6mm) outside the drawn outline. Stick this on to card and then cut out the exact outline through both tracing paper and card. Try to cut just inside the drawn lines as this keeps the measurements accurate as you draw round the template on the fabric. Alternatively, make the templates from clear template plastic.

TIP

Try using freezer paper as an alternative to tracing paper (available from most quilt shops). Trace the shape on to the non-shiny side of the freezer paper. Cut the shape out roughly as described above. Place the cut shape shiny-side down on a piece of card and iron it with a medium-hot iron. The freezer paper will bond on to the card and you can then cut out the template in the usual way.

Using the Sewing Machine

When I first explored Cathedral Window I treated it as a hand technique from start to finish. I used to construct the folded squares by hand using a steam iron, but over the years I have switched to the envelope method and to stitching by machine, although all the stitching may be done by hand if preferred. I like the machine for this part of the job because it is more secure and speeds up the tedious preliminary processes, giving me more time for the delicious hand-work with the windows.

I have always joined the folded squares together by oversewing or whip stitching the folded edges by hand, much like English patchwork over papers. This is a process that I really enjoy, finding the gentle oversewing very restful and therapeutic. I am very aware, however, that such activities are not everyone's pleasure. I realized that if I wanted Cathedral Window to have as wide an appeal as possible, I needed to find alternative ways of doing the preliminary stages more quickly by machine – that way both the hand workers and the machinists can explore the technique in the medium that they most enjoy. Although I believe that the final stage of stitching the rolled edge over the added window fabric is essentially a hand process, I know that clever machinists will enjoy themselves perfecting it by machine. Well, they would do, wouldn't they? Meanwhile what I have done is take the stitching together of the folded background squares or rectangles and offer a machined method as an alternative to oversewing by hand (see Joining Square Blocks by Machine, page 20). For the machining, a basic straight stitch with an accurate ¼in (6mm) seam allowance is all that is required, so even an ancient hand machine would do. Use a new 80/11 size needle for medium-weight cotton fabrics or a 70/9 for lightweight fabric.

Classic Cathedral Window

Mastering the basic technique of making a classic Cathedral Window folded square is the basis of all the other Cathedral Window variations described in this section. It is not difficult at all – you just need each part of the process set down clearly and explained step by step. So the section that follows is the key to the treasure that is Cathedral Window.

Classic Cathedral Window

Classic Cathedral Window is a wonderful technique that uses folded squares joined together to make a background on to which smaller pieces of fabric are stitched to create a second design layer of squares on point. Coupled with striking fabrics, the effect can be stunning, as seen by the Bright Batiks wall hanging opposite. This basic principle can be developed in many exciting ways, allowing you to create some gorgeous effects, as you will see throughout this book.

Before embarking on a larger project it is a good idea to make one Cathedral Window unit to get your hands and head round the technique and the following section describes this process in detail. This finished block can be developed into a simple pincushion project – see page 24.

If you are happy to join the folded squares in the traditional way by hand, oversewing or whip-stitching the blocks together, follow the instructions given here. If you would like to try the totally machined technique, follow steps 1–7 overleaf and then turn to the unit Joining Square Blocks by Machine on page 20 and follow that instead.

'When making your first Cathedral Window block, start with a simple pincushion, which if not perfect technically, can be swiftly passed on to a less judgemental non-quilter friend.'

Marbled and batik fabrics in beautiful colours were used to create this striking wall hanging, Bright Batiks, which showcases the Cathedral Window technique perfectly in the central area. It also features two variations – Secret Garden and a final border of Twisted Windows. See the instructions on page 53 and also the picture on page 54.

Making a Cathedral Window Unit

1 To make a single Cathedral Window unit as in Fig 1, cut from the chosen background fabric two squares each measuring 8in × 8in (20.3cm × 20.3cm). This size is a good one to learn with and perfect for a pincushion. It was also used by Janet Covell for her wall hanging on page 32.

Fig 1

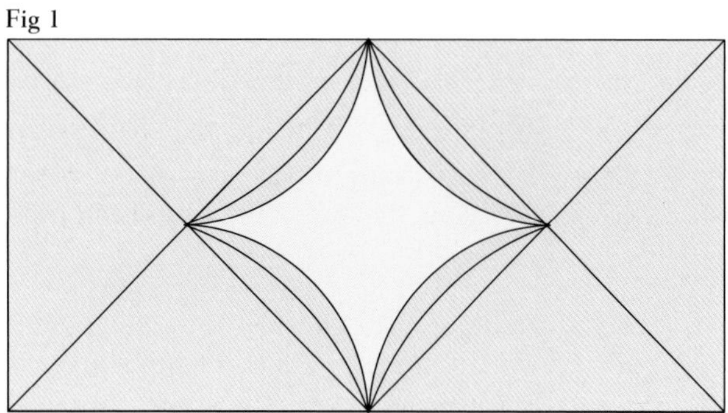

2 Fold each cut square in half with right sides facing. Pin and stitch an exact ¼in (6mm) seam at either end (Fig 2). I use the machine to do this and stitch both squares at once, stringing them through the machine in a chain, one after the other. Leave about 1½in (3.8cm) of thread between each stitched square. Cut the linking threads after stitching to separate the folded squares (see Tip below).

Fig 2

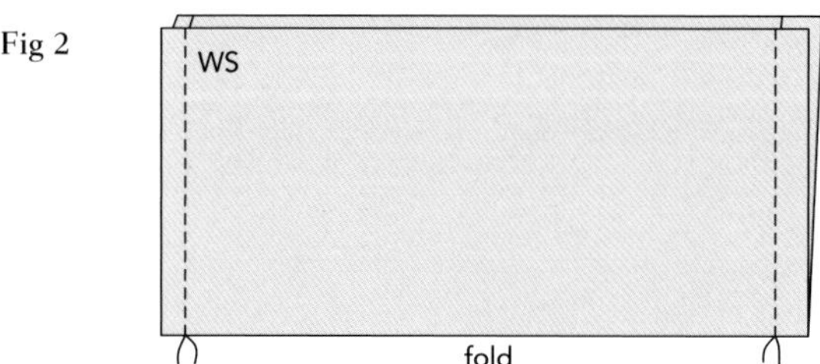

3 Trim the two folded corners diagonally to within ⅛in (3mm) of the stitching to reduce the bulk of the fabric (Fig 3). Finger-press the two stitched seams open.

Fig 3

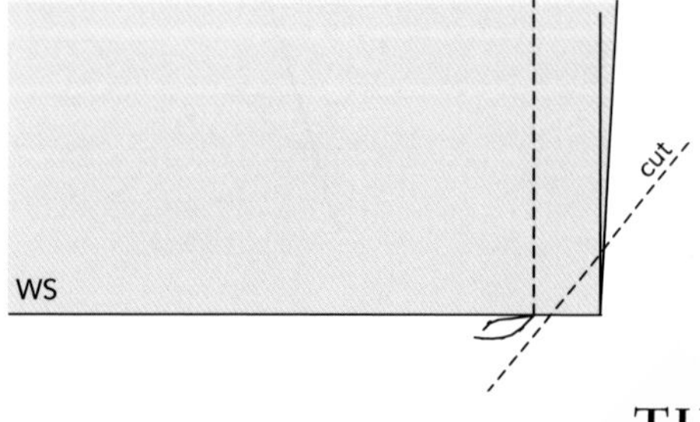

TIP

Leave about ¾in (1.9cm) of machine threads hanging at the folded end of each seam. Use the threads to help pull the corner out as you finger-press the seam open.

Cutting the Squares

Each folded square of background fabric starts out as a larger cut square. There is an easy way to calculate this: choose the finished size of the folded square, e.g., 3in × 3in (7.6cm × 7.6cm). Double this measurement and then add ½in (1.3cm) for the seam allowances – this will be the size of the cut square of fabric needed at the start. For example, a 3in x 3in (7.6cm × 7.6cm) folded square will need 3in + 3in + ½in (7.6cm + 7.6cm + 1.3cm) = a 6½in (16.5cm) cut square of fabric.

I use this size for most of my projects, especially for those mixing squares and rectangles as the calculations are simpler. Alternatively I like to use a larger square (cut 8in × 8in / 20.3cm × 20.3cm) which is a nonsense mathematically as it finishes up as a 3¾in × 3¾in (9.5cm × 9.5cm) folded square, but is visually very satisfying and a comfortable size to work with. Refer to the table below for other cutting and finishing sizes.

Cut size of fabric square	Finished size of block
4½in × 4½in (11.4cm × 11.4cm)	2in × 2in (5.1cm × 5.1cm)
6½in × 6½in (16.5cm × 16.5cm)	3in × 3in (7.6cm × 7.6cm)
8½in × 8½in (21.6cm × 21.6cm)	4in × 4in (10.2cm × 10.2cm)
10½in × 10½in (26.7cm × 26.7cm)	5in x 5in (12.7cm × 12.7cm)
12½in × 12½in (31.8cm × 31.8cm)	6in x 6in (15.2cm × 15.2cm)

4 Pull the open edges of the folded square apart and refold with the seamlines matching. Pin, then stitch from each corner to within 1in (2.5cm) of the centre seam, leaving longer threads at the folded ends as before (Fig 4).

Fig 4

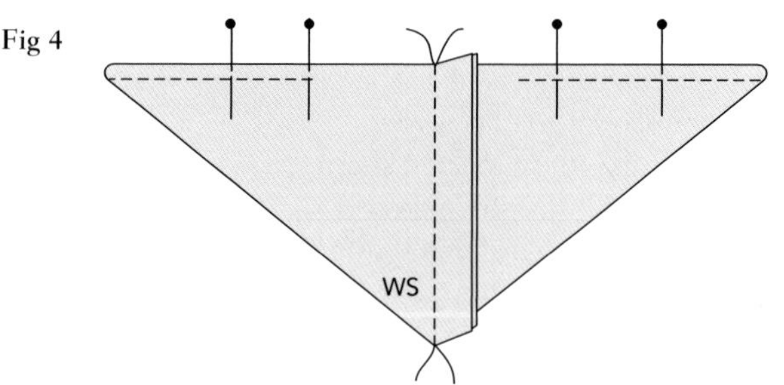

5 Trim the two remaining corners and pull the threads as before while finger-pressing the seams open, including the unstitched section across the centre of the square (Fig 5).

Fig 5

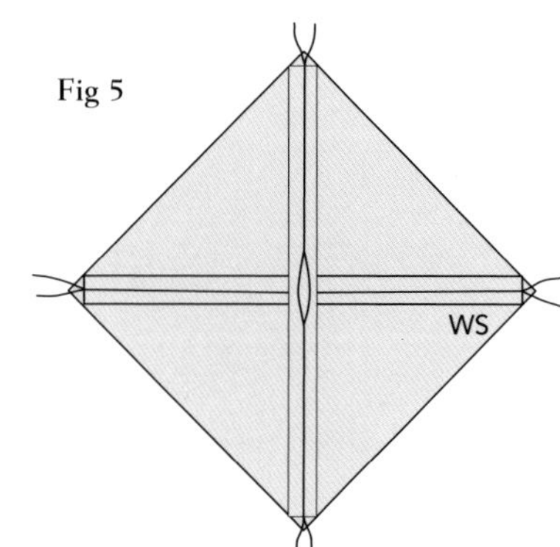

6 Turn each folded square right side out through the centre opening. Use a large pin (i.e., one that isn't too sharp and doesn't do too much damage) to ease out each corner. Hold the opened seam allowances firmly between thumb and forefinger as you turn so that they stay open. The aim is to finish up with the corners of the square as flat and pointed as possible (Fig 6).

Fig 6

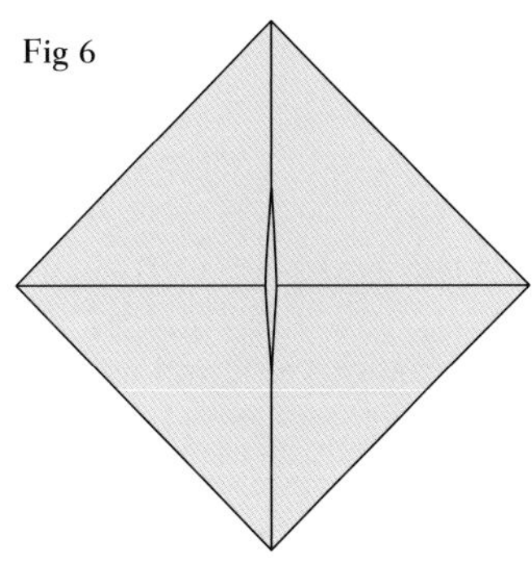

7 Using a steam iron, take one square of fabric and press lightly around the outer folded edges, pulling the corners out as much as possible as you do so. Don't expect the shape to lie flat at this stage – fabric seldom behaves as you wish it to! If you wish to join blocks by machine, turn to steps 1–12 Joining Square Blocks by Machine page 20.

8 Bring two adjacent corners (A and B in Fig 7) to meet at the centre of the folded square. Ideally they will meet at the centre and make a sharp outer corner. If not, and the outer corner is blunt, don't worry – this often happens. To correct it, pull corners A and B together over the centre area a little, keeping them level with each other. Pinch the outer corner to make it sharp and press firmly with the steam iron, ironing from the outer corner in towards the centre. The two folded edges of fabric being pressed are on the bias

Fig 7

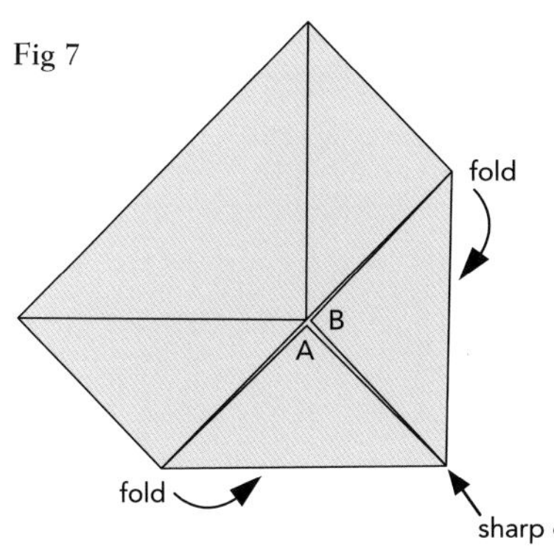

Fig 8

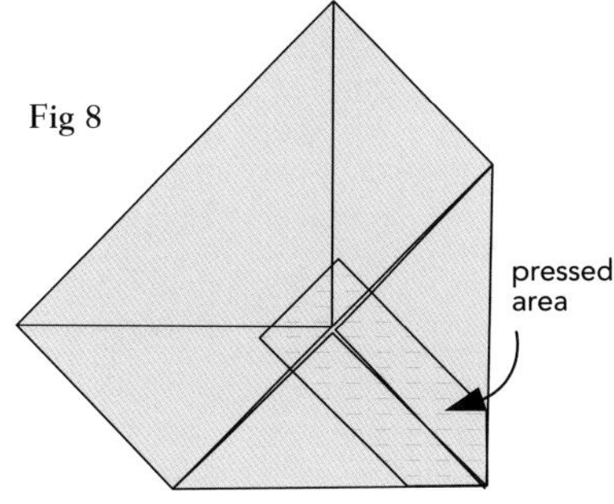

and can be shrunk slightly with a steam iron. Restrict the pressing area to a narrow strip between the outer corner and the centre. Leave the rest of the outer folded sides unpressed at this stage (Fig 8). The important thing is to have a really sharp outer corner. Never press from the centre of the square outwards or you will lose those sharp corners. If corners A and B do not reach the centre of the square but seem too short, just pull them – they are bias and will stretch easily.

9 Bring corner C in to the centre. Adjust corner B if necessary so B and C are level with each other. Pinch the outer corner to sharpen it and press in the same way as the first corner. Treat problems in the same way as before (Fig 9). Press, ironing only a narrow strip from the new sharp corner into the centre. If corners A, B and C are not all meeting dead centre, don't worry too much – it's sharp outer corners that matter.

Fig 9

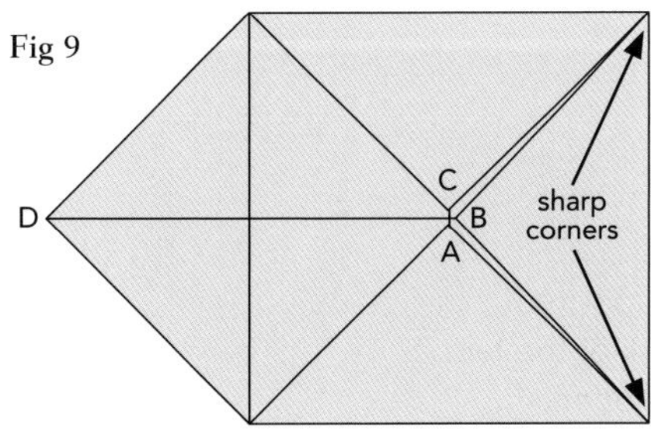

10 Repeat the process with corner D, making a sharp corner between C and D first, then tackling the corner between D and A (Fig 10).

Fig 10

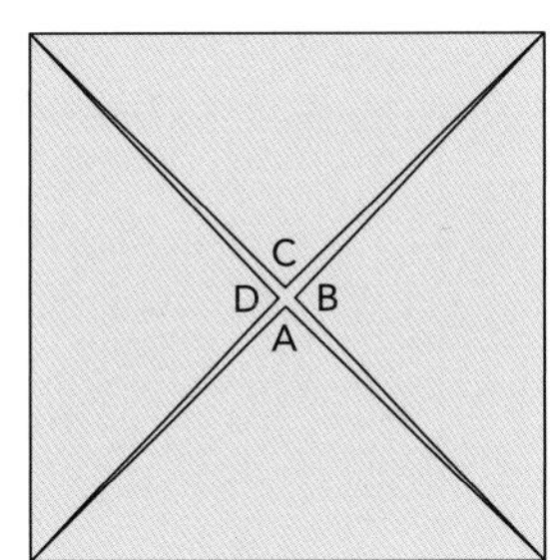

11 Once all the corners are fixed, press the whole block with the steam iron, pressing along the outside edges and then from the outer corners towards the centre.

Stitching the Folded Square

1 Open out the folded corners to reveal the centre with its unstitched section. If necessary pull the folded edges together at the centre until they meet.

2 Using a thread that matches the fabric and a fine sewing needle, knot the end of the thread and pass the needle through the open area into the fabric from front to back at the centre of the folded square (Fig 11). The knot will be hidden under the top layers of fabric. To close the opening in the centre, draw the two edges together and take two tiny stitches to make a cross at the centre through all layers, ending with the needle at the back of the work (Fig 12).

Fig 11

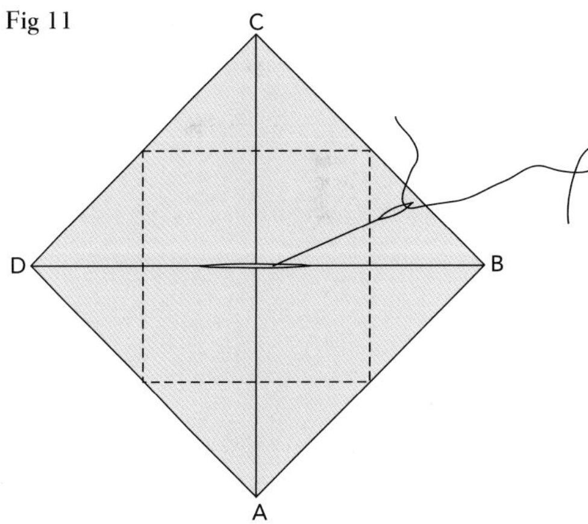

Fig 12

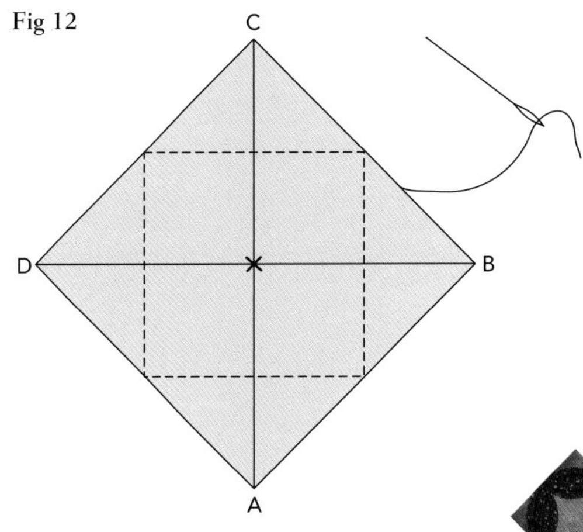

3 Bring the four corners into the centre as previously pressed. Stitch the two opposite corners A and C down with one small stitch though all the layers at the centre. Arrange corners B and D so that they fit snugly alongside A and C, not sitting on top of them. Stitch these two corners down with one stitch through all the layers. The stitches will form a tiny cross at the centre of the folded square. Pull the stitches really firmly and repeat (Fig 13).

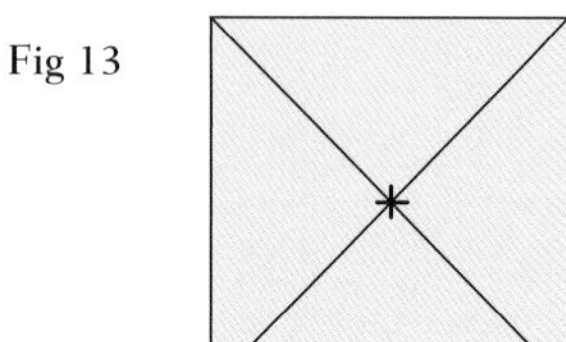
Fig 13

4 Finish off at the back with two tiny stitches through the back layer only and run the needle into the back layer for about 1in (2.5cm) before cutting off the thread to keep the back looking neat.

5 Repeat this folding, pressing and stitching on the other 8in × 8in (20.3cm × 20.3cm) square of background fabric.

Joining Folded Squares by Hand

1 The folded squares can be joined by hand or machine – see right for machine instructions. To join by hand, place the two folded squares together with folded sides facing. It is important that the corners match exactly. If this presents a problem, try turning the squares round until you find two sides that match. If one of the sides to be stitched is still shorter than the other, place the squares together with the shorter side on top, nearer to you. Match the corners and fix them with a pin (Fig 14). As you hand stitch, the top fabric will stretch slightly and ease to fit the longer bottom edge.

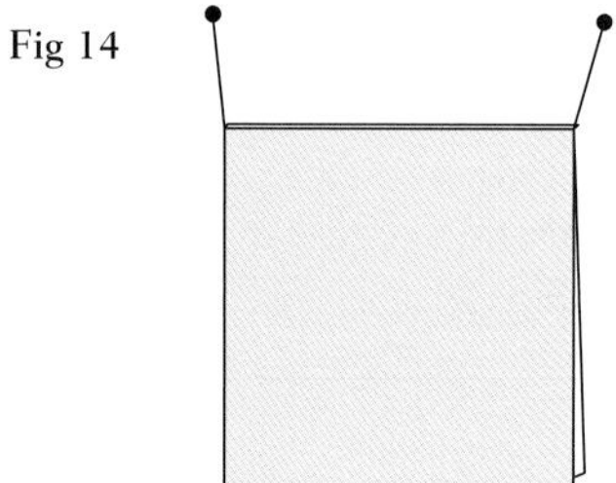
Fig 14

'Don't ask why when two identical squares will not fit together: fabric is totally wayward. Most problems in quilt-making are with trying to get badly behaved fabric to do what we want. Never blame yourself, always blame the fabric. . .'

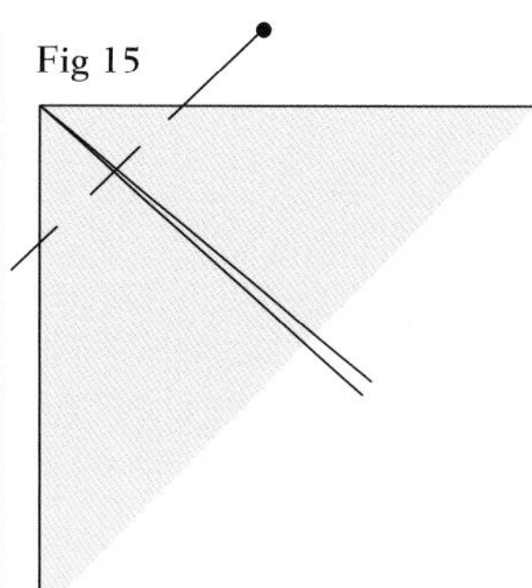
Fig 15

TIP

If a corner has lost sharpness, pinch it into shape and pin it about ¼in (6mm) from the corner (Fig 15). Keep the pin in position until the folded square has been joined to another.

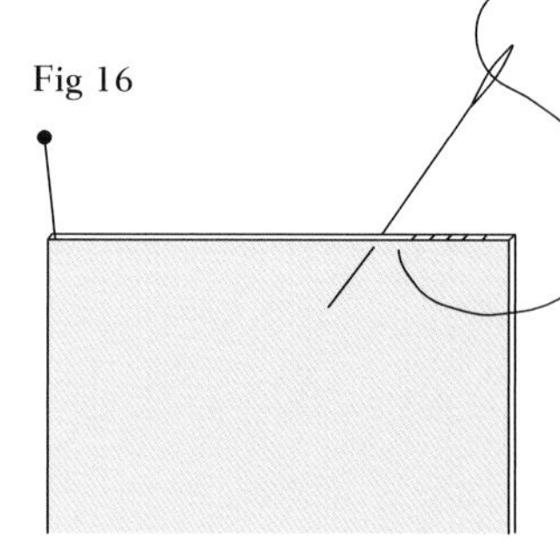
Fig 16

2 Start with a double stitch at the corner, not a knot as this will pop through to the front and show. Oversew the two edges together, spacing the stitches regularly about 1/16in (1.5mm) apart (Fig 16). This stitch is also known as whip-stitching and is used to join together hexagons and other shapes that have been tacked over papers as English patchwork.

3 Remove the end pin as you approach it. Finish with two stitches on top of each other and then stitch back a couple of stitches before running the needle through just the bottom layer of fabric for ½in (1.3cm) or so and cutting the thread. Once the two folded units are joined together, move on to Adding the Windows on page 22.

Joining Square Blocks by Machine

1 Cut and stitch the background squares in the usual way, following steps 1–7 from Making a Cathedral Window Unit on page 18. Do not press the corners into the centre the second time – leave them as in Fig 6 on page 19.

Marking the Stitching Lines

2 Measure along each side of the stitched square of fabric. A square that started out as 8in × 8in (20.3cm × 20.3cm) should now measure approximately 5¼in (13.3cm) along each side. A square that started out as 6½in (16.5cm) should now measure approximately 4¼in (10.8cm) along each side. If your squares are not this measurement, or are slightly different on each side, don't worry. You just need to find the exact mid-point of each side and mark it lightly with a marking pencil as in Fig 17.

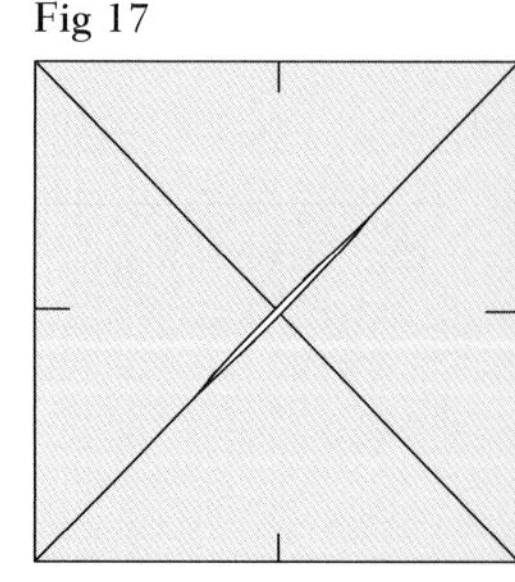
Fig 17

3 Join the marked points with a marking pencil, keeping the marking as light as possible, especially in the corners, where the marks may show slightly when the edges are rolled back and stitched later (Fig 18).

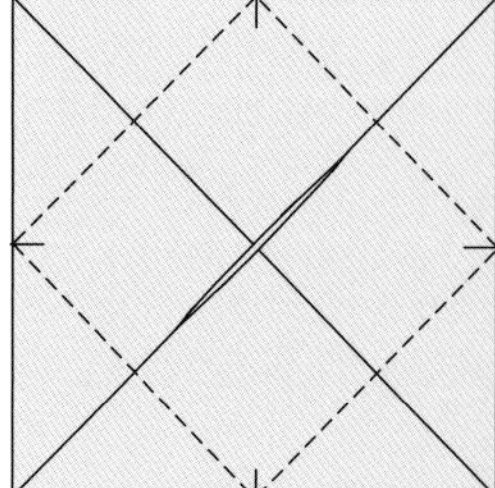
Fig 18

4 Mark every background square in the same way, keeping the pencil marks really light at all times.

TIP

If you are creating an original design and are not sure where each folded background square should be positioned in the final design, arrange them on a design board in their final smaller folded shape. Bring the corners of each marked square into the centre and pin them into place without pressing (Fig 19). Now you can place them on the board and make design decisions.

Fig 19

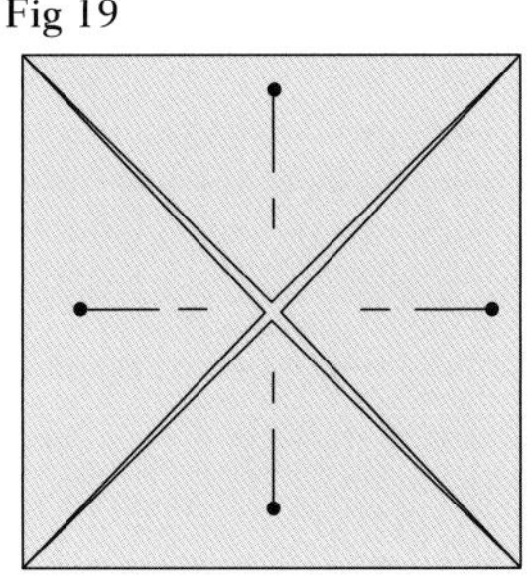

Machining the Blocks Together

5 Take the squares to be used in the top row of the design. Arrange them in a line as in Fig 20. If you need to check how they will look finally, pin the corners of each block into its centre as described in the tip above.

Fig 20

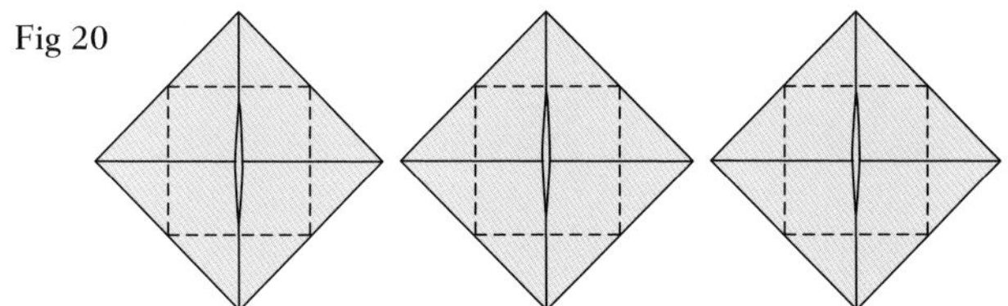

6 Take the first two blocks in the row to be joined together. They will be stitched together along the marked lines indicated in Fig 21. Place the two squares together with the unmarked sides facing and the two marked stitching lines positioned on top of each other. Match the marked mid-line points at either end of the stitching lines exactly and pin together (Fig 22). The corners of the blocks should also match each other, but this is less important – don't worry too much if they don't. Pin through all layers in two more places, checking that the marked lines are exactly matched.

Fig 21

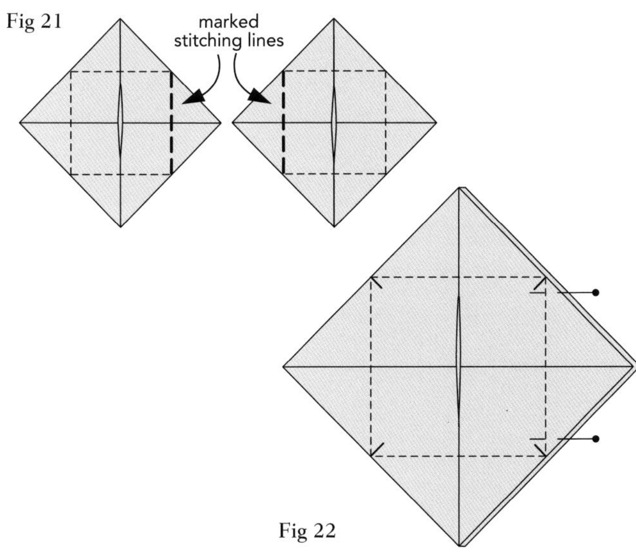

Fig 22

7 Use a thread on the machine that matches as closely as possible the fabric of the folded squares. If the two squares to be joined are different colours, use a matching thread for the top square of the layer and a different colour thread in the bobbin to match the bottom square of fabric. Fiddly, I know, but necessary if the stitching is to remain unseen in the final design.

8 It is the stitching at either end of the marked lines that is the most visible in the finished design, so it is best not to start and finish stitching at these places. I begin about ¼in (6mm) from the end of the marked line and stitch *towards* the outer edge (Fig 23). At the end of the marked line, absolutely on the edge of the fold, I sink the needle into the fabric, lift the pressure foot of the machine and turn the fabric round through 180°. Then I stitch along the marked line until I get to the other end. Again, I stop right on the folded edge, lift the foot, turn the work through 180° and stitch back along the line for about ¼in (6mm) before finishing and cutting the threads.

Fig 23

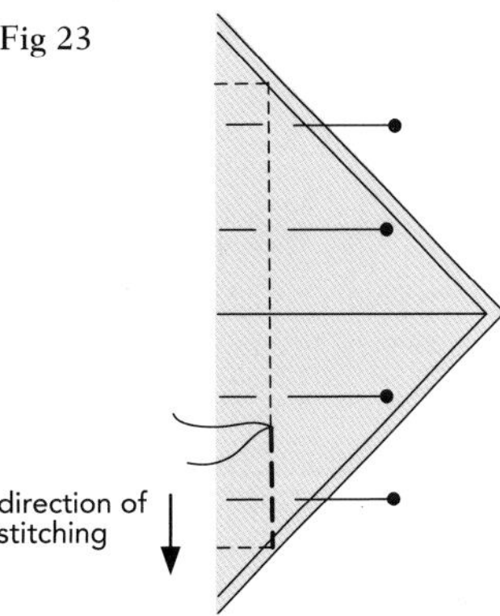

9 Repeat this to join the next fabric square to the joined pair. Continue to pin and stitch the whole row of squares together to make the top row of the design.

10 Pin and stitch the design in horizontal rows. Press the corners of the stitched seams to the centre of each block and pin in place (Fig 24).

Fig 24

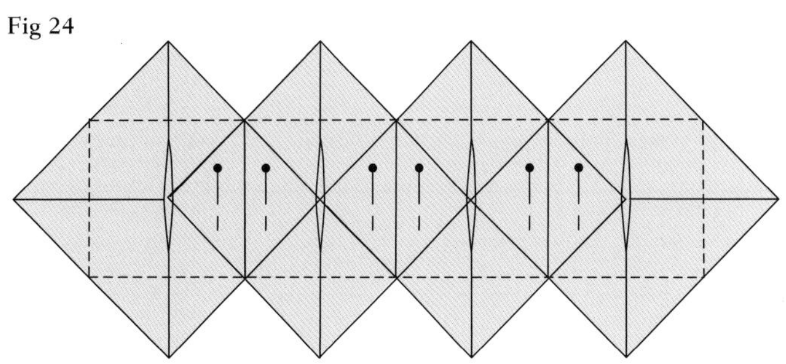

'I thought the stage of joining the rows by machine was going to be really tricky, but it proved to be surprisingly easy.'

Joining the Rows by Machine

11 Take the top two rows of the design and place them together with the unmarked sides facing and the marked stitching lines positioned on top of each other as before. Match the mid-point marks exactly and pin either side as in Fig 25. Add more pins to fix the two marked lines exactly on top of each other and stitch as before, stitching across the matched mid-point marks from one end of the pinned squares to the other. Start and finish ¼in (6mm) from the ends as in step 8. If the stitching does not always run exactly through the drawn lines on both sides of the work, don't worry – all that matters is that it is a perfect match at the junctions where the mid-point markings lie.

Fig 25

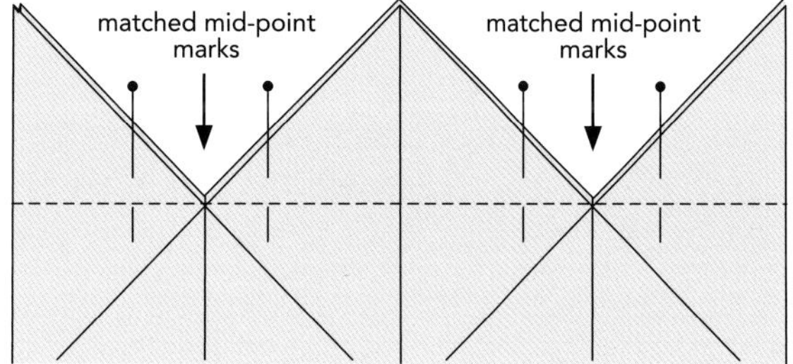

12 Repeat this to join the next row of squares to the design. Join all the rows together in this way to complete the background design. Once done, the corners of the blocks can be pressed to the centre and stitched into place, following steps 1–5 in Stitching the Folded Square on page 19. Now move on to Adding the Windows, below.

Adding the Windows

1 Measure from the centre of a folded square diagonally to one corner. Subtract ¼in (6mm) from this measurement. This is the size of the square of fabric that will make the window. For the folded square that began as an 8in × 8in square cut one window measuring 2⅜in × 2⅜in (6cm × 6cm).

2 Two background folded squares when joined together create a centre square on point (Fig 26). This is where the extra square of window fabric is positioned. Pin the window in place, keeping the pins in the centre area, not around the edge (Fig 27).

Fig 26

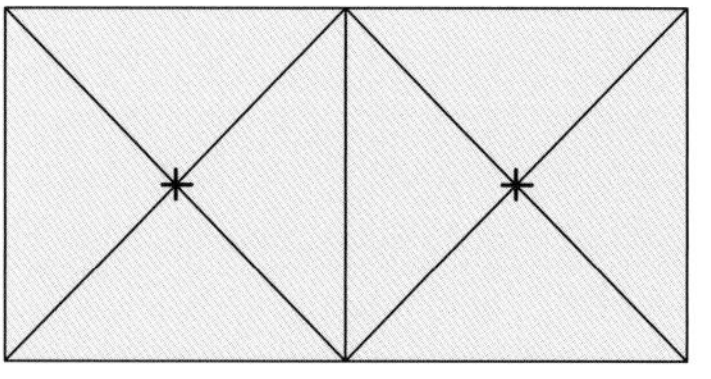

Fig 27

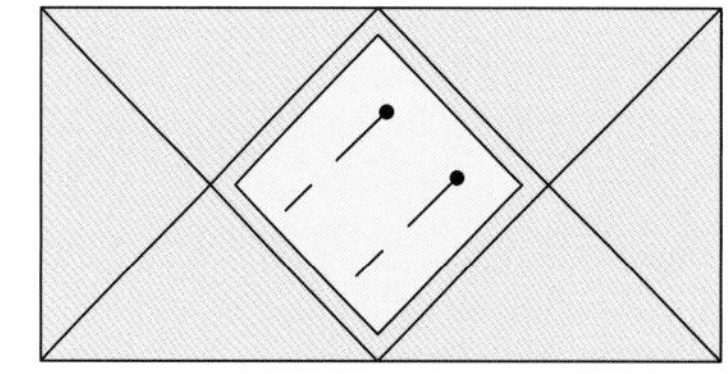

TIP

If you want to use a specific area of a piece of fabric in the window such as a flower or star, you need to cut a square template in the appropriate size from template plastic so that you can position it exactly in the right position on the fabric before drawing round it and cutting it out. Remember that the window is arranged on point as in Fig 27, so place the template on the fabric to match this. The outer ¼in (6mm) of the cut square will be lost when it is covered by the curved edge of the background fabric (Fig 28). For most fabrics I just cut squares of the required size with a rotary cutter and ruler as usual.

3 Trim the window fabric down if necessary until about ⅛in (3mm) of the background fabric shows on all sides. If your fabric is bulky you may like to cut a slight curve along each side to reduce the bulk when the background fabric is rolled over it. If so, do not trim away at the corners of the window fabric – leave them at the original ⅛in (3mm) distance from the background fabric.

TIP

To give the window a smooth, slightly rounded finish I sometimes cut a smaller square (about 1½in × 1½in/3.8cm × 3.8cm) of thin wadding and place it on to the background square before laying the window square on top of it. This is especially useful when the window is a fine fabric or silk, which tends to sink into the centre seam and show a slight crease along it.

4 Starting at the top centre corner (the corner that has the seam joining the two folded squares underneath it), roll the surrounding border on one side of the window over it, stretching the bias edge to create a curve. Don't be afraid to really stretch that edge so that the curve measures at least ¼in (6mm) in the centre. Pin the curved edge at the centre as in Fig 28.

Fig 28

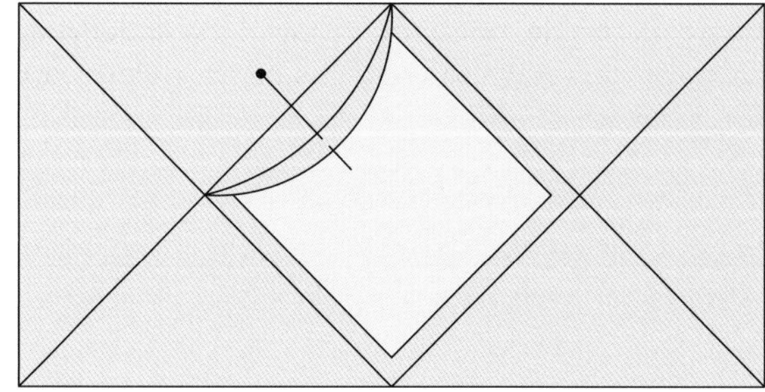

5 Beginning about ½in (1.3cm) from the corner, stitch the rolled edge down with a hemming stitch or tiny spaced backstitches placed close to the folded edge. I prefer backstitch but choose whatever stitch gives the best effect (Fig 29). The trick with the backstitch is to place the needle virtually back in the place where the thread is emerging, but just behind it, so that the stitch made looks like a tiny pinprick without any real length. I do not take my needle through to the back of the work, just into the background fabric below the window. Every few stitches I dig a little deeper to fix the curved edge on to the background layers to make it more secure and less vulnerable to wear and tear.

Fig 29

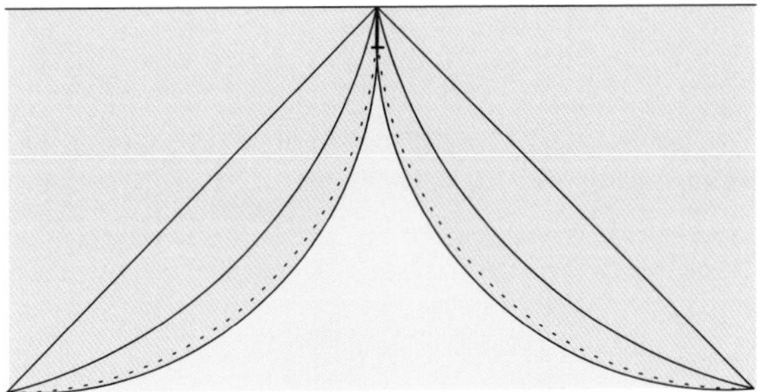

6 Since all raw edges of the window fabric need to be covered, stop stitching about ⅜in (9mm) from the corner and bring both bias edges over the window. Some of the corners can be quite bulky and resist being pulled over the window fabric. I use the side of a fine pair of scissors or the edge of a hera (a Japanese marking tool) or even the blunt edge of an old butter knife to press a central groove in the layers to encourage the rolled edges to meet in a balanced way when pulled over the window. Don't be gentle with this – place the piece of work flat on a work surface and push very hard with the side of the scissors or hera to flatten the fibres in the layers of fabric along the centre groove.

7 When you are happy with the look of the rolled edges at the corner, stitch a bar stitch a good ¼in (6mm) from the corner (Fig 30). Stitch straight across both rolled edges from side to side, not through any of the underlying layers. Often quilters stitch too near the corner before making the bar stitch, which risks the window fabric fraying out. I think ¼in (6mm) is the safest distance from the corner to keep the window fabric in place and protect its raw edges. Pull the stitch firmly and repeat it, this time bringing the needle up into the next rolled edge ready to begin stitching this side of the window in place.

Fig 30

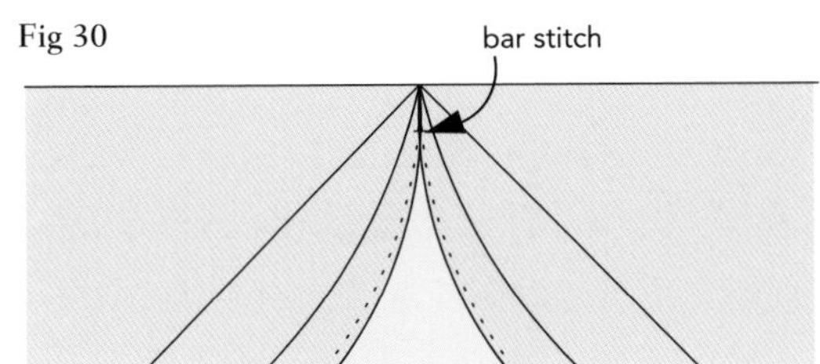

8 Stitch all four sides of the rolled edges around the window, treating each corner in the way just described. When the final corner is reached, the original stitching began ½in (1.3cm) from the corner, so there is room to make the final double bar stitch ¼in (6mm) from the corner to match the others.

9 Bring the needle to the back of the work in the joining seam between the two blocks. Make a couple of tiny stitches into the back layer of fabric only and run the needle into this layer for 1in (2.5cm) before cutting off the thread.

10 Turn the work over to the right side. Of course it won't be perfect – a first attempt never is, and of course it takes so long at this stage to do just one window. Remember though that anything learned for the first time takes about four times as long as when you are comfortable with the technique. You may see poor corners and flawed stitches, but no one else will.

'I defy you not to pat the window fondly and give a sigh of contentment at the way the window fabric is framed so nicely by the curved edges. I shall now say what most quilters say when anyone admires their work – "Don't look too closely…".'

Summer Skies Pincushion

The elegant curves of Cathedral Window are shown to great effect in this pretty pincushion – the perfect practice piece! The summery fabrics provide a good contrast between the blues and yellows and reveal the 'window' effect beautifully. The picture opposite shows other colourways.

Pincushion finished size: 3¾in × 3¾in (9.5cm × 9.5cm).

'If you turn your first attempt into a pincushion and give it to a non-quilter they will be thrilled, you will have got rid of your beginner piece and everyone is happy.'

Construction

1 Make the Cathedral Window unit as described previously on pages 18–23. Bring the two shorter sides of the unit (marked A and B in Fig 31) round to meet each other with the right side facing *outwards*. If you try to do it with right side facing inwards, it is very difficult to turn the whole thing right side out again after stitching. Stitch the two shorter sides A and B together, slipstitching as when the two folded squares were originally joined. This will make a tube rather like a napkin ring which is just about big enough for you to get your hand inside (Fig 32).

Fig 31

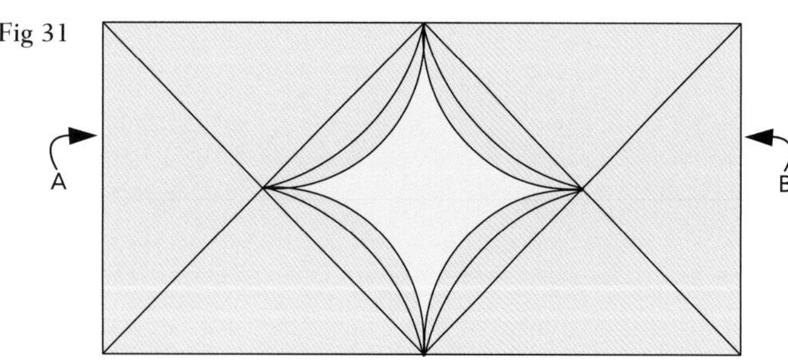

Fig 32

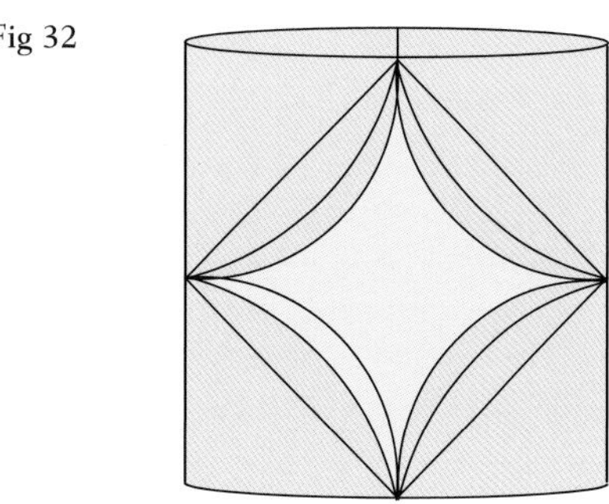

2 Cut a second square of window fabric 2⅜in × 2⅜in (6cm × 6cm) to match the one already stitched in place. This can be the same fabric or a different one similar in tone.

3 Turn the fabric tube round to show the seam that you have just stitched. Place the square of window fabric over this seam on point, positioning it as you did the first window square, with ⅛in (3mm) of the background fabric showing on all sides (Fig 33). To stitch the window into place follow steps 3–9 from Adding the Windows on page 22.

Fig 33

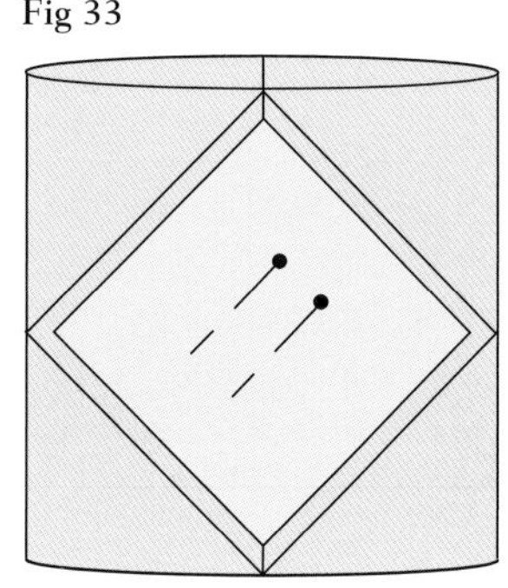

4 Flatten the ring as shown in Fig 32, matching the joining seams. Stitch together one side of the pincushion, either with ladder stitch or by over-sewing as before. Stitch from the centre outwards to one corner, then start again from the centre and stitch to the other corner.

5 Stuff the pincushion very firmly, especially in the corners, with scraps of wadding or other filling. Finally, pin and stitch the edges of the open end together, again working from the centre outwards. This allows extra stuffing to be added at the sharp corners at the last minute before stitching to keep them firm.

Designing with Classic Cathedral Window

Making a Nine-square Block

Now you have made one Cathedral Window unit it is a simple matter to add to it to make a larger design. The three Nine-square blocks shown below use the same fabric throughout as the folded background squares with different arrangements of fabrics in the windows. I used a textured blue fabric for the background and a combination of starry fabric and silver silk fabric for the windows to create an elegant look.

Nine-square block finished size: 11¼in × 11¼in (28.6cm × 28.6cm).

REQUIREMENTS (FOR ONE NINE-SQUARE BLOCK)

- **For the folded background squares:** nine squares each 8in × 8in (20.3cm × 20.3cm)
- **For the windows:** two fabrics approx. 9in x 9in (22.9cm × 22.9cm) of each

Construction

1 Using the 8in (20.3cm) fabric squares, construct nine folded squares and join them together into three rows of three squares each, either by hand or by machine (Fig 1).

Fig 1

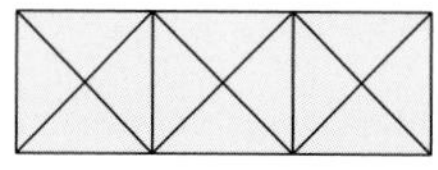

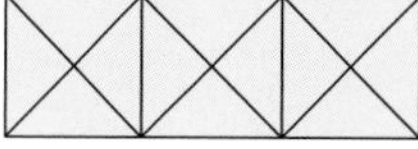

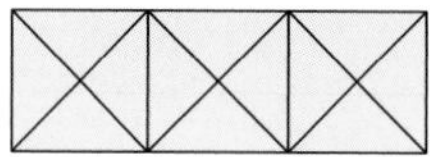

2 Stitch the rows together, matching seams carefully to complete the block as in Fig 2.

Fig 2

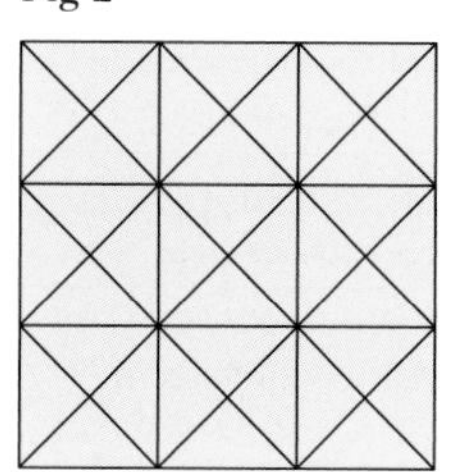

3 Press the block carefully, keeping outer edges as sharp as possible.

TIP

When joining rows of blocks together by hand, sew a tiny cross of two stitches at each seam junction and pull them firmly to match the seams and to prevent any little gaps appearing at the junctions. If the outer edges of the joined line of blocks are not all level with each other, just stroke the higher edges down with your needle until they are all level and then stitch.

Adding the Windows

4 If you prefer to cut with templates, make a template for the window (see Tip after step 2 on page 22). If you are cutting squares with rotary cutting equipment, cut squares measuring 2⅜in × 2⅜in (6cm × 6cm) for the windows.

5 The window layout designs are shown in Fig 3. Each design has a total of twelve windows cut from the two chosen fabrics. The first design has

Fig 3

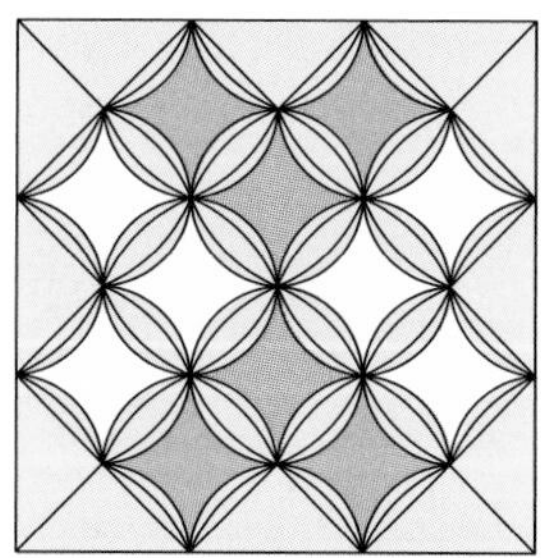

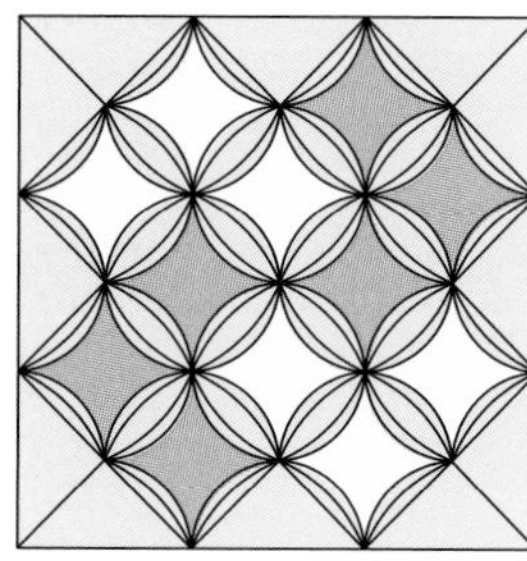

four windows from one fabric in the centre with the other eight arranged around the edge of the block. The other two designs use six windows in each fabric in two different arrangements. Choose one of the designs or create an original one for yourself and cut the twelve windows for that design. Lay the window squares in place on the background to check that you like the arrangement before stitching.

6 Working from the centre out, stitch each window in place, matching the sewing thread to the background fabric. Follow the directions for Adding the Windows on page 22.

Alternative Edging Treatments

When I make Cathedral Window block designs I tend to leave the outer bias edges flat, without curving them back as is usual, as this gives a straight-edged frame to the design (Fig 4). These outer edges can be curved back if preferred to continue the Cathedral Window effect right to the edges of the design as in Fig 5. If you do this, take care to keep the outer edge and the corners of the block in shape.

Fig 4

Fig 5

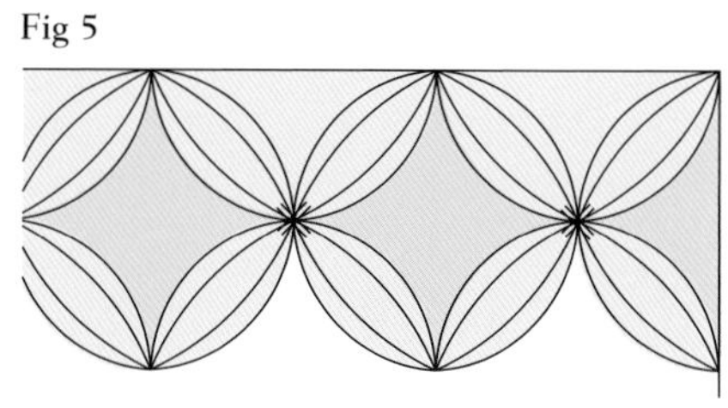

Displaying the Design

Cathedral Window has a big bonus over more conventional techniques in that the outer edges are completely finished – no borders or binding needed before you can just hang it up and admire! A sleeve can be stitched in place on the back to take a hidden hanging rod, but the simplest way of displaying a small design like the Nine Square block is to stitch a curtain ring on the back ½in (1.3cm) from one of the corners and hang it on the wall on point, with the corners at top, bottom and either side, as shown here.

Adding More Background Fabrics

To use just one background fabric throughout a Cathedral Window piece can mean a lot of fabric and it is likely that you won't have enough for the whole design. It was when this happened to me many years ago that I decided to use a combination of different fabrics for the folded background squares, making a simple design from them as well as with the overlying windows. This was a major breakthrough, as it immediately enriched the visual effect, creating two levels of design. The Cathedral Window Nine-patch piece shown below has a background of three different fabrics arranged as in Fig 6a. The arrangement of the two window fabrics is shown in Fig 6b. It is quite hard to relate one view to the other, and this is one of the most exciting things about Cathedral Window designs – the effect is multi-layered and the non-quilter has no idea how the effect is achieved.

Fig 6a

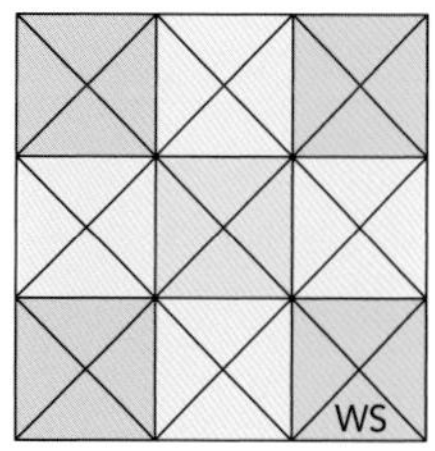

Fig 6b

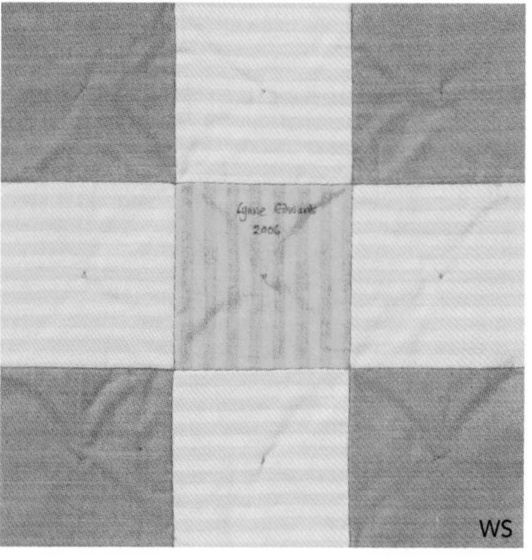

The two pictures here show the value of adding more background fabrics.

Back view (left): when folded squares using several different fabrics are arranged and joined together to make a background, they make a formal design of toning or contrasting squares.

Front view (left): However, once windows are laid on top of these squares, the vertical and horizontal seams where the squares were joined are hidden. This creates a subtle change of background colour behind the windows rather than the sharply defined pattern which is evident before windows are added.

Cool and Classic Cushion

This delicately shaded cushion of classic Cathedral Window uses alternating folded squares of two fabrics as a background with three different fabrics as the windows. The finished effect is elegant and sophisticated. The windows are a mixture of hand-dyed silk noile (a thick, textured fabric) and fine Liberty lawn. The windows are totally supported by the underlying layers, so different weights and textures can be used without any problems.

Cushion finished size: 18½in × 18½in (47cm × 47cm).

TIP

If you just have ½yd (0.5m) of each of the background fabrics and really want to use them in this cushion, use a third fabric just for the centre background folded square. This means you will only need twelve cut squares of each of the two main fabrics, which can easily be cut from ½yd of each fabric.

REQUIREMENTS

- **For folded background squares:**
  Fabric A: 21in (53.3cm) of 42in–44in (107cm–112cm) wide;
  Fabric B: ½yd (0.5m)
- **For the windows** (see Fig 8):
  Fabric C: 6in × 6in (15.2cm × 15.2cm);
  Fabric D: 9in × 9in (22.9cm × 22.9cm);
  Fabric E: 12in × 12in (30.5cm × 30.5cm)
- For borders and cushion back ¾yd (0.75m)
- To line cushion front 20in × 20in (61cm × 61cm) lightweight calico (muslin)
- Cushion pad 20in (50.8cm) square

Construction

1 From background fabric A cut thirteen squares each measuring 6½in × 6½in (16.5cm × 16.5cm). From background fabric B cut twelve squares each measuring 6½in × 6½in (16.5cm × 16.5cm).

2 Follow the directions in Making a Cathedral Window Unit beginning on page 18 to construct twenty-five folded background squares, using your choice of the hand or machine methods. Each folded square should measure 3in × 3in (7.6m × 7.6cm) when completed.

3 Arrange the squares in the design shown in Fig 7. Stitch the folded squares into five rows each of five folded squares, either by hand or by machine (see Joining Folded Squares on page 20). Remember that if you are using the machine throughout follow the method given in Joining Square Blocks by Machine on page 20. Finally, stitch the five rows together to make the design shown in Fig 7. Press the block carefully, keeping the outer corners as sharp as possible.

Fig 7

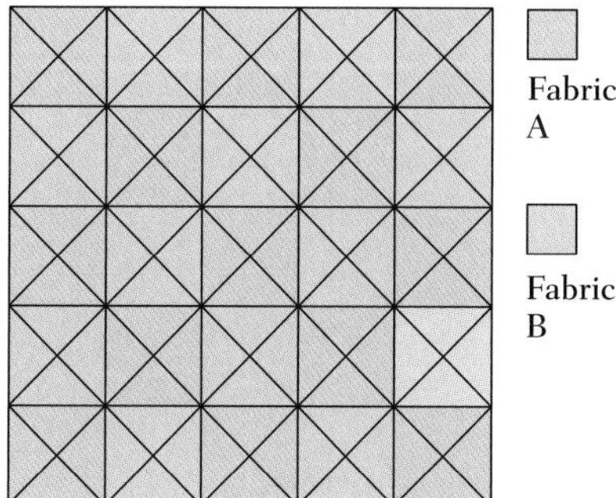

Adding the Windows

4 For a 3in (7.6cm) folded square the windows need to measure 1⅞in × 1⅞in (4.7cm × 4.7cm). If you prefer to use a template, trace Template 1 on page 73 and make a template in the usual way. The windows are arranged as shown in Fig 8. From the chosen fabrics for the windows cut four squares from fabric C for the centre of the design, twelve from fabric D and twenty-four from fabric E.

Fig 8

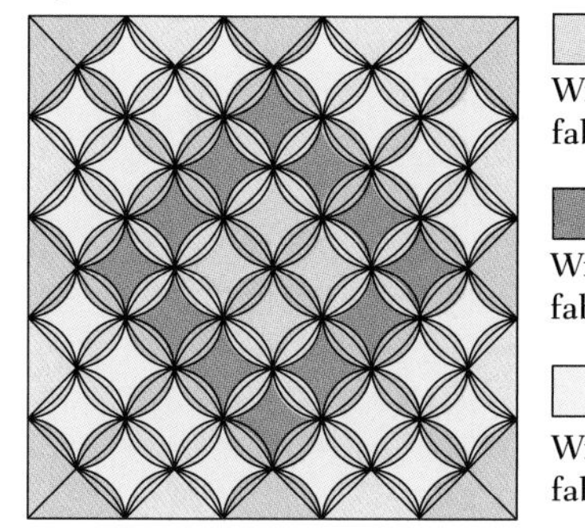

5 Working from the centre and following the instructions given in Adding the Windows on page 22, pin and stitch each window in place following the arrangement in Fig 8.

TIP

Lay each cut square window in place to check that you like the arrangement before you begin to stitch them. You may wish to alter the design or substitute a different window fabric and now is the time to do it.

Adding the Borders

6 Cut four strips of border fabric each 2½in (6.4cm) wide, referring to the section, Adding Borders on page 130 for measuring and cutting directions. Stitch the borders to the cushion top as shown in that section, mitring the corners.

Completing the Cushion

7 Place the cushion front face up on top of the calico (muslin) square, trim both the cushion top and the calico to a square 19in × 19in (48.3cm × 48.3cm) and then tack (baste) the two layers together. I used a piped edging on my cushion, but a much easier alternative is just to top-stitch ½in (1.3cm) within the finished edge of the cushion after it is completed, which is the method I have described here.

8 For the cushion back, cut two pieces of fabric each 19in × 13in (48.3cm × 33cm). Press a ¼in (6mm) turning to the wrong side of the fabric on one long side of each piece. Fold over this edge again to make a ½in (1.3cm) turning (Fig 9a). Machine stitch along this edge close to the fold (Fig 9b).

Fig 9a

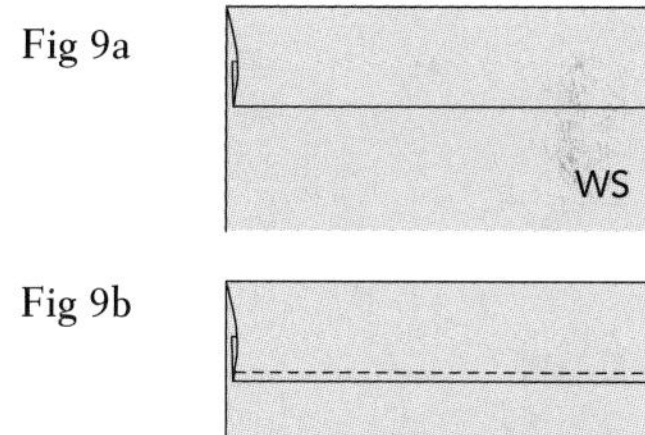

Fig 9b

9 Place the cushion front right side up on a flat surface. Arrange the two back pieces right side down, with their raw edges matching the edges of the cushion front and the folded edges overlapping across the centre (Fig 10).

Fig 10

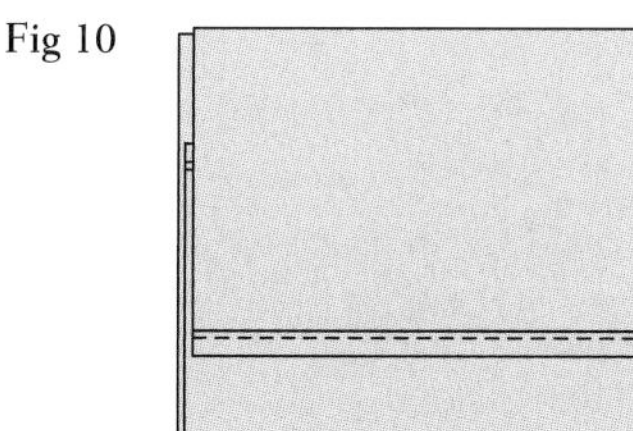

10 Pin the front and back together and machine stitch all around the outer edges with a ¼in (6mm) seam. Trim the corners a little to reduce the bulk of the fabric.

11 Turn through to the right side and press the outer seam. Machine stitch a line about ½in (1.3cm) from the edge all round the cushion, to give an extra finish around the outer edges. Insert the cushion pad to finish.

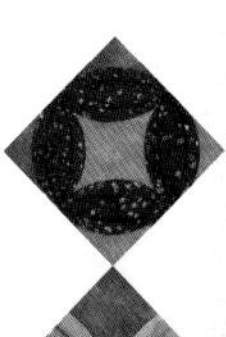

Mandarin Dreams Wall Hanging

This striking wall hanging by Jane Gaddas began with a mandarin duck fabric, which Jane wanted to use as a feature in the windows, so she increased the size of her folded blocks to 4in × 4in (10.2cm × 10.2cm) to allow more of the birds to show in the windows. She also used a contrasting gold thread for the stitching on some of the windows to great effect.

Folded square finished size:
4in × 4in (10.2cm × 10.2cm).
Wall hanging finished size:
16in × 16in (40.6cm × 40.6cm).

'I have always tried to make the stitching of the windows as invisible as possible but now that I've seen in Jane's design how effective a contrast can be, it has opened up yet another area of possible design.'

REQUIREMENTS

- **For twelve folded background squares: Fabric A:** ¾yd (0.75m)
- **For four folded background squares: Fabric B:** ¼yd (0.25m)
- **For the windows:**
  Fabric (a): one fat quarter
  Fabric (b): one fat quarter

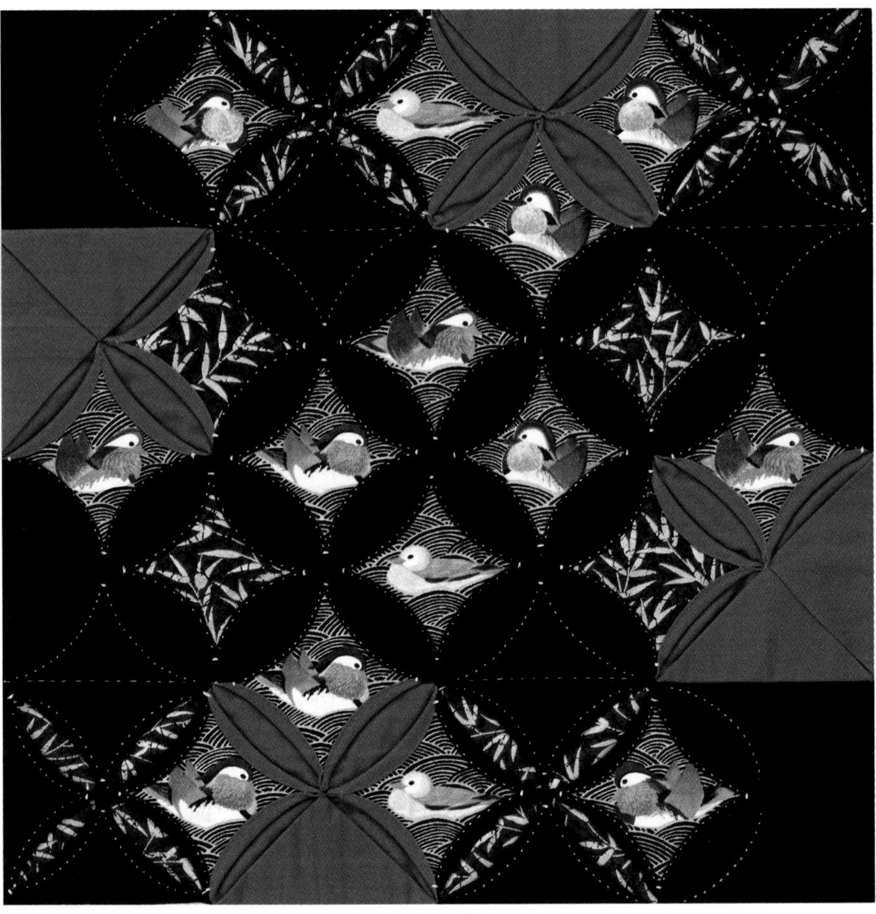

Construction

1 From background fabric A cut twelve squares each measuring 8½in × 8½in (21.6cm × 21.6cm). From background fabric B cut four squares each measuring 8½in × 8½in (21.6cm × 21.6cm). The arrangement used by Jane is shown in Fig 11a.

Fig 11a

2 Follow the directions in Making a Cathedral Window Unit beginning on page 18 to construct eight folded background squares only from fabric A and all four from fabric B, using your choice of the hand or machine methods. Each folded square should measure 4in × 4in (10.2cm × 10.2cm) when completed.

3 The remaining four cut squares of fabric A have an extra piece of fabric inserted during the construction to give added depth to the design. From the window fabric (a) cut four squares each measuring 4½in × 4½in (11.4cm × 11.4cm). Use a steam iron to press a ¼in (6mm) seam allowance to the wrong side of the fabric on all sides (Fig 12).

Fig 12

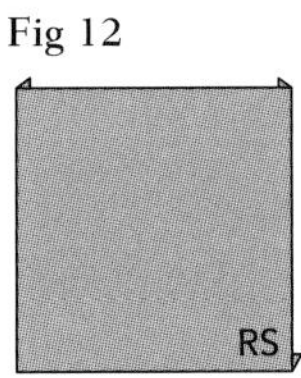

4 Stitch and fold the remaining four background squares of fabric A as far as the final folding in to the centre (see Stitching the Folded Square page 19 as far as steps 1 and 2). Remove the needle and leave the thread at the back of the work ready to pick up later.

5 Take a square of fabric (a) with its pressed-under seam allowance around all sides and place it right side up on top of the background square, using the fold lines as a guide for positioning (Fig 13). It should fit snugly to the fold lines. Use thread that matches the window fabric to appliqué the extra square on to the background fabric. The stitches do not have to be through all the layers or be very close together, but should secure the four corners in particular into place on the background as these are the areas that will be on show when the top layers are curved back later.

Fig 13

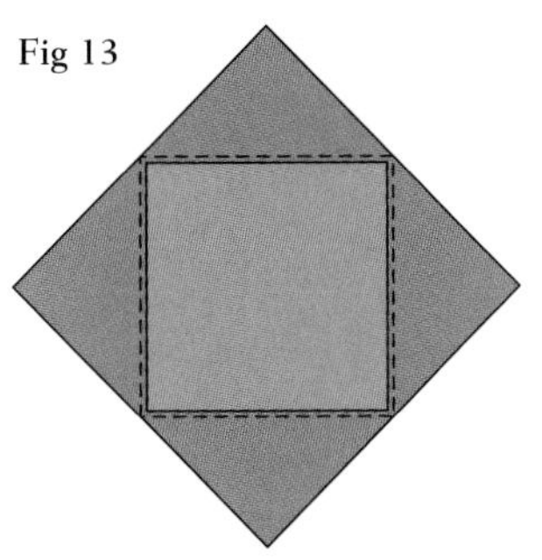

6 Bring the four outer corners of the background folded square back into the centre over the extra square of fabric (a). Re-thread the length of thread at the back of the block and use it to stitch the four corners of the block into the centre as usual (see Stitching the Folded Square page 19 steps 3 and 4 on page 20). Repeat this on all the four remaining folded background squares of fabric A.

7 Arrange the sixteen folded background squares into the design shown in Fig 11a, noting the position of the four squares with the extra layer of fabric (a) inserted.

8 Stitch the folded squares into four rows each of four folded squares, either by hand or machine (see Joining Folded Squares page 20). If you are using the machine throughout follow the method given in Joining Square Blocks by Machine on page 20. Finally, stitch the four rows together to make the design in Fig 11a. Press the block carefully, keeping the outer corners as sharp as possible.

Adding the Windows

9 Make a square template for the window from clear template plastic measuring 2½in × 2½in (6.4cm × 6.4cm). Place this on the front of your fabric to select a specific area of the fabric for the window (Jane used duck fabric as her feature fabric). Remember that the window is placed on to the background *on point* (that is, with the corners pointing north, south, east and west). You will lose about ¼in (6mm) all around the outer edge of the window fabric when the background is rolled over on to it, so keep the image in the centre of the cut window. Draw round the template on the front of the fabric and cut it out on the drawn line. Draw and cut fourteen of these 'fussy-cut' windows.

10 From the fabric (a), which was used as the extra layers in the four background folded squares (steps 3–6), cut four windows. These do not need to be fussy-cut so you could just cut 2½in (6.4cm) squares with the rotary cutter if you prefer.

11 Place the eighteen windows in position on the joined background squares in the arrangement shown in Fig 11b. There are six places where the background squares are left without a window.

Fig 11b

12 Working from the centre and following the instructions given in 'Adding the Windows' on page 22, pin and stitch each window in place as in Fig 11b.

The stitching on background fabric B was done in a matching thread, which is not noticeable in the final design. Jane also turned back and stitched in the contrast thread the curved edges of fabric A in the squares that did not have the window added and stitched across the centre. Fabric B was left unturned and unstitched.

Rose Window Wall Hanging

This gorgeous classic Cathedral Windows wall hanging by Janet Covell uses silk as the surrounding border to echo the silk windows, which together add richness and a lovely shimmering effect to the finished piece. She used the larger folded background square in an arrangement of four fabrics with five silk shades as the windows.

Folded square finished size: 3¾in × 3¾in (9.5cm × 9.5cm).
Wall hanging finished size: 35in × 35in (88.9cm × 88.9cm).

REQUIREMENTS

- **For the background folded squares:**
  Fabric A: ½yd (0.5m);
  Fabric B: ¼yd (0.25m);
  Fabric C: ¾yd (0.75m);
  Fabric D: 1¼yd (1.25m)
- **For the windows:**
  Fabric a: 12in x 12in (30.5cm × 30.5cm);
  Fabric b: 6in × 6in (15.2cm × 15.2cm);
  Fabric c: ¼yd (0.25m);
  Fabric d: ¼yd (0.25m);
  Fabric e: ¼yd (0.25m)
- Border and binding 1yd (1m)
- Thin wadding four strips each 36in × 4½in (91.4 × 11.4cm)
- Backing fabric 36in × 36in (91.4cm × 91.4cm)

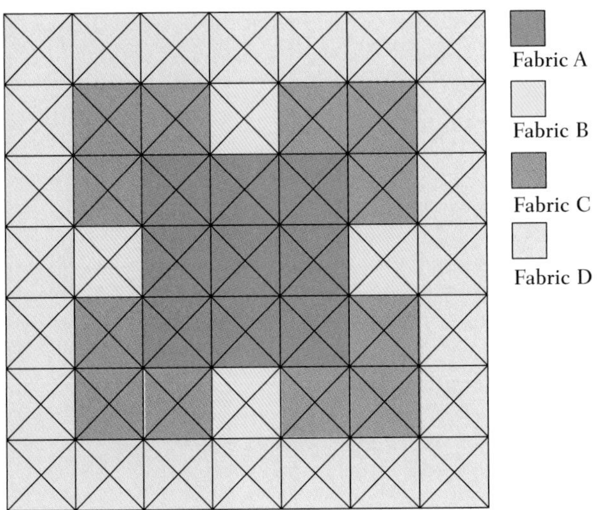

Fig 14a *This shows the background plan of folded square, shaded to indicate fabrics*

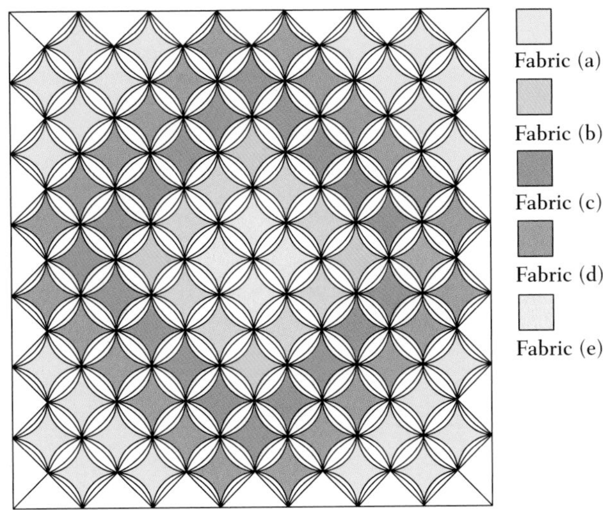

Fig 14b *The plan of the windows*

Construction

1 All the background squares are cut 8in × 8in (20.3cm × 20.3cm). The arrangement used by Janet is shown in Fig 14a above. From background fabric A cut nine squares. From background fabric B cut four squares. From fabric C cut twelve squares. From fabric D cut twenty-four squares.

2 Follow the directions in Making a Cathedral Window Unit beginning on page 18 to construct all forty-nine folded background squares. The finished squares should all measure 3¾in × 3¾in (9.5cm × 9.5cm) when completed.

3 Arrange the folded squares in the arrangement shown in Fig 14a above.

4 Stitch the folded squares into seven rows, each of seven folded squares, either by hand or machine (see Joining Folded Squares on page 20). Remember that if you are using the machine throughout follow the method given in Joining Square Blocks by Machine on page 20. Finally, stitch the seven rows together to make the design in Fig 14a. Press the block carefully, keeping outer corners as sharp as possible.

Adding the Windows

5 If you prefer to cut with templates, make a template – see Tip after step 2 on page 22. If you are simply cutting squares with rotary cutting equipment you will need to cut squares measuring 2⅜in × 2⅜in (6cm × 6cm) for the windows. From window fabric (a) cut eight windows. From window fabric (b) cut four windows. From window fabric (c) cut twenty windows. From window fabric (d) cut twenty-four windows. From window fabric (e) cut twenty-eight windows. Fabric (e) is used as the windows in the outer corners and in the centre four windows.

6 Arrange the windows on the background squares in the design shown in Fig 14b above.

7 Working from the centre out, stitch each window in place, matching the sewing thread to the background fabric. Follow directions for Adding the Windows on page 22.

Adding the Borders

8 Cut four strips of the silk chosen for the border each measuring 4½in × 36in (11.4cm × 91.4cm). Also cut four strips of thin wadding in the same measurements. Follow the instructions on page 130 Adding Borders to join the border strips to the quilt and to back it before quilting.

Quilting the Design

9 Janet tied the quilt at regular intervals in the central Cathedral Window section and then quilted the border in diagonal lines to echo the diagonal fold lines in the main design (see Knotting or Tying a Quilt on page 132 and Quilting the Border on page 133). Finally, the outer edges of the borders were bound in the usual way (see page 133 Binding the Quilt).

Cathedral Window – Secret Garden

I found this simple four-petal variation of Cathedral Window mentioned in an American patchwork and quilting book many years ago. There they called it Cathedral Window, but it was not the version I knew. It was suggested that the simple folded square should be made in a variety of different green fabrics with floral prints laid within the layers to be revealed as the petal shapes, like flowers in a garden. This is why I gave it the name 'Secret Garden'.

Classic Cathedral Window uses folded squares stitched together, on to which the smaller window squares are laid. These overlying windows mask the regular vertical and horizontal seams so that the background fabrics seem to change mysteriously without any obvious joins. This effect can be seen in Figs 1a and 1b, where the diagram in Fig 1a shows nine folded squares joined into rows with vertical and horizontal seams (shown as dotted lines). Fig 1b shows how these seams, still shown as dotted lines, are hidden beneath the added windows.

Secret Garden has a different effect: each individual folded square contains the window within its folded layers, which is revealed as four petal shapes when the top bias edges are rolled back (see Fig 2 and detail picture, right). To make a sample of Secret Garden it is not necessary to fold and stitch two background squares and join them together, as with classic Cathedral Window. Just one cut square of background fabric is needed with its own contrasting window square to make an individual unit of Secret Garden.

Fig 1a

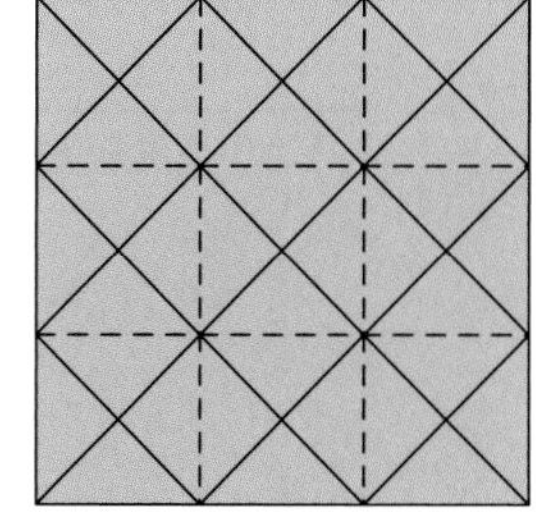

Fig 1b

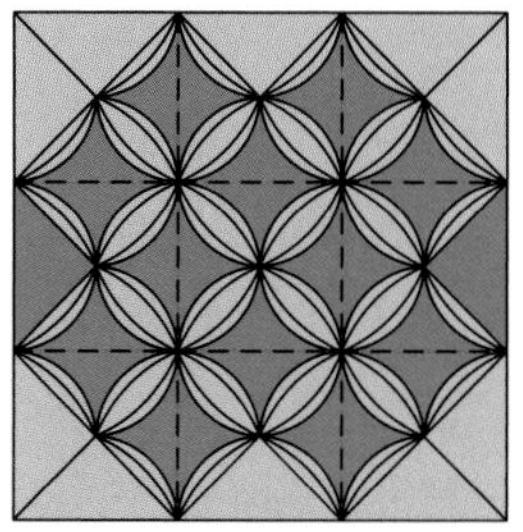

Fig 2

'Quilters often really like the effect of a single Secret Garden square when it is finished – lots of contented sighing and patting goes on. There is actually more stitching involved in this block than in the Classic Cathedral Window, but if you like the stitching part, as I do, the more the better!'

The folded background squares for both Cathedral Window and Secret Garden are the same size, so why not combine them to make rich and striking designs? This colourful wall hanging called Peacock Windows, uses Secret Garden squares in the centre of the design, surrounded by squares of Cathedral Window.

Cutting the Squares

All the details for cutting the folded background squares given for classic Cathedral Window apply to Secret Garden (see Cutting the Squares page 18). I suggest you use squares cut 8in × 8in (20.3cm × 20.3cm) for trying out the technique but if you prefer to use the smaller 6½in × 6½in (16.5cm × 16.5cm) square that will be fine.

Making a Secret Garden Unit

1 From the chosen background fabric cut one square measuring 8in × 8in (20.3cm × 20.3cm). Follow the directions given in Making a Cathedral Window Unit steps 2–11, pages 18–19, and then continue with step 2 below.

Stitching the Square

2 This is where the technique differs from classic Cathedral Window. Open out the folded corners to reveal the centre with its unstitched section. If necessary pull the folded edges together at the centre until they meet.

3 Using a thread that matches the fabric as nearly as possible and a fine sewing needle (sharps 9 or 10), knot the end of the thread and pass the needle through the open area into the fabric from front to back at the centre of the folded square (Fig 3). The knot will be hidden under the top layers of fabric. To close the opening in the centre, draw the two edges together and take two tiny stitches to make a cross at the centre through all layers, ending with the needle at the back of the work (Fig 4). Leave the needle and thread pinned temporarily into the back of the work for the moment.

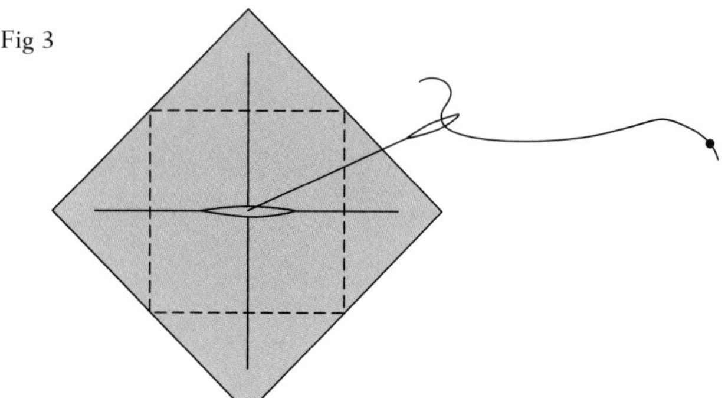

Fig 3

Fig 4

Adding the Windows

4 Measure the folded background square along one side and cut a square of window fabric in the same measurement. For the folded square that began as an 8in × 8in (20.3cm × 20.3cm) square cut one window measuring 3¾in × 3¾in (9.5cm × 9.5cm).

TIP

This hidden square of fabric will be revealed only as narrow petals when the bias edges of the background fabric are rolled back, so small prints or textured fabrics work best for these, rather than larger designs.

5 Place the cut square of fabric on top of the background block, using the fold lines as a guide for positioning (see Fig 5). You will probably have to trim the window square of fabric slightly so that it just fits inside the fold lines. Fold the four corners of the background fabric square back to the centre and check that the trimmed window fits snugly within the folded block. It needs to be just touching the fold lines but not too large to lie completely flat when the four outer corners of the background are folded to the middle of the block. If working by hand rather than machine, move on now to step 6.

Fig 5

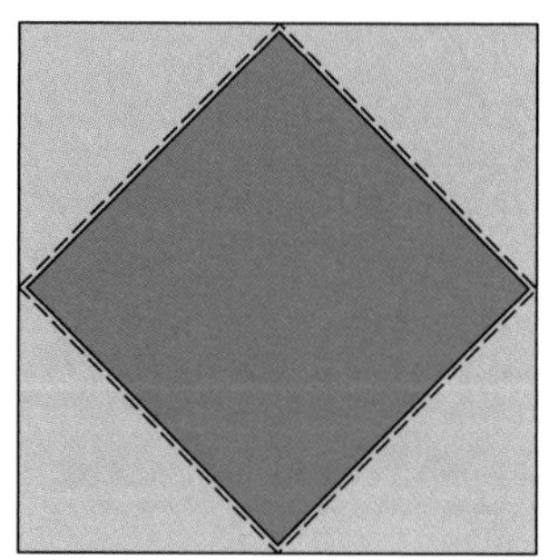

If you want to join the blocks together all by machine, follow the instructions in Joining Square Blocks by Machine on page 20 before inserting the windows, which should fit exactly to the lines of machine stitching that join the folded blocks together. Once this is done, the corners of the blocks can be pressed to the centre and stitched into place, following steps 1–5 in Stitching the Folded Square on page 19. Machinists should then continue from step 7 (opposite page), to roll back the bias edges of the block.

6 Bring the four outer corners of the folded square back to the centre. Use the thread still at the back of the block to stitch the four corners into position at the centre (see steps 3–5 in Stitching the Folded Square beginning on page 20).

7 The bias edges of the background folded square are now rolled back without a contrast fabric square being added, and stitched down either with a hemming stitch or with a series of tiny backstitches, as for Cathedral Window. The bias edges must not be turned right up to the outside corners as this would reveal the raw edge of the contrast fabric beneath. Instead, place a pin through all the layers about ¼in (6mm) in from each corner (Fig 6).

Fig 6

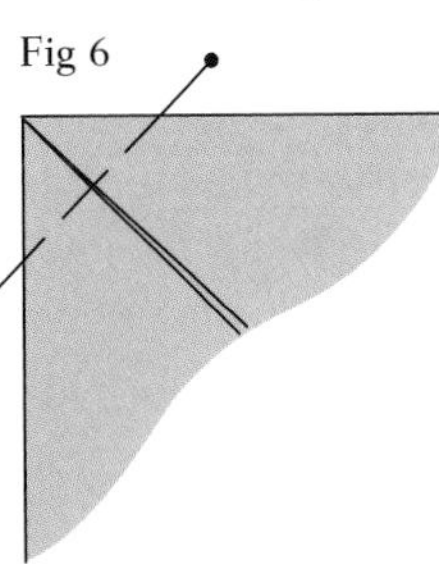

8 Begin stitching at a corner of the block. Knot the thread and slide the needle between the window fabric and the lower layer of the background folded square. Remove the pin and sew a double bar stitch where the pin had been, stitching across the two bias edges through all the layers with a tiny stab stitch (Fig 7). This keeps the corner of the folded square sharp and protects the raw edges of the window fabric.

Fig 7

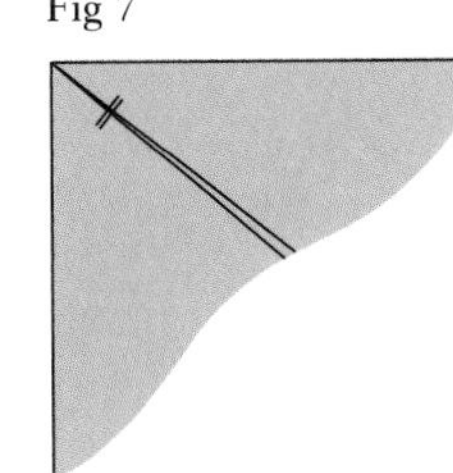

9 Pull one bias edge back to form a curve, stretching it so that the curve measures at least ¼in (6mm) in the centre. Pin the curved edge at its centre as in Fig 8.

Fig 8

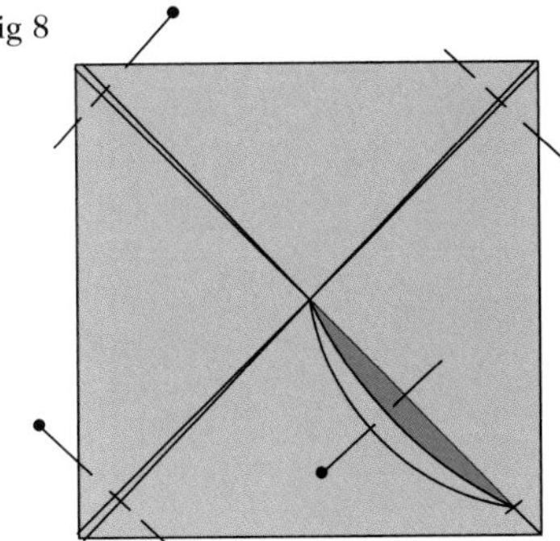

10 Run the needle into the rolled edge and stitch along it, keeping the stitches towards the outer edge as in Fig 9 (for the stitching technique, see step 5 Adding the Windows on page 23).

Fig 9

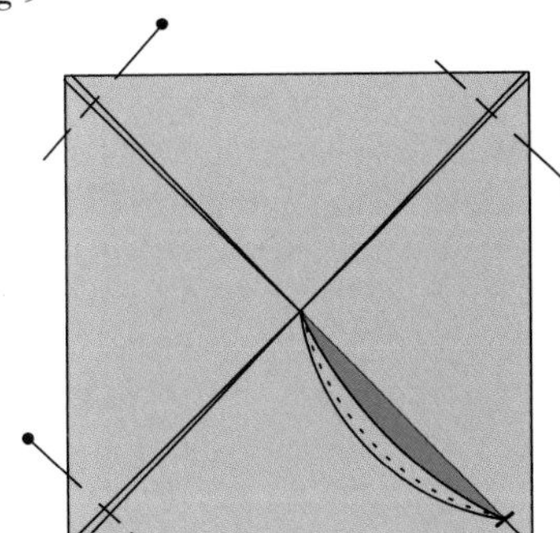

11 About 3/8in (1cm) from the centre of the block, stop stitching and roll the adjacent bias edge over to meet the stitched bias edge. This is the same tricky corner that you had with Cathedral Window, with the same bulk to deal with. At least here there is no window fabric to keep in place at the same time. Follow steps 6 and 7 in Adding the Windows on page 23 to link the two bias edges together with a double bar stitch (Fig 10). Do not stitch right through the block here – it's only necessary on the outer corners of the block to protect the window fabric.

Fig 10

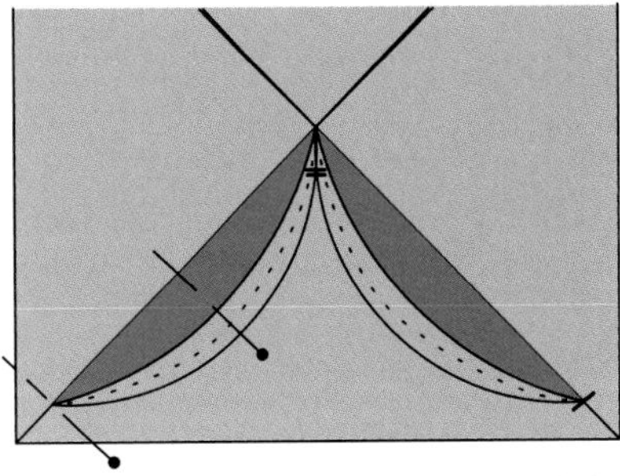

12 Continue to stitch along the second rolled bias edge until you reach the outer corner with its protecting pin. Remove the pin and stitch a double bar stitch through all layers as you did with the first corner.

13 In this way pin and stitch all the rolled edges until you get back to the starting point.

14 To finish, bring the needle to the back of the work where the bar stitches can be seen ¼in (6mm) from the corner of the block. Make a couple of tiny stitches alongside these stitches through the back layer of fabric only and run the needle into this layer for about 1in (2.5cm) before cutting off the thread. Turn over the finished block and do the usual pat-and-sigh ritual.

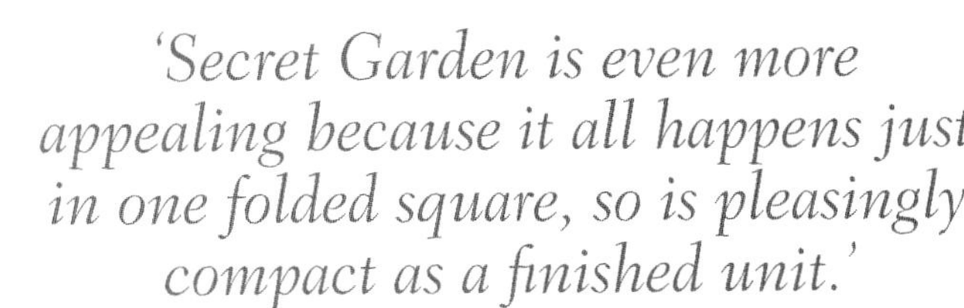

'Secret Garden is even more appealing because it all happens just in one folded square, so is pleasingly compact as a finished unit.'

Using Secret Garden Units

To practise this variation you could simply make one unit with two contrasting Christmas fabrics, add a few beads, stitch a loop on to one corner and hang it on the Christmas tree.

Alternatively, make two identical units and use them as the front and back of a needle case to match the pincushion described on page 24.

Birgitte Bennett added small Secret Garden squares as hanging tails from three corners of a Cathedral Window nine-square design. The nine-square block was her interpretation of the design in Designing with Classic Cathedral Window on page 26, using 8in (20.3cm) cut squares for the folded units. The little Secret Garden squares were made from cut squares of fabric 3½in × 3½in (8.9cm × 8.9cm), finishing up 1½in × 1½in (3.8cm × 3.8cm). The inner squares were cut 1½in (3.8cm) square to match this measurement.

Making an attractive Christmas decoration will allow you to practise your Secret Garden technique – try making a single unit (see above) using some sparkly gold or silver fabrics. In the main picture, Birgitte Bennett's simple nine-square block has been turned on point and hung from one corner with small Secret Garden squares strung from the other three corners.

The first pieces that I made with Secret Garden blocks were simple nine-patch blocks either using the same fabric throughout as the background folded squares or using two fabrics alternately as the background and the windows, as in Fig 11. The green check nine-patch piece shown below uses two rustic check fabrics in this arrangement.

Fig 11

This green check nine-patch arrangement of Secret Garden features two different check fabrics. Fig 11 shows the design in diagram form.

Designing with Secret Garden

Blocks made from the Secret Garden variation give a pleasing and formal effect with the vertical and horizontal joining seams adding to the final design. The design breakthrough for me, however, was when I realized that the same size folded square could be used for both Cathedral Window and Secret Garden and the two effects combined to make original designs, as shown in the Sea Spray Nine-patch design here.

The nine-patch design (right), called Sea Spray Nine-patch has Secret Garden in the four corners, with Cathedral Window in the centre. The picture below shows the back of the block.

TIP

If you are joining everything together by machine, then leave all the windows, both small for Cathedral Window and large for Secret Garden, until the folded squares are joined into the complete design (see Joining Square Blocks by Machine on page 20).

Fig 12a

Fig 12b

When making a piece that combines the two techniques of Cathedral Window and Secret Garden, complete the Secret Garden squares as individual units before stitching them into rows with the other folded squares (Fig 12a). Once the block is assembled then the overlying Cathedral Windows are stitched in place (Fig 12b). Marjory Dench's attractive wall hanging called Coral Batiks (shown right), uses the arrangement shown in Figs 12a and 12b to great effect.

Cathedral Window and Secret Garden combined in an attractive wall hanging by Marjory Dench called Coral Batiks. Using a batik fabric for each of the Cathedral Window folded squares gives depth and richness to this design, as the colours in the fabric shift from coral to yellow, green and mauve. The four Secret Garden blocks provide strength and interest at the corners of the piece.

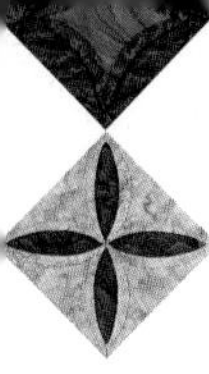

An alternative combination of both techniques is shown in Figs 13a and 13b. Fig 13a shows sixteen folded squares stitched together in rows, with the centre four Secret Garden units already completed with their hidden windows and all the surrounding Cathedral Window squares folded and stitched together ready for the windows to be applied. Fig 13b shows the finished block with these windows added. I have made two blocks using this design, shown below in African Blues and opposite in Batik Beauty. What makes these blocks so effective is the use of the lighter and brighter fabric in the centre for the four Secret Garden folded squares, with the less dominant fabric as the surrounding folded squares, making a darker border around the bright centre.

Fig 13a

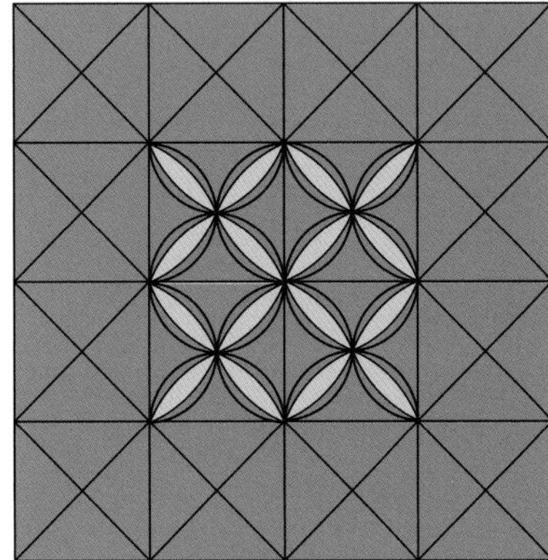

Fig 13b

African Blues combines Cathedral Window and Secret Garden using African indigo prints with a plain blue fabric. The second picture shows the back of the piece.

Batik Beauty uses two contrasting batik fabrics plus a hand-dyed fabric for the outer windows in an attractive combination of Cathedral Window and Secret Garden. The second picture shows the back of the piece.

Cathedral Window and Secret Garden may be combined in the same folded square by adding the extra Secret Garden layer with an extra ½in (1.3cm) for seam allowances. This is what Jane Gaddas did in her Mandarin Dreams Wall Hanging (see picture below and steps 3–6 Construction on page 30). This allows the usual windows to be added as for classic Cathedral Window and the curved edges turned back right to the corner as usual, revealing the extra fabric beneath. Different effects can be achieved by changing the fabrics of the Secret Garden windows to produce different coloured petal shapes, which is how the Peacock Windows wall hanging was created – see project details overleaf.

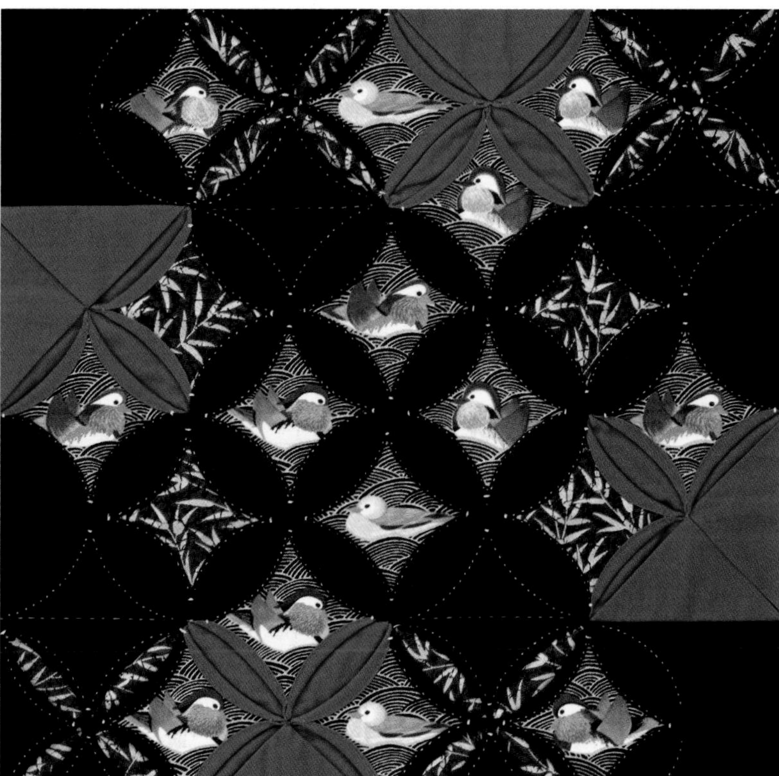

In this piece, Mandarin Dreams, Jane Gaddas 'fussy-cut' the windows for her design so that the Mandarin ducks are framed beautifully by the curved edges of the background fabrics.

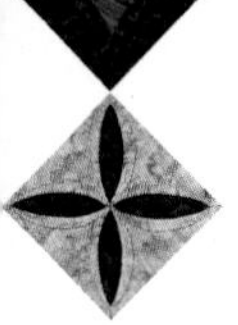

Peacock Windows Wall Hanging

For my Peacock Windows piece, shown opposite, I used the Secret Garden Squares in the centre of the design and surrounded it with squares of classic Cathedral Window. The Secret Garden units seem to be on a larger scale than the Cathedral Window but in reality they are all the same size, which is an intriguing illusion. Using patterned fabric for the central Secret Garden folded squares gives a richer and stronger centre. The diagonal diamond-shaped emphasis of the petal windows is achieved by using pieced four-patch squares for the Secret Garden windows (see Fig 14 below). When the completed Secret Garden units are joined in a design, a secondary design with the petal windows is revealed (see Fig 15).

Folded square finished size: 3in × 3in (7.6cm × 7.6cm).
Wall hanging finished size: 38in × 38in (96.5cm × 96.5cm).

REQUIREMENTS

- **For the folded background squares:**
  Fabrics A, B, C, D: ½yd (0.5m) each;
  Fabrics E: 1½yd (1.5m)
- **For the windows:**
  ½yd (0.5m) each of five fabrics (window fabrics a, b, c, d and e)
- Border and binding 1yd (1m)
- Wadding (batting) four strips each cut 4½in × 40in (11.4cm × 101.6cm)
- Backing fabric 40in (101.6cm) square

Fig 14

Fig 15

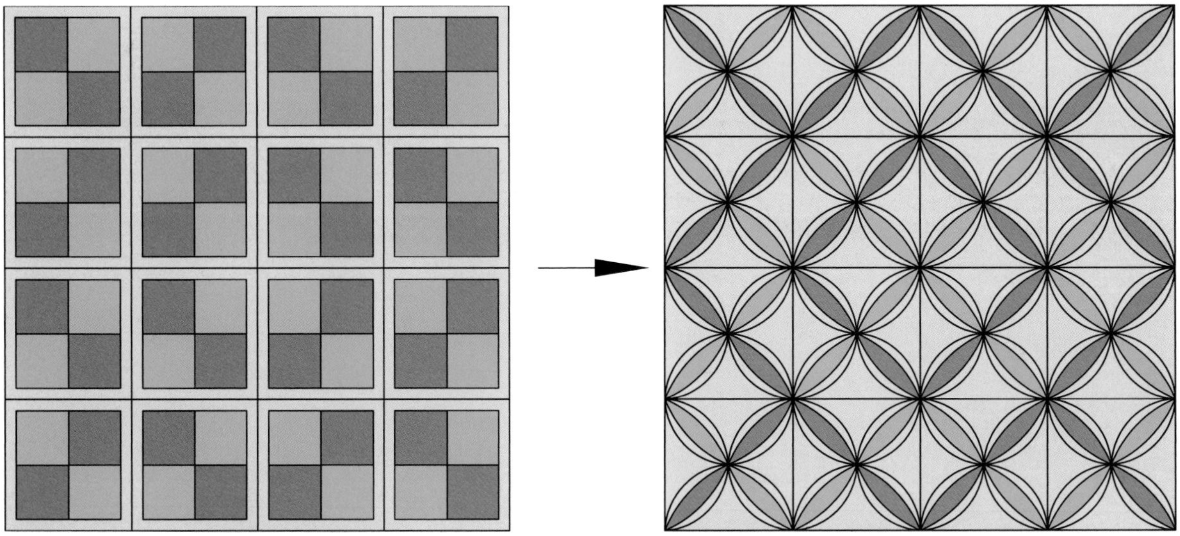

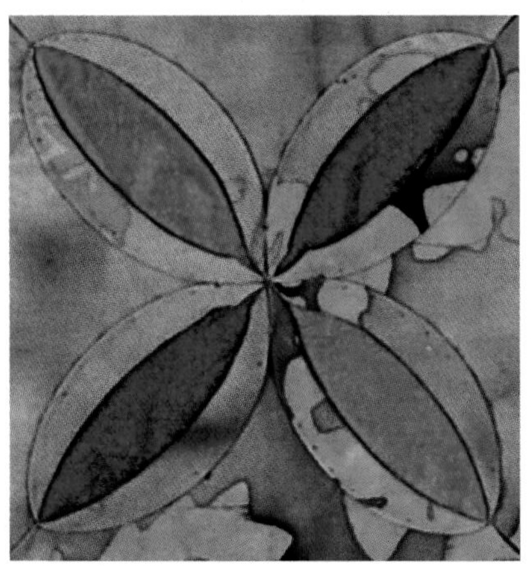

A Secret Garden block from the central section of the Peacock Windows wall hanging.

A classic Cathedral Window block from the surrounding sections of the Peacock Windows wall hanging.

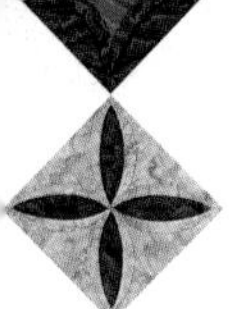

Fig 16a *Quilt plan*

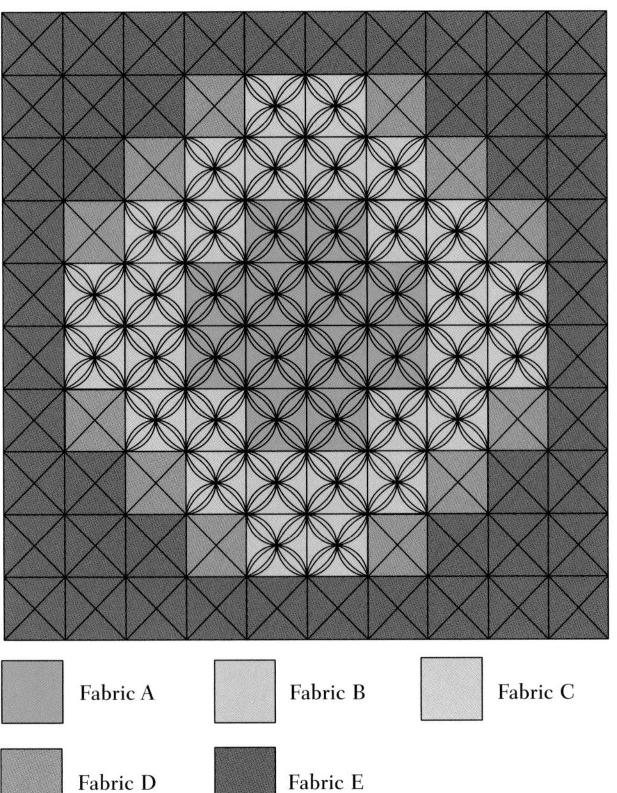

Fabric A
Fabric B
Fabric C
Fabric D
Fabric E

Fig 16b *Window plan*

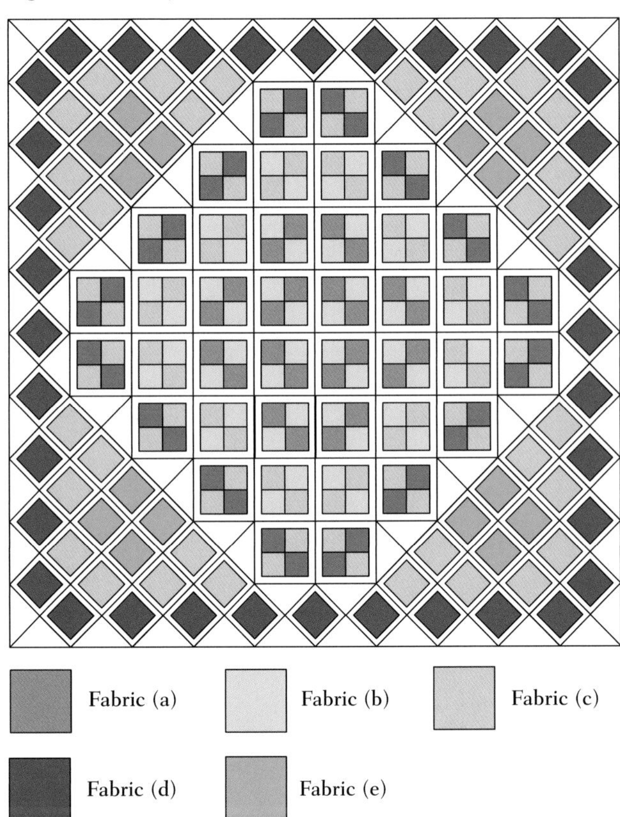

Fabric (a)
Fabric (b)
Fabric (c)
Fabric (d)
Fabric (e)

Construction

1 Cut the required number of 6½in × 6½in (16.5cm × 16.5cm) squares from each of the following fabrics:
Fabric A: twelve squares;
Fabric B: twelve squares;
Fabric C: sixteen squares;
Fabric D: twelve squares;
Fabric E: forty-eight squares.
Fig 16a shows the arrangement of background squares.

2 Using the cut squares of fabrics A, B and C, construct the Secret Garden folded background squares, following steps 1–3 Making a Secret Garden Unit on page 36.

3 The windows in the Secret Garden units are made of four-patch squares, each 3in × 3in (7.6cm × 7.6cm). Fig 16b shows the various fabric combinations and positions in the design. For the twelve centre windows, cut one strip of fabric (a) and one strip of fabric (b), both measuring 1¾in × 43in (4.4cm × 109.2cm). Stitch the two strips together with a ¼in (6mm) seam. Press the seam towards the darker strip, ironing from the front of the work (Fig 17).

Fig 17

4 From the stitched strip cut twenty-four pieces, each 1¾in (4.4cm) wide (Fig 18).

Fig 18

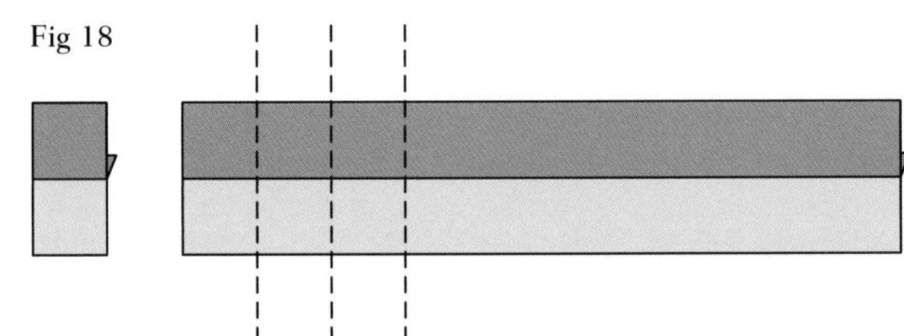

5 Take two cut pieces and arrange them in a four-patch as in Fig 19. Pin and stitch the pieces together, matching seams carefully. Press the seam to one side, ironing from the front (Fig 20). Assemble the other eleven four-patch units in the same way.

Fig 19

Fig 20

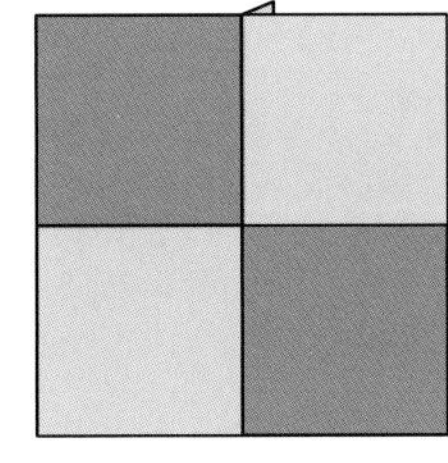

6 For the next set of four-patch windows cut one strip of fabric (b) and one strip of fabric (c), both measuring 1¾in × 43in (4.4cm × 109.2cm). Follow steps 3–5 above to make twelve four-patch windows in these fabrics (Fig 21).

Fig 21

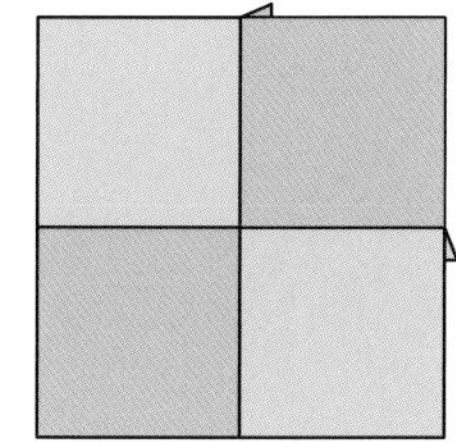

7 For the outer set of four-patch windows, cut one strip 1¾in × 43in (4.4cm × 109.2cm) and one strip 1¾in × 15in (4.4cm × 38.1cm) from each of fabrics (c) and (d). Follow steps 3–5 above to cut thirty-two pieces and make sixteen four-patch windows in these fabrics (Fig 22).

Fig 22

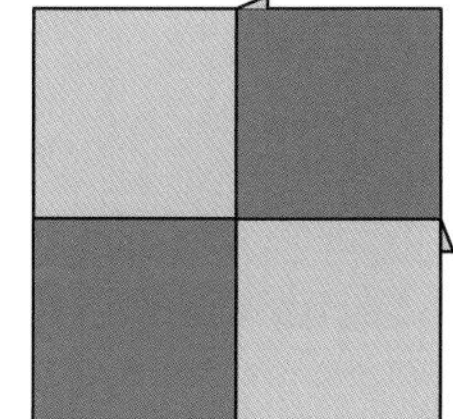

8 Place the four-patch windows in the folded background squares.
The centre twelve windows – fabrics (a) and (b) – are placed in the background squares of fabric A.
The next set of windows – fabrics (b) and (c) – are place in the background squares of fabric B.
The outer set of window – fabrics (c) and (d) – are placed in the background squares of fabric C.

9 Follow the instructions for stitching the windows in steps 4–14 Making a Secret Garden Unit on page 36.

TIP

If you are stitching the folded squares together by machine, leave adding the four-patch windows until all the background squares are joined together to make the design shown in Fig 16a.

10 Construct twelve Cathedral Window background folded squares from fabric D and forty-eight from fabric E, following the instructions given in Making a Cathedral Window Unit on page 18.

11 Arrange the completed squares, following the background and window plans in Figs 16a and 16b.

12 Join the squares into rows, and then stitch the rows together, matching seams carefully.

Adding the Windows

13 If you prefer to cut with templates, make a template for the window from Template 1 on page 73. If you are simply cutting squares with rotary cutting equipment you will need to cut squares measuring 1⅞in × 1⅞in (4.7cm × 4.7cm) for the windows.

14 Arrange the windows on the Cathedral Window background squares in the design in Fig 16b.

15 Stitch each window in place, matching the sewing thread to the background fabric. Follow the directions for Adding the Windows on page 22.

Adding the borders

16 Cut four strips of fabric for the border each measuring 4½in × 40in (11.4cm × 101.6cm). Cut four strips of thin wadding in the same measurements. Follow the instructions in Adding Borders on page 130 to join the border strips to the quilt and to back it before quilting.

Quilting the Design

17 I tied the quilt at regular intervals in the central Cathedral Window/ Secret Garden section and then quilted the border in diagonal lines to echo the diagonal fold lines in the main design (see Knotting or Tying a Quilt on page 132 and Quilting the Border on page 133. Finally, bind the outer edges of the borders – see page 133.

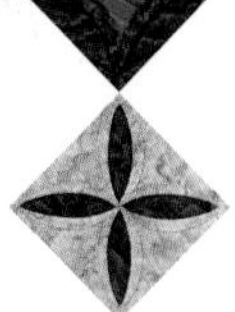

Playing With Colour

Cathedral Window/Secret Garden designs do not have to be formal and symmetrical – they can be far looser and more impressionistic, both in the background area of folded squares and also in the added windows. In my wall hanging Silver Blue Tower, shown opposite, I created a shimmering tower of Cathedral Window squares and set it against a 'sky' of Secret Garden, all in the smaller 3in × 3in (7.6cm × 7.6cm) folded squares. I wanted to keep the sky area less dominant than the tower, so limited the petal shapes to just two (as Fig 23) to give a background diagonal effect. The unopened edges were anchored with a bar stitch through all layers about ¼in (6mm) from the corners. The folded Cathedral Window squares for the tower were arranged in individual squares so the colour flows from dark at the base up to the lighter shades, as did the colours of the overlying windows. The Secret Garden squares for the sky were all of the same grey silk fabric, but the petal windows were graded diagonally from the palest in the bottom right corner to darkest in the top left corner.

Fig 23

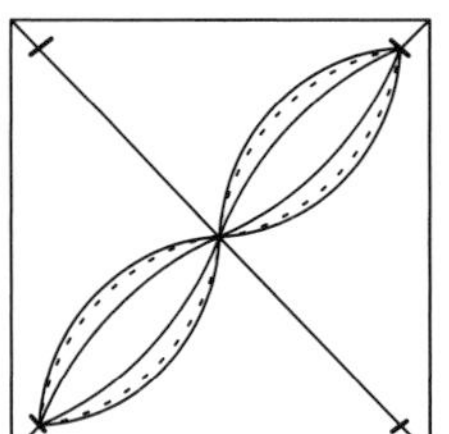

This impressionistic, almost colour-washed design is very different from the balanced symmetrical designs shown so far and shows the scope within Cathedral Window and its variations for innovative designs that flow across the quilt. Fig 24a shows the arrangement of the folded Cathedral Window tower background squares and Fig 24b the added windows. Fig 24c shows the Secret Garden 'sky'.

Fig 24a

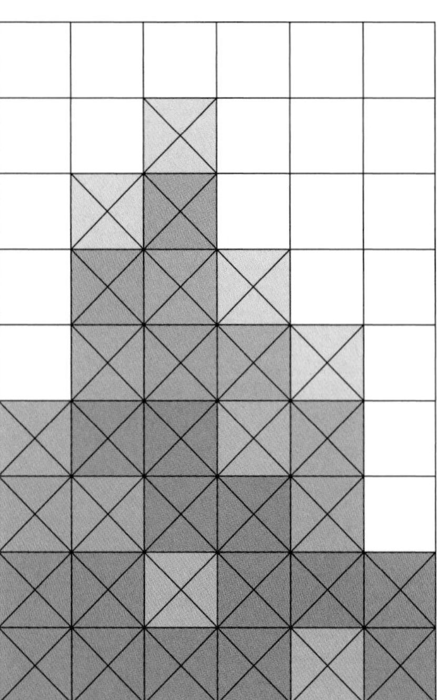

Fig 24b

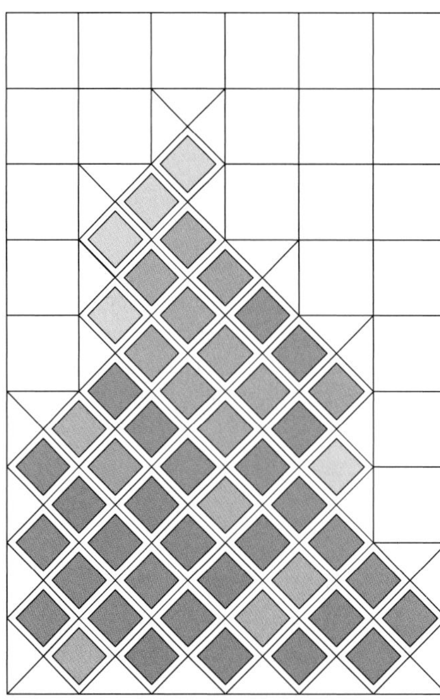

Fig 24c

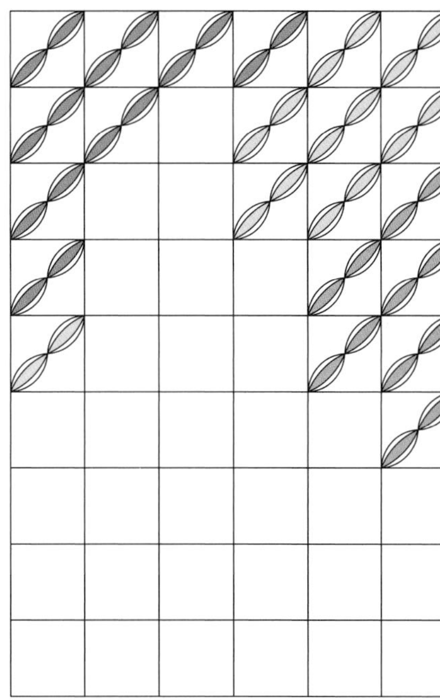

In Silver Blue Tower (opposite), all the folded background squares as well as the windows were of silk, which was not an easy task with all the folding and pressing, and also very extravagant. The extra shimmery quality made it all worth it though, creating an almost ethereal effect, which I love.

Cathedral Window – Twisted Windows

I first picked up this twisted-back variation of Cathedral Window some years ago from a quilter friend Ann Larkin, who had learned it on a fabric manipulation workshop for embroiderers and played with it, combining it with the other Cathedral Window techniques to make her own exciting designs. I used several of these in my original book on Cathedral Window (now out of print) and it was then that I started to explore it for myself and got hooked.

Twisted Windows can be used on its own in a design or combined with classic Cathedral Window. In the Winter Solstice wall hanging shown opposite (instructions on page 60), I edged a complex centre of classic Cathedral Window with a border of Twisted Windows. I also used Twisted Windows in the Bright Batiks wall hanging on pages 17 and 54 as a final border to frame the central design of Cathedral Window and Secret Garden. I find it most effective when plain or lightly textured fabrics are used for the complex folding, as the folds and edges are not then lost in the patterns of the fabrics. Like Secret Garden, this variation uses just one folded square of fabric. No extra windows of fabric are added: instead the corners of the folded background square are twisted and pressed back to make intriguing kite shapes.

'The variety of ways in which the folded corners can be twisted and stitched into position are endless. Play with the blocks and see what you can discover for yourself as well as using the samples in Fig 3 overleaf as guides.'

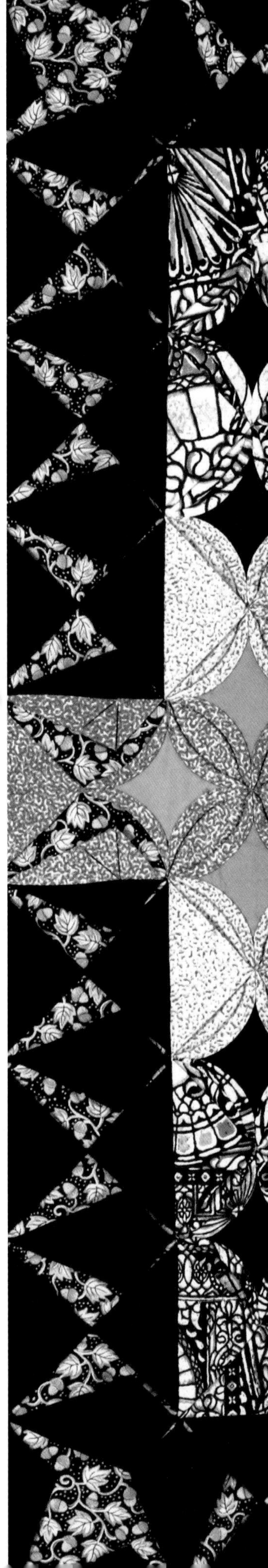

This gorgeous quilt, with its striking black, cream and gold colouring, has a complex centre of classic Cathedral Window with a border of Twisted Windows.

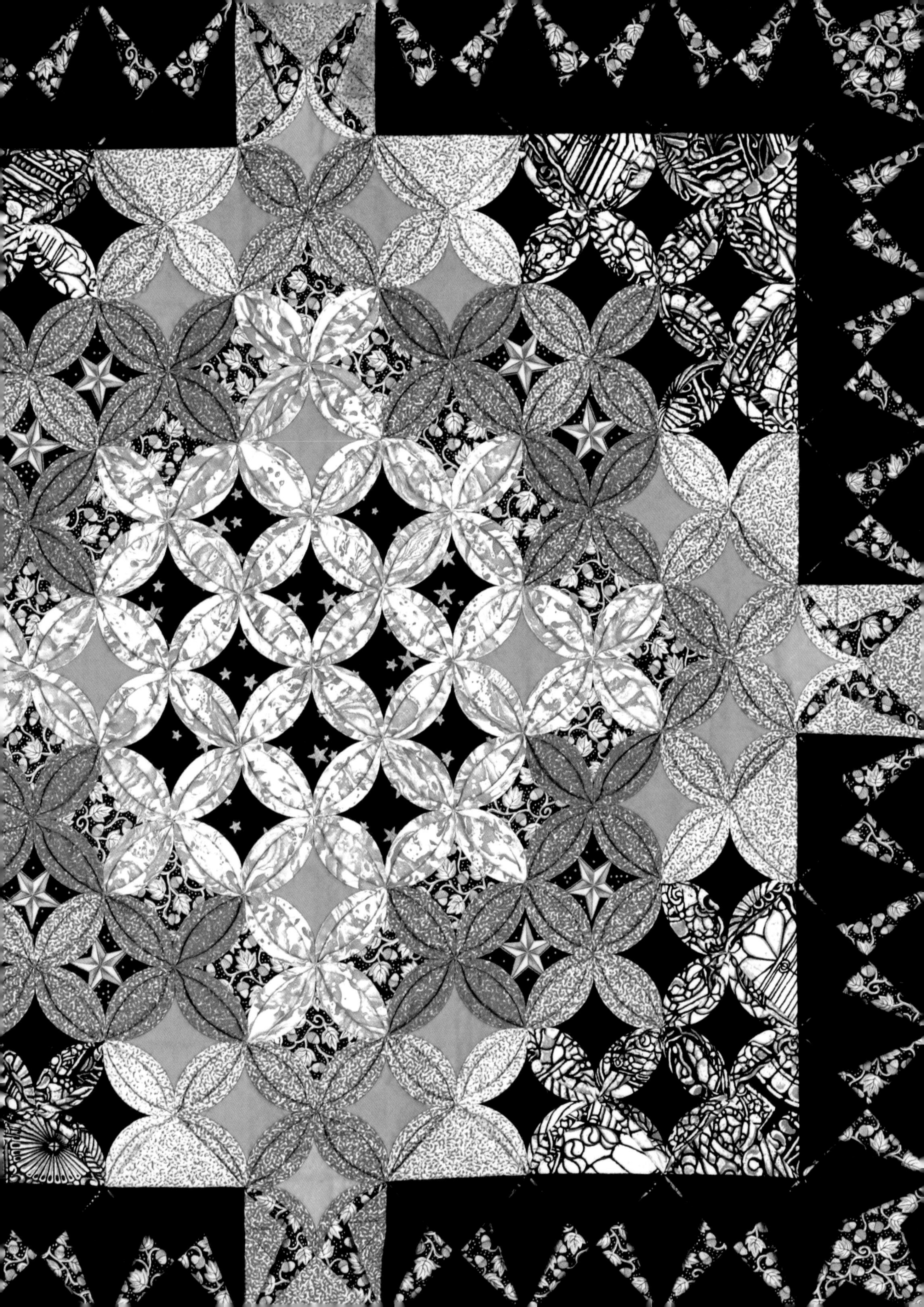

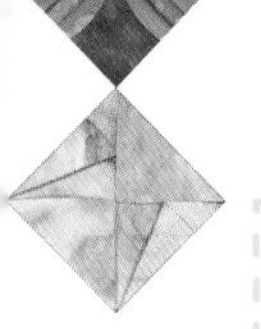

Cutting the Squares

All the details for cutting the folded background squares given for classic Cathedral Window apply to Twisted Windows (see Cutting the Squares on page 18). I suggest you use squares cut 8in × 8in (20.3cm x 20.3cm) for trying out the technique but if you prefer to use the smaller 6½in × 6½in (16.5cm × 16.5cm) square that will be fine.

Making a Twisted Windows Unit

1 From the chosen fabric cut one square measuring 8in × 8in (20.3cm x 20.3cm). Follow the instructions given in steps 2–11 in Making a Cathedral Window Unit on page 18.

2 Open out the folded corners of the square to reveal the unstitched section. Stitch the centre of the square as described in step 2 Stitching the Folded Square on page 19. Also stitch up the small opening so that the folded square is completely sealed. Keep the stitching as nearly invisible as possible, as some of these seams will show in the final design (Fig 1). Finish off the stitching at the back of the work.

Fig 1

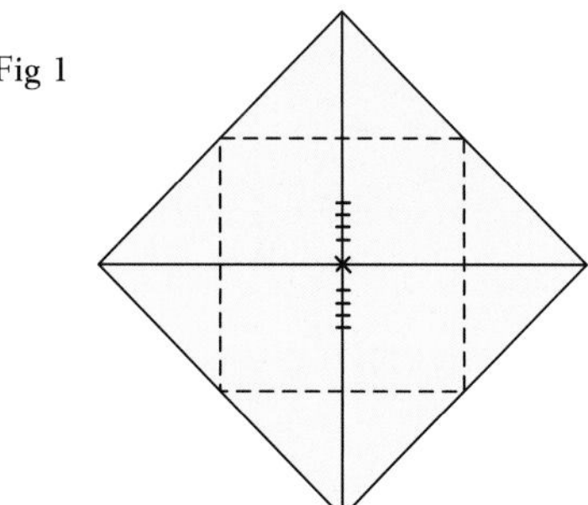

3 Bring the four corners into the centre as previously pressed. Do not stitch them down, but pin each corner in place as shown in Fig 2.

Fig 2

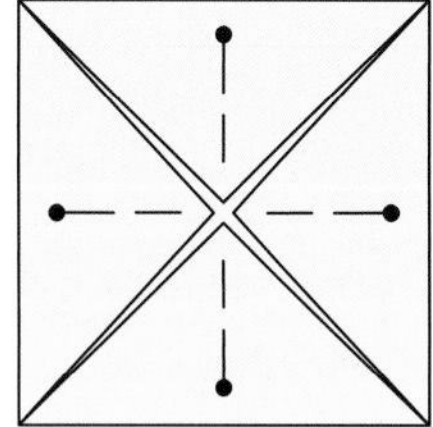

TIP

When stitching several of these folded squares together, you may find the pins a nuisance. An alternative is to stitch the corners at the centre into place temporarily with two large tacking (basting) stitches through the layers. Remove these once the whole design is joined.

4 Before pulling back the corners of the block to make the Twisted Windows, the folded square must be stitched in place with all the other blocks in the design. To make the four-patch designs shown in Fig 3, four folded squares are made and joined together.

Fig 3

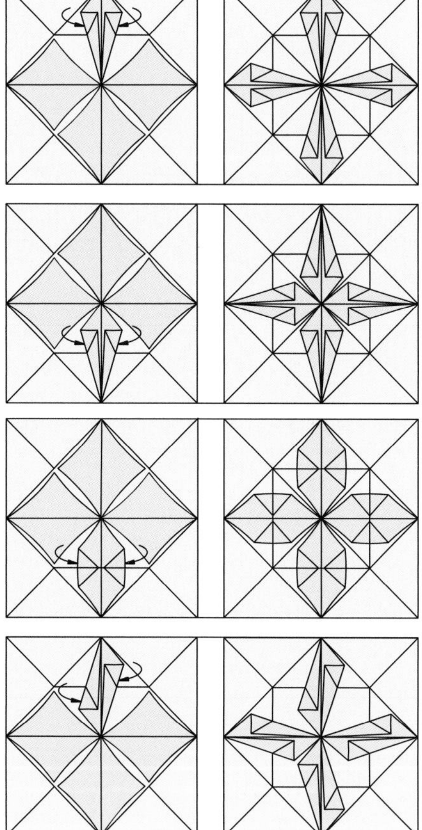

TIP

If you are joining the blocks together by machine, stitch the centres of each block by hand as in step 2 above and then follow Joining Square Blocks by Machine on page 20. After stitching together, press the four corners into the centre of each folded square and pin as in Fig 2.

5 Now oversew the squares together in the usual way, matching corners carefully and keeping the corners of the squares as sharp as possible (Fig 4).

Fig 4

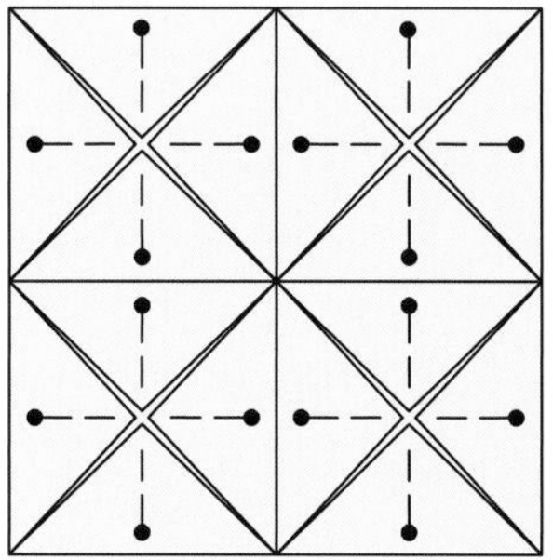

6 To make any of the four-patch designs shown in Fig 3 remove the pins from the eight central triangles (the shaded sections in Fig 5). Ignore these flapping triangles and secure the remaining two corners at the centre of each folded square, (marked A and B), with a pair of tiny stitches through all the layers.

Fig 5

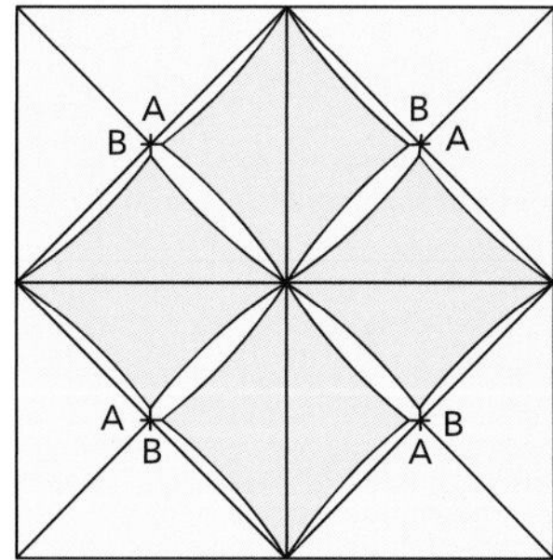

7 Try all the folded designs in Fig 3 to see which you find the most effective. Fold the loose triangles back, as shown, and pin them in position. Stitch them into place by catching the loose corners with two tiny stitches through all the layers. Press the folded block after stitching.

Bright Batiks Wall Hanging

This beautiful design (see overleaf and page 17) combines all three square variations of Cathedral Window – a centre of classic Cathedral Window has corners of Secret Garden and a final border of Twisted Windows. The use of gorgeous batik fabrics adds an extra dimension and certainly makes it eye-catching. Fig 6a shows the arrangement of the folded background squares and Fig 6b shows the window plan.

Folded squares finished size: 3¾in × 3¾in (9.5cm × 9.5cm).
Wall hanging finished size: 26¼in × 26¼in (66.7cm × 66.7cm).

REQUIREMENTS

- **For the background folded squares:**
  Fabric A: five squares each 8in × 8in (20.3cm × 20.3cm)
  Fabric B: eight squares each 8in × 8in (20.3cm × 20.3cm) – ½yd (0.5m) will be plenty
  Fabric C: twelve squares each 8in × 8in (20.3cm × 20.3cm) – ¾yd (0.75m)
  Fabric D: twenty-four squares each 8in × 8in (20.3cm × 20.3cm), plus twelve smaller squares for the inside of the Secret Garden units each 3¾in × 3¾in (9.5cm × 9.5cm) – ½yd (1.4m) in total (I didn't have enough of one fabric, so used two very similar batik fabrics in alternating squares for this outer border)
- **For the windows:**
  Fabric (a): the centre four windows – one square of fabric 6in × 6in (15.2cm × 15.2cm)
  Fabric (b): the surrounding sixteen windows – one square of fabric 12in × 12in (30.5cm × 30.5cm)

Fig 6a *Background squares plan*

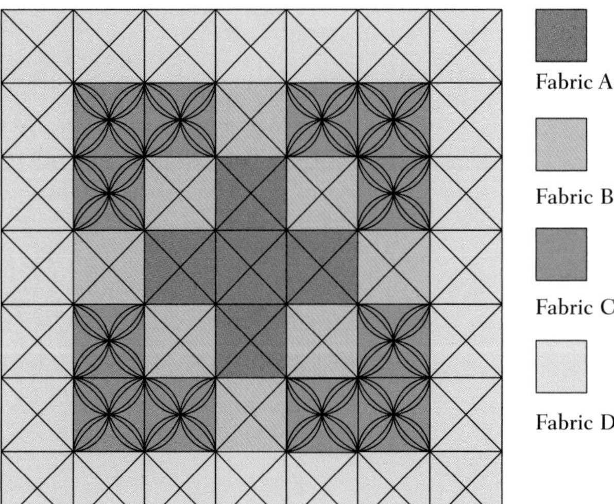

Fig 6b *Window plan*

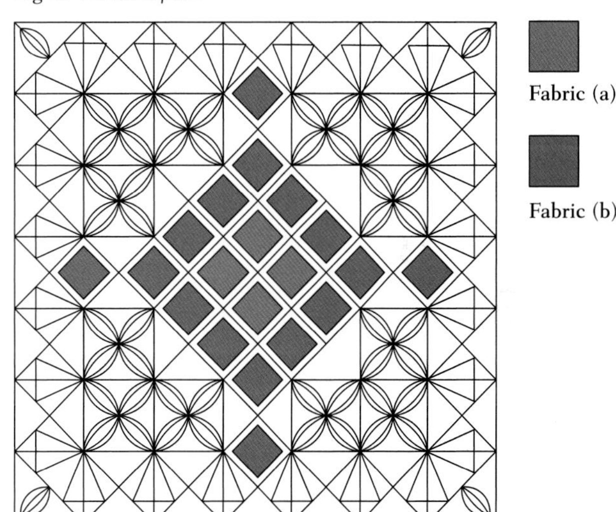

Construction

The centre section of twenty-five folded squares (5 × 5 rows) is made first, before the outer border of Twisted Windows is added.

TIP

If you are stitching the folded squares together by machine, do not add any windows at all until all the background folded squares are joined together in the arrangement shown in Fig 6a.

Making the Centre Section

1 Cut five squares from fabric A, eight squares from fabric B and twelve squares from fabric C, all measuring 8in × 8in (20.3cm × 20.3cm).

2 Cut twelve squares from fabric D, each measuring 3¾in × 3¾in (9.5cm × 9.5cm) for the Secret Garden windows. Using the twelve squares of fabric C, construct the Secret Garden folded background squares with their inner windows of fabric D, following steps 1–14 Making a Secret Garden Unit on page 36.

3 Take the five squares of fabric A and the eight squares of fabric B and follow the directions in Making a Cathedral Window Unit beginning on page 18 to construct thirteen folded background squares. The finished squares should all measure 3¾in × 3¾in (9.5cm × 9.5cm).

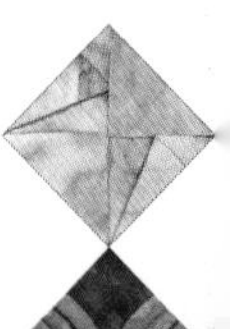

4 Arrange the folded squares and the completed Secret Garden units in the design shown in Fig 7. Join the squares into rows, and then stitch the rows together, matching seams carefully.

Fig 7

Adding the Windows

5 If you prefer to cut with templates, make a template for the window (see Tip after step 2 on page 22). If you are simply cutting squares with rotary cutting equipment cut squares measuring 2³/₈in × 2³/₈in (6cm × 6cm) for the windows. Cut four windows from fabric (a) and twelve windows from fabric (b), each measuring 2³/₈in × 2³/₈in (6cm × 6cm).

6 Arrange the windows on the Cathedral Window background squares as shown in Fig 8.

Fig 8

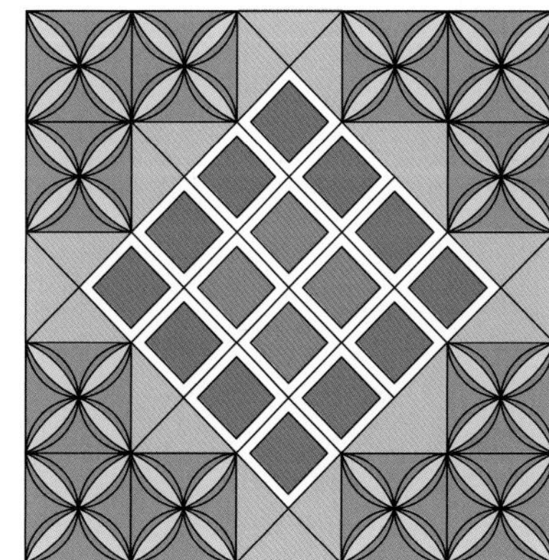

7 Stitch each window in place, matching the sewing thread to the background fabric. Follow the directions for Adding the Windows on page 22.

Making the Twisted Window Blocks

8 From fabric D cut twenty-four squares, each measuring 8in × 8in (20.3cm × 20.3cm). I didn't have enough of one fabric, so used two very similar batik fabrics and used them alternately as fabric D in the Twisted Window border.

9 Follow the instructions given in steps 1–3 earlier on page 52 to make the twenty-four folded squares. These will have their outer corners folded into the centre and pinned or tacked temporarily in position as in Fig 2 on page 52.

10 Arrange five of the folded squares into a strip and stitch them together by oversewing them in the usual way (see Joining Folded Squares on page 20). Repeat this with another five squares to make a second strip.

TIP

When arranging the folded squares into a row, place each one so that the hand-stitched section of the centre seam is vertical on the block. This keeps the hand-stitching nicely hidden when the windows are twisted back later as in Fig 11 and 12.

11 Pin and stitch one of these strips to either side of the main quilt (Fig 9).

Fig 9

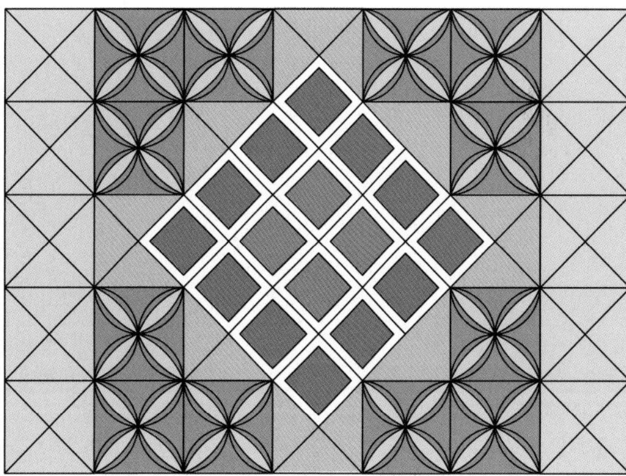

12 Arrange seven folded squares into a strip, pinning and stitching them together. Repeat this with the remaining seven folded squares to make a second strip.

13 Pin and stitch these strips to the top and bottom of the quilt (Fig 10).

Fig 10

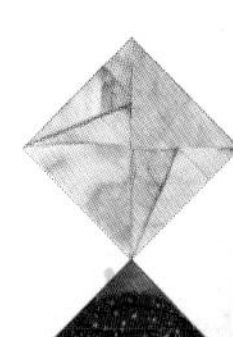

14 Remove the pins or tacking from all the folded squares except those in each of the four corners of the wall hanging. Leave these until last, as they have a different folded design. The other twenty folded squares are all folded back in exactly the same arrangement as in Fig 11. Two of the corners at the centre of each folded square (marked A and B in Fig 12) will be stitched down while the other two are left, ready to be twisted back.

Fig 11

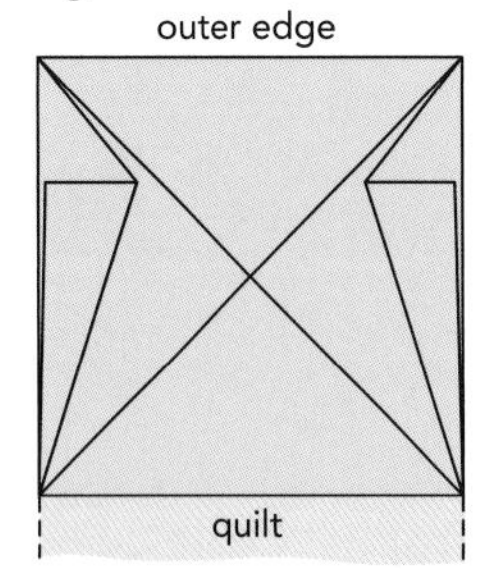

15 Secure the two corners at A and B as in Fig 12 with two tiny stitches through all the layers.

Fig 12

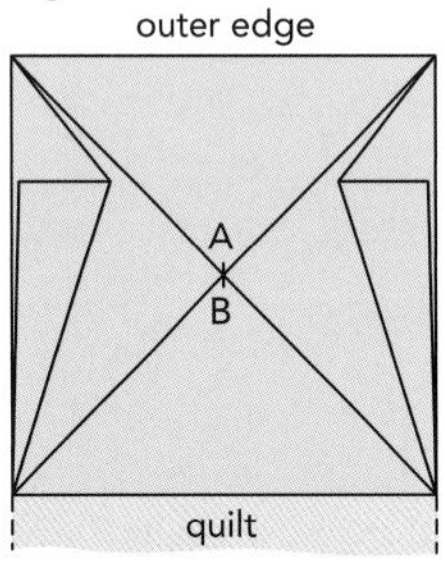

outer edge

A

B

quilt

16 Fold the two loose corners of each block back as in Fig 12 and pin in position. Stitch them down as in step 7 of Making a Twisted Window unit on page 52.

17 Remove the pins or tacking from the four corner squares. Stitch down the two corners on the outer edges of each square as in Fig 13. Twist back the other two corners in the arrangement in Fig 13 and stitch them down as the other Twisted Window corners.

Fig 13

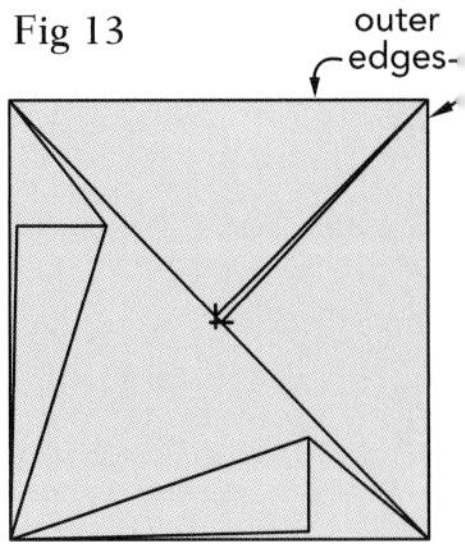

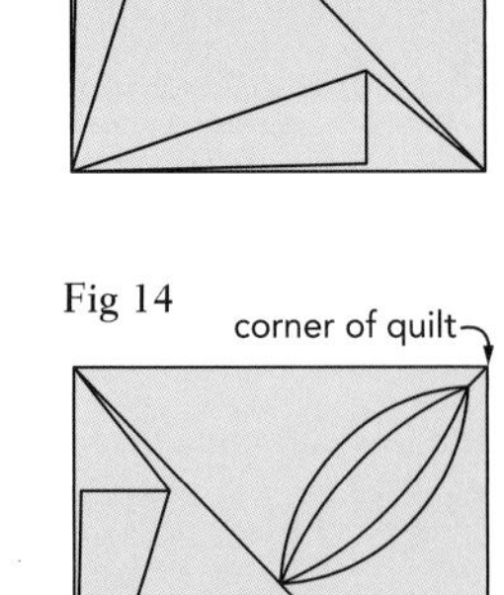

18 The outer corners of the wall hanging are given an extra emphasis with the addition of a Secret Garden treatment to the diagonal folded edges (Fig 14). The bias edges are rolled back and stitched to give the characteristic petal effect (see steps 7–10 Making a Secret Garden Unit on page 37). The wall hanging is now complete. No framing border or binding is needed, just a sleeve on the back for hanging it in pride of place.

Fig 14

corner of quilt

This shows the reverse side of the Bright Batiks wall hanging, which is a quilt design in its own right. Because the backs are so interesting, giving an insight into the construction of the piece, in my recent pieces I have joined the folded squares together by machine to give the back a cleaner finish.

Les Nunn used the Bright Batiks quilt design and reinterpreted it with his own choice of fabrics to great effect in his creation, Amethyst Twist. The fabrics used are softer and create less contrast than those in the Bright Batiks wall hanging, so that the design flows into the final border of Twisted Windows, rather than being set within a contrasting frame. An extra layer was inserted in the Twisted Windows border to give more contrast to the design. *See also Playing with Twisted Windows overleaf.*

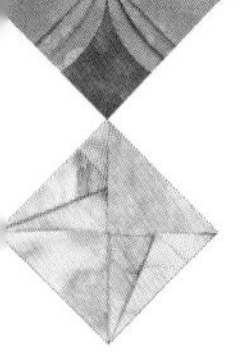

Playing with Twisted Windows

Using a dark or busy fabric for the folded background squares, can mean that the twisted shapes lose their visual impact. This can be counteracted by adding an extra square of contrasting light fabric between the layers like Secret Garden, with an extra ½in (1.3cm) added for seam allowances to eliminate the raw edges, and stitching it in place. Jane Gaddas did this in her Mandarin Dreams wall hanging on page 30 (see steps 3–6 Construction on page 30–31). When the corners are turned back to make the kite shapes, they are highlighted against the contrast inner layer.

Jean Campbell also used this strategy in her lively African Windows piece, shown opposite, where she created yet more twisted variations around the outer edge of the design. She calmed the busy African fabric she used for the folded squares with centres of black fabric that she over-printed with fabric paint to add interest to the design.

A detail from Jean Campbell's African Windows design, showing three of the Twisted Windows blocks (see also Fig 16). Fabric paints were used on the black fabric to give further interest.

Fig 15

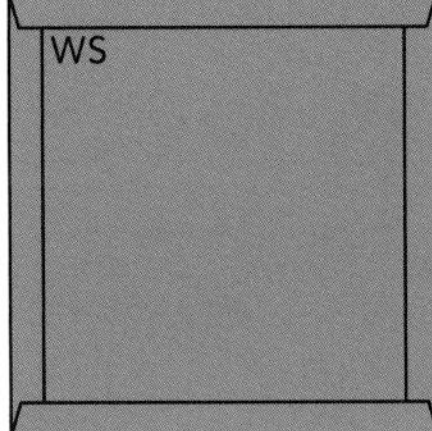

Fig 16

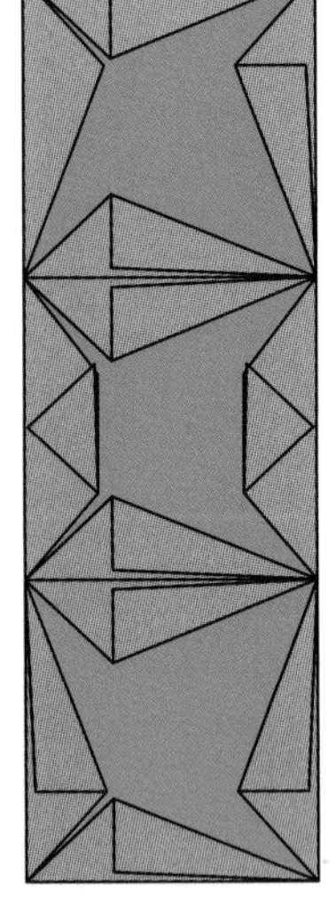

For African Windows the squares of black fabric were cut 4¼in × 4¼in (10.8cm × 10.8cm), which is ½in (1.3cm) larger than the folded background square. A seam allowance of ¼in (6mm) was ironed to the back of the cut square on all sides (Fig 15). The inner square of black fabric was then laid right side up within the background folded square like Secret Garden and stitched into place. The stitches should be just into the top layer of the background square, not right through all the layers to the back. The four corners of the background square were then folded back and stitched in the arrangements shown in Fig 16.

'Sometimes when I am laboriously adding extra layers and turning in seam allowances within the folded squares, I think I must be mad. Then, as the windows are revealed and the extra effects shine through, I know exactly why I am doing it.'

Jean Campbell is an embroiderer at heart and cannot resist embellishing her work with beads, decorative thread work and even printing and overdyeing, as seen in the design above. She can be found crooning and stroking, not just the fabric, but box after box of gleaming threads and shimmering beads – we're all the same at heart…

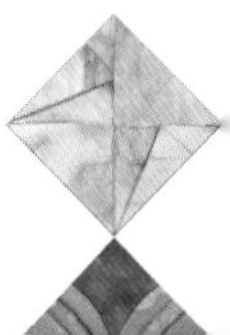

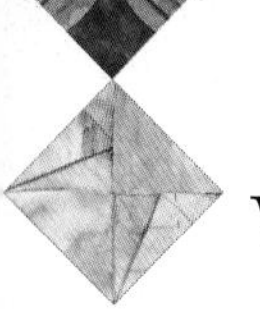

Winter Solstice

For this eye-catching wall hanging, Winter Solstice (also shown on page 8), I edged a complex centre of classic Cathedral Window with a border of Twisted Windows. Like Jean in her African Windows, I used an inner layer of fabric with an extra seam allowance stitched in place between the layers to help highlight the black Twisted Window folded squares. The centre design of seven rows each of folded squares (forty-nine in total) was made from four fabrics as shown in Fig 17a below. The windows were cut from five fabrics and arranged and stitched as in Fig 17b. The final four windows of gold fabric, which give the piece real impact, were added after the black Twisted Window border was added.

Folded square finished size: 3in × 3in (7.6cm × 7.6cm).
Wall hanging finished size: 27in × 27in (68.6cm × 68.6cm).

REQUIREMENTS

- **For the folded background squares:**
  Fabric A: ½yd (0.5m);
  Fabric B: ¾yd (0.75m);
  Fabric C: ½yd (0.5m);
  Fabric D: ¾yd (0.75m);
  Fabric E: 1yd (1m) for the Twisted Windows border
- **For the windows:**
  One 12in x 12in (30.5cm x 30.5cm) square each of five different fabrics;
  For the inner layer of Twisted Windows border 12in (30.5cm) of fabric 42in–44in (107cm–112cm) wide

Fig 17a *Background squares plan*

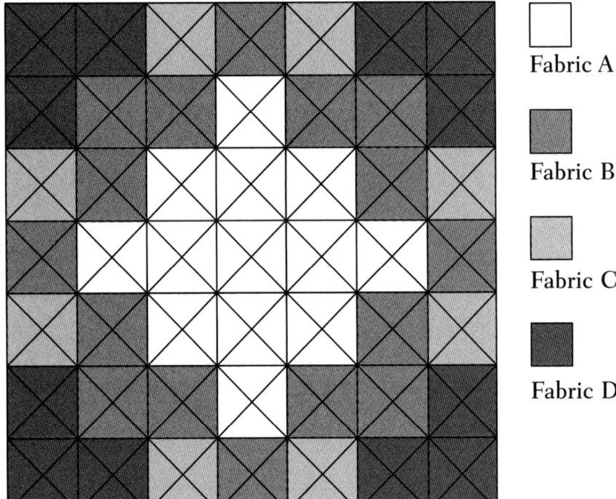

Fig 17b *Window plan*

Construction

1 Cut the following squares, all 6½in × 6½in (16.5cm × 16.5cm): thirteen squares from fabric A, sixteen from fabric B, twelve from fabric C and twelve from fabric D. Set four of the fabric C squares aside for the Twisted Windows border.

2 Follow the directions in Making a Cathedral Window Unit beginning on page 18 to construct forty-nine folded background squares from the remaining cut squares.

3 Arrange the folded squares in the design shown in Fig 17a above and stitch them together.

Adding the Windows

4 If you prefer to 'fussy-cut' some of the windows (see page 31) using a clear plastic template, make a template for the window from Template 1 on page 73. Remember to place the template on point.

5 If you are simply cutting squares with rotary cutting equipment you will need to cut squares measuring 1⅞in × 1⅞in (4.7cm × 4.7cm) for the windows. I used five different fabrics and fussy-cut starry fabric to make the windows more interesting, but just choose whatever fabric you like and arrange them to suit your ideas and fabrics.

6 Arrange the windows on the Cathedral Window background squares in the design shown in Fig 17b.

7 Stitch each window in place, matching the sewing thread to the background fabric. Follow the directions for Adding the Windows on page 22.

Making the Twisted Window Blocks

8 From fabric E cut twenty-eight squares each measuring 6½in × 6½in (16.5cm × 16.5cm).

9 Follow the instructions given in steps 1–3 on page 52 to make the twenty-eight folded squares from fabric E and also four folded squares from the remaining cut squares of fabric C. Cut thirty-two squares of fabric for the inner layer each measuring 3½in × 3½in (8.9cm × 8.9cm). For cutting and stitching the inner layers see steps 3–6 Construction page 30. After adding the inner layers, fold the outer corners of each square into the centre and pin or tack them temporarily into position as in Fig 2 on page 52.

10 Arrange seven of the folded squares into a strip, three squares of fabric E either side of one square of fabric C, and stitch them together by oversewing them in the usual way. Repeat this with another seven squares to make a second strip.

11 Pin and stitch one of these strips to either side of the main quilt.

12 Arrange nine folded squares into a strip, four squares of fabric E on either side of one square of fabric C. Pin and stitch them together. Repeat this with the remaining nine folded squares to make a second strip. Pin and stitch them to the top and bottom of the quilt.

13 Remove pins or tacking from all the folded squares except those in the four corners of the wall hanging. The other twenty-eight folded squares are all folded back in exactly the same arrangement as shown in Fig 18. Two of the corners at the centre of each folded square (those marked A and B in Fig 19) will be stitched down while the other two are left ready to be twisted back.

Fig 18

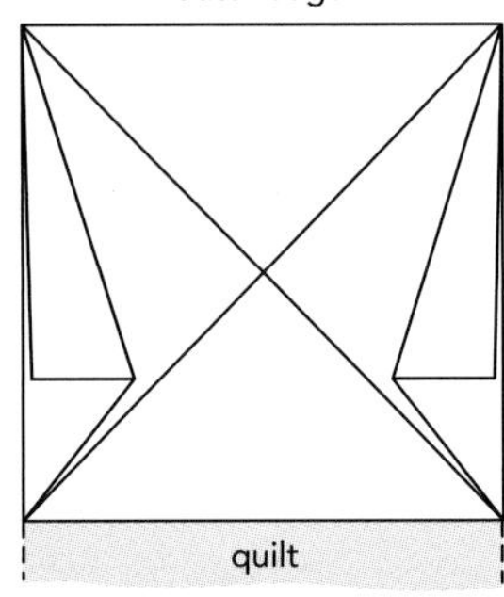

14 Secure the two corners at A and B as Fig 19 with two tiny stitches through all layers.

Fig 19

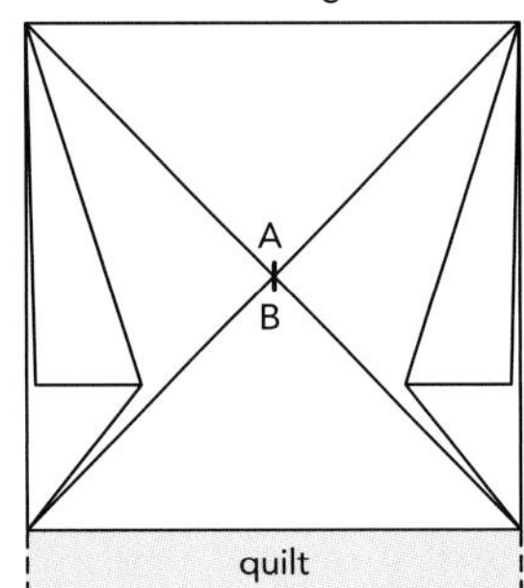

15 Fold the two loose corners of each block back as in Fig 19 and pin in position. Stitch them down as described earlier in step 7 of Making a Twisted Window Unit on page 52.

16 Remove the pins or tacking from the four corner squares. Stitch down the two inner corners of each square to make the usual kite shape as in Fig 20. To keep the outer corner of the block sharp, sew a double bar stitch ¼in (6mm) from the corner, stitching across the two folded edges through all the layers in a stab stitch like Secret Garden corners. Fold back two corners from the bar stitch level with the outer edges of the block as in Fig 21. Stitch them down as the other Twisted Window corners and also stitch the corners marked X to keep the design in place.

Fig 20

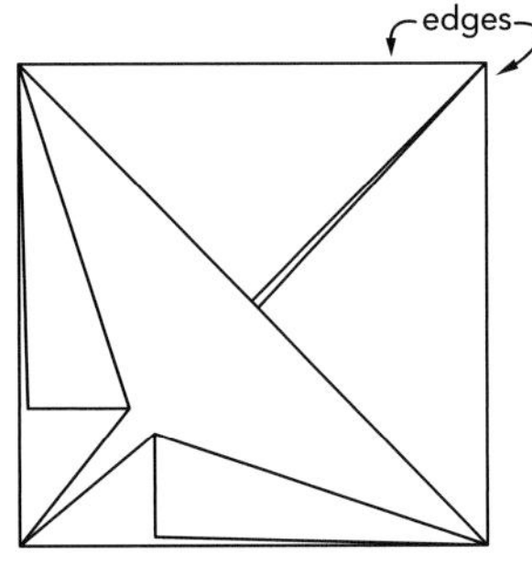

Fig 21

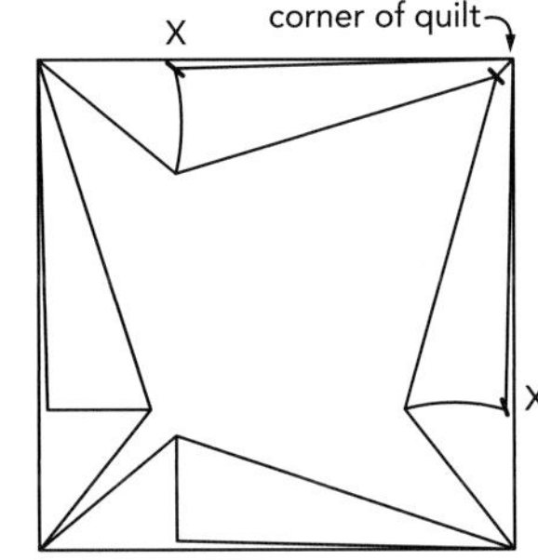

17 Finally, add four extra windows to link the centre design to the Twisted Windows border as shown in Fig 22 in the positions marked A.

Fig 22

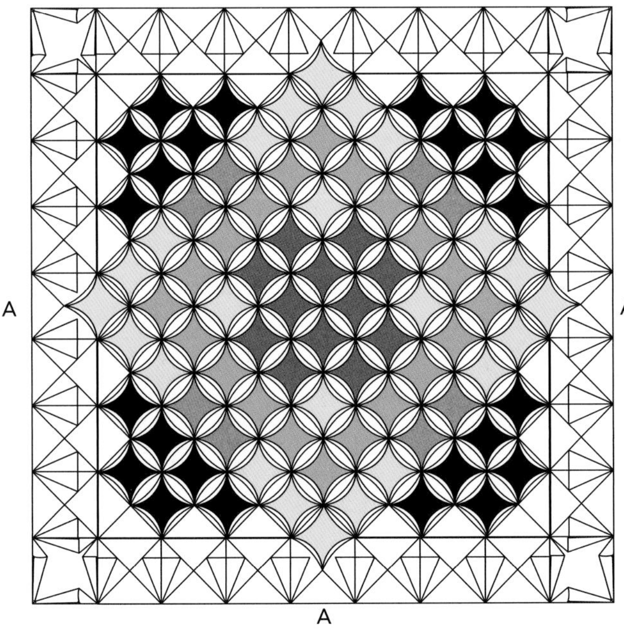

Another Combination-Block Design

The same 5 × 5 block design is shown here in two very different colour interpretations. Twinkle, Twinkle (see picture below) is a baby version of Winter Solstice, with Twisted Window corners as in Fig 21, opposite. The other picture is Glowing Batik, a strikingly coloured version, with corners as in Fig 14 on page 56.

The 5 x 5 block plan.

Window plan for Twinkle, Twinkle 5 x 5 block.

Window plan for Glowing Batik 5 x 5 block.

I so enjoyed playing with all those stars in Winter Solstice that I couldn't resist making a smaller version,Twinkle, Twinkle.

I tried the same arrangement as Twinkle, Twinkle with some of the wild fabrics in my batik collection to make this piece, Glowing Batik. What fun it is to step out of character sometimes!

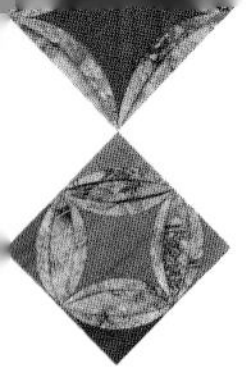

Cathedral Window – Using Rectangles

I often incorporate folded rectangles in my Cathedral Window work, combining them with the folded squares to create depth and movement in the designs. You may ask, why bother with different shapes when the simple Cathedral Window square is so effective? Perhaps the impressive piece, Dawning Rose, shown opposite shows you why. This quilt is also shown in full on the inside covers of the book.

The two designs in Fig 1 and Fig 2 show what a difference the addition of rectangles can make to a design. Figs 1a and 2a show the plan of folded squares and rectangles, while Figs 1b and 2b show the overlying windows added. The small folded square in the centre of the first design gives a density to the central windows, while in the second design the large folded square in the centre makes the shapes of the central windows seem to curve outwards towards us.

Quilt finished size: 63in x 92in (160cm x 233.7cm).

Fig 1a

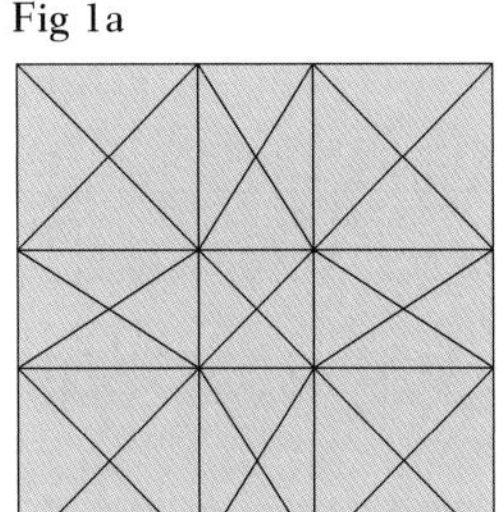

Fig 1b

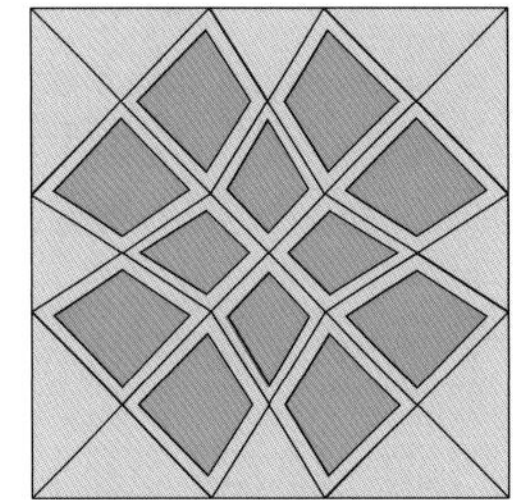

Fig 2a

Fig 2b

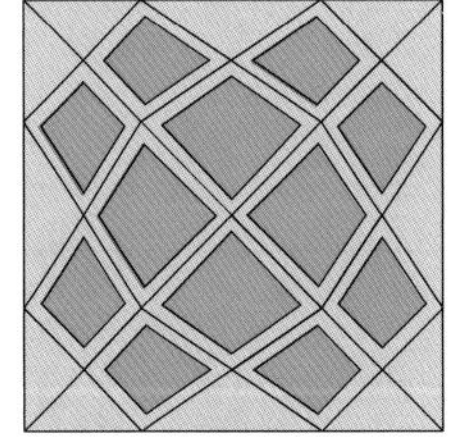

This detail picture shows an example of a single rectangular Cathedral Window block.

I was asked to make a Cathedral Window quilt for a contemporary quilt show at Shipley Art Gallery in North East England. Only bed-size pieces would be included, so I took a smaller design that had ground to an unfinished halt and developed it into this large, landscape-format piece. The silk windows in their varying shapes float and shimmer on a multitude of background fabrics, giving depth and movement. It is the largest Cathedral Window quilt I have made and the one, I admit, of which I am most proud.

Making the Rectangular Shape

The template for a rectangular Cathedral Window unit is not the rectangle that you would expect it to be. Instead it is a very odd shape indeed. I have given templates for the folded rectangles used in the projects, but it is useful to know how a rectangle is drafted on graph paper to give the unexpected starting shape. Those with good mathematical skills will doubtless know the technical steps to achieve the template outline with a ruler and a pair of compasses, but this method is for those more geometrically challenged. The shape for the initial template to be used for drawing round on the fabric is found by drawing out the final rectangle shape and working back through the folding procedures until you get the required template shape.

'I have tried to approach the technical drawing aspect of the rectangles from a practical rather than a theoretical viewpoint, so there's no need to be frightened...'

1 Draw the finished rectangle full size on graph paper. Draw diagonal lines from corner to corner. This is what the fabric rectangle will look like after all the folding (Fig 3).

Fig 3

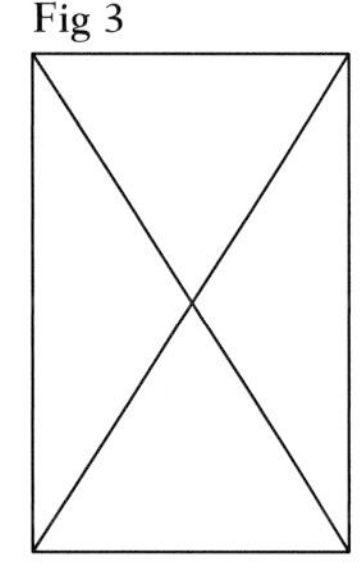

2 Draw a horizontal and vertical line through the centre of the rectangle and well beyond it. Measure from the centre (O) to point A, and then mark this distance from A to AA and from C to CC. Now measure from the centre (O) to point B, and then mark this distance from B to BB and from D to DD (Fig 4).

Fig 4

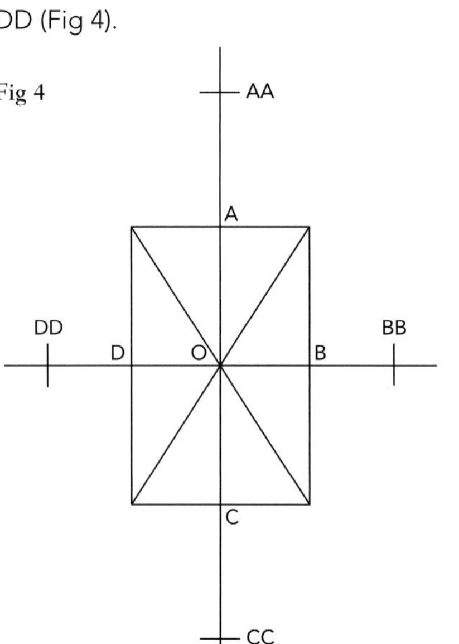

3 Join the points AA, BB, CC, and DD to form a diamond (Fig 5).

Fig 5

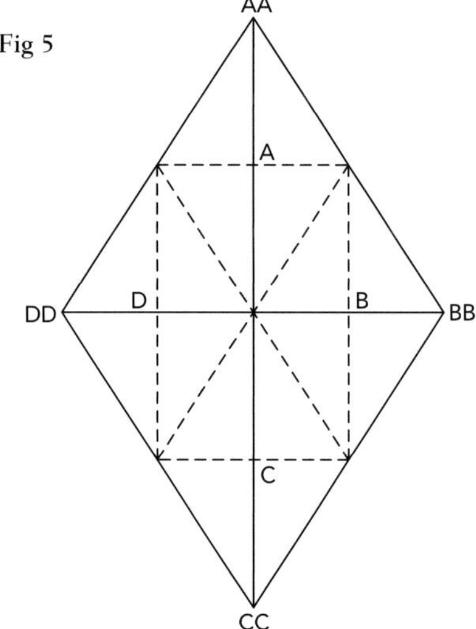

4 Erase all the lines of the original drawn rectangle and its diagonals so that you finish up with Fig 6.

Fig 6

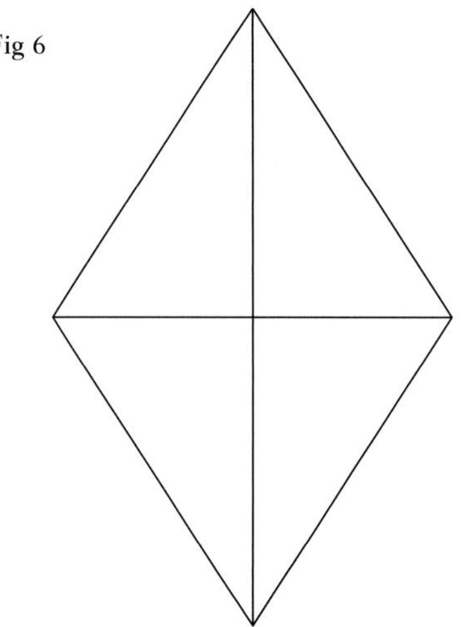

5 Make a template of one triangular quarter section of the diamond (the shaded area in Fig 7) by tracing it, cutting it out and sticking it on to card, or by using template plastic. Flip the template over on to its *wrong* side and place the longest edge against one side of the diamond. Draw around the other two sides (Fig 8).

Fig 7

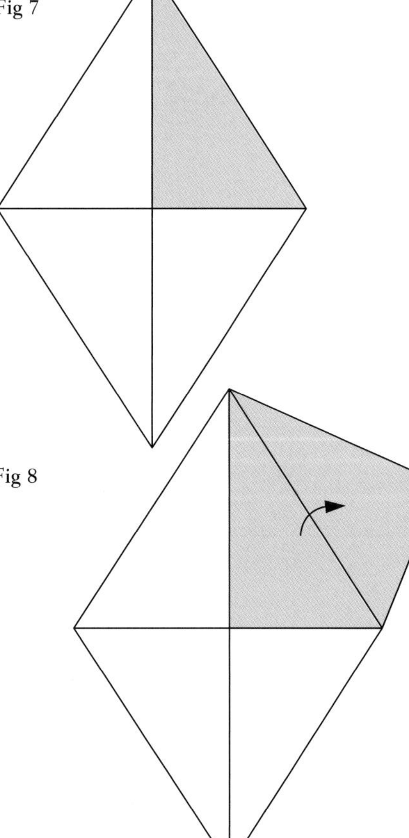

Fig 8

6 Repeat this on the remaining three sides of the diamond. This makes the complete shape for a rectangular Cathedral Window template (Fig 9). All that is needed now is the extra ¼in (6mm) on all sides for the seam allowance (Fig 10).

Fig 9

Fig 10

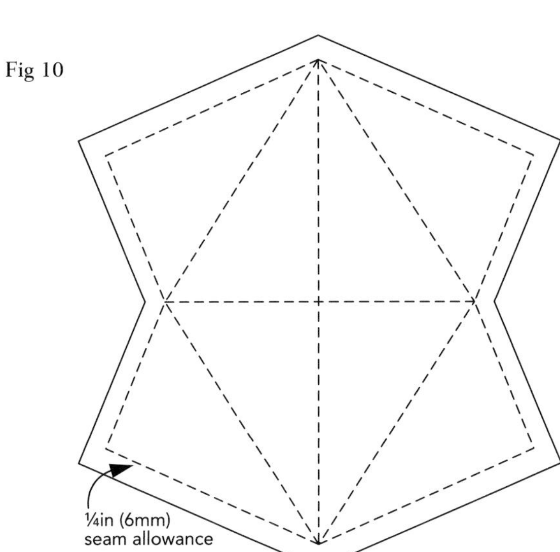

What Size Rectangle?

The rectangle I use most measures 3in × 4½in (7.6cm × 11.4cm) – a short rectangle that is half as long again as it is wide. It combines with a small square that measures 3in × 3in (7.6cm × 7.6cm) finished size and a larger square 4½in × 4½in (1.4cm × 11.4cm) finished size, as in the designs in Figs 1 and 2 on page 64. A variety of shapes for the overlying windows will result from combining the squares and rectangles in different arrangements. Most of the designs in this section of the book use this size of rectangle together with the two sizes of folded squares. It is relatively easy to make this shape so that the resulting design looks good, even the first time you attempt it.

Because this size rectangle is the most useful for exploring designing with Cathedral Window, I have designed a special ruler which will enable you to cut the strange shape more quickly and efficiently using rotary cutting (see the picture on page 11). However, this is not an absolute essential, just an aid to the addict. If you prefer to use the template overleaf, follow the instructions there for cutting the rectangle starting shapes.

TIP

The way to calculate the starting size of the folded squares is given in the classic Cathedral Window section on page 18. The small square of finished size 3in x 3in (7.6cm x 7.6cm) is cut 6½in x 6½in (16.5cm x 16.5cm). The larger square of finished size 4½in x 4½in (11.4cm x 11.4cm) is cut 9½in x 9½in (24.1cm x 24.1cm).

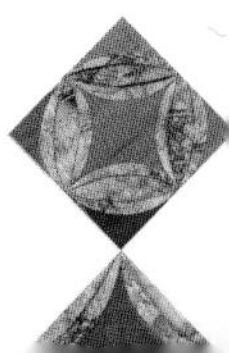

Making a Rectangular Cathedral Window Unit

1 The template to use here is given in Fig 11. Half of the shape is given at actual size. Trace the shape on to a large sheet of paper, flip the tracing over and trace the mirror image to create the full template. Cut out the completed shape and stick it on to card (or use template plastic).

2 Place the template on to the back of the fabric and draw around it, using a sharp marking pencil. Cut the shape out, using scissors or a rotary cutter and ruler.

TIP

Several rectangle units can be cut at once using a rotary cutter and ruler. I draw around the template on the top layer only, and then cut along the drawn lines through all the layers. Take care at the inner corners to cut only to the marked corners, not further into the drawn shape.

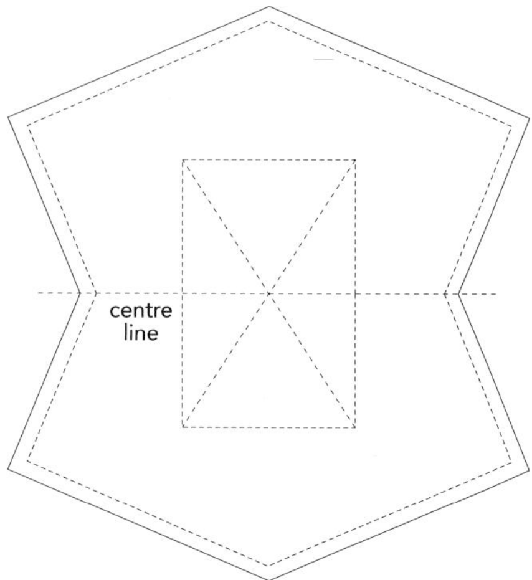

The complete template shape.

Fig 11

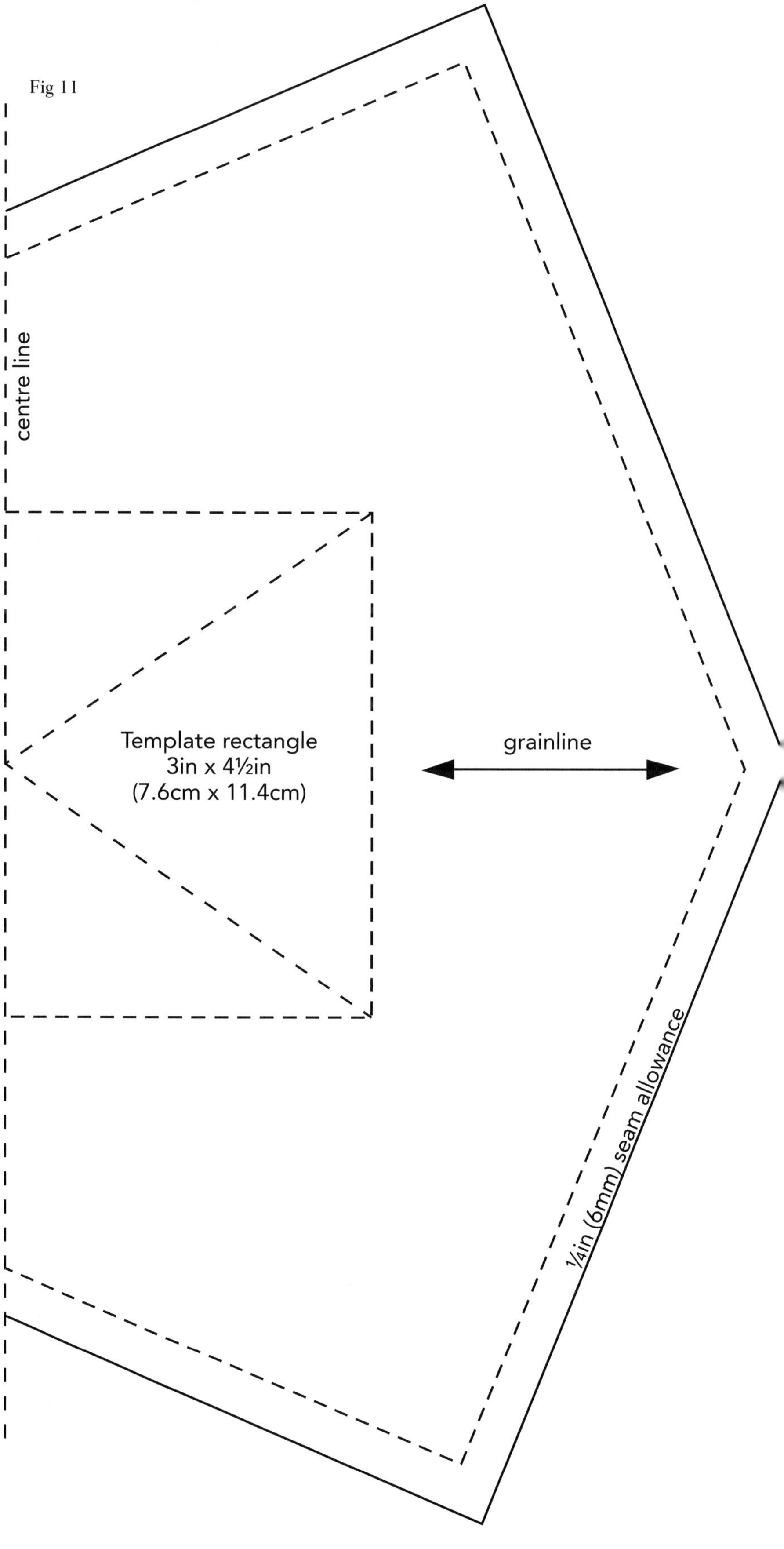

centre line

Template rectangle
3in x 4½in
(7.6cm x 11.4cm)

grainline

¼in (6mm) seam allowance

3 Fold the fabric in half with right sides facing along the line AB (Fig 12). Machine the shorter edges together with a ¼in (6mm) seam as in Fig 13. Trim the corner to reduce the bulk and finger-press the two seams open.

Fig 12

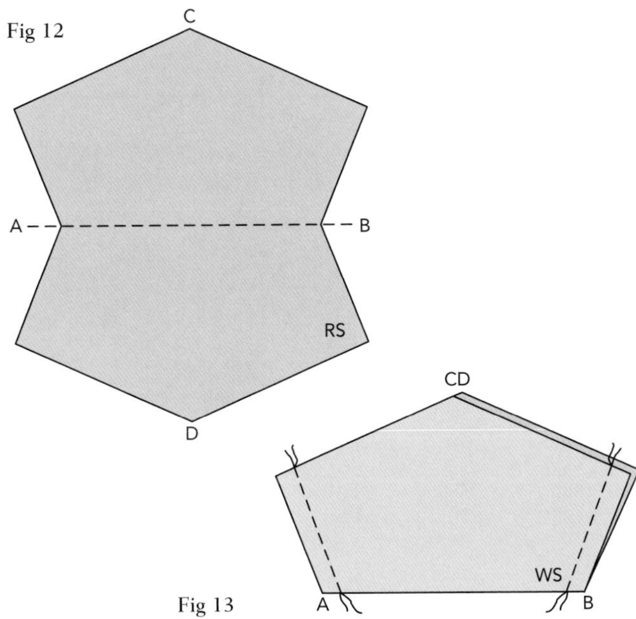

Fig 13

4 Open the stitched shape out and fold it from C to D so that the machined seams lie on top of each other. Pin the edges together, matching the centre seams. Starting about 1in (2.5cm) from the centre, stitch to point C, leaving a length of double machine threads at C (about 3in/7.6cm long). Repeat from about 1in (2.5cm) from the centre to point D, again leaving a 3in (7.6cm) length of threads (Fig 14).

Fig 14

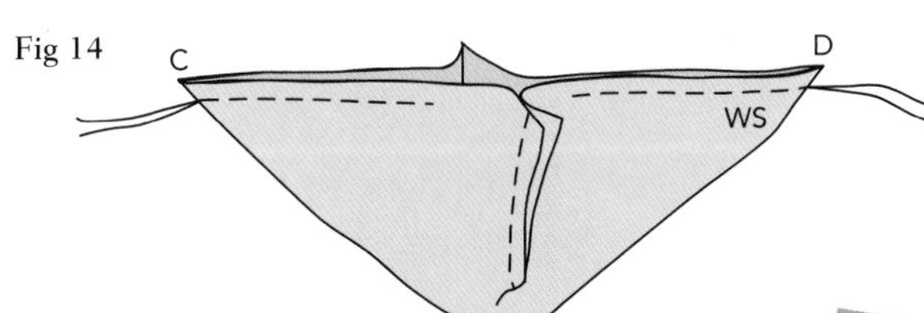

5 Trim the corners at C and D to reduce the bulk of fabric in the seam allowances. Finger-press the seams open, including the centre unstitched section (Fig 15).

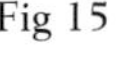

Fig 15

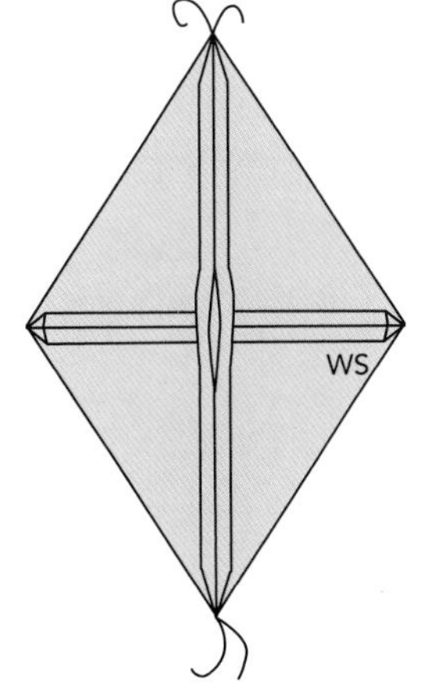

6 Turn the envelope right side out. The long corners at C and D can be pulled out more accurately if you thread up a needle with the machine threads at C and reinsert it into the fabric as near the corner of the fold as possible (Fig 16). Pull the corner through to its right side with the needle and threads, pulling really hard to bring the corner out as much as possible. Repeat at D and trim off the threads. It should now look like Fig 6.

Fig 16

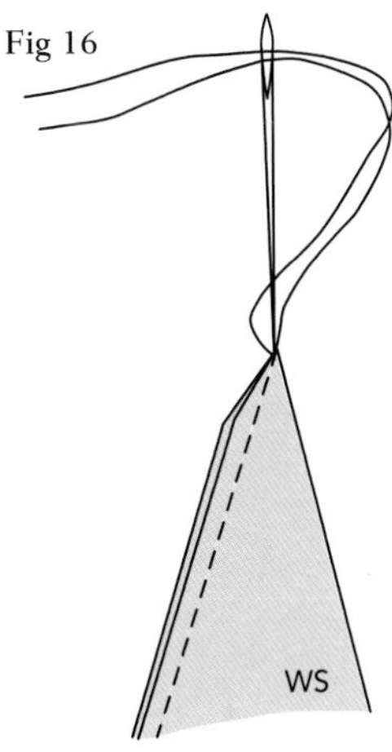

7 Press around the edge of the diamond-shaped block. Fold and press the four corners to the centre as with classic Cathedral Window (steps 7–11 Making a Cathedral Window Unit on page 19), so that it looks like the rectangle in Fig 3, page 66.

TIP

The finished size of the rectangle should be 3in × 4½in (7.6cm × 10.8cm), which is not as easy to press into this exact shape as is the usual Cathedral Window square. I have a piece of calico with a grid of 1in (2.5cm) and ½in (1.3cm) squares drawn on it, which I lay on the ironing board underneath my piece of fabric to use as a handy guide for pressing the folded rectangle to the right dimensions.

8 Stitch the centre of the folded rectangle down in the same way as the classic Cathedral Window (steps 1–4 Stitching the Folded Square on page 19). The rectangular unit is now complete and ready to be combined with other rectangles and squares in a design.

TIP

If you wish to stitch the whole design together by machine before adding windows, the folded rectangle can be treated in exactly the same way as a folded square (see Joining Square Blocks by Machine on page 20).

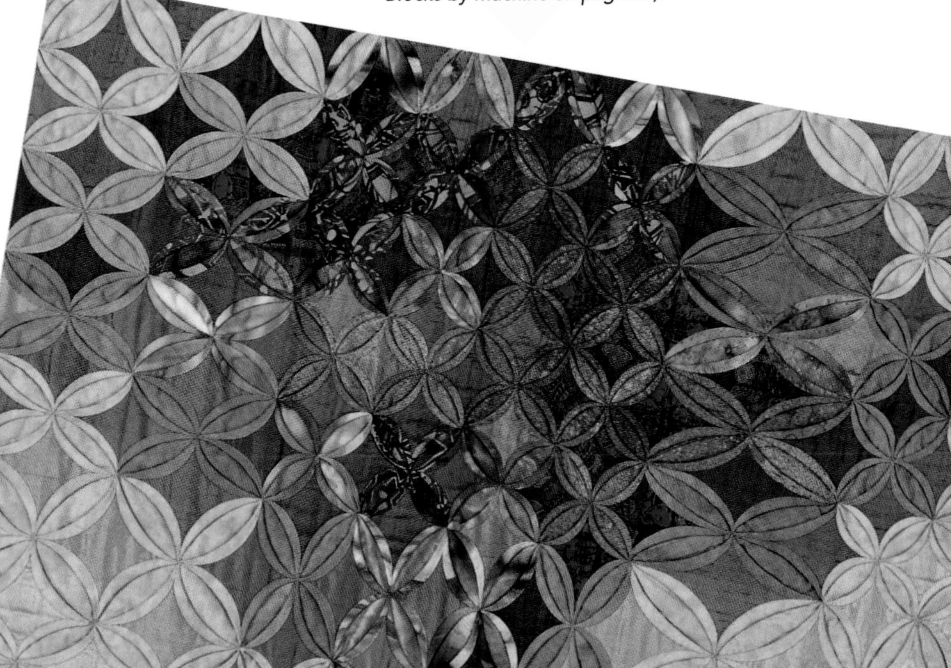

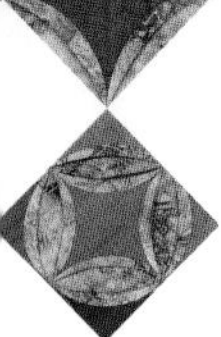

Using Rectangles with Squares

It is important to keep the final measurement of the folded squares and rectangles accurate so that they will fit together in the design. Check each shape with a ruler as you construct it (see previous Tip) and also with the other folded shapes to make sure that they are all the same size. Matching squares and rectangles is quite simple: the smaller square links with itself and with the short side of the rectangle; the large square links with itself and with the long side of the rectangle (Fig 17).

Fig 17

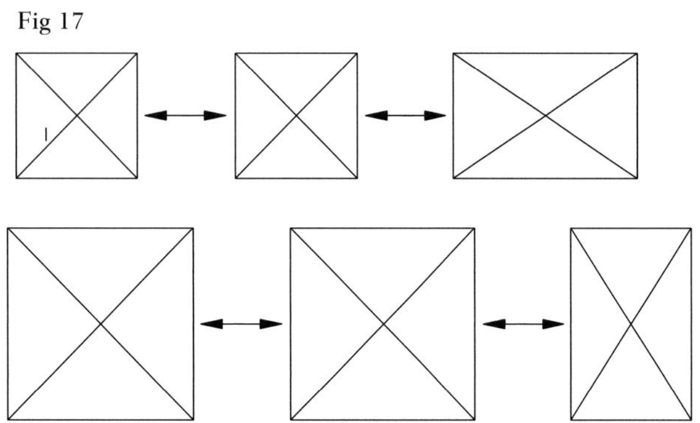

Adding Windows

A variety of window shapes occur, depending on which folded shapes are stitched together. All of the window shapes for the designs in this book are included (see page 73). If you are making original designs with different sized squares and rectangles you need to know how to draw the special window shapes for your design.
First make the folded squares and rectangles and stitch them together. To make a window template, trace the four-sided shape formed over two adjoining folded shapes. This may be symmetrical or asymmetrical as shown in the examples in Fig 18. Trim the shape down by about 1/8in (3mm) on all sides.

Fig 18

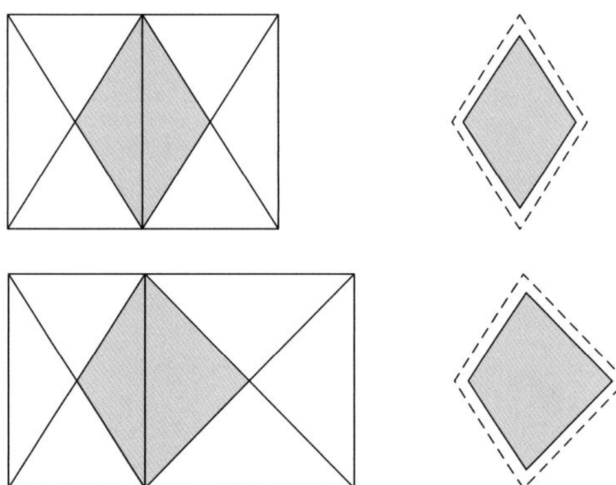

Creating Accurate Windows

The positioning and stitching of the various shaped windows is outlined in the instructions for classic Cathedral Window (see Adding the Windows on page 22), but there are a few areas that need special attention. If the window fabric needs trimming down to fit the background folded shapes, do not cut it down too much at the corners, especially if those corners are not simple square corners. Some corners will be wider than 90°. When making the bar stitches across these corners, the fabric must be pulled across the windows *firmly*, as the two bias edges have to stretch across the wider angle of the corner. Be careful not to trim the window fabric too much in case it frays out at this corner (Fig 19).

Fig 19

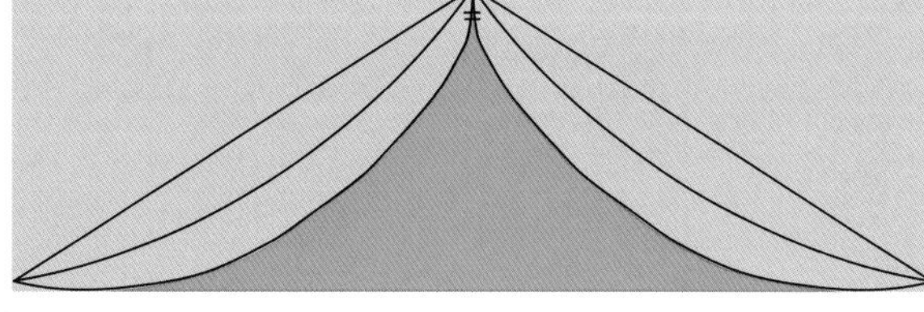

When turned, the seam allowances in the sharper, narrower corners are compressed inside and are more bulky than the square corners. Use the side of a pair of small scissors or a hera to compress the layers to help persuade the edges to roll over with both sides balanced (see step 6 Adding the Windows on page 23). Even with this assistance, the turned edges may not lie completely flat. Often they make a slight petal shape beyond the bar tack (Fig 20). This cannot be avoided, so just make sure the petal shapes balance on each side and that no tufts of window fabric show in this petal.

Fig 20

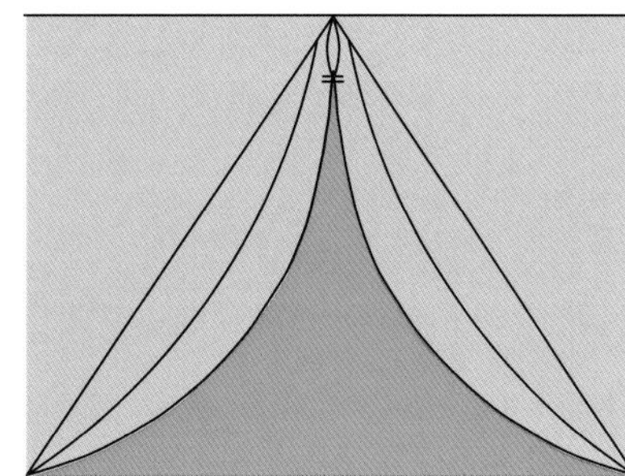

Designing with Three Shapes

The two simple symmetrical designs shown at the beginning of this section of the book are a great way to start combining rectangles and squares. Figs 21a and 22a show the plan for the background folded shapes while Figs 21b and 22b show the positioning of the various windows. The numbers on the window diagrams refer to the window templates required for each shape (these templates are on page 73).

Fig 21a

Fig 21b

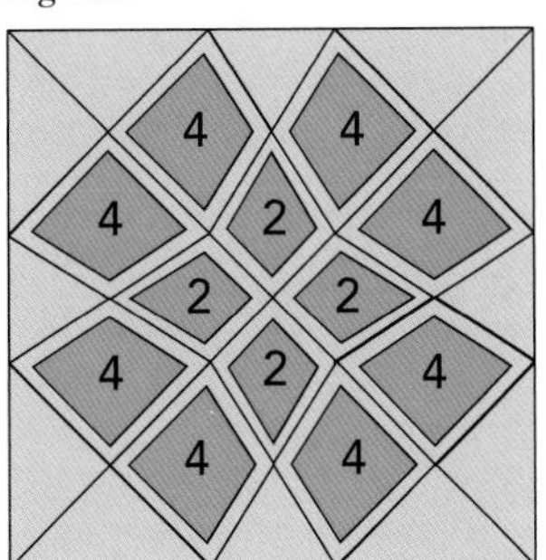

Fig 22a

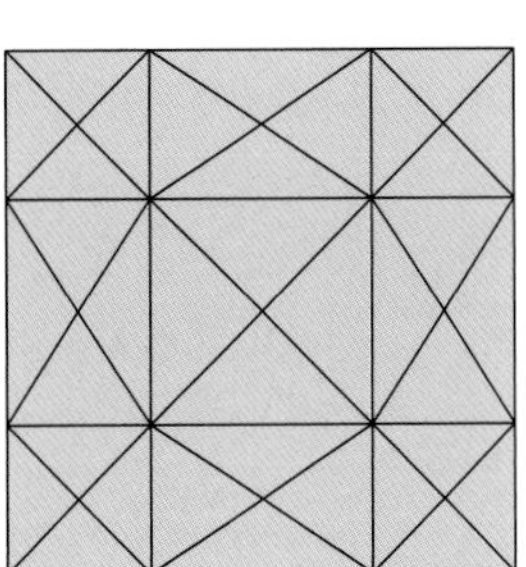

Fig 22b

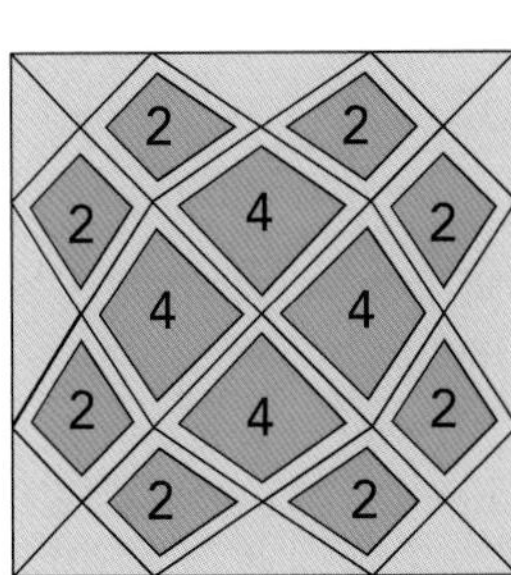

The small asymmetrical design shown in Figs 23a and 23b can be made on its own or used as repeating block for a larger design. Fig 23a shows the plan of background folded shapes and 23b the positioning of the numbered windows (window templates page 73).

Fig 23a

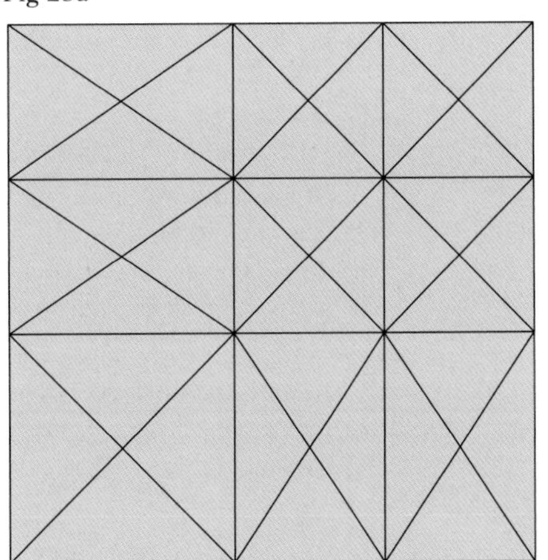

Fig 23b

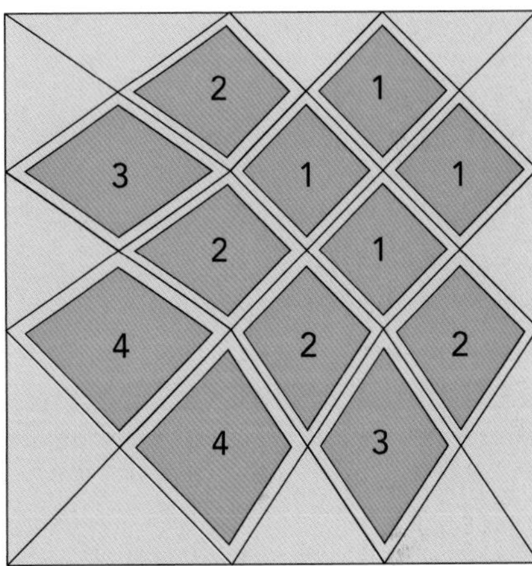

Four of the blocks shown above can be combined to make a larger design. If the large squares are placed together in the centre (Fig 24a), the central windows give the illusion of an outward-curving dome shape (Fig 24b). If the small squares are grouped in the centre (Fig 25a), the effect is of concentrated depth in the central area (Fig 25b).

Fig 24a

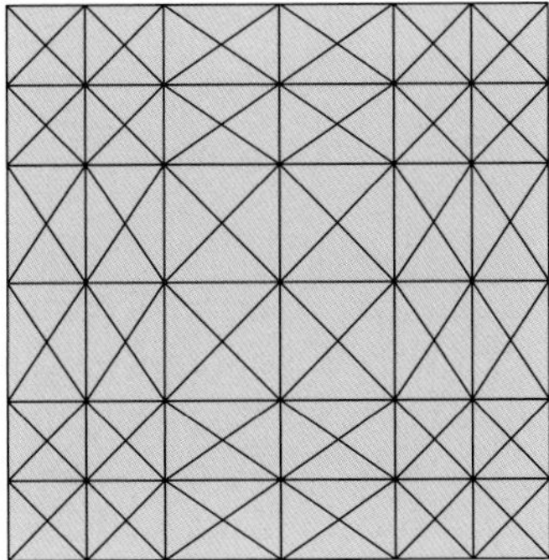

Fig 24b

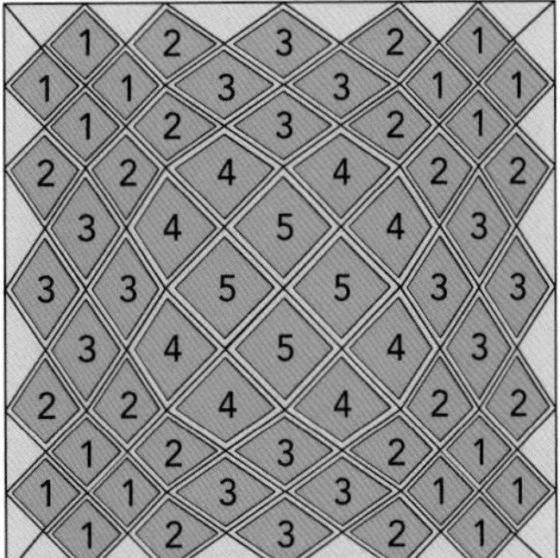

Fig 25a

Fig 25b

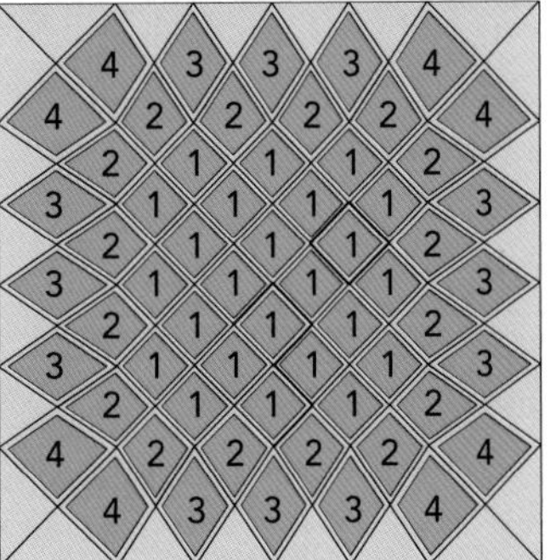

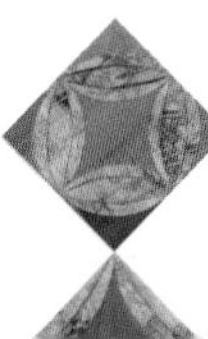

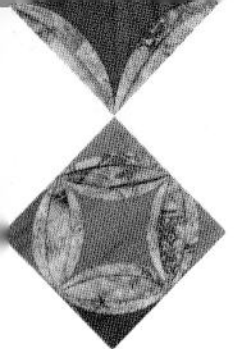

The simple design shown in Fig 23b on the previous page is a lovely project to start with, as it uses both sizes of square plus the rectangle, and can be transformed by the choice of fabrics. It looks really effective hung on point, which gives a more symmetrical look to the block. This first design sample uses one background fabric throughout with hand-dyed cotton fabrics used for the windows.

The same design as that above but using three fabrics for the background folded shapes, as in Fig 23a, and a variety of silks for the windows.

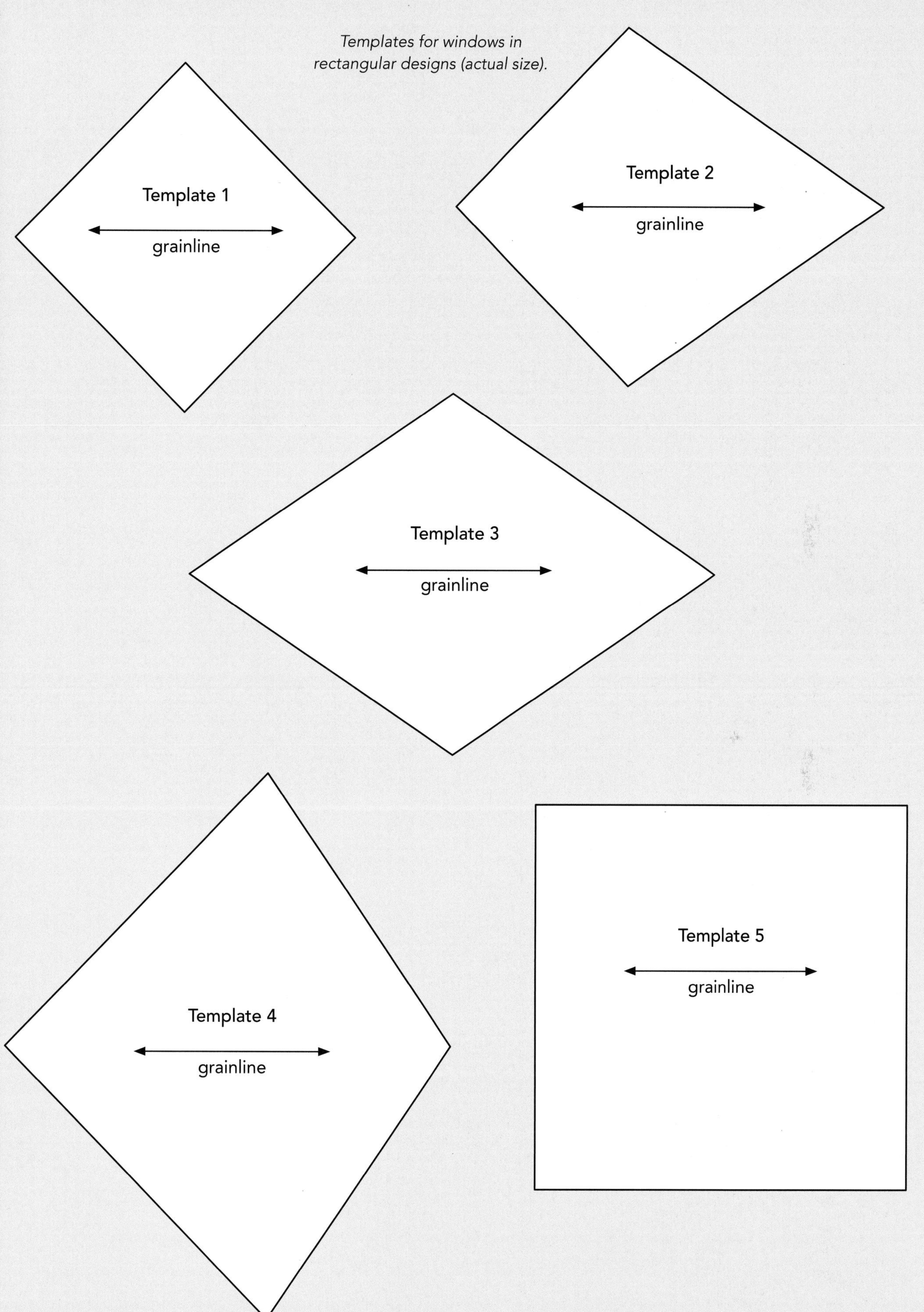

Templates for windows in rectangular designs (actual size).

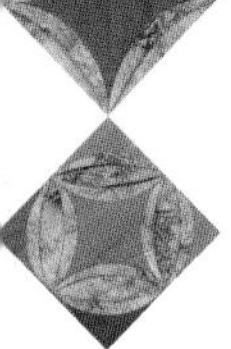

Candyfloss Wall Hanging

I staggered all my students by breaking out into lime green and shocking pink in this design. I *can* do bright, just not often... The wonderful singing shades currently available in batiks are just too delicious to resist. It's also great fun to work in colours that are outside your comfort zone just occasionally – a bit like fancy dress!

This delightful design is a combination of the short rectangle which measures 3in × 4½in (7.6cm × 11.4cm) finished, a small square measuring 3in × 3in (7.6cm × 7.6cm) and a larger square measuring 4½in × 4½in (11.4cm × 11.4cm). The smaller squares are cut 6½in × 6½in (16.5cm × 16.5cm), and the larger squares are cut 9½in × 9½in (24.1cm × 24.1cm). Fig 26a below shows the placement of each fabric in the design of folded shapes before the windows are laid in place over them. Fig 26b shows the arrangement of the overlying windows. The numbers refer to the template shapes on the previous page.

Wall hanging finished size: 24in × 24in (61cm × 61cm).

Fig 26a

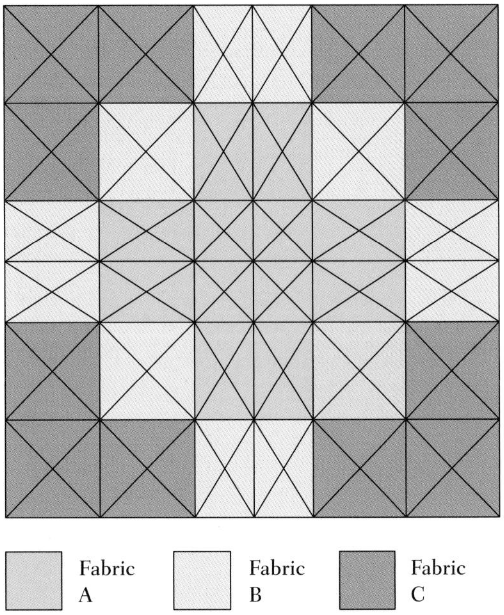

Fig 26b

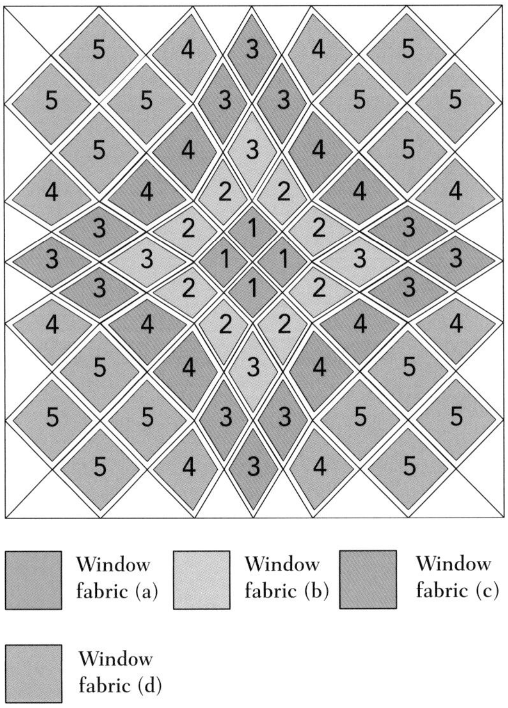

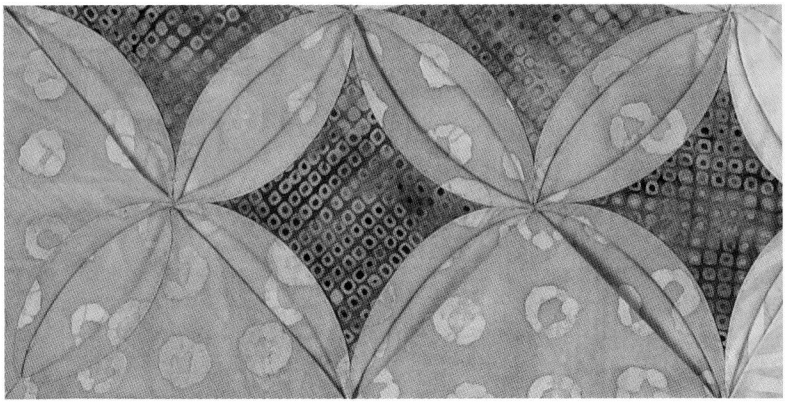

This delicious pink confection, aptly titled Candyfloss, daringly teams up a selection of pink and lime shades in a bright combination of batik fabrics in square and rectangular windows.

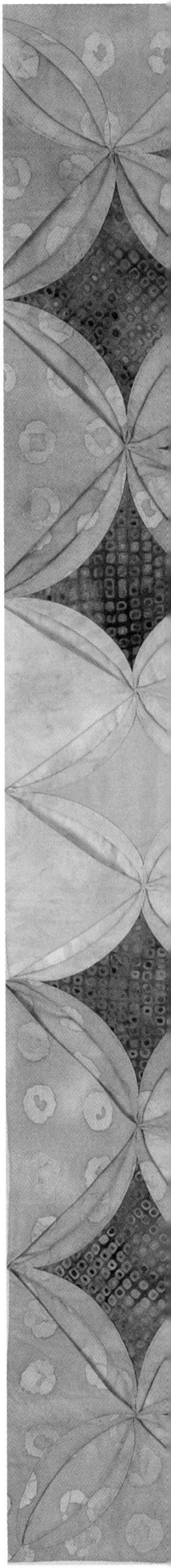

REQUIREMENTS

- **For the folded background squares and rectangles:**
  Fabric A: four small squares each cut 6½in × 6½in (16.5cm × 16.5cm) and eight rectangle cut shapes (see Fig 11 on page 68) – ¾yd (0.75m) in total;
  Fabric B: four large squares each cut 9½in × 9½in (24.1cm × 24.1cm) and eight rectangle cut shapes (see Fig 11) – 30in (76cm) in total of 42in–44in (106.7cm x 111.8cm) wide fabric
  Fabric C: twelve large squares each cut 9½in × 9½in (24.1cm × 24.1cm) – 30in (76cm) in total
- **For the windows:**
  Fabric (a): the centre four windows, one square of fabric 6in × 6in (15.2cm × 15.2cm);
  Fabric (b): surrounding twelve windows, ¼yd (0.25m);
  Fabric (c): twenty pink windows, ¼yd (0.25m);
  Fabric (d): twenty-four corner windows, ¼yd (0.25m)

Making the Folded Background Units

1 To make the Cathedral Window folded background units, following the instructions on page 18. From fabric A make four small folded squares units, each measuring 3in × 3in (7.6cm × 7.6cm) when finished. Following the instructions given earlier on page 68, from fabric A make eight rectangular units each 3in × 4½in (7.6cm × 11.4cm).

2 In the same way, from fabric B make four large folded square units, each measuring 4½in × 4½in (11.4cm × 1.4cm) when finished, and eight rectangular units each measuring 3in × 4½in (7.6cm × 11.4cm).

3 From fabric C make twelve large folded square units, each 4½in × 4½in (11.4cm × 11.4cm) when finished.

4 Arrange these folded background shapes in the design shown in Fig 26a on page 74.

5 Join the squares and rectangles in rows by hand or machine, following the instructions for joining units in Classic Cathedral Window (Joining Folded Squares page 20).

Cutting the Windows

6 A variety of window shapes occurs, depending on which folded shapes are stitched together. See page 73 for the five window templates used in this project design.

7 Make templates by tracing the windows, cutting them out and sticking them on card, or use template plastic.

8 Draw round the templates on the back of each fabric, using a sharp marking pencil and matching the grainline arrow on the template with the fabric grain or weave.

9 From fabric (a) cut four shapes from template 1.
From fabric (b) cut eight shapes from template 2 and four shapes from template 3.
From fabric (c) cut twelve shapes from template 3 and eight shapes from template 4.
From fabric (d) cut eight shapes from template 4 and sixteen shapes from template 5.

Stitching the Windows

10 Arrange the windows on the background, following the plan in Fig 26b on page 74 and stitch them into place (see Adding the Windows on page 22).

11 This design has no added border or backing, so once the windows are stitched, press the whole piece from the back and then add a sleeve and hang it in place ready for general admiration.

Shades of Gill

The outward-curving effect of large folded squares in the centre of a design is developed in this quilt Shades of Gill, shown overleaf. It was named for friend and student Gill Sharman, whose liking for weary shades of mauves and greys is as odd as my own colour preferences. The central design is composed of Cathedral Window units while the corners are Secret Garden squares.

The design combines the short rectangle which measures 3in × 4½in (7.6cm × 11.4cm) finished, the small square 3in × 3in (7.6cm × 7.6cm) and the larger square measuring 4½in × 4½in (11.4cm × 11.4cm). The smaller squares are cut 6½in × 6½in (16.5cm × 16.5cm) and the larger squares are cut 9½in × 9½in (24.1cm × 24.1cm). Fig 27a shows the placement of each fabric in the design of folded shapes before the windows are laid in place over them. Fig 27b shows the arrangement of the overlying windows.

Wall hanging finished size: 35in × 35in (88.9cm × 88.9cm).

'The fabrics used in this design were very lightweight sari cottons in grey/mauve shades with shimmery silks for the windows, plus a wonderfully weary flowered Liberty Lawn that I had about my person – well, what a surprise…'

Fig 27a *Quilt plan*

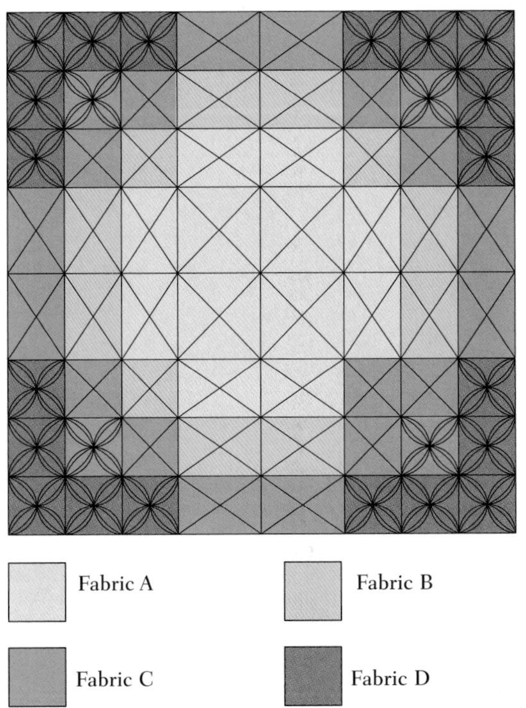

Fig 27b *Window plan*

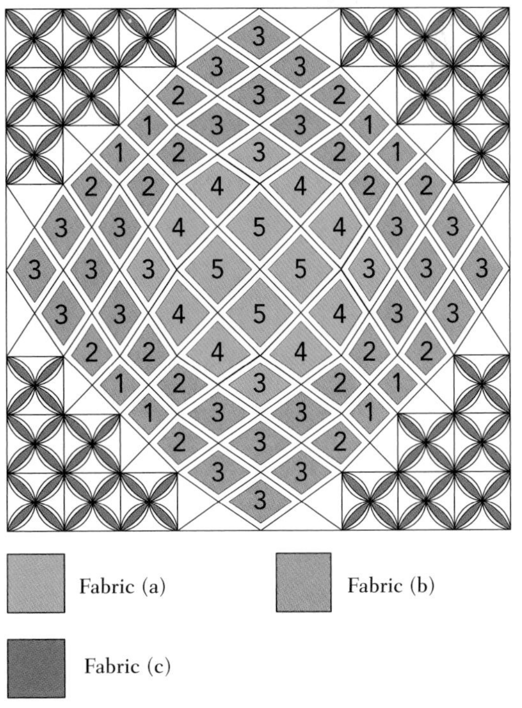

The positioning of four large background folded squares at the centre of this Shades of Gill design is the key to the rounded effect of the piece. The large silk windows lie on a background of folded shapes made from a beautiful faded lavender coloured Liberty lawn print – almost too good to use...

REQUIREMENTS

- **For the folded background squares and rectangles:**
  Fabric A: four large squares each cut 9½in × 9½in (24.1cm × 24.1cm) and eight rectangle cut shapes (see Fig 11 on page 68) – 30in or (76cm) in total of 42in–44in (106.7cm x 111.8cm) wide fabric;
  Fabric B: four small squares each cut 6½in × 6½in (16.5cm × 16.5cm) and eight rectangle cut shapes (see Fig 11) – ¾yd (0.75m) in total;
  Fabric C: twelve small squares each cut 6½in × 6½in (16.5cm × 16.5cm) and eight rectangle cut shapes (see Fig 11) – 1yd (1m) in total;
  Fabric D: twenty squares each cut 6½in × 6½in (16.5cm × 16.5cm) – ¾yd (0.75m) in total
- **For the windows:**
  Fabric (a): the centre sixteen windows – ¼yd (0.25m);
  Fabric (b): surrounding forty-eight windows – ½yd (0.5m);
  Fabric (c): within the Secret Garden folded squares – ¼yd (0.25m)
- For the border: four strips each measuring 4in × 36in (10.2cm × 91.4cm)
- Thin wadding (batting): four strips each measuring 4in × 36in (10.2cm × 91.4cm)
- Backing fabric: 36in x 36in (91.5cm × 91.5cm)

Making the Folded Background Units

1 To make the Cathedral Window folded background units, follow the instructions starting on page 18. From fabric A make four large folded squares units, each measuring 4½in × 4½in (11.4cm × 11.4cm) when finished. Following the instructions on pages 68/69, from fabric A make eight rectangular units each 3in × 4½in (7.6cm × 11.4cm) finished.

2 In the same way, from fabric B make four small folded square units, each measuring 3in × 3in (7.6cm × 7.6cm) when finished and eight rectangular units each measuring 3in × 4½in (7.6cm × 11.4cm).

3 From fabric C make eight small folded square units, each measuring 3in × 3in (7.6cm × 7.6cm) when finished (leaving four cut squares of fabric C to be used as Secret Garden units) and eight rectangular units each measuring 3in × 4½in (7.6cm × 11.4cm).

Making the Secret Garden Units

4 Following the instructions on page 36, make four Secret Garden units measuring 3in × 3in (7.6cm × 7.6cm) finished size from fabric C and twenty from fabric D. The extra squares of fabric between the layers are all cut from window fabric (c).

5 Arrange both the Cathedral Window folded background shapes and the finished Secret Garden units in the design shown in Fig 27a on page 77.

6 Join the squares and rectangles in rows by hand or machine, following the instructions for joining the units together in Classic Cathedral Window (Joining Folded Squares on page 20).

Cutting and Stitching the Windows

7 Follow steps 6–8 in the instructions for the Candyfloss Wall Hanging on page 76. From fabric (a) cut four shapes from template 3, cut eight from template 4 and cut four from template 5. From fabric (b) cut eight from template 1, cut sixteen from template 2 and cut twenty-four from template 3.

8 Arrange the windows on the background, following the plan in Fig 27b and stitch them into place (see Adding the Windows on page 22).

Adding the Borders

9 Cut four strips of the fabric chosen for the border each measuring 4in × 36in (10.2cm × 91.4cm). Also cut four strips of thin wadding (batting) in the same measurements. Follow the instructions for Adding Borders on page 130 to join the border strips to the quilt and to back it before quilting.

Quilting the Design

10 I tied the quilt at regular intervals in the central Cathedral Window/Secret Garden section and then quilted the border in diagonal lines to echo the diagonal fold lines in the main design (see Knotting or Tying a Quilt on page 132 and Quilting the Border on page 133. Finally, the outer edges of the borders were bound in the usual way.

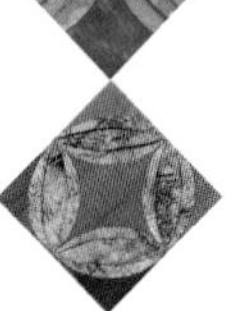

Dawn to Dusk Quilt

This is one of my very favourite pieces, where I have mixed fabrics of different weights and textures even for the background folded shapes. If a design is destined for the wall as opposed to the bed, you can really set aside the hard-wearing aspect and concentrate on the visual effect. A focus of light in the centre of the background folded shapes moves outwards, becoming darker towards the top left side. The windows follow the same route.

I used seven shades of silk and also created subtle variations in shading by turning the silk through 180°.

The design combines the short rectangle that measures 3in × 4½in (7.6cm × 11.4cm) finished, the small square measuring 3in × 3in (7.6cm × 7.6cm) and the larger square 4½in × 4½in (11.4cm × 11.4cm). The smaller squares are cut 6½in × 6½in (16.5cm × 16.5cm) and the larger squares are cut 9½in × 9½in (24.1cm × 24.1cm). Fig 28a shows the placement of each fabric in the design of folded shapes before the windows are laid in place over them. Fig 28b shows the arrangement of the overlying windows. The numbers refer to the template shapes on page 73.

Size of finished quilt: 34in × 40½in (86.4cm × 102.9cm).

Fig 28a *Quilt plan*

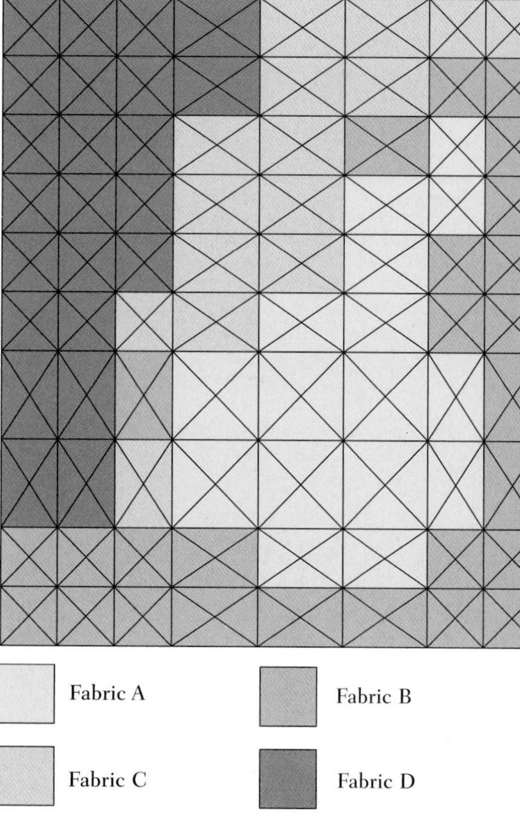

Fig 28b *Window plan*

Creating Impressionistic Designs

The designs so far have combined the three shapes in quite formal arrangements. They may also be used to create flowing designs where the colours shift subtly across both background and windows to create an impressionistic effect of shade and movement, as in the design Dawn to Dusk opposite.

You may want to follow this design exactly or use it as a starting point for your own ideas. Much will depend on the fabric you collect for the project. Pin the folded shapes into place on a design wall and add or discard some as needed. Once the background layout is to your liking, cut windows and pin them in place. Don't rush – getting something right usually takes time. Get on with other things but look at the design as you walk past it, pinning on a couple of windows and letting it cook gently for a time while you ponder the effect. When you feel comfortable with what you see, make a plan of the design before dismantling it for stitching. It is easier to stitch a piece this size in sections, as the windows are then easier to reach and the weight of all those folded fabrics can be considerable.

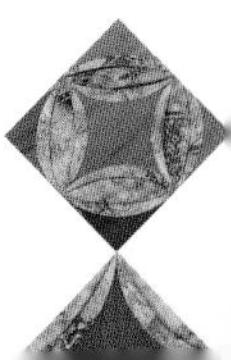

Construction

REQUIREMENTS

- **For the background folded shapes (A, B, C, D):** 1yd (1m) each of four different fabrics
- **For the windows (a, b, c, d, e, f, g):** about 1yd (1m) in total of seven fabrics in graduated shades
- For the border plus binding: 1yd (1m)
- Wadding/batting: four strips each cut 4½in x 42in (11.4cm × 106.7cm)
- Backing fabric: 36in × 42in (91.4cm × 106.7cm)

1 For the background folded squares and rectangles cut the following:
From fabric A: two small squares each cut 6½in × 6½in (16.5cm × 16.5cm); six large squares each cut 9½in × 9½in (24.1cm × 24.1cm) and eight rectangle cut shapes (see Fig 11, page 68).
From fabric B: eighteen small squares each cut 6½in × 6½in (16.5cm × 16.5cm) and eight rectangle cut shapes (see Fig 11).
From fabric C: three small squares each cut 6½in × 6½in (16.5cm × 16.5cm) and twelve rectangle cut shapes (see Fig 11).
From fabric D: seventeen small squares each cut 6½in × 6½in (16.5cm × 16.5cm) and six rectangle cut shapes (see Fig 11).

Making the Folded Background Units

2 To make the Cathedral Window folded background units, following the instructions given in Stitching the Folded Square on page 19, from fabric A make two small folded squares each measuring 3in × 3in (7.6cm × 7.6cm) when finished and six large folded squares units, each measuring 4½in × 4½in (11.4cm × 11.4cm). Following steps 1–8 on page 68, from fabric A make eight rectangular units each measuring 3in × 4½in (7.6cm × 11.4cm).

3 In the same way, from fabric B make eighteen small folded square units, each measuring 3in × 3in (7.6cm × 7.6cm) when finished and eight rectangular units each measuring 3in × 4½in (7.6cm × 11.4cm).

4 From fabric C make three small folded square units, each measuring 3in × 3in (7.6cm × 7.6cm) when finished and twelve rectangular units each measuring 3in × 4½in (7.6cm × 11.4cm).

5 From fabric D make seventeen small folded square units, each measuring 3in × 3in (7.6cm × 7.6cm) when finished and six rectangular units each measuring 3in × 4½in (7.6cm × 11.4cm).

6 Arrange the folded background shapes in the design shown in Fig 28a on page 80.

7 Join the squares and rectangles in rows by hand or machine, following the instructions for joining the units together in Classic Cathedral Window (see Joining Folded Squares on page 20).

Cutting the Windows

8 Follow the instructions in steps 6–8 on page 76.
From fabric (a): cut four windows from template 3, seven from template 4 and seven from template 5.
From fabric (b): cut three windows from template 1, four from template 2, five from template 3 and two from template 4.
From fabric (c): cut twenty-four windows from template 1, nine from template 2 and sixteen from template 3.
From fabric (d): cut two windows from template 1, seven from template 2, thirteen from template 3 and one from template 4.
From fabric (e): cut six windows from template 1, four from template 2 and five from template 3.
From fabric (f): cut seven windows from template 1 and one from template 3.
From fabric (g): cut twelve windows from template 1, two from template 2 and one from template 3.

Stitching the Windows

9 Arrange the windows on the background as Fig 28b and stitch into place (see Adding the Windows on page 22).

Adding the Borders

10 I chose a damask linen fabric for my border. Cut four strips of the fabric chosen for the border each measuring 4½in × 42in (11.4cm × 106.7cm). Also cut four strips of thin wadding in the same measurements. Follow the instructions for Adding Borders on page 130 to join the border strips to the quilt and to back it before quilting.

Quilting the Design

11 I tied the quilt at regular intervals in the central Cathedral Window/Secret Garden section and then quilted the border with decorative stitches in a variety of silk and metallic threads and also in diagonal lines to echo the diagonal fold lines in the main design (see Knotting or Tying a Quilt on page 132 and Quilting the Border on page 133). Finally, the outer edges of the borders were bound in the usual way (see Binding the Quilt on page 133).

Developing Designs

Once you get the hang of the way the different shapes can be combined to create movement and also how to draft the plans of background shapes and overlying windows, this technique can be used in original and exciting designs. Kate Badrick's design Sun Arise (right) was inspired by my piece Dawn to Dusk but uses more dynamic colours to create a sunrise effect.

Like Kate Badrick, Avril Ellis used countless fabrics for the individual folded shapes and the windows of her design Sunrise over the Rock Pools at Westward Ho (below).

Sun Arise by Kate Badrick. Kate built up her design using many fabrics for both background shapes and windows.

Sunrise over the Rock Pools at Westward Ho – an original design by Avril Ellis. Avril made each folded shape and arranged them on a design board, moving them around and changing them until she had the design she felt worked best. Only then did she stitch the folded shapes together and start adding the windows. *See also Borders for Cathedral Window pages 128–129.*

Fronds

Here's another piece that might inspire you. For my wall hanging entitled Fronds (shown opposite), I have given the variety of fabrics used for both background folded shapes and windows in the plans below. It uses the same two squares and short rectangle to create flowing lines of colour across the quilt.

Quilt plan for the Fronds design.

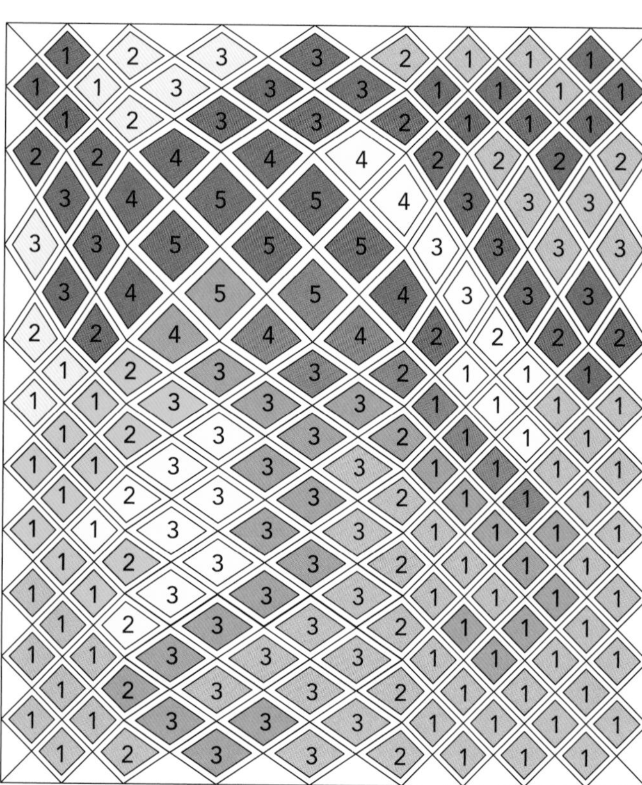

Window plan for the Fronds design.

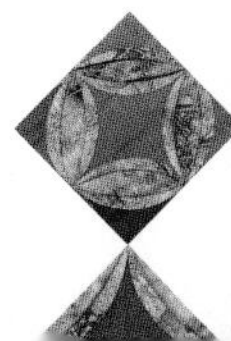

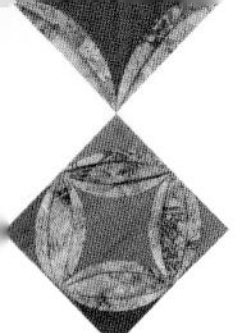

Using Longer Rectangles

A more distorted shape can be achieved by using a longer rectangle, one that is twice as long as it is wide. This more extreme shape is developed in exactly the same way as the shorter rectangle (see Making the Rectangular Shape on page 66). The double-length rectangle can be used with large and small squares to make many designs, and can also be combined with shorter rectangles to create subtle distortions of the window shapes as in Fig 29a. A template for a long rectangle that measures 3in × 6in (7.6cm × 15.2cm) is given in Fig 30 opposite, which can be combined with the 3in × 4½in (7.6cm × 11.4cm) short rectangle given in Fig 11 on page 68. The longer the rectangle, the narrower and wider the corner points will be. Follow the directions given in Creating Accurate Windows on page 70 for handling these types of corners. Note that Fig 30 gives half the actual size template – see its caption for making the full template.

Fig 29a *Quilt plan* Fig 29b *Window plan*

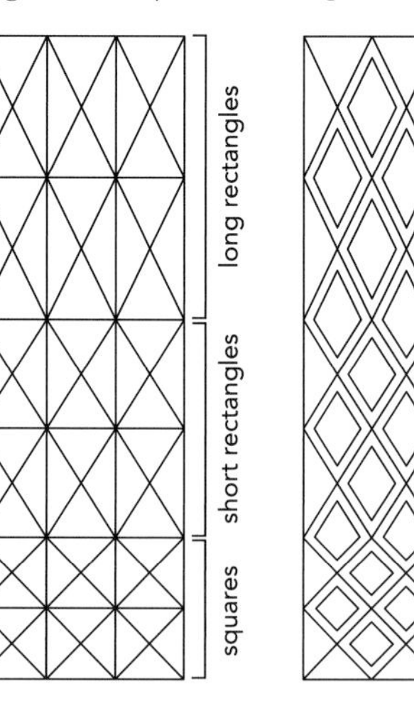

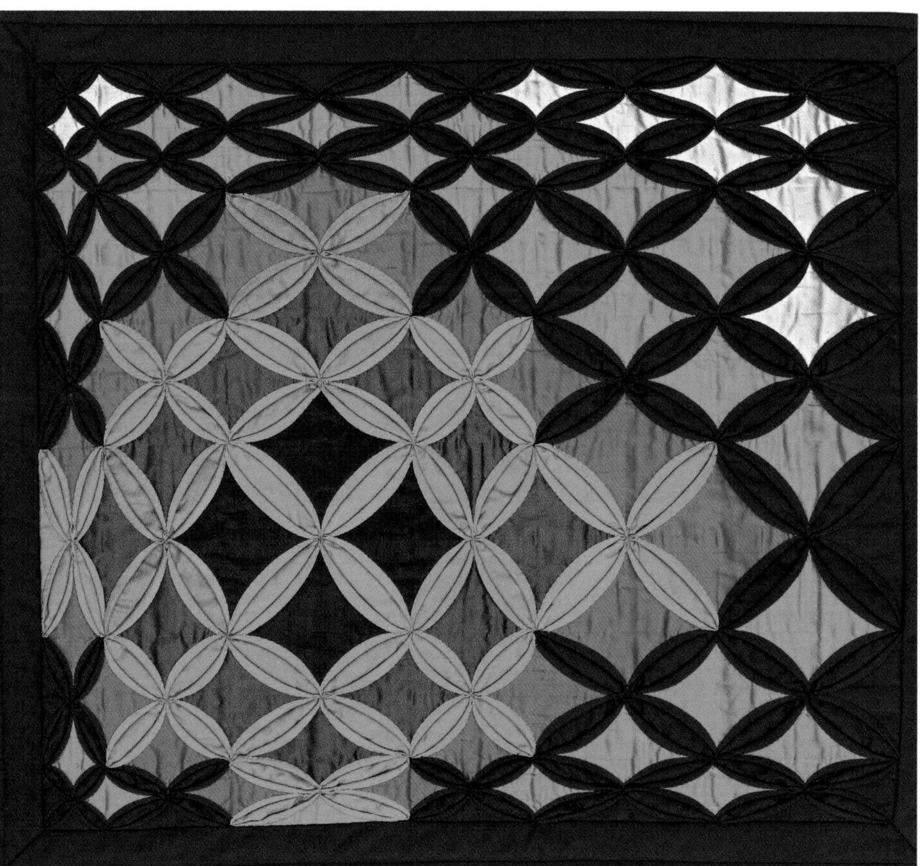

Maggie Burman's piece called Into the Depths combines squares and rectangles in a rich design. Different shades and shapes flow out from the four purple windows.

Fig 31a *Quilt plan*

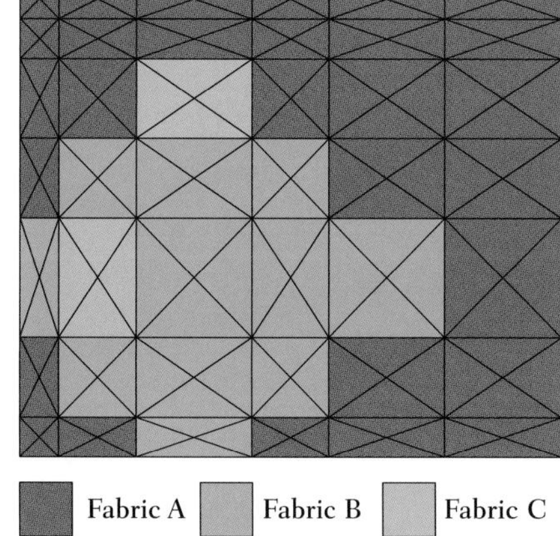

Fig 31b *Window plan*

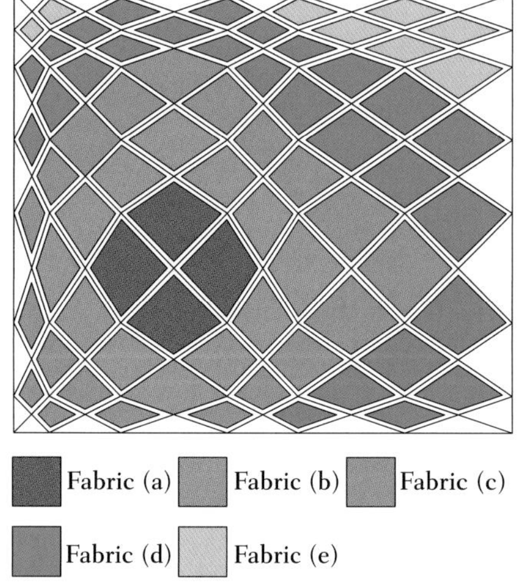

Wonderful designs can be created by experimenting with combinations of all these shapes. If you enjoy the drafting of templates, be adventurous and explore even more shapes and sizes. This is an area of patchwork where the traditional can be moved forward in totally original ways. Maggie Burman drafted her own templates in several different squares and rectangles to make the rich design, Into the Depths, shown above. The focus of the design is marked by four large purple windows and the different shapes and shades flow from this area across the piece. Fig 31a and 31b show her background plan and that of the overlying windows.

Fig 30 *Trace this actual size template on to a large sheet of paper. Flip the tracing over and trace the shape again to create the complete shape. Cut out the completed shape and stick it on to card (or use template plastic).*

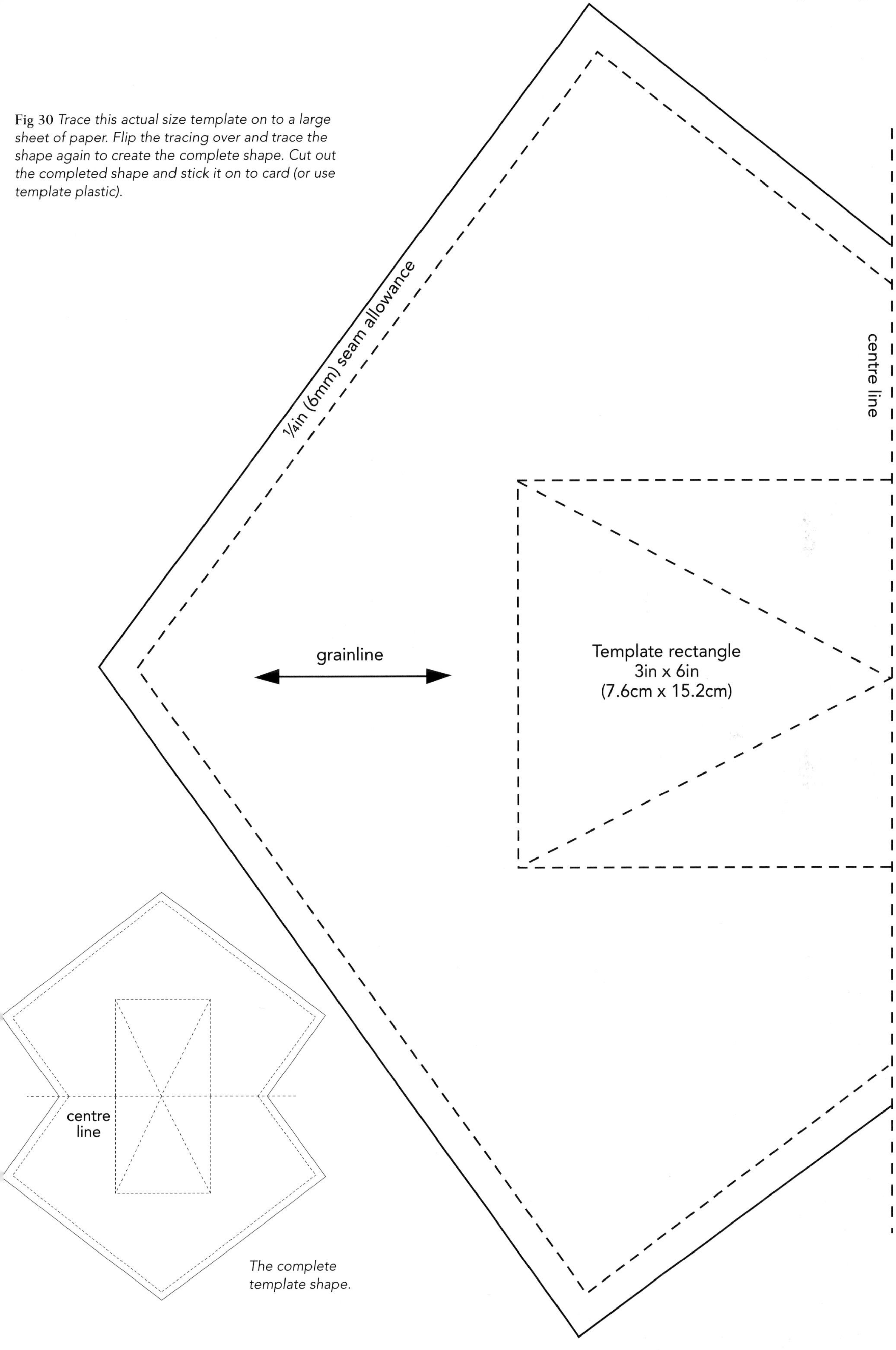

The complete template shape.

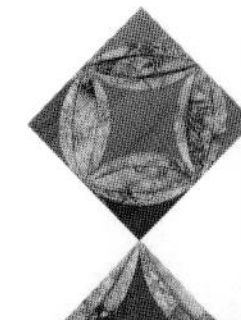

Keep on Folding

One of the main limitations of Cathedral Window patchwork is the lack of raw edges, which makes it difficult to combine with borders, sashing or other forms of patchwork. The great advantage of the techniques shown in this section of the book is that while most look much like the original Cathedral Window, they *do* all have seam allowances and can be joined together or to other fabrics in the conventional way.

One-square Folded Cathedral Window

This is my favourite look-alike technique. The designs made with this one-square variation differ from classic Cathedral Window in that the windows sit in the centre of each square block rather than lying across two folded squares. The blue Pastel Twist cushion shown opposite has nine folded blocks, each with a window placed centrally on it and stitched in place in the usual way. Extra interest is added at the corners of each square block by folding one layer back to give a similar effect to Twisted Windows (see page 50). When blocks are joined together these twisted areas combine to make an origami-style pinwheel between the stitched windows, which is a real bonus! Brenda Scragg's cushion (shown opposite and on page 103) is made using a different technique, which I've called Two-shade Folded Window – see page 100 for details.

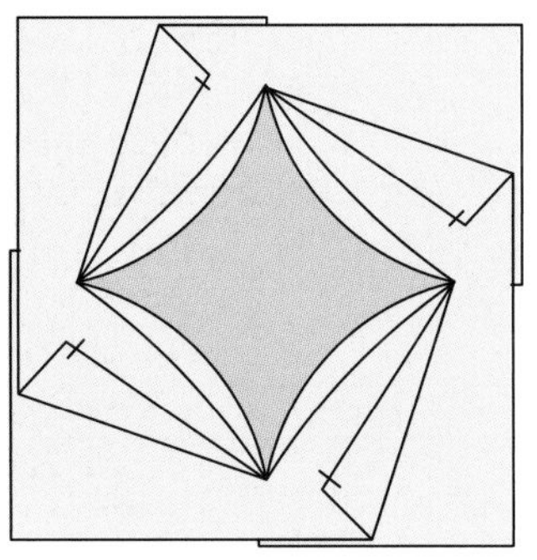

A single one-square folded block

Nine blocks joined in a nine-patch arrangement

These two cushions are a long way from the image in people's minds when you say the word patchwork. They use a limited palette of colours and subtle shades of silk that would grace any minimalist décor. The folded triangle details down two sides of Brenda's cushion add to the interest in the border, which is finished with a narrow, piped edging. My past attempts at stitching a piped edging have not been so successful, and I much prefer the safer option of a stitched, flat edging to my cushion. If I can't do something that looks really good, I would rather choose an alternative technique that works well for me! This is the method that I have given for all the cushions in this book as I like the look and find it easy to do.

'When teaching Cathedral Window I never show the one-square alternative version in case the students all abandon their projects and switch instantly to this easily achieved variation!'

Cutting the Squares

Each block is made from one square of fabric for the folded background square and one square of contrast fabric for the window. As with classic Cathedral Window, each folded square of background fabric starts out as a larger cut square. There is an easy way to calculate this: choose the finished size of the folded square, e.g. 3in × 3in (7.6cm × 7.6cm). Now double this measurement and then add 1in (2.5cm) for the seam allowances – this will be the size of the cut square of fabric needed at the start. Note: this technique has a *½in (1.3cm) seam allowance* when joining the blocks together rather than the usual ¼in (6mm). For example, a 3in × 3in (7.6cm × 7.6cm) folded square will need 3in + 3in +1in (7.6cm + 7.6cm + 2.5cm) = a 7in (17.8cm) cut square of fabric.

Like Cathedral Window, I often use an 8in × 8in (20.3cm × 20.3cm) cut square that finishes up as a 3½in (8.9cm) finished block, which is visually satisfying and comfortable to work with. Smaller sizes can be used in miniature designs as the rolled-back bias edges are less bulky to handle than Classic Cathedral Window.

Making a One-square Folded Block

1 From the chosen background fabric cut one square measuring 8in x 8in (20.3cm × 20.3cm), or any size to suit your project.

2 Place the square right side *up* on a surface and mark along the top edge the exact mid-point (mark this as A). Also mark ½in (1.3cm) from the left corner (mark this as B), as in Fig 1a.

Fig 1a

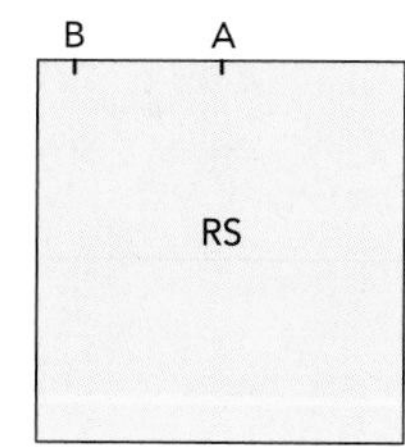

3 Rotate the fabric square through 90° and mark the top edge in the same way (Fig 1b).

Fig 1b

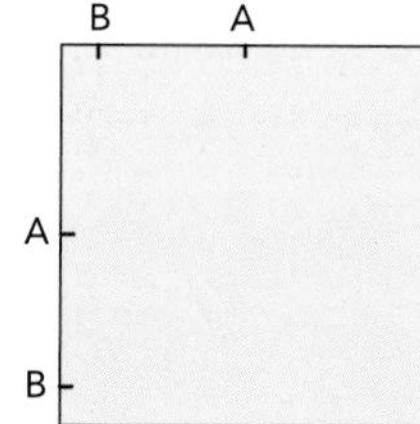

4 Turn and mark the remaining two sides of the fabric square in the same way (Fig 1c).

Fig 1c

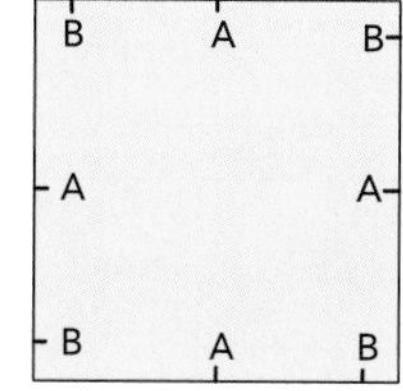

5 Working on one edge of the fabric square, bring mark A over to the left to lie exactly on mark B, keeping raw edges level. Pin the edges as in Fig 2a. Pin the left-hand pleat as in Fig 2b.

Fig 2a Fig 2b

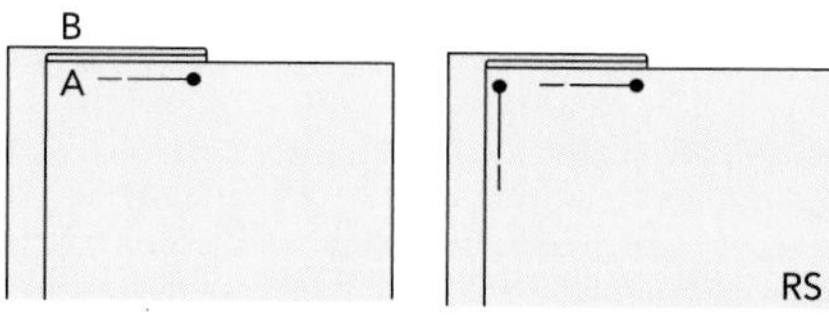

Repeat this on each side of the fabric square, keeping the outer edges flat while the central area becomes puffed up. Work round each side in a clockwise direction as this helps to control the centre puffiness (Fig 3).

Fig 3

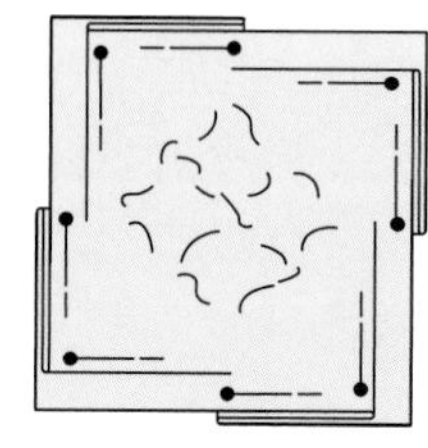

6 Working on a flat surface, carefully pull the edges of the block into a square. Smooth the fabric from the pinned pleats towards the centre in an anti-clockwise direction, turning the block each time as you do so until a square-on-point forms in the centre (Fig 4). The four corners should lie over the midway folds that are on the back of the block.

Fig 4

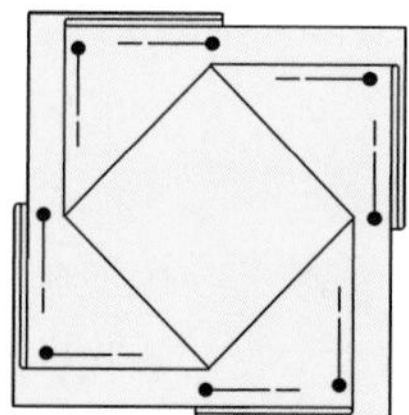

TIP

If you hold the block up against the light, you should be able to check that each corner of the square-on-point is in the correct position.

7 Thread a needle with thread in a shade that matches the background fabric square and knot the end. To secure each corner of the square-on-point, take the needle down the centre fold that lies at the back of one side of the fabric square and bring it out just behind the corner as in Fig 5.

Fig 5

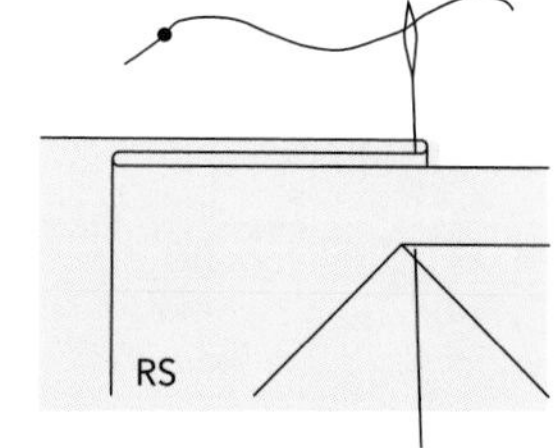

8 Secure the point with a few stitches through all the layers, taking care not to stitch the front of the pointed corner, just the pleat behind it (Fig 6).

Fig 6

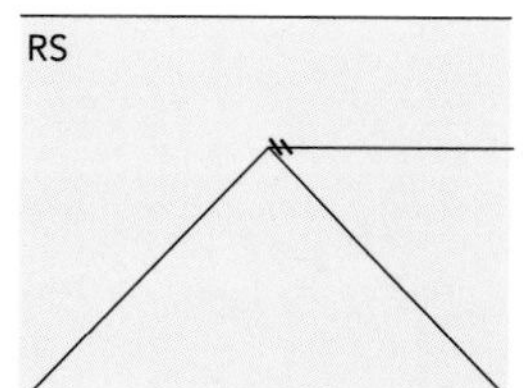

9 Take the needle to the back of the work, stitch two or three stitches on the back fold to secure the thread and run the needle up inside the fold to the outer raw edge of the block. Cut the thread.

10 Repeat this on all four sides of the block and then remove the pins.

Folding Back the Pleat

11 Working on one side of the block, fold back the left-hand pleat as in Fig 7. The original folded edge should lie midway between the edge of the centre square on point and the new folded edge.

Fig 7

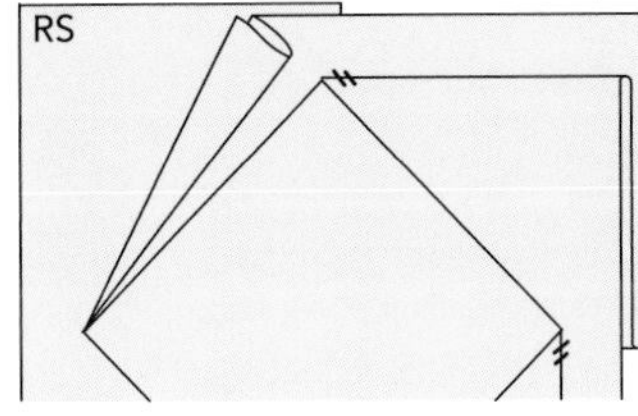

Pull the folded pleat slightly so that its top corner lies no more than ¼in (6mm) from the outer raw edge of the block (Fig 8). The dotted line in Fig 8 shows where the ½in (1.3cm) seam will be when the blocks are joined, so the raw edges of the folded section need to be within that ½in (1.3cm) seam allowance. Pin the folded wedge shape in position and secure it with two or three small stitches through all the layers within the ½in (1.3cm) seam allowance (Fig 9).

Fig 8

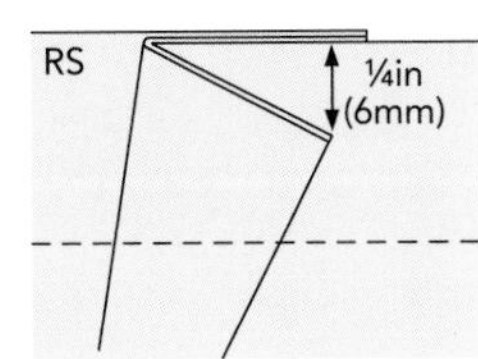

Fig 9

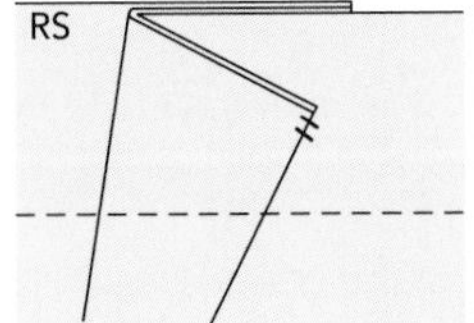

12 Repeat this on all four sides to make the twisted block ready for the window to be added (Fig 10).

Fig 10

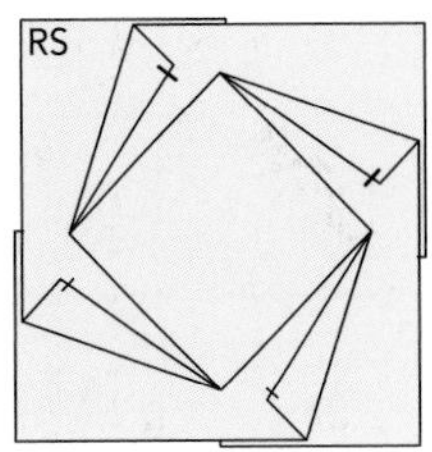

Adding the Window

13 Measure the centre square-on-point from corner to corner. Subtract ¼in (6mm) from this measurement. This is the size of the square of fabric that will make the window. For the folded square that began as an 8in x 8in square cut one window measuring 2¼in × 2¼in (5.7cm × 5.7cm). Trim the window fabric down a little if it needs it once it is pinned into place (Fig 11). There should be 1/8in (3mm) of backing fabric showing around the window on all sides.

Fig 11

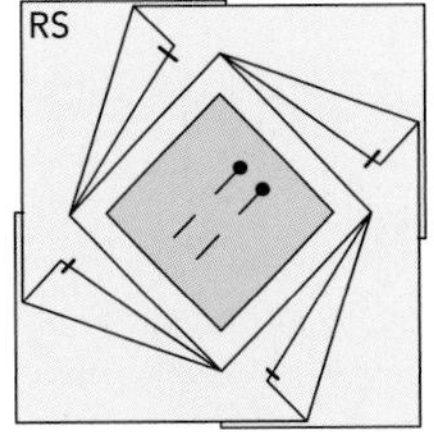

14 Pin the window in position and stitch as for the classic Cathedral Window (see page 22).

'This technique really is a fabric form of origami, with the bonus that the bias edges can be stretched into a lovely curve, which paper just won't do.'

Designing with One-square Folded Cathedral Window

Pastel Twist Cushion

This pretty nine-block cushion uses alternating folded squares of two fabrics as a background with two different silk fabrics as the windows. The colours are subtle, enhanced by the lovely marbled batik fabric used. A mitred border provides a stylish finish.

Cushion finished size: 16½in × 16½in (42cm × 42cm).

Construction

1 From fabric A make five blocks of the One-square folded Cathedral Window with windows in the chosen silk fabric as described in steps 1–14 beginning on page 92.

2 From fabric B make four blocks of the One-square folded Cathedral Window and add windows in the second silk fabric.

3 Arrange the nine blocks in the design shown in Fig 12. Machine stitch the folded squares into three rows each of three blocks. Press the seams open from the back of the work to reduce the bulk. Finally, stitch the three rows together. Press the long seams open as before.

Fig 12

TIP

Remember that the seam allowance when stitching the blocks together is ½in (1.3cm), not ¼in (6mm). Match the corners of the stitched windows exactly – they should virtually touch each other when the blocks are joined.

REQUIREMENTS

- **Background Fabric A:** five squares each cut 8in × 8in (20.3cm × 20.3cm)
- **Background Fabric B:** four squares each cut 8in × 8in (20.3cm × 20.3cm)
- **For the windows:** one square of silk fabric 8in × 8in (20.3cm × 20.3cm) from each of two fabrics
- Fabric for borders and cushion back, ½yd (0.5m)
- Fabric to line the cushion front, lightweight calico (muslin) 18in x 18in (45.7cm × 45.7cm)
- Cushion pad 18in (45.7cm) square

Adding the Mitred Borders

4 Cut four strips of border fabric each 3¾in (9.5cm) wide and 18in (45.7cm) long. Pin and stitch two strips to opposite sides of the cushion block, matching the centres and stitching with a ½in (1.3cm) seam as before, beginning and ending the stitching ½in (1.3cm) from either end of the cushion. The border strips will extend beyond the cushion at both ends ready to be mitred (Fig 13).

Fig 13

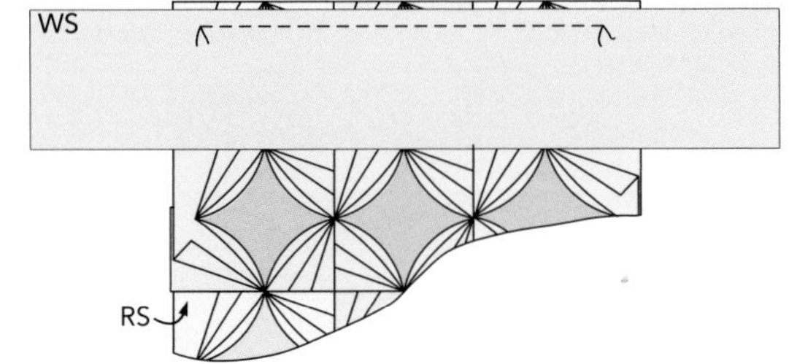

5 Pin and stitch the remaining two border strips to the other sides of the cushion in the same way.

Making the Mitre

6 Place the cushion right side down on a cutting board. Working on one corner, push the seams towards the quilt and fold both border strips back at an angle of 45° so the folded edges are butted together – use the 45° markings on the cutting board to help you with this (Fig 14). Finger-press the folded edges to crease them along these lines. Repeat this on all four corners.

Fig 14

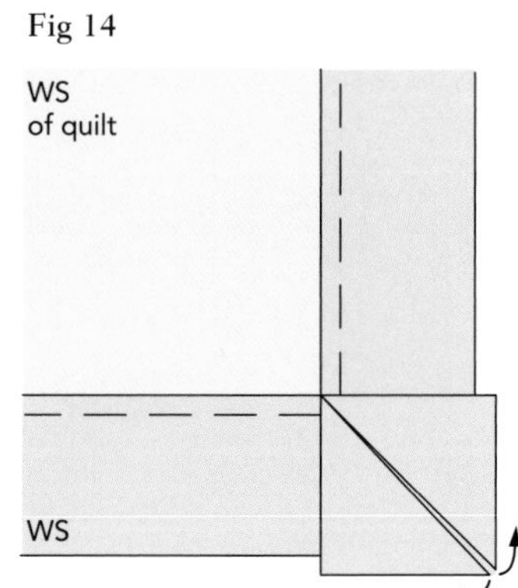

7 To stitch the mitres, fold the cushion diagonally with right sides facing at one corner so that the two border strips are lying on top of each other.

8 Pushing the seam allowance towards the cushion, position the two fold lines on the border strips exactly on top of each other and pin (Fig 15). Stitch along these lines towards the cushion from the outer edges of the border strips. Repeat this on all four corners of the cushion.

Fig 15

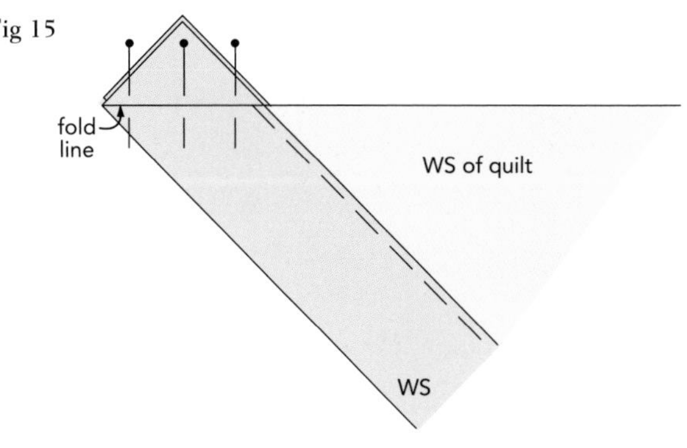

9 Trim the mitre seam allowances to ½in (1.3cm) and then press the seam open.

Completing the Cushion

10 Place the cushion front face up on top of the calico (muslin) square, trim both the cushion top and the calico to a square 17in × 17in (43.2cm × 43.2cm) and tack (baste) the two layers together.

11 For the back of the cushion, cut two pieces of the chosen fabric each 17in × 11in (43.2cm × 27.9cm). Press a ¼in (6mm) turning to the wrong side of the fabric on one long side of each piece. Fold over this edge again to make a ½in (1.3cm) turning (Fig 16a). Machine stitch along this edge, close to the fold (Fig 16b).

Fig 16a

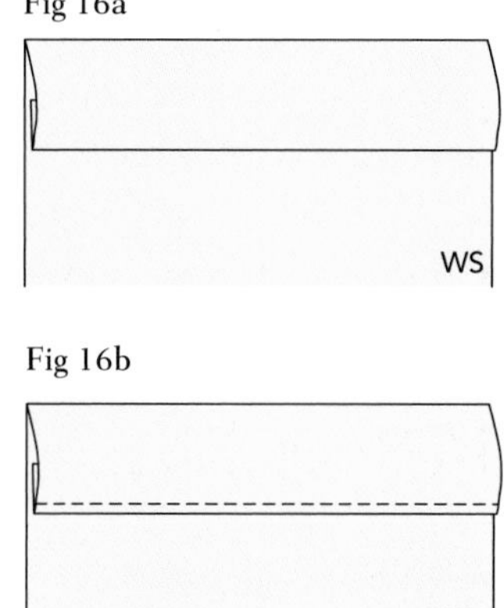

Fig 16b

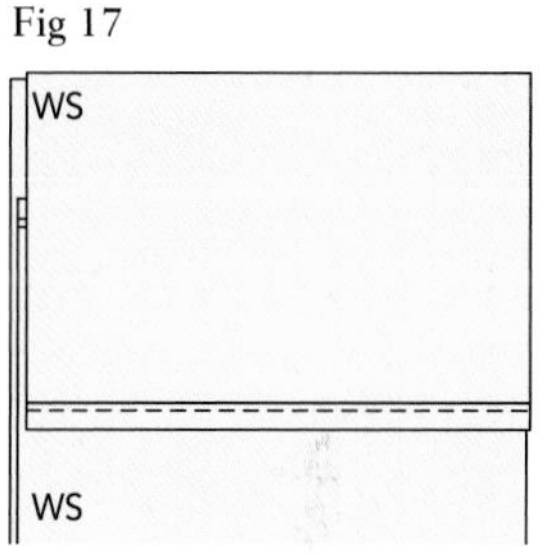

12 Place the cushion front right side *up* on a flat surface. Arrange the two back pieces right side *down* with their raw edges matching the edges of the cushion front and the folded edges overlapping across the centre (Fig 17).

Fig 17

WS

WS

13 Pin the front and back together and machine stitch all around the outer edges with a ¼in (6mm) seam. Trim the corners a little to reduce the bulk of the fabric.

14 Turn the cushion through to its right side and press the outer seam. Machine stitch a line about ½in (1.3cm) from the edge all around the cushion – this gives it an extra finish around the outer edges.

'This really is a wonderful way to fool the public about your amazing talent as a quiltmaker. All those intricate folds and twists and curving windows framing delicious fabric – yet so easily made! This is the perfect choice for a very special cushion or small wall hanging.'

Drama Queen Wall Hanging

This dramatic piece was made by Joni Cramp using two different sizes of the one-square folded Cathedral Window, pieced together with sashing and larger pieces of fabric to make a lovely Amish-looking design. Unlike classic Cathedral Window, Joni was able to make a conventional layering of top, wadding and backing fabric and quilt it to enhance the overall design.

Wall hanging finished size: 32in × 32in (81.3cm × 81.3cm).

REQUIREMENTS

- **Fabric A:** ½yd (0.5m) for folded Cathedral Window background squares plus windows
- **Fabrics B and C:** ¼yd (0.25m) each for folded Cathedral Window squares plus windows
- **Fabric D:** one square cut 6in × 6in (15.2cm × 15.2cm) for the four centre windows
- **Fabric E:** 1¾yd (1.75m) for sashing, quilt corners, borders and binding
- Thin wadding 33in × 33in (83.8cm × 83.8cm)
- Backing fabric 33in x 33in (83.8cm x 83.8cm)

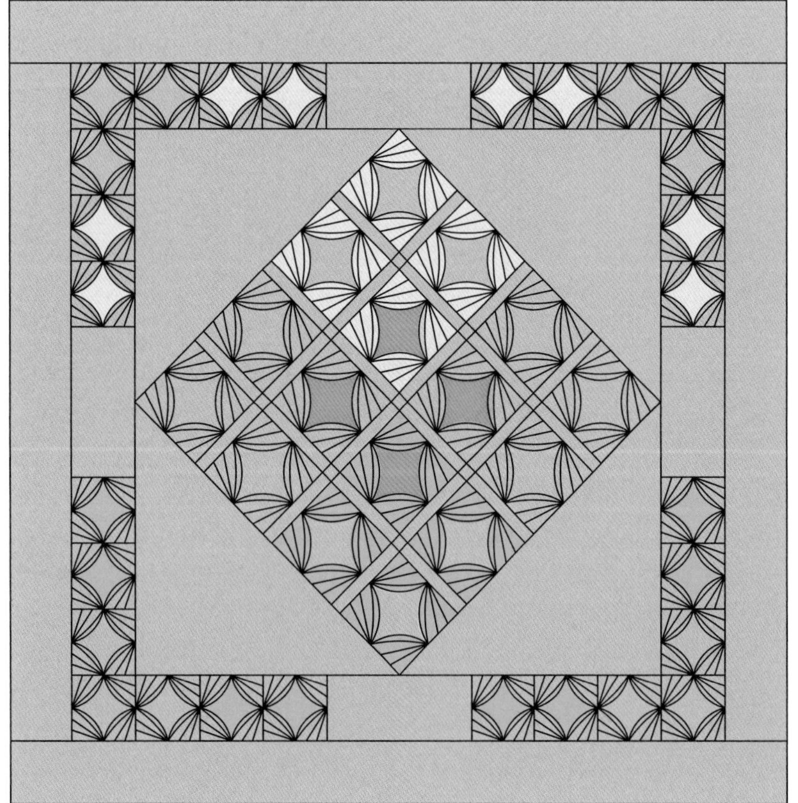

Fabric A

Fabric B

Fabric C

Fabric D

Fabric E

Layout plan of Joni Cramp's Drama Queen wall hanging.

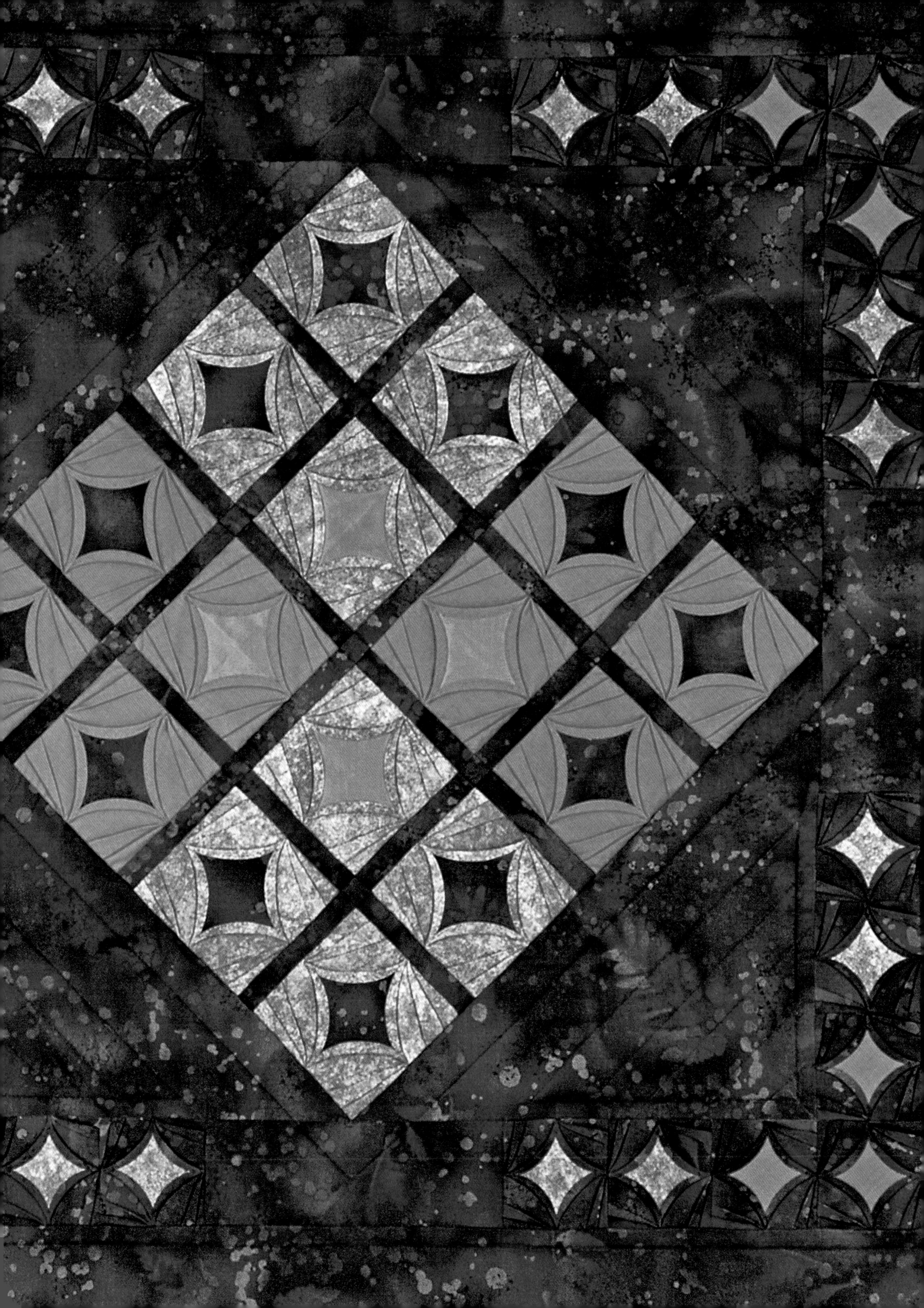

Construction

This project works best if you complete the sixteen centre one-square blocks with their windows and the smaller, outer twenty-eight blocks with their windows first, before assembling the whole design.

Making the Larger Central Blocks

1 From background fabric A cut eight squares, each 8in x 8in (20.3cm x 20.3cm). From background fabric B cut four squares to the same measurements and then four squares from background fabric C to the same measurement.

2 Follow Making a One-square Folded Block on page 92 steps 1–12 to make the sixteen blocks ready for the windows to be added.

3 From the 6in x 6in (15.2cm x 15.2cm) of fabric D cut four squares for the centre windows each measuring 2¼in x 2¼in (5.7cm x 5.7cm). From the sashing fabric E cut twelve squares each measuring 2¼in x 2¼in (5.7cm x 5.7cm).

4 Working on the eight folded squares of fabric A, pin and stitch two windows of the centre window fabric D and six windows of the sashing fabric E into place on the blocks.

5 Working on the four folded squares of fabric B, pin and stitch one window of fabric D and three windows of fabric E into place on the blocks.

6 Repeat this to add windows to the four folded squares of fabric C.

Making the Smaller Outer Blocks

7 From the sashing fabric E cut twenty-eight squares each measuring 6in x 6in (15.2cm x 15.2cm).

8 Follow steps 1–12 in Making a One-square Block page 92 to make the blocks ready for the windows to be added.

9 From fabric A cut twelve windows, each measuring 1½in x 1½in (3.8cm x 3.8cm). From fabric B cut eight windows each measuring 1½in x 1½in (3.8cm x 3.8cm). From fabric C cut eight windows 1½in x 1½in (3.8cm x 3.8cm).

10 Pin and stitch these twenty-eight windows to the twenty-eight folded squares made from fabric E.

TIP

Before joining the centre larger sixteen blocks together with the sashing, trim ¼in (6mm) from each side of all sixteen blocks. This reduces the seam allowance to ¼in to fit under the narrow sashing strips. The blocks should now measure 4in x 4in (10.2cm x 10.2cm).

Assembling the Design

11 For the sashing cut from fabric E twelve strips measuring 1in x 4in (2.5cm x 10.2cm) and three strips measuring 1in x 16in (2.5cm x 40.6cm).

12 Arrange the sixteen blocks in four rows each of four blocks as in Fig 18a.

Fig 18a

13 Pin and stitch three short strips of the cut sashing between each of the four blocks in the top row (Fig 18b). Press the seams towards the sashing, ironing from the front to the work. The blocks should butt together under the sashing strip. Repeat this on all four rows of blocks.

Fig 18b

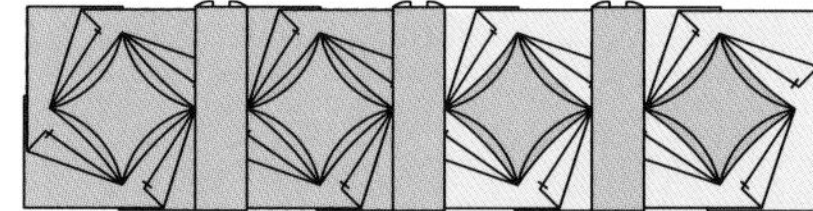

14 Pin and stitch the three long sashing strips between the four rows of blocks to join them together (Fig 18c). Press the seams towards the sashing as before.

Fig 18c

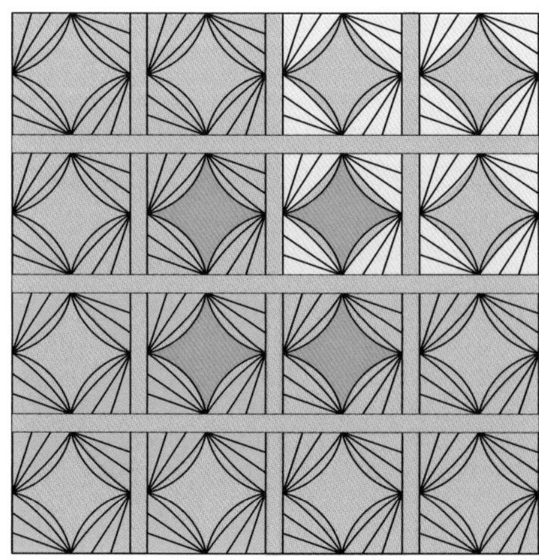

Adding the Corners

15 From the sashing fabric E cut two squares each measuring 12in x 12in (30.5cm x 30.5cm). Cut each square in half diagonally.

16 Pin and stitch the long side of one triangle to one side of the joined blocks. It should be slightly longer than the blocks, so balance the extra length equally at either end (Fig 19). Press the triangle back with seams outwards from the blocks. Repeat this on the opposite side of the blocks. Finally, pin and stitch the two remaining triangles to the other two sides of the blocks. Press the triangles out from the centre blocks.

Fig 19

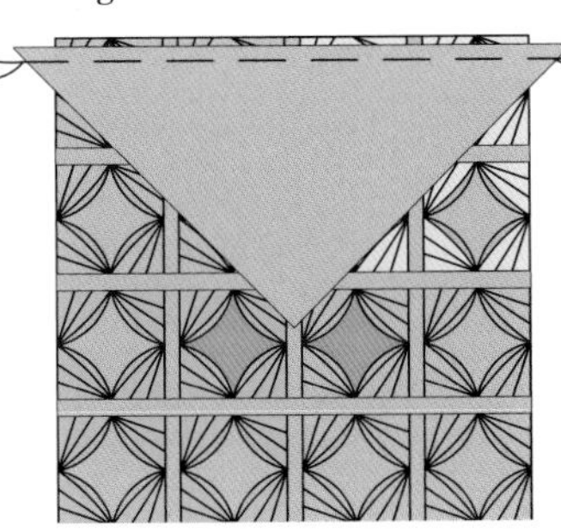

17 Working from the front, trim the sides of the quilt down to ½in (1.3cm) beyond the four corners of the centre area.

Adding the Borders

18 From fabric E cut four strips each measuring 3½in x 8in (8.9cm x 20.3cm). Place six of the smaller folded Cathedral Window blocks plus one of the cut strips of fabric E in the arrangement shown in Fig 20. Pin and stitch these together with *½in (1.3cm) seams* (*not* the usual ¼in seams). Match the corners of the stitched windows exactly – they should virtually touch each other when the blocks are joined. Press all the seams open to reduce the bulk. Repeat this process with a second strip of blocks arranged as in Fig 20 and pin and stitch them together as before.

Fig 20

19 Pin and stitch each of the joined strips to the sides of the quilt, following the arrangement shown in the layout plan on page 96, stitching a ½in (1.3cm) seam. Press the seams towards the quilt, ironing from the front of the work.

TIP

If the side strips do not exactly match the sides of the quilt, adjust the centre piece of fabric between the small Cathedral Window blocks to make the side strips fit.

20 Arrange the remaining blocks and pieces of fabric E into two strips as shown in Fig 21. Pin and stitch them to make two strips as before, pressing the joining seams open.

Fig 21

21 Pin and stitch the two strips to the top and bottom of the quilt with a ½in (1.3cm) seam, matching seams carefully. Press the seams towards the quilt.

22 For the final border, from fabric E cut two strips measuring 3in × 28in (7.6cm × 71.1cm) and two strips 3in × 32in (7.6cm × 81.3cm). Pin and stitch the two shorter lengths to the sides of the quilt with a ½in (1.3cm) seam. Press the seams towards the final border strips, ironing from the front of the work.

23 Pin and stitch the two longer lengths to the top and bottom of the quilt as before. Press the seams towards the border strips.

Quilting the Design

24 Joni layered her wall hanging with wadding and backing fabric in the usual way and then quilted by machine in the seams of the narrow sashing in the centre area and diagonally across the large corner triangles. Finally, she quilted ½in (1.3cm) away from the border strips by machine. The quilt was bound in fabric E (see Binding the Quilt page 133).

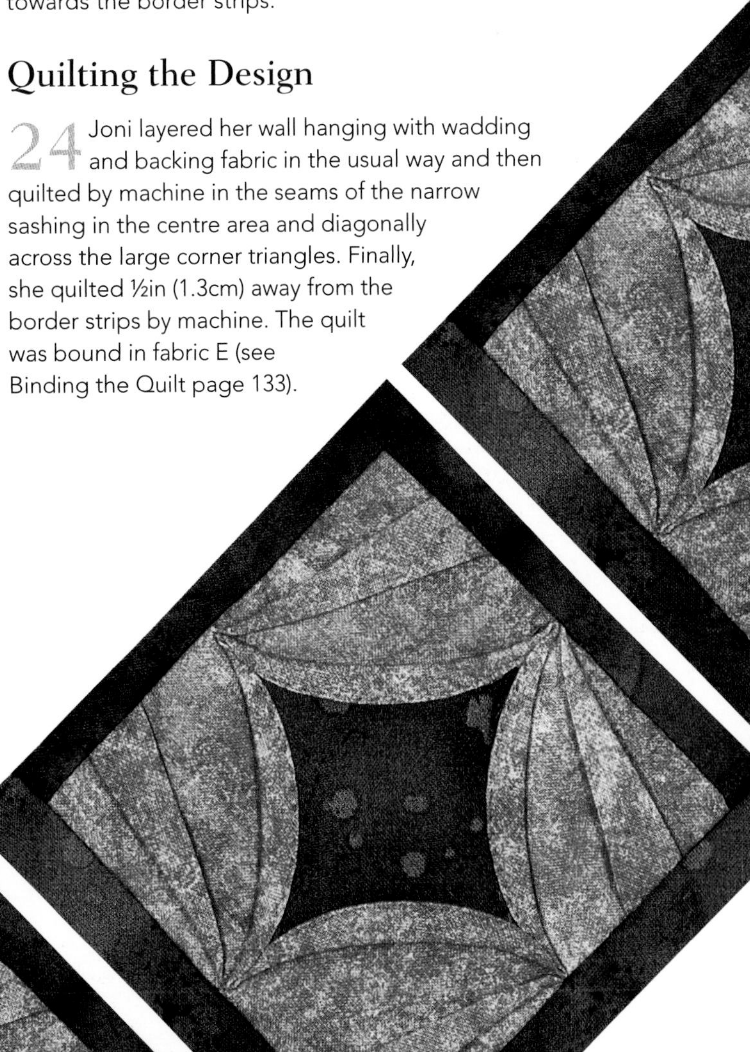

Two-shade Folded Cathedral Window

I so enjoyed experimenting with rolled edges and adding windows when making this striking piece. I was also able to quilt it, as the layers are thinner than Cathedral Window, which has added more depth to the design and enriched the borders.

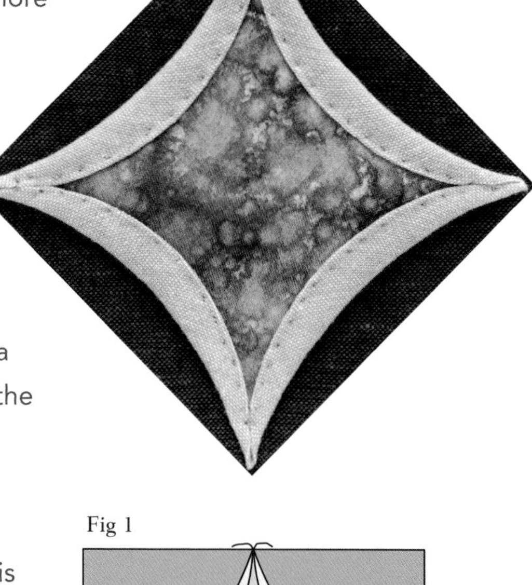

This folded look-alike version of Cathedral Window, like the Folded One-patch on page 90, has the huge advantage of having a proper seam allowance and raw edges of fabric around the outer edge, so it can easily be combined with other patchwork techniques to create original designs. It adds interest without the layering and bulk of classic Cathedral Window. This variation is very like classic Cathedral Window in appearance but with the bonus of a second colour fabric used for the rolled-over curved edges around the centre windows (see the single block here and Fig 1).

Each block is constructed from a large square of fabric for the centre plus four smaller squares that make up the corners of the block. An extra square of fabric is used to make the window, which is added to the block in the usual way. The large square finishes up as a folded square on point in the centre of the block. The fabric for the window is placed on this centre as in classic Cathedral Window so that the only areas of the original large square to be seen in the final design are the curved edges that are rolled over the window and stitched into place.

Fig 1

'Those of you who enjoy fiddling will like the option of adding extra folded triangles at each corner, which can then be played around with – called "Fabric Manipulation" in the trade rather than "fiddling around". I like the way this technique looks so complex but is surprisingly easy to do and very stable – the perfect candidate for a cushion or wall hanging.'

My Purple Windows wall hanging is a nine-patch design in Two-shade Folded Cathedral Window with small folded triangles inserted in the seams to add interest.

Making the Folded Block

1 A good size to try as a sample is the block that measures 4in × 4in (10.2cm × 10.2cm) finished size. From the fabric chosen to make the rolled curved edges of the Cathedral Window design (see Fig 1 page 100) cut one square measuring 4½in × 4½in (11.4cm × 11.4cm). From the fabric chosen for the background corners cut four squares each measuring 2½in × 2½in (6.4cm × 6.4cm).

2 Fold the centre large square in half, right side outwards (Fig 2).

Fig 2

3 Place one small square on a flat surface with right side *upwards*. Place the folded square on it, matching the raw edges along the top and side of the squares as in Fig 3. The folded edge should lie ¼in (6mm) away from the bottom edge of the small square.

Fig 3

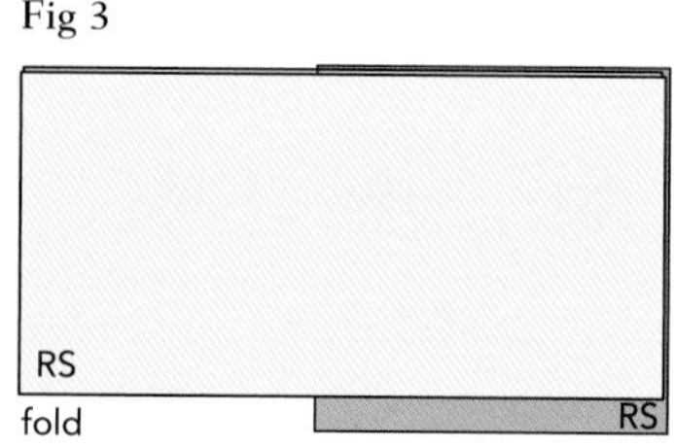

4 Place a second small square on top of the large folded square with right side *down* exactly on top of the first small square (Fig 4).

Fig 4

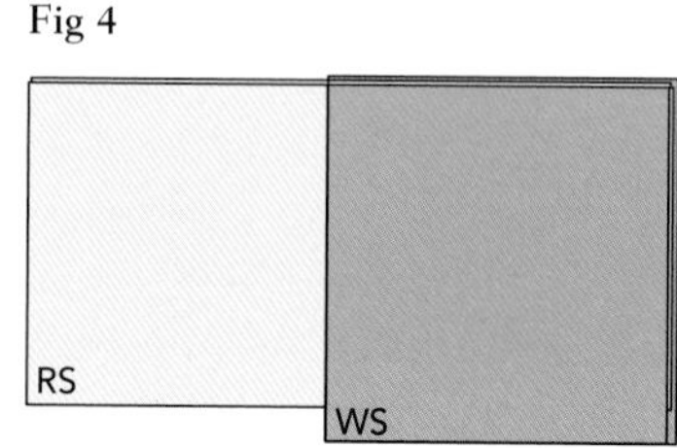

Choosing the Block Size

This block can be made in any size for the planned design. First choose the size needed for the finished block e.g., 4in × 4in (10.2cm × 10.2cm). The centre square is cut this size plus ½in (1.3cm). The four corner squares that make the background corners of the block are cut half the final size of the finished block plus ½in (1.3cm) e.g., the four corner squares of a 4in × 4in (10.2cm × 10.2cm) block will be cut 2in + ½in = 2½in (5.1cm + 1.3cm = 6.4cm). Cutting details for several sizes of blocks are given below:

3in × 3in (7.6cm × 7.6cm) – centre square cut 3½in × 3½in (8.9cm × 8.9cm) and four corner squares cut 2in × 2in (5.1cm × 5.1cm).
4in × 4in (10.2cm × 10.2cm) – centre square cut 4½in × 4½in (11.4cm × 11.4cm) and four corner squares cut 2½in × 2½in (6.4cm × 6.4cm).
5in × 5in (12.7cm × 12.7cm) – centre square cut 5½in × 5½in (14cm × 14cm) and four corner squares cut 3in × 3in (7.6cm × 7.6cm).
6in × 6in (15.2cm × 15.2cm) – centre square cut 6½in × 6½in (16.5cm × 16.5cm) and four corner squares cut 3½in × 3½in (8.9cm × 8.9cm).

5 Pin and stitch a ¼in (6mm) seam along the right-hand edge as in Fig 5.

Fig 5

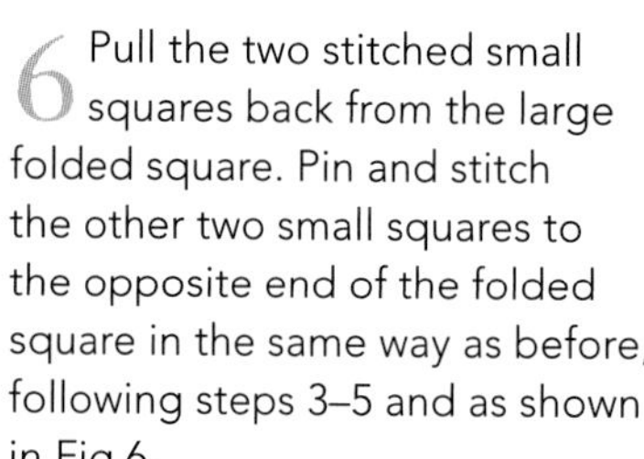

6 Pull the two stitched small squares back from the large folded square. Pin and stitch the other two small squares to the opposite end of the folded square in the same way as before, following steps 3–5 and as shown in Fig 6.

Fig 6

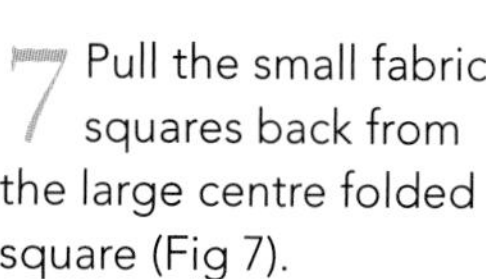

7 Pull the small fabric squares back from the large centre folded square (Fig 7).

Fig 7

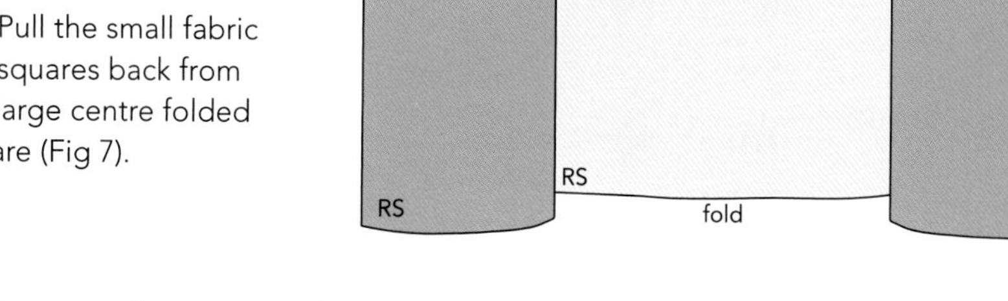

8 Separate the two raw edges of the centre folded square of fabric. Pull them apart and match the two opposite seams, each marked as A in Fig 7. Finger-press these seams open (Fig 8). Pin the two seams together, matching them carefully.

Fig 8

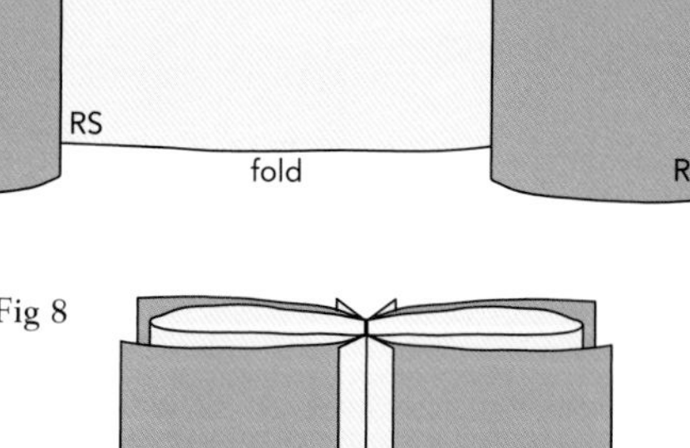

9 Match the top edges of the squares and of the folded layer that is sandwiched between them, taking care not to catch in any odd folds of fabric. Pin these edges (Fig 9).

Fig 9

Stitch through the layers with the usual ¼in (6mm) seam (Fig 10).

Fig 10

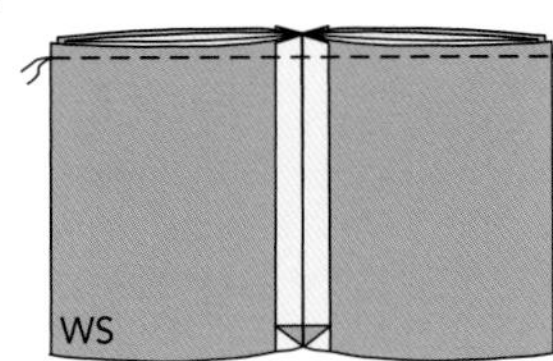

Now open out the block and pull the folded square into shape. Press the long seam on the back of the block open to reduce the bulk (Fig 11).

Fig 11

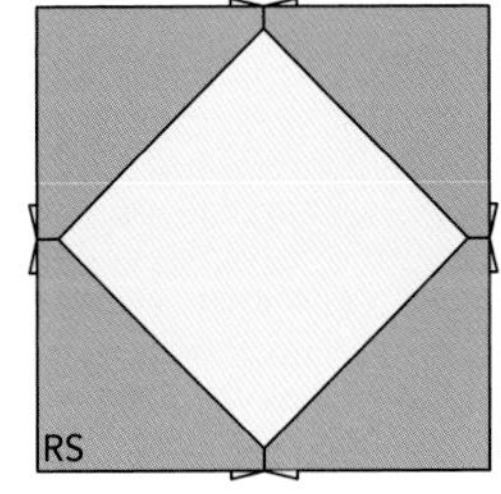

TIP

To prevent catching folds of the inner layers in this seam, you might find it easier to pin and stitch just from the centre to one side. Turn the block over and pin and stitch the other half of the long seam, starting again at the centre and stitching towards the outer edge of the block.

Adding the Window

10 Measure the centre square-on-point from corner to corner and then subtract ¼in (6mm) from this measurement. This is the size of the square of fabric that will make the window. Trim the window fabric down a little if it needs it once it is pinned into place. The window measurements for several sizes of block are given below:

3in × 3in (7.6cm × 7.6cm) – window cut 1⅞in × 1⅞in (4.7cm × 4.7cm).
4in × 4in (10.2cm × 10.2cm) – window cut 2⅝in × 2⅝in (6.6cm × 6.6cm).
5in × 5in (12.7cm × 12.7cm) – window cut 3¼in × 3¼in (8.3cm × 8.3cm).
6in × 6in (15.2cm × 15.2cm) – window cut 4in × 4in (10.2cm × 10.2cm).

11 Pin the window in position and stitch as for the classic Cathedral Window (see page 22).

Joining the Blocks

12 Several blocks can be joined together or mixed with other techniques to make a design. The seam allowance is the usual ¼in (6mm) but take care not to let the stitched seam joining the blocks cut off part of the window corners. Extra interest can be made by changing the fabric used for the four corners of each block to give different effects – see Figs 12a and 12b.

Fig 12a

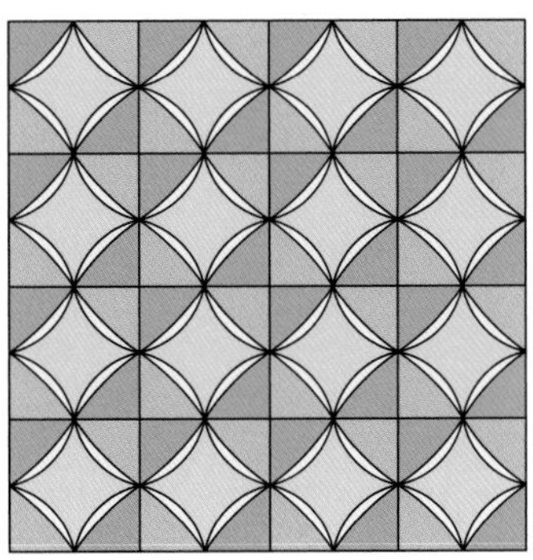

Fig 12b

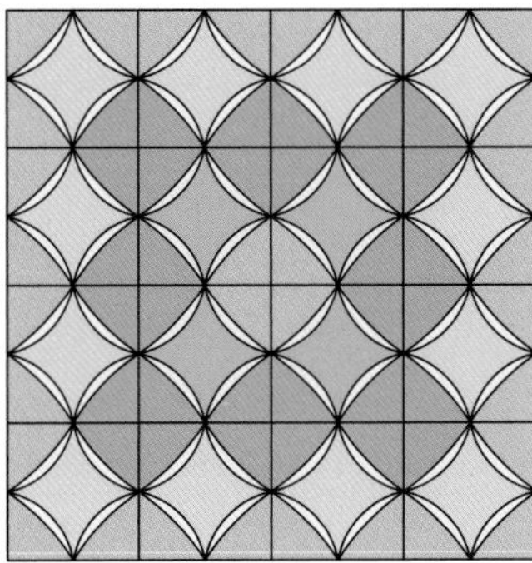

13 Another way to give interest to empty areas where blocks meet is to pin folded triangles on each corner before the blocks are joined. Cut a square of contrast fabric for each corner. For the 4in × 4in (10.2cm × 10.2cm) finished blocks used in Purple Windows (shown on page 101) I cut pink squares 1½in × 1½in (3.8cm × 3.8cm), folded each in half with right side outwards and pressed (Fig 13a).

Fig13a

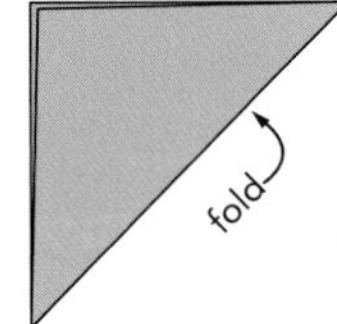

Fig13b

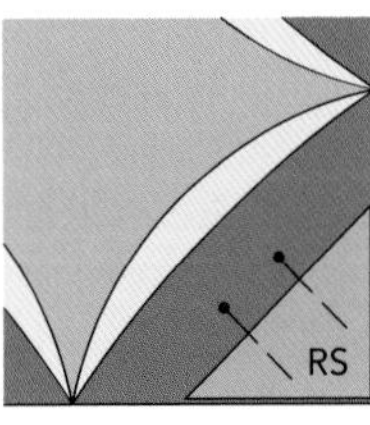

Fig13c

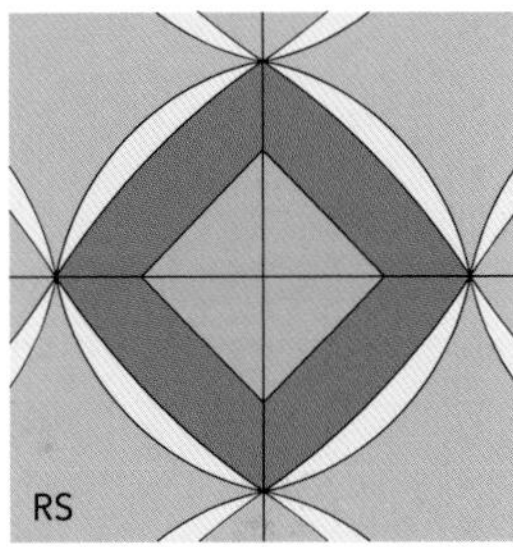

Each folded triangle was pinned in position on a corner of each block with the cut edges of the triangle matching the cut edges of the block and the folded edge of the triangle running diagonally across the corner (Fig 13b). When the blocks are then stitched together in the usual way, a little square on point is revealed at the junction of the seams (Fig 13c). This can be left as it is in Brenda Scraggs' cushion (right) or the folded edges can be rolled back like Cathedral Window, as in Purple Windows. An extra layer can be inserted as a window.

Brenda Scraggs' elegant cushion in cotton and silk (also shown on page 91) uses an arrangement of Two-shade Cathedral Window blocks with added folded triangles of silk in the corners.

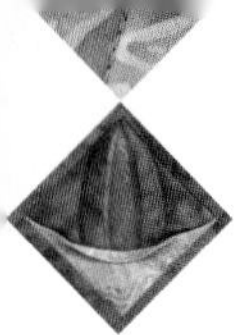

Folded Squares

This technique does not imitate Cathedral Window in its looks but uses the principle of the rolled-back bias edge to create a variety of designs, such as the bright Flowering Folds wall hanging by Pauline Bugg shown opposite. Squares of fabric are folded in half and layered on a background square. The folded bias edges are then rolled back to make the deep curve that we associate with Cathedral Window blocks. The number of folded squares used in each block can vary from just one to four as shown in Figs 1a–1d. They can also be combined with plain squares of the same size in a design. The blocks may be made in any size you choose, just adding on the usual ¼in (6mm) for the seam allowances, i.e., ½in (1.3cm) in total for each block. See pages 108–111 for a gallery of wall hangings showing the use of the Folded Square technique in some original designs. You can use one of the designs in this section as a project or learn the technique and create your own original pieces, for which, of course, I will take all the credit...

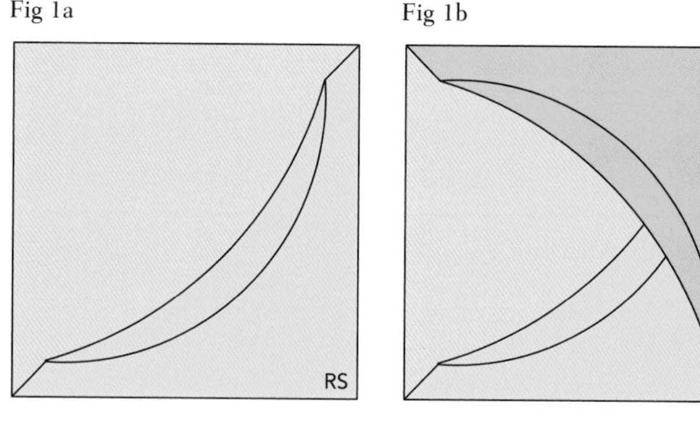

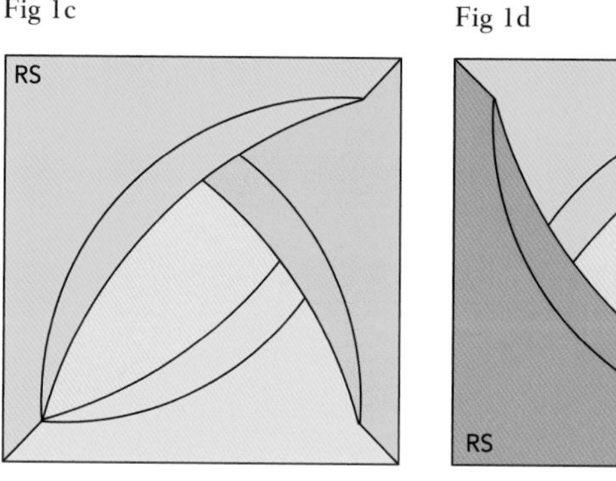

'This is such a versatile and elegant technique. You can make it any size, in any fabric; use it in a bag, quilt or wall hanging and change the effect totally by using fewer or more layers of curved folds. It can be made totally by machine (hooray! I hear some of you cry) or stitched tranquilly by hand while on holiday, so it really is a crowd-pleaser.'

In this pretty design called Flowering Folds, Pauline Bugg uses the Folded Square technique to create flowers in a slightly three-dimensional design – see page 109 for more information on this piece.

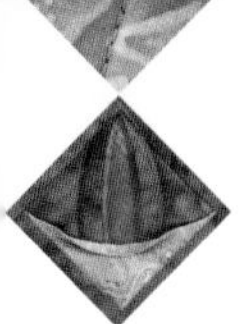

Making a Block of Folded Squares

1 Choose a block size to suit your design – I used a block measuring 5in × 5in (12.7cm × 12.7cm) final size for my Lavender Folds design (shown overleaf), and so cut all the squares 5½in × 5½in (14cm × 14cm).

2 Cut one square for the background. How much this fabric shows will depend on how many layers you are adding on top of it (see Fig 1 page 104). Cut one square in this same size from each of the fabrics chosen for the layers. I will give the instructions for building up a background square with four layers, but the number of layers used for your block is entirely up to you.

TIP

As each folded square is added to the design, the lower layers become partially covered. The last folded square to be added usually shows the most.

3 Place the background Square 1 right side *up* on a flat surface. Fold and press Square 2 in half diagonally as accurately as possible, right side outwards. Place the folded Square 2 on the background Square 1 (Fig 2).

Fig 2

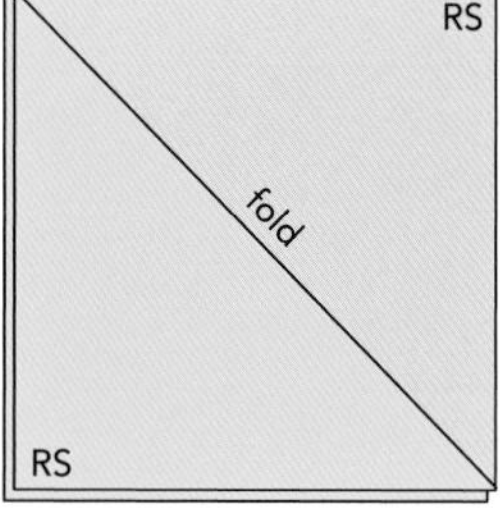

4 Pin the sides and anchor the corners (Fig 3). The corner pins should anchor the folded edges ¼in (6mm) from the square's outer edges (Fig 4).

Fig 3

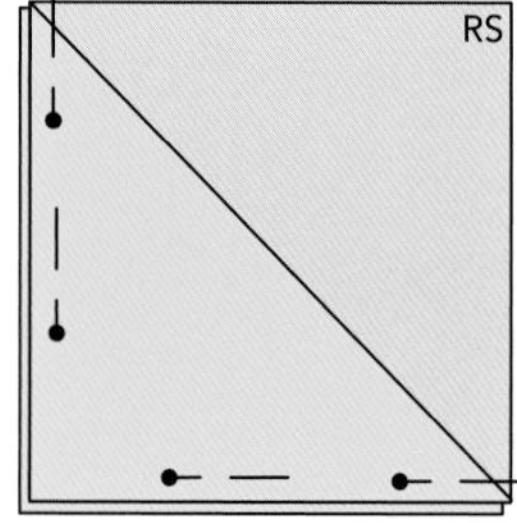

Fig 4

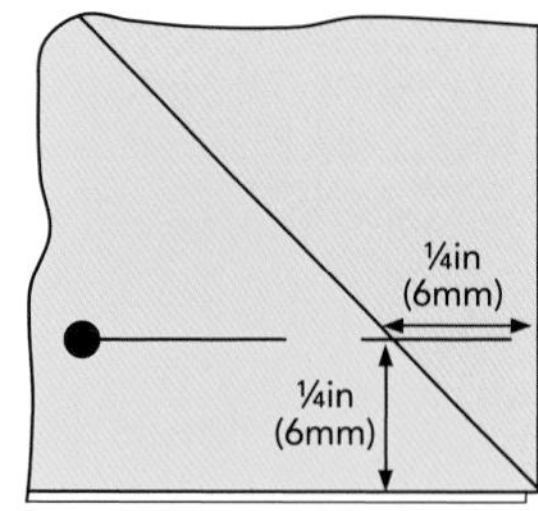

5 Pull the folded edge back in the centre as far as it will go, much like Cathedral Window. Pin it with just one pin as in Fig 5.

Fig 5

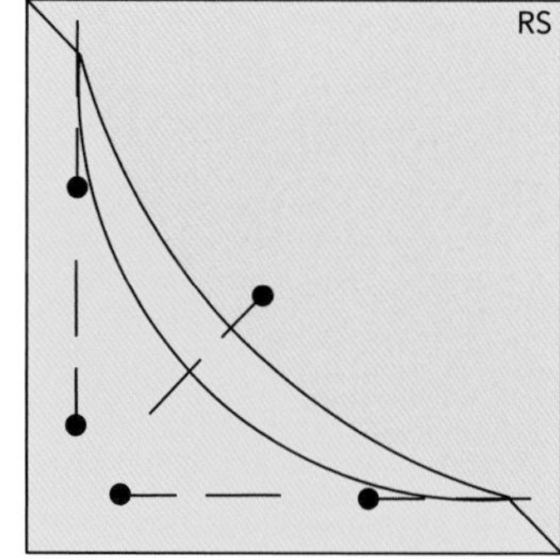

6 Stitch along the rolled edge as for Cathedral Window (see step 5 Adding the Windows on page 23).

TIP

This is a very easy edge to top-stitch by machine if you prefer rather than hand stitching in the usual way. Start stitching from the corner of the background square, stitching along the edge of the folded square up until the point where the folded edge starts to curve back. Keep the corner pins in position for as long as possible as you stitch. Position the needle in the curved edge and top stitch along it to the other end of the curve. Continue to stitch on the background fabric alongside the folded edge and finish at the corner of the background square (Fig 6).

Fig 6

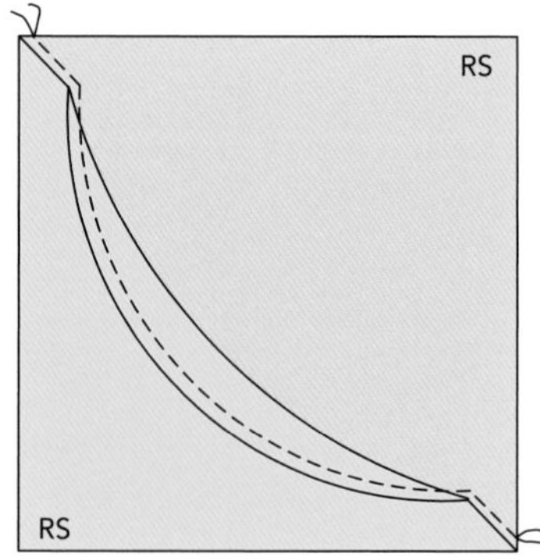

7 Remove the pins. Reduce the bulk of the folded square by pulling back the top layer and trimming the under layer of this folded square about ⅛in (3mm) from the stitching.

8 Fold and press Square 3 in half diagonally, right side outwards. Place it on the block either on the opposite corner as in Fig 7a or overlapping it as in Fig 7b. Pin as before and pull back the folded edge to make a curve. Stitch the curve as before.

Fig 7a

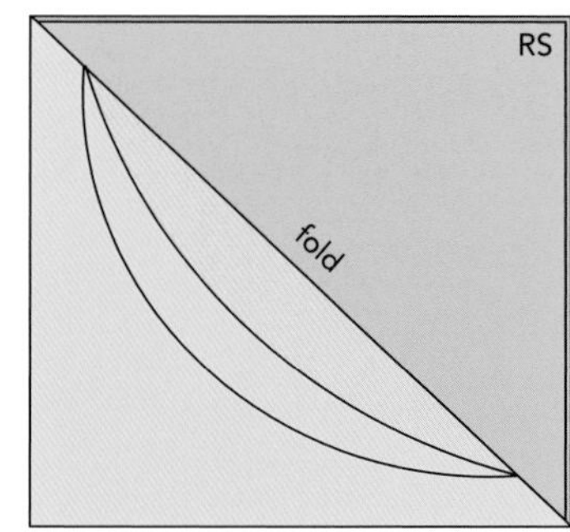

Fig 7b

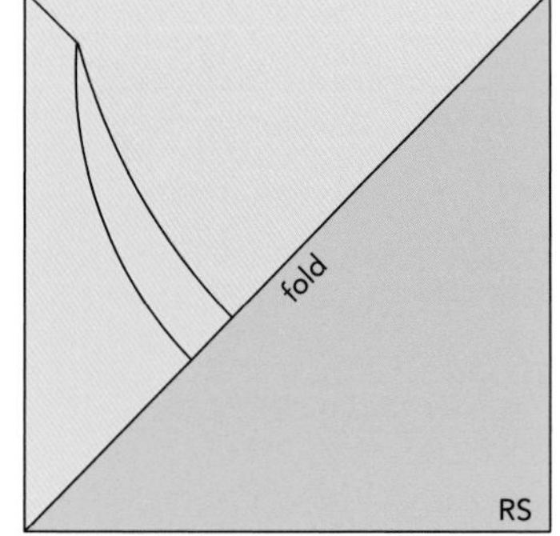

9 Remove the pins and trim the under layer of this folded square to reduce the bulk.

10 Fold and press Square 4 in half diagonally, right side outwards. Place it on the block so that it overlaps the previous layers as in Fig 8a or 8b. Pull back and stitch the curve as before. Trim the under layer to reduce the bulk.

Fig 8a

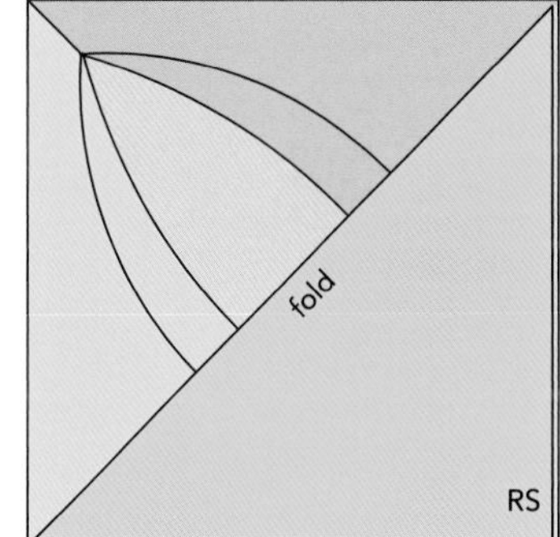

Fig 8b

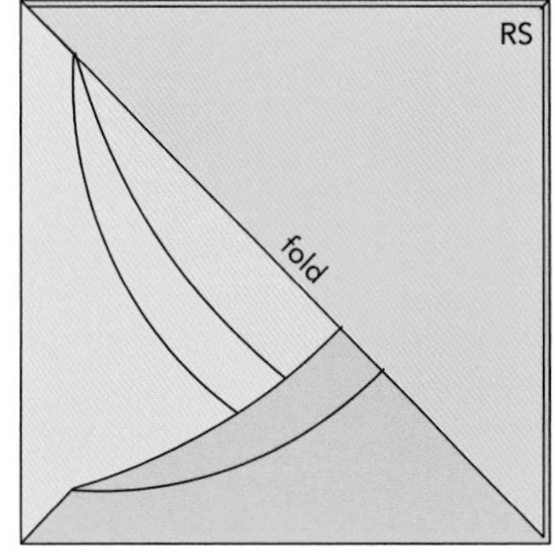

11 Add the final folded square to the design in the way described in steps 4–7 opposite.

'I am amazed that I had these bright, glowing colours in my collection, especially yellow and red! I don't dye fabric myself as it's too messy for our little house, but I love to use it with other commercial fabrics in my quilts.'

Creating a Design

Many different designs can be created by joining Folded Square blocks together. The joining seams need to be pressed *open* from the back to reduce the bulk of all the layers. I then add a layer of thin wadding (batting) and a backing fabric even if I do not intend to quilt the piece, as the wadding absorbs the thickness of the seam allowances and makes the back of the design smooth. The piece needs to be tied or quilted to hold the layers in place before the outer edges are bound (see Knotting or Tying a Quilt on page 132).

Glowing Squares

This little wall hanging repeats the four-layer folded square described left in a nine-block design. Each block is identical in design but the colours of the fabrics shift gradually from sharp yellow in the top-left corner row by row to red in the bottom-right corner. All the fabric was hand dyed so I was able to graduate the shades across the piece. Each block used cut squares of fabric measuring 5in × 5in (12.7cm × 12.7cm). This was not a conscious design choice but due to the fact that all the squares of dyed fabric measured 10in (25.4cm), so this way I was able to cut four squares from each piece. All the top stitching on the curved edges was by machine.

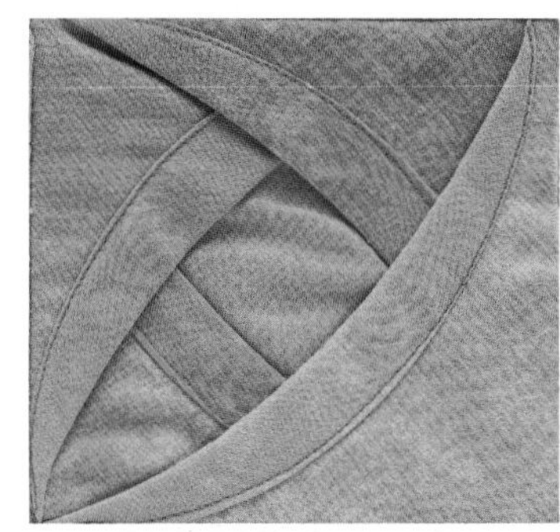

This aptly named Glowing Squares wall hanging uses vivid colours shaded in brightness from top left to bottom right. Finished size of this sample is 13½in (34.3cm) square.

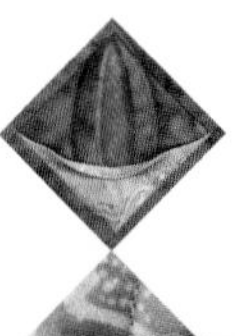

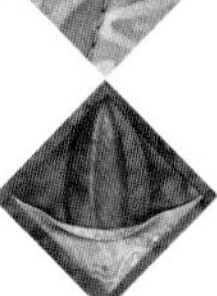

Lavender Folds

This design uses sixteen blocks of folded squares that vary in the arrangement of layers, none using more than two folded layers on the background. I did this because I loved the batik fabric used for the background and wanted it to show in the design as much as possible. Fig 9 shows the arrangement of the blocks.

Pink, mauve and soft blue fabrics were used in addition to a patterned batik for the background squares. The four centre blocks used two folded squares, one of pink and one of mauve on the background as shown in Fig 10a. The four corner blocks used one blue folded square on the background (Fig 10b). The remaining eight outer blocks used two folded squares, one of pink and one of mauve arranged as in Fig 10c.

Fig 9

Fig 10a

Fig 10b

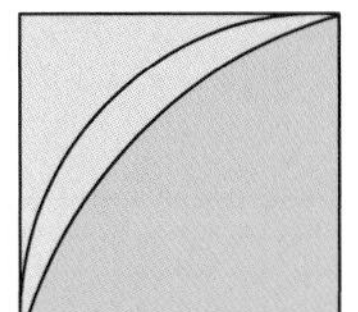

Fig 10c

Flowering Folds

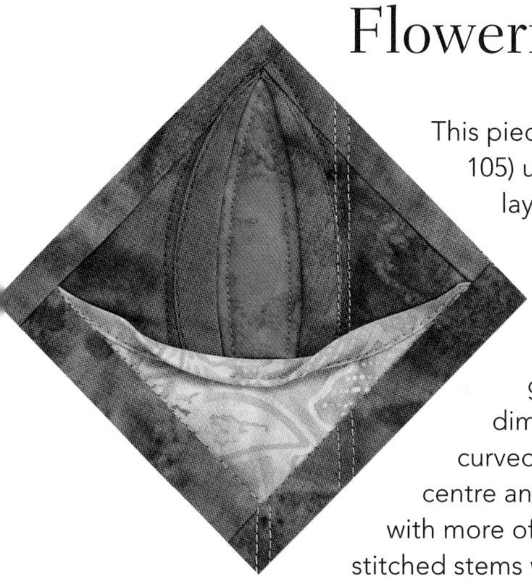

This piece made by Pauline Bugg (also shown on page 105) uses 3in (7.6cm) finished Folded Squares with three layers which are placed on point in the design to create flowers (Fig 11). The background purple fabric becomes the centre column of the flower with the two first folded layers as a green background. The final folded layer in a paler green becomes the base of the flower. A three-dimensional effect is achieved by folding the top curved edge of the pale green fabric back on itself in the centre and stitching it with a few machine stitches. The six blocks are then joined together with more of the same green background fabric to make the design. Appliquéd leaves and stitched stems were added, with extra machine quilting to enhance the raised look of the design.

Fig 11

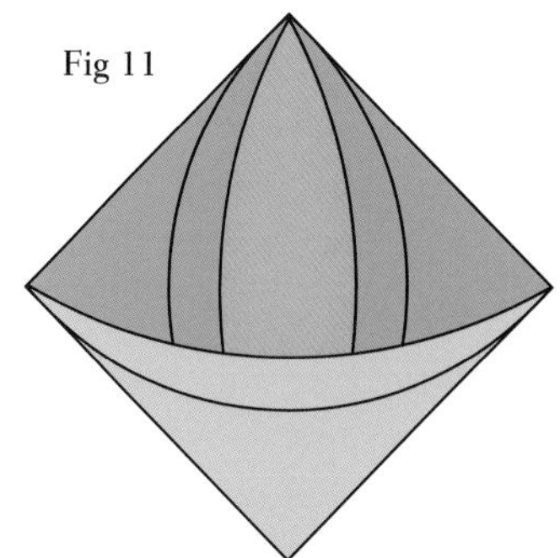

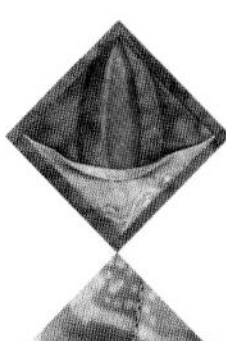

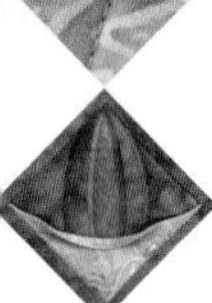

Folded Leaves

This second wall hanging by Pauline Bugg creates yet another variation of this block. Pauline has used the fabric she wants as the leaf for the unfolded base square. The two folded squares are not whole pieces of fabric but two half-square triangles joined on the diagonal, where they will eventually be folded in the usual way (Fig 12a). One half of the square is the same leaf fabric, the other half is the background neutral shade. The best way to make these pieced squares is to cut two squares, one from each fabric, in the chosen finished size plus ⁷⁄₈in (2.2cm). Pauline's blocks were finished size 3½in × 3½in (8.9cm × 8.9cm) so the squares to be pieced were cut 3½in + ⁷⁄₈in = 4³⁄₈in (11.1cm).

Fig 12a

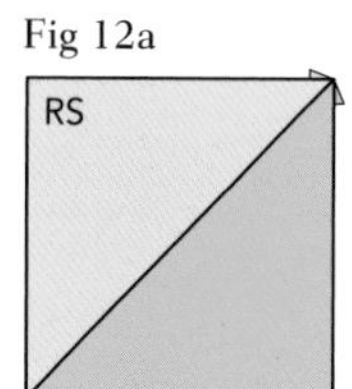

1 Pin the two cut squares together with right sides facing, matching the edges carefully. Draw a line diagonally across the top square with a sharp marking pencil (Fig 12b). Machine a line of stitching on either side of the drawn line at a distance of exactly ¼in (6mm) (Fig 12c).

Fig 12b

Fig 12c

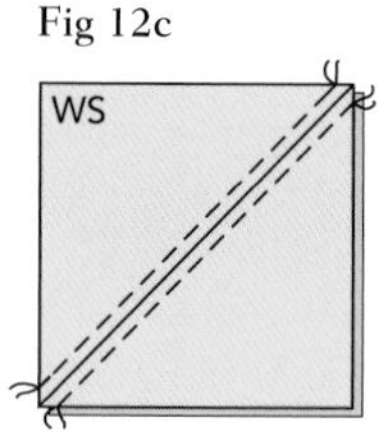

Fig 12d

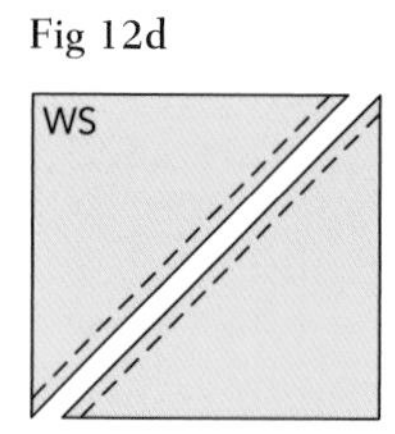

2 Cut along each drawn line between the stitched lines (Fig 12d). Open out each square and press the diagonal seam open – this makes it much easier to fold in half exactly along the seamline.

3 Fold each pieced square along the seamline with right side outwards and press it to make the usual triangle used as a layer in the Folded Square block (Fig 13a).

Fig 13a

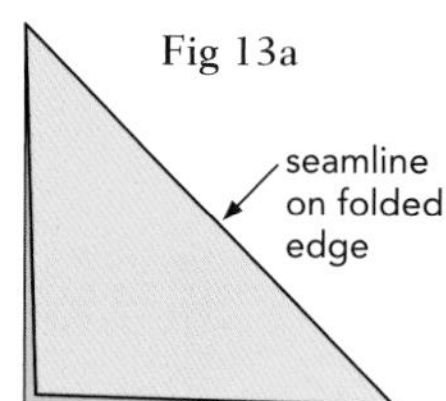

4 Place the two folded squares on opposite corners of the base square of leaf fabric as in Fig 13b with the background fabric uppermost. Follow steps 4–7 Making a Block of Folded Squares on page 106, to pin and stitch the curved edges as usual. The pulled-back curves will be in the leaf fabric and add extra width to the centre leaf shape, while the rest of the top folded squares make a neutral background (Fig 13c).

Fig 13b

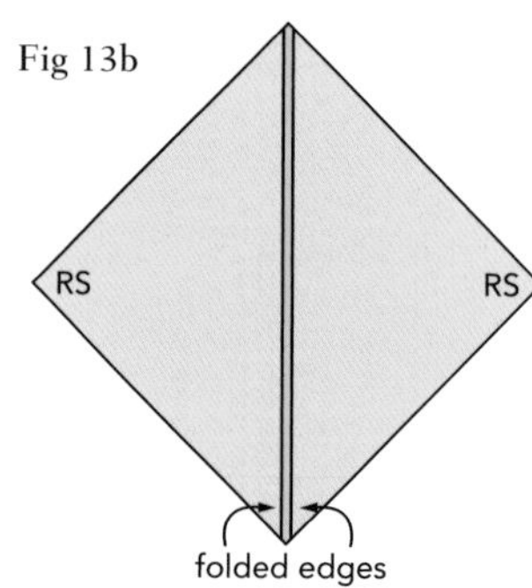

Fig 13c

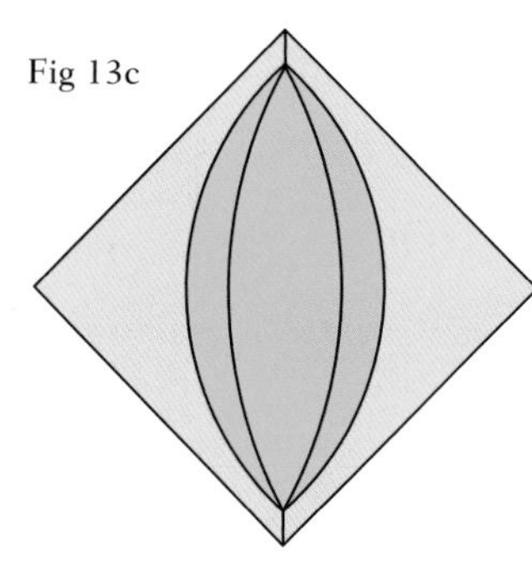

5 Pauline enriched her piece with hand quilting, stitching leaf outlines on the background areas in contrasting thread.

Quilt for Barbara

This dramatic wall hanging by Jenny Lyons uses the Folded Square technique in an original design that plays with different tones and textures of fabric in the layers to great effect. The piece uses sixteen blocks, some with three folded layers and some with four. Further interest is created by arranging the design on point.

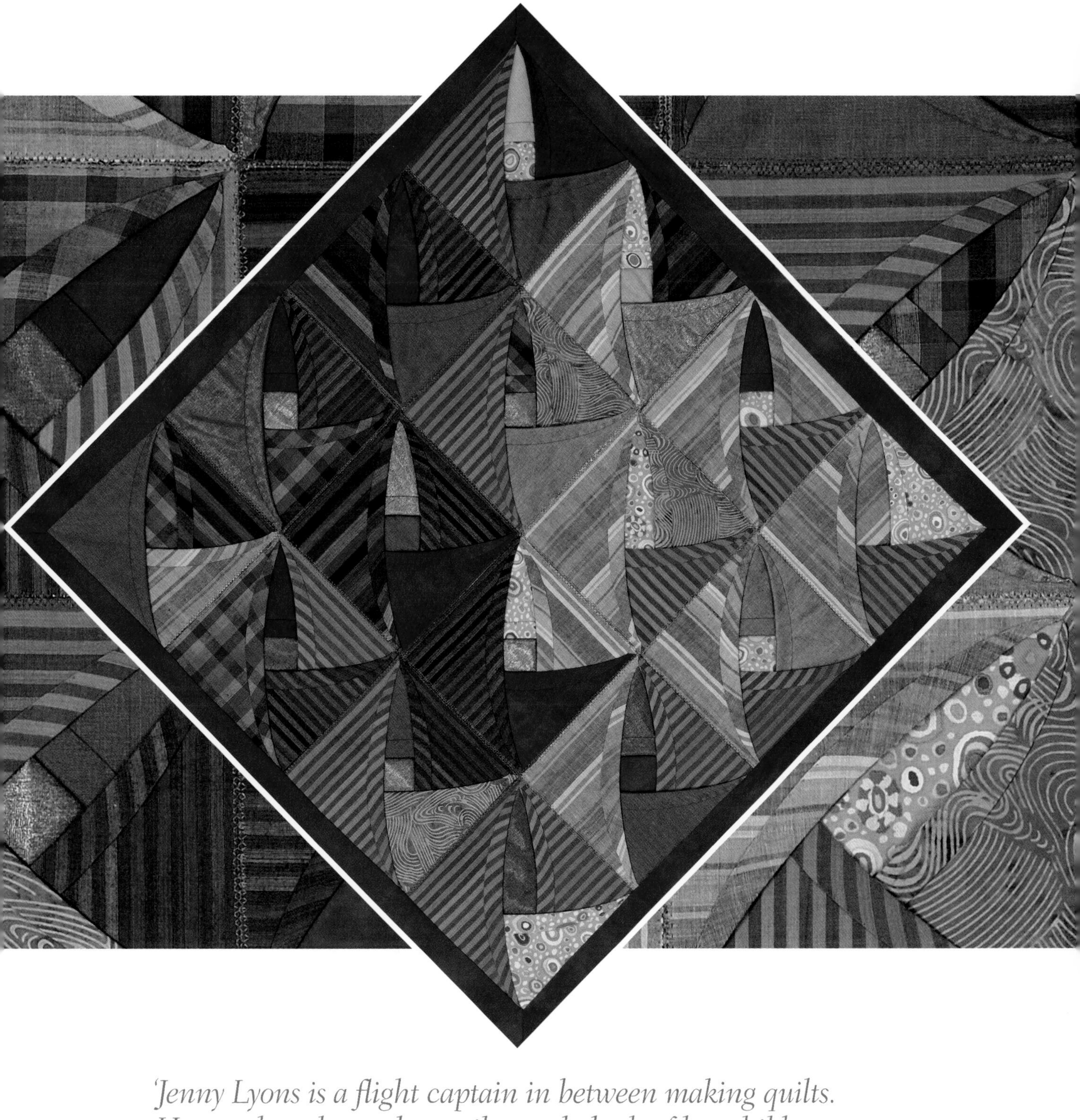

'Jenny Lyons is a flight captain in between making quilts. Her mother also makes quilts, as do both of her children, so that's three generations all playing with fabric.'

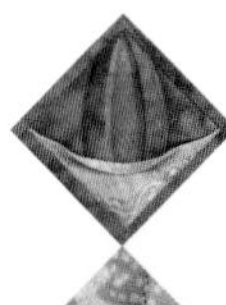

Folded Flowers

This fascinating layered design really does resemble origami paper-folding, with the addition of some final curving back of folded edges to soften the flower design. The folded flower is made from one square of fabric, which floats on a background fabric. The maths involved in the various folded and diagonal elements of the design means that to alter the sizing from a finished 5½in x 5½in (14cm x 14cm) block is not an easy option, but this seems fine to me, as the balance of folds and background layers works well in this size and looks good combined with other folded designs, as in Avril Ellis' Christmas Windmills quilt on page 126.

Because the folding process is done with a steam iron to give really sharp edges and corners, chose a fabric for the flower that responds well to folding and pressing. I have used the technique to create the stylish Four Flowers cushion shown here – instructions for the cushion are on page 116.

Block finished size: 5½in × 5½in (14cm × 14cm).

Fig 1

'A cushion is just one way to use this intriguing block. Once you have mastered the very simple folding and pressing process, you can move on to create your own designs. I'm sure there are many wonderful interpretations out there waiting to be made.'

This elegant cushion uses four Folded Flower blocks of yellow silk on a patterned black cotton background framed with yellow silk. Folded corners of silk are stitched back into a curve to add interest. Silk lends itself to the central folded flower as it folds crisply with the help of a steam iron, and the raw edges, so vulnerable to fraying, are covered by triangles of the background cotton fabric. The combination of the sheen of the silk with the matt surface of the cotton works really well in this design.

Making a Folded Flower Block

Cutting the Squares

For each block cut the following pieces of fabric:
From the flower fabric – one square cut 8in × 8in (20.3cm × 20.3cm);
From the background fabric – one square cut 6in × 6in (15.2cm × 15.2cm) and two squares each cut 4in × 4in (10.2cm × 10.2cm).

1 From the fabric chosen for the folded flower cut a square measuring 8in × 8in (20.3cm × 20.3cm). Fold it into four as in Fig 2a, to mark the centre. If possible use a steam iron at all times for the folding.

Fig 2a

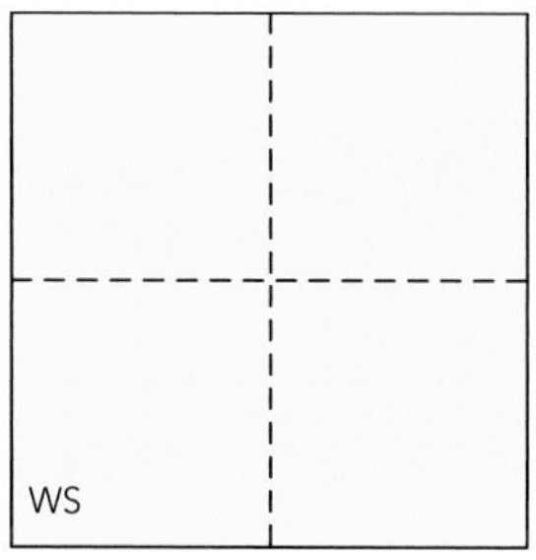

2 With the wrong side of the fabric square upwards, fold one corner into the centre, pressing firmly with the iron (Fig 2b).

Fig 2b

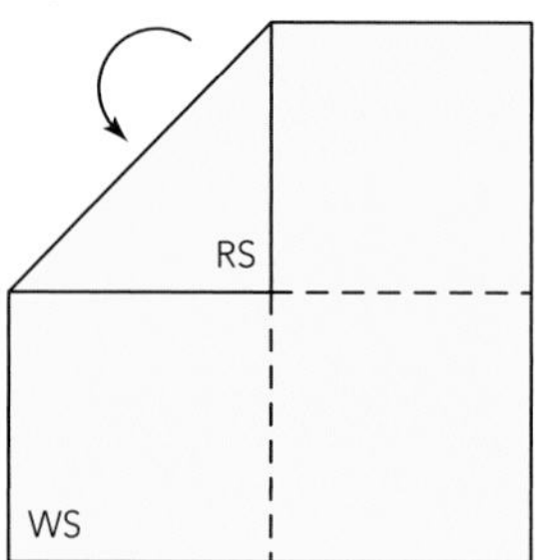

3 Repeat this on all four corners, pressing firmly as before (Fig 2c).

Fig 2c

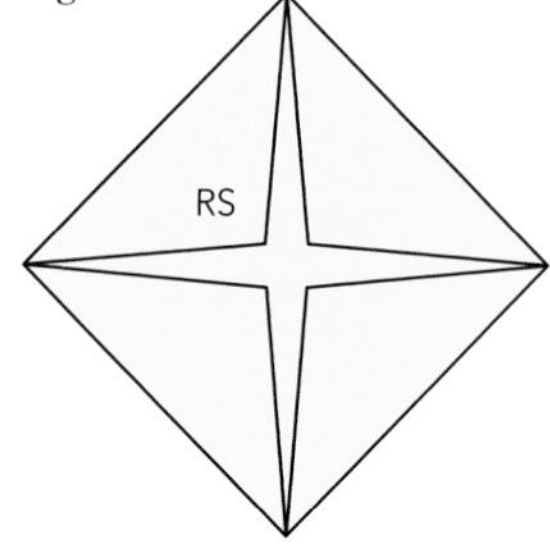

4 Turn the block over. Press one corner into the centre, pressing firmly (Fig 3a).

Fig 3a

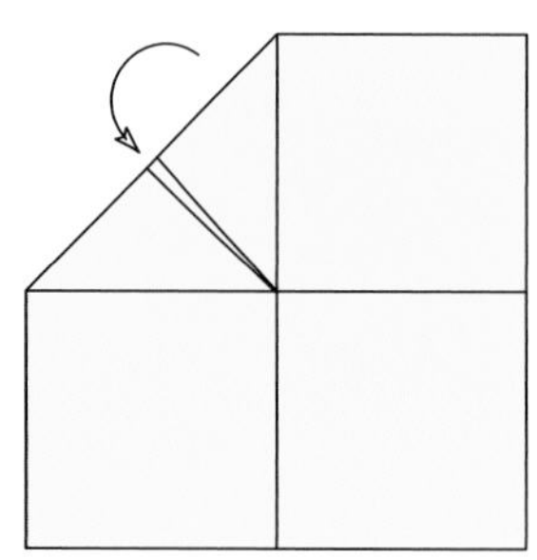

5 Repeat this on all four corners, pressing firmly (Fig 3b).

Fig 3b

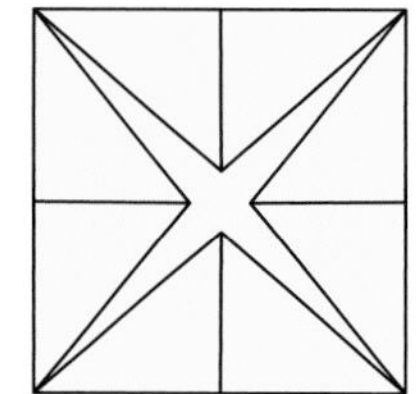

6 Turn the block over again – it should look like Fig 4a. Press one corner to the centre and press (Fig 4b).

Fig 4a

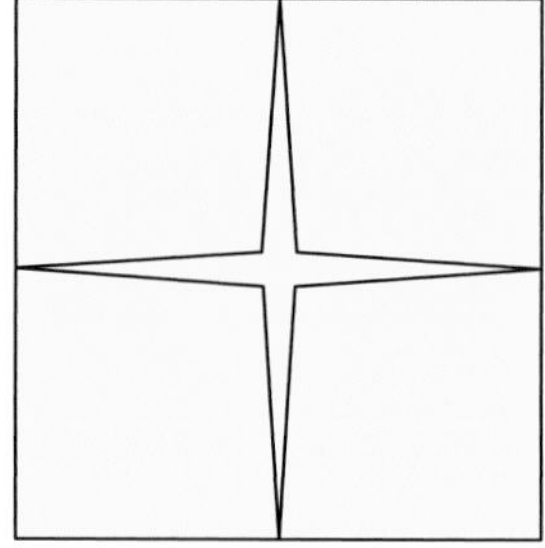

Fig 4b

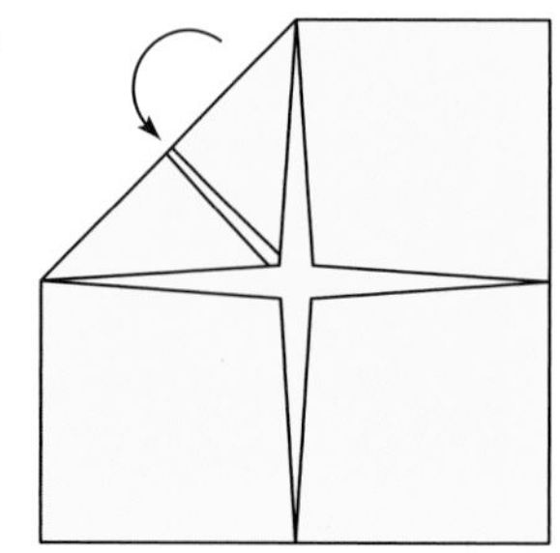

7 Repeat this on all four corners, pressing firmly (Fig 4c).

Fig 4c

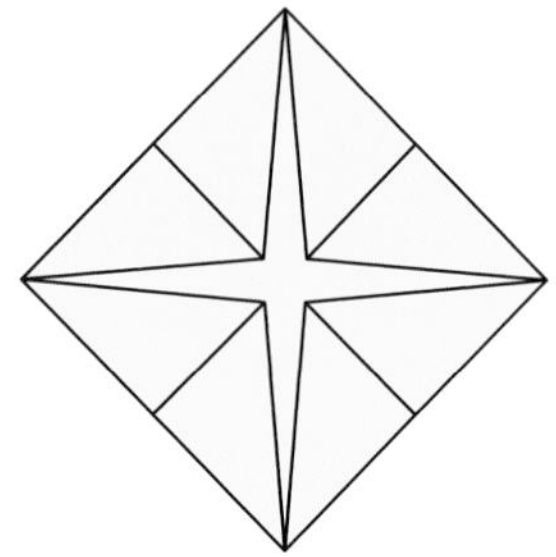

8 Turn the block over once more. Here comes the origami/fabric manipulation bit: place both thumbs under the flap of fabric at the place marked A in Fig 5a and push the corner at A towards the corner at B. At the same time, pull apart the two raw edges of fabric that run from A to B and spread them sideways to make a rectangle (Fig 5b). Press firmly with the steam iron.

Fig 5a

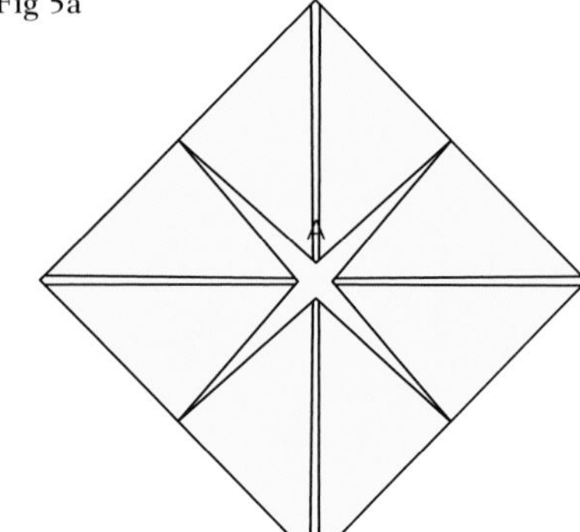

Fig 5b

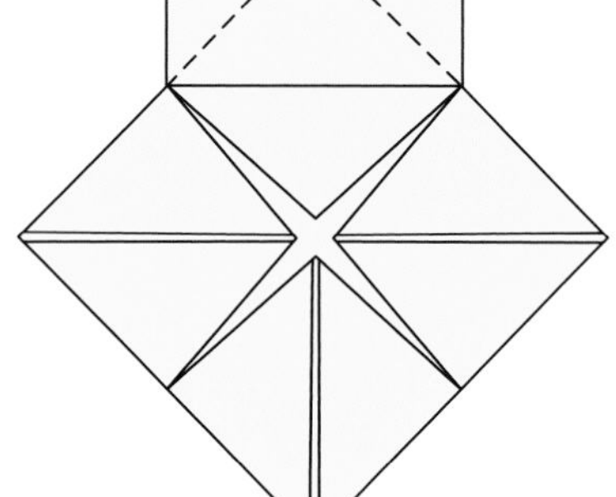

9 Repeat this on all sides of the block (Fig 5c).

Fig 5c

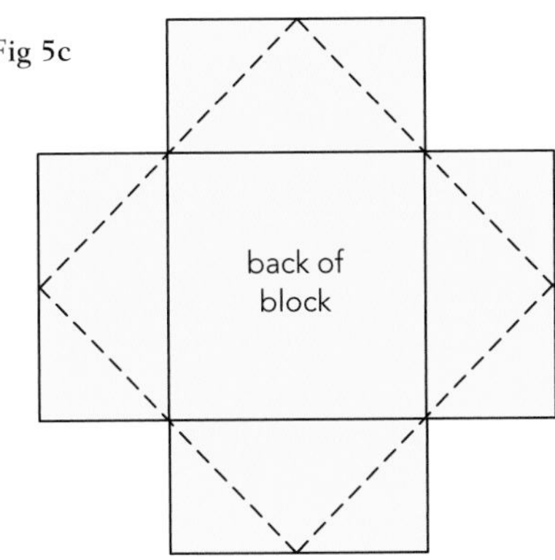

10 Turn the block over to its correct side to show the folded flower (Fig 5d).

Fig 5d

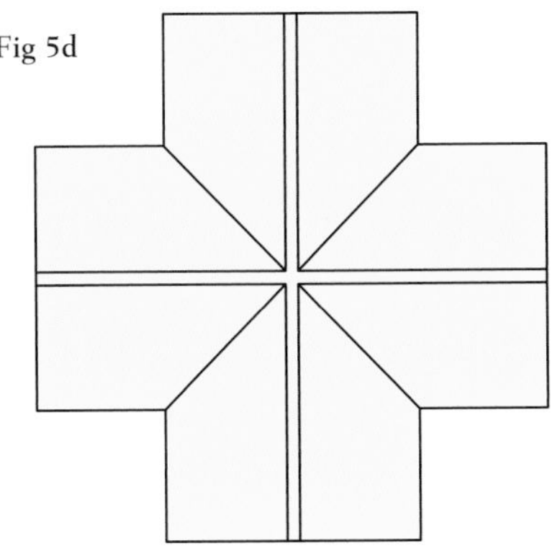

Setting the Flower on its Background

11 From the background fabric cut one square measuring 6in × 6in (15.2cm × 15.2cm). On the *right* side of the fabric use a sharp marking pencil to draw the two diagonal lines from corner to corner (Fig 6). These are guidelines for positioning and will not show in the final design.

Fig 6

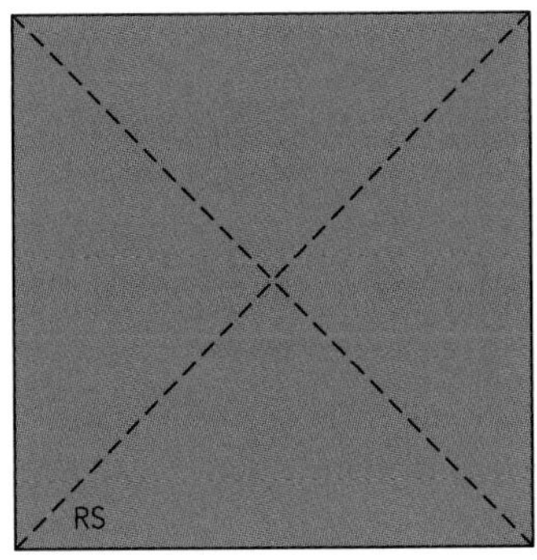

12 Use these lines to help position the folded flower in the centre of the background square – the drawn lines should match up with the centre folds on each side of the flower as in Fig 7. Pin the flower into place on the background square.

Fig 7

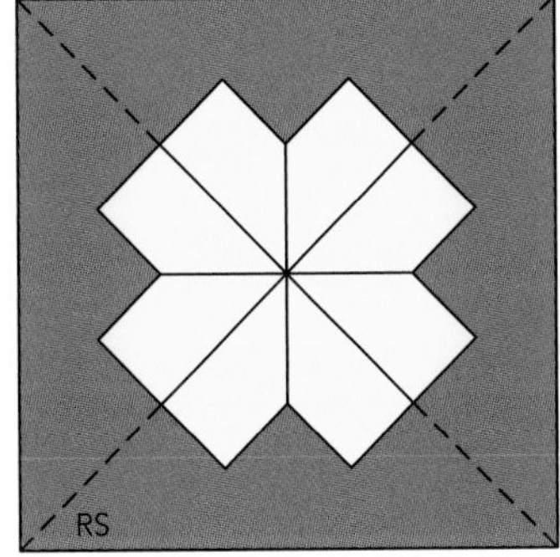

13 From the background fabric cut two squares each measuring 4in × 4in (10.2cm × 10.2cm). Cut both squares in half diagonally to make four triangles (Fig 8).

Fig 8

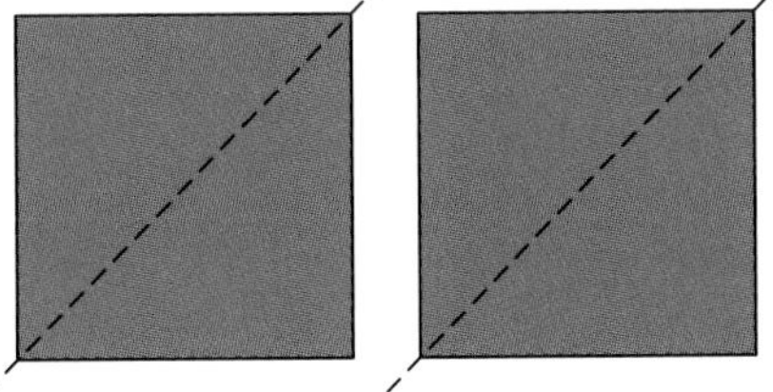

14 Fold one triangle in half and finger-press to mark the centre (Fig 9).

Fig 9

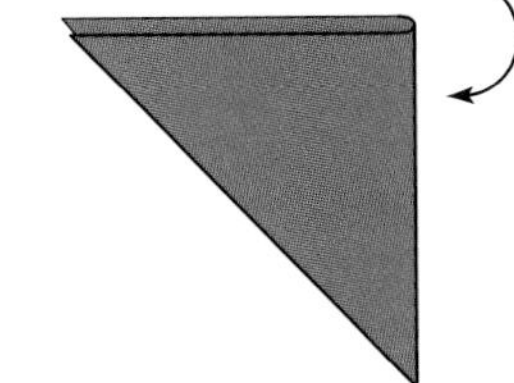

15 Place the triangle right side *down* with its longest side level with one side of the folded flower (Fig 10). Match the centre crease on the triangle with the drawn diagonal line on the background square. The corners of the triangle should extend slightly over the sides of the background square so that a ¼in (6mm) seam exactly hits the edge of the background square. Pin and stitch this seam (Fig 11). Flip the triangle of fabric back on to the background, pressing firmly.

Fig 10

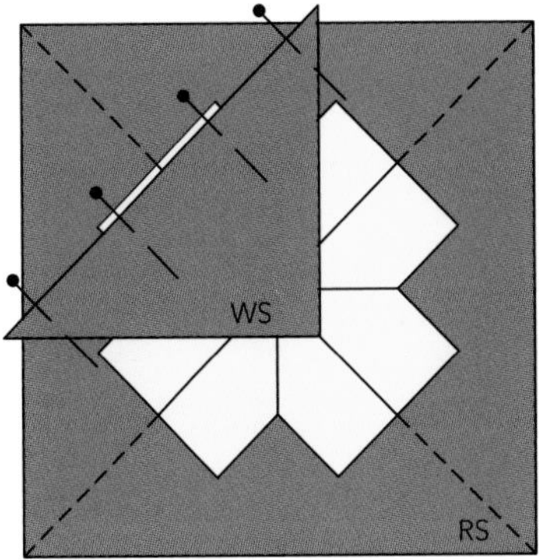

Fig 11

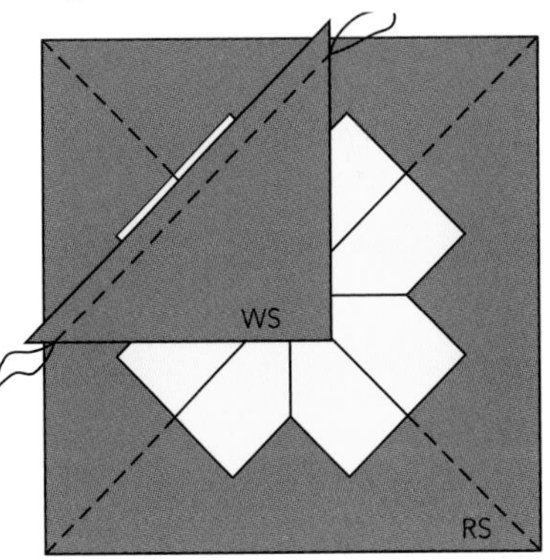

16 Repeat this with a second cut triangle of background fabric pinned and stitched on to the opposite corner of the block. Press back firmly (Fig 12).

Fig 12

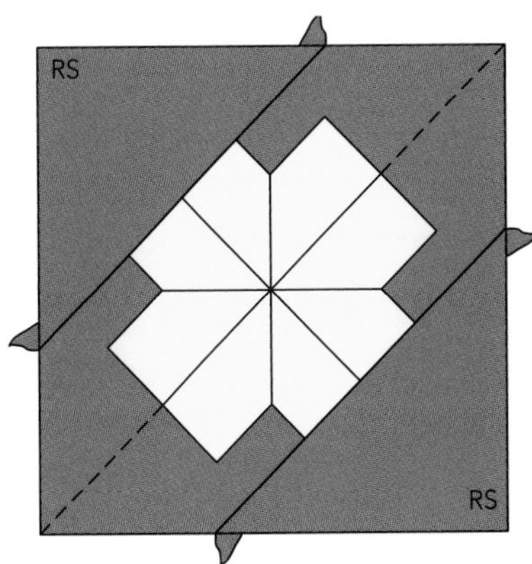

17 Repeat this with the two remaining cut triangles on the other two corners of the block. Press back firmly (Fig 13).

Fig 13

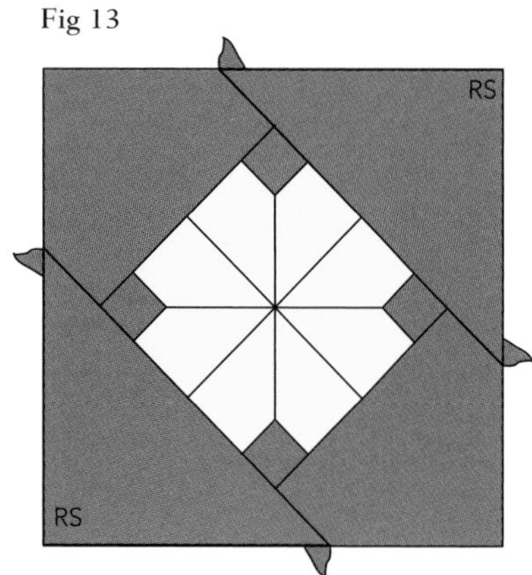

18 Finally, turn the block to its back and trim any edges of the pressed-back corners that are overhanging the 6in (15.2cm) backing square. Try not to trim this background square at all as it was cut 6in × 6in (15.2cm × 15.2cm) and will make the final 5½in × 5½in (14cm × 14cm) finished block.

19 Fix the centre of the flower in place with a few tiny invisible stitches through all the layers, or make a feature of the centre by stitching a cross of stitches in thicker decorative thread.

20 Curve back and stitch the folded bias edges of the flower as shown in Fig 14.

Fig 14

Designing with the Folded Flower Block

Four Flowers Cushion

This elegant cushion (also shown on page 113) uses four Folded Flower blocks of yellow silk on a patterned black cotton background framed with a border of the same yellow silk. Folded corners of the silk add interest to the design. These may be left as folded triangles or stitched back into a curve as I have. If you have a collection of silk fabric brought back from afar that you have been longing to use, the Folded Flowers would work well, as silk, being a natural fibre, responds well to an iron and even steam-pressing. I would avoid very floppy silk or spray starch it to give it body, but the textured dupion type silk is fine. Combine the silk with a cotton fabric for the background and four corners if you wish as it frays less, or use silk throughout.

Cushion finished size: 15in × 15in (38.1cm × 38.1cm).

'Silk in a cushion adds a note of real sophistication and combining it with cotton for the background keeps the vulnerable silk edges from fraying and gives stability.'

REQUIREMENTS

- For the folded flowers, corners and borders ½yd (0.5m) of fabric
- For the background and cushion back ¾yd (0.75m) of fabric
- Lightweight calico (muslin) to line cushion front 16in × 16in (40.6cm × 40.6cm)
- Cushion pad 16in (40.6cm) square

Construction

1 From the two fabrics for the flowers and the background follow steps 1–20 on page 114 to make four Folded Flower blocks, as in Fig 14 opposite.

2 From the fabric used for the folded flowers cut eight squares each measuring 2in × 2in (5.1cm × 5.1cm). Fold each square in half with right side outwards and press (Fig 15a). Pin a folded triangle on two opposite corners of each block with the cut edges of the triangle matching the cut edges of the block and the folded edge of the triangle running diagonally across the corner (Fig 15b).

Fig 15a

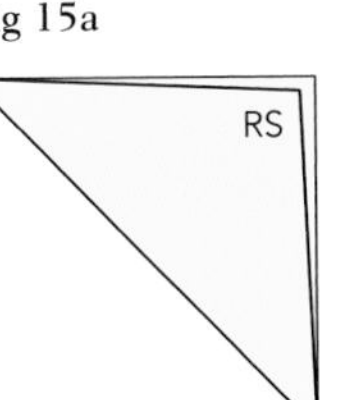

Fig 15b

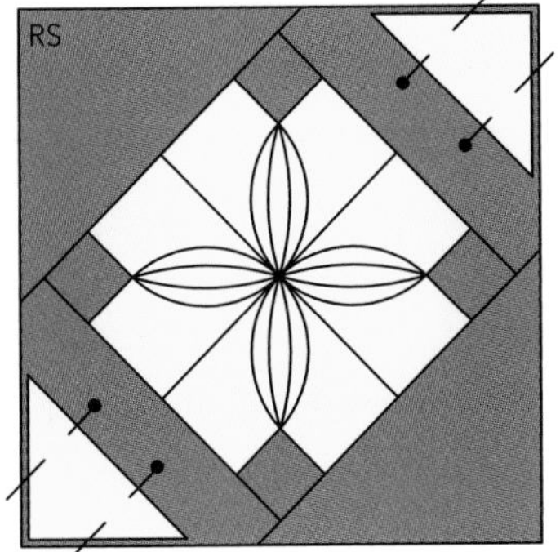

3 Arrange the four blocks as in Fig 16. Pin and stitch the folded flower blocks into two rows each of two blocks, matching the corners of the two little folded triangles in the centre of the design exactly before stitching. Press the seams open from the back of the work to reduce the bulk. Finally, stitch the two rows together to make the design in Fig 16. The four folded triangles in the centre should make a little square on point while the four triangles on the outer corners soften the corners of the design. Press the long seams open as before.

Fig 16

TIP

Once the corner folded triangles have been secured by the surrounding border strips, the folded edges may be rolled back and stitched into curves as in the Four Flowers cushion. The centre four folded triangles may be curved back at any time.

Adding the Border Frame

4 From the folded flower fabric cut four strips each measuring 2½in × 11½in (6.4cm × 29.2cm) and four cornerstone squares each cut 2½in × 2½in (6.4cm × 6.4cm). Stitch one long strip to each side of the cushion design. Press the strips out from the design, ironing from the front of the work (Fig 17a).

Fig 17a

5 Pin and stitch a cut square to either end of each of the two remaining long strips. Press the seams towards the long strips (Fig 17b).

Fig 17b

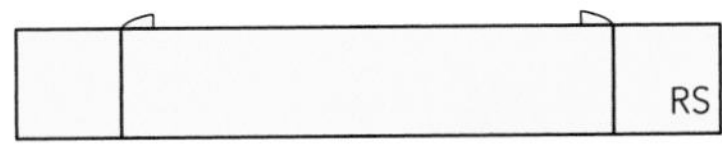

6 Pin and stitch the two lengths to the top and bottom of the cushion, matching the seams carefully (Fig 17c).

Fig 17c

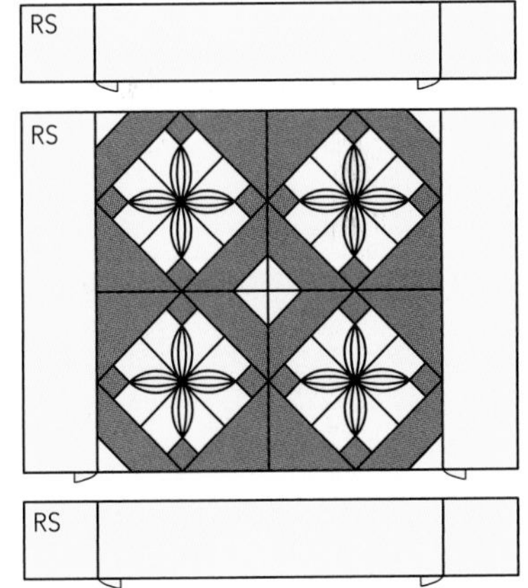

Completing the Cushion

7 Place the cushion front face up on top of the calico (muslin) square, trim both the cushion top and the calico to a square 15½in × 15½in (39.4cm cm × 39.4cm) and tack (baste) the two layers together.

8 For the back of the cushion, cut two pieces of the chosen fabric each 15½in × 11in (39.4cm × 28cm). Follow steps 8–11 (Completing the Cushion on page 29).

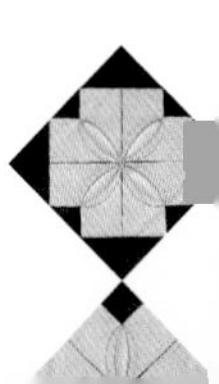

Folded Windmill

I saw this simple design in a shop in Spain and desperately held it in my head until I got back home and could try to fathom it out. Based on a classic four-patch block, the Folded Windmill is made from two layers of cut squares. The top layer of squares makes the windmill, the bottom layer the background. Each windmill square is folded, pressed and pinned on to a square of background fabric before they are joined to make the block. The 'blades' of the windmill may be left as straight folded edges (Fig 1a), curved back and stitched on one bias folded edge (Figs 1b and 1c) or on both bias folded edges (Fig 1d).

The charming Windmills baby quilt shown opposite was made by Chris Laudrum. Pauline Bugg used the Folded Windmill block in a charming bag (see page 121), while Avril Ellis created a bright, festive wall hanging (see page 126).

Windmill block finished size: 6in × 6in (15.2cm × 15.2cm).

Fig 1a

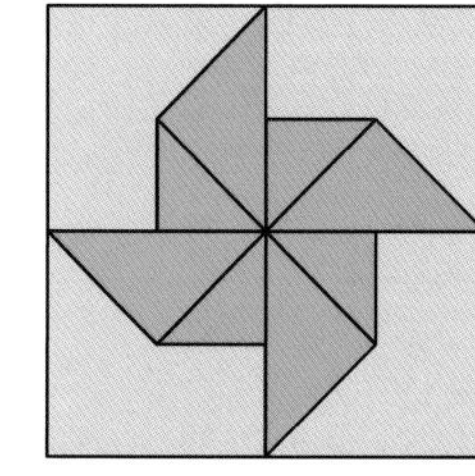

Fig 1b

Fig 1c

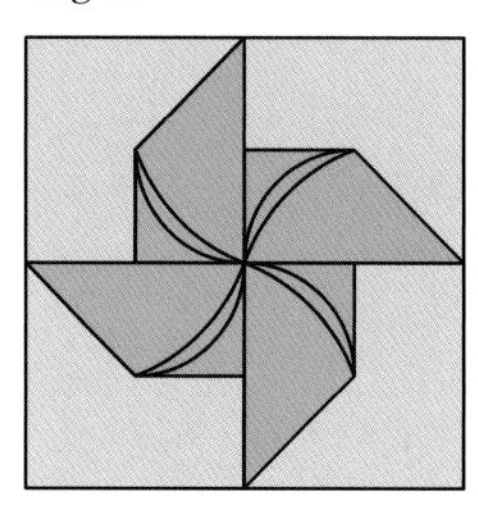

Fig 1d

'I usually carry a small notebook with squared paper around in my bag ready to record an interesting shape or design or even technique that I spot on my travels. During this trip to Spain, we had so many warnings about pickpockets and bag theft that I was travelling light and was reduced to scribbling what I could with a borrowed pencil on the back of a till receipt – no wonder I had such trouble working the design out!'

Chris Laudrum used the Folded Windmill block with sashing strips for this gorgeous baby quilt. The block can also be used alternately with Four-patch blocks or other blocks of the same size in a quilt design – quick and easy and very effective. *See page 126 for more information.*

Making a Folded Windmill block

1 These instructions are for a 6in (15.2cm) finished block. Cut four squares of background fabric and four squares of windmill fabric each measuring 3½in × 3½in (8.9cm × 8.9cm).

TIP

Smaller blocks may be made by simply reducing the size of the cut squares.
For a 5in × 5in (12.7cm × 12.7cm) finished block, cut all squares 3in × 3in (7.6cm × 7.6cm).
For a 4in × 4in (10.2cm × 10.2cm) finished block, cut all squares 2½in × 2½in (6.4cm × 6.4cm).
For a 3in × 3in (7.6cm × 7.6cm) finished block, cut all squares 2in × 2in (5.1cm × 5.1cm).

2 Fold the four windmill squares in half diagonally, right sides *outwards* (Fig 2). Press firmly, using a steam iron if you have one.

Fig 2

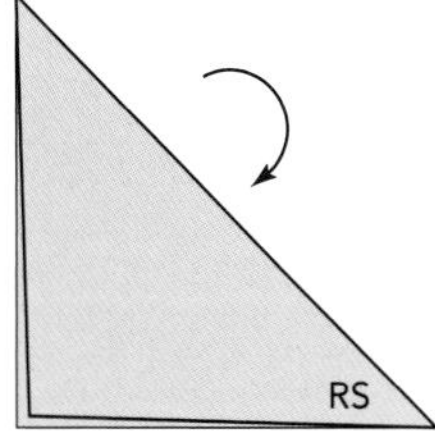

3 Fold each of these four triangles once more as in Fig 3, matching the raw edges exactly. Press firmly.

Fig 3

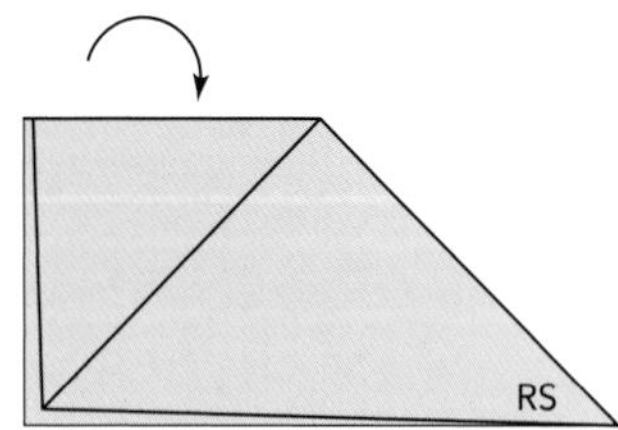

TIP

Make sure each folded square is folded in exactly the same arrangement as Fig 3. If some are folded one way and some the other, the arms of the windmill will not be pointing in the same direction and the design will not work.

4 Place each folded shape on to the *right* side of a square of background fabric as Fig 4. Match the corners of both shapes carefully. Pin with two pins as shown – this keeps the pins clear of the seams when the background squares are stitched together.

Fig 4

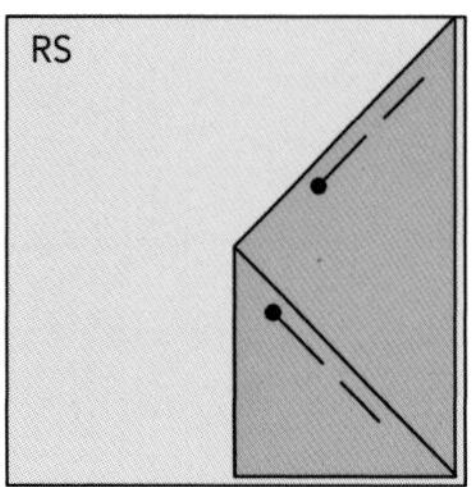

5 Take the layered squares and arrange them into two rows each of two squares (Fig 5).

Fig 5

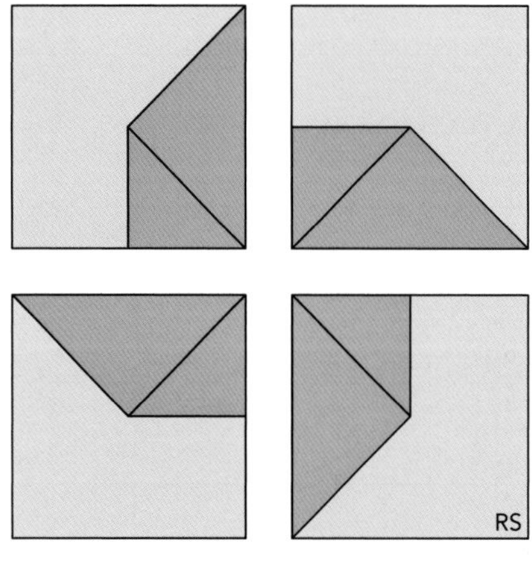

6 Pin the top two squares together, matching the edges of the layered fabrics exactly. Make sure the folded corners butt together to make a diagonal mitre at the centre corner of the block.

7 Stitch a ¼in (6mm) seam through all the layers. Press the seam *open* to reduce the bulk of the seam (Fig 6).

Fig 6

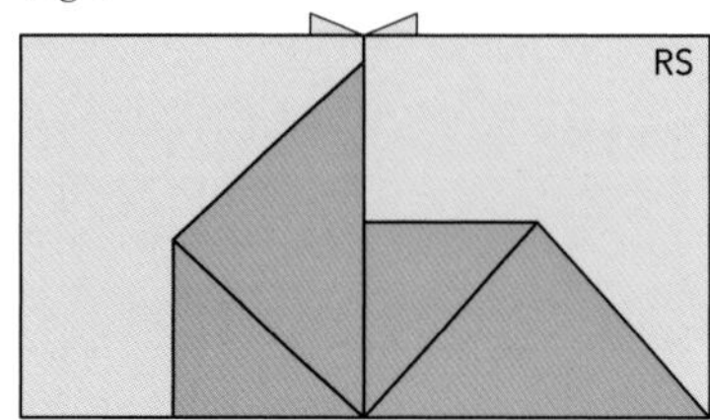

8 Repeat this with the bottom row of two squares.

9 Pin and stitch the two rows of layered squares together, matching the centre seams and mitred folded edges carefully. Press the long seam open (Fig 7).

Fig 7

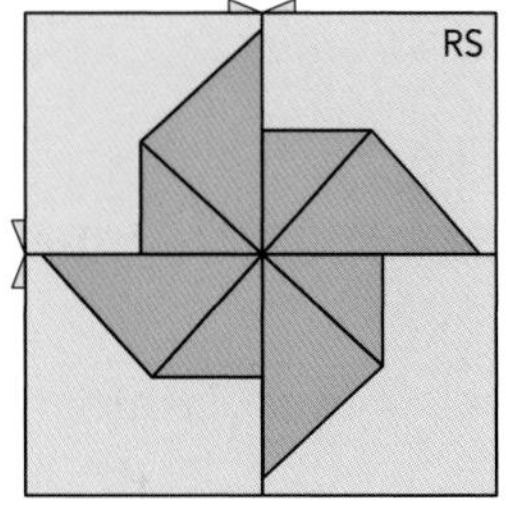

10 If desired, catch the outer corner of each arm of the windmill with two small stitches through all the layers to secure it (Fig 8).

Fig 8

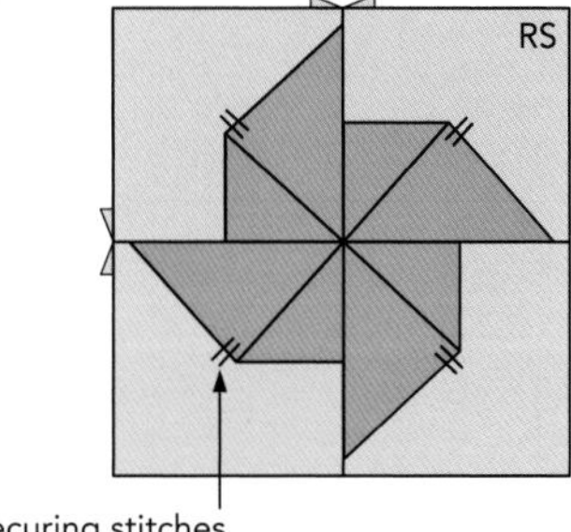

Curving the Bias Folds

11 The bias edges of each arm of the windmill may be curved back and stitched in the usual Cathedral Window way to soften the design if you wish. Either one edge may be curved or both (see Figs 1a–1d on page 118).

TIP

To give a different effect two fabrics can be used for the windmill blades instead of one.

Designing with the Folded Windmill Block

Seaside Bag

This charming seaside bag was made by Pauline Bugg and features a smaller version of the Folded Windmill block. It is a really useful and versatile bag pattern, which Pauline designed herself, in that, having made the bag, you can superimpose other patchwork patterns instead of the windmill sections and then just continue to follow the basic assembly instructions (see overleaf).

Avril Ellis also used the Folded Windmill block in her Christmas Windmills, shown in full on page 126, but in a larger 6in (15.2cm) size. As you can see by the picture of a single block below, she curved the two bias folded edges to give a softer curved look to the windmill.

Bag finished size: 12½in (31.8cm) high × 16in (40.6cm) wide.

'The quilters in my classes have fallen upon this bag with relish and dozens have appeared throughout East Anglia. They have also gone on to make variations using Seminole patchwork for the top sections, appliquéd flowers and even sunshine one side and rain and umbrellas on the other side!'

A single Folded Windmill block in a larger 6in (15.2cm) size, used for Avril Ellis' bright Christmas design, shown in full on page 126.

REQUIREMENTS

- Fabric for the 'sky' and handles: ½yd (0.5m)
- Fabric for the 'sand': a fat ¼yd (0.25m)
- Bright fabrics for windmills, one square about 5in × 5in (12.7cm × 12.7cm) of each of eight different fabrics
- Fabric to line the bag: 18in × 30in (45.7cm × 76.2cm), plus a strip for top lining 2½in × 32½in (6.4cm × 82.6cm)
- Wadding (batting) 18in × 30in (45.7cm × 76.2cm) and two strips each 2in × 30in (5.1cm × 76.2cm)

Making the Folded Windmill Blocks

Eight blocks are needed, four for the front of the bag and four for the back. Each block measures 3in × 3in (7.6cm × 7.6cm) finished size.

1 From the sky fabric cut thirty-two squares each measuring 2in x 2in (5.1cm × 5.1cm). From each of the eight windmill fabrics cut four squares each 2in × 2in (5.1cm × 5.1cm).

2 Follow steps 2–9 on page 120 to construct eight Folded Windmill blocks each measuring at this stage 3½in x 3½in (8.9cm × 8.9cm). Do not stitch the bias folded edges in a curve – leave them as Fig 1a on page 118.

3 Arrange the windmill blocks in two rows each of four windmills. Pin and stitch them together. Press the joining seams open to reduce the bulk.

4 From the sky fabric cut four strips each 2½in x 3½in (6.4cm × 8.9cm). Pin and stitch a cut strip to either ends of both rows of windmill blocks (Fig 9). Press the seams away from the windmill blocks, ironing from the front of the work.

Fig 9

RS

5 From the sky fabric cut two strips measuring 2in × 16½in (5.1cm × 42cm) and two strips measuring 2½in × 16½in (6.4cm × 42cm). Pin and stitch a wider strip to the top of each row of blocks and a narrower strip to the bottom of each row of blocks (Fig 10). Press the seams away from the row of blocks, ironing from the front.

Fig 10

6 From the sand fabric cut a piece measuring 15½in × 16½in (39.4cm × 42cm). Pin and stitch a band of blocks to each of the longer sides of the piece of sand fabric, stitching the narrower strip of sky fabric to the blocks as in Fig 11. Press the seams towards the sand fabric.

Fig 11

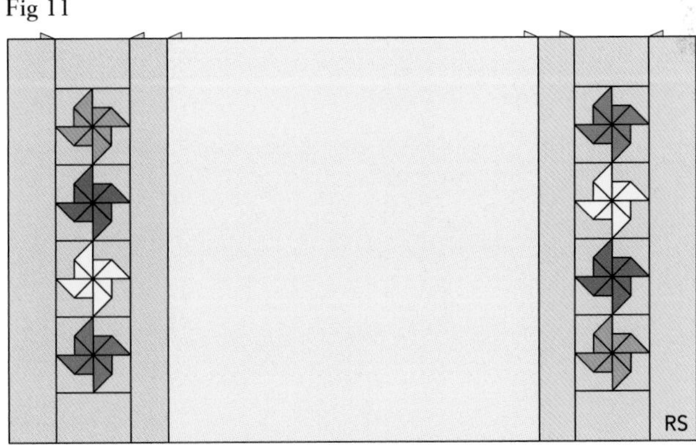

7 Cut a piece of lining fabric and a piece of wadding (batting) both 18in × 30in (45.7cm × 76.2cm). Place the lining fabric down on a surface with right side downwards. Place the wadding on to it and finally the pieced rectangle with right side upwards. The edges of the wadding and lining should be level with each other and show all around the edges of the bag rectangle. Pin or tack the layers together ready for quilting.

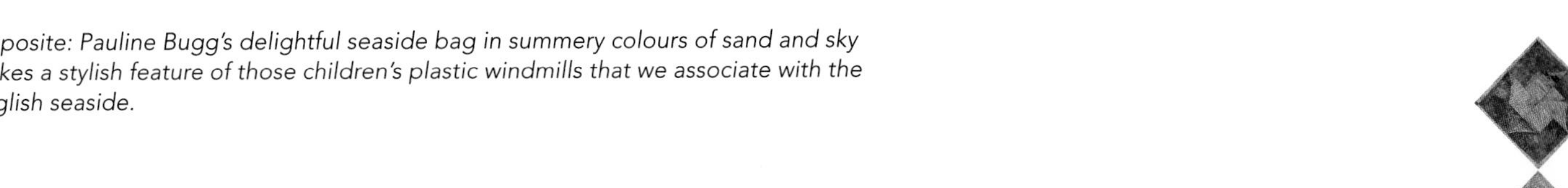

Opposite: Pauline Bugg's delightful seaside bag in summery colours of sand and sky makes a stylish feature of those children's plastic windmills that we associate with the English seaside.

Quilting the Design

8 Use a marking pencil or hera to mark across the centre of the sand fabric from top to bottom. Machine quilt this line and then three lines on either side of it at ½in (1.3cm) intervals, making seven lines altogether (Fig 12a). This forms the base of the bag. Quilt the sand and sky as desired with random wavy lines to give texture. Finally, stitch the windmill 'sticks' with machine satin stitch or hand stitching (Fig 12b).

Fig 12a

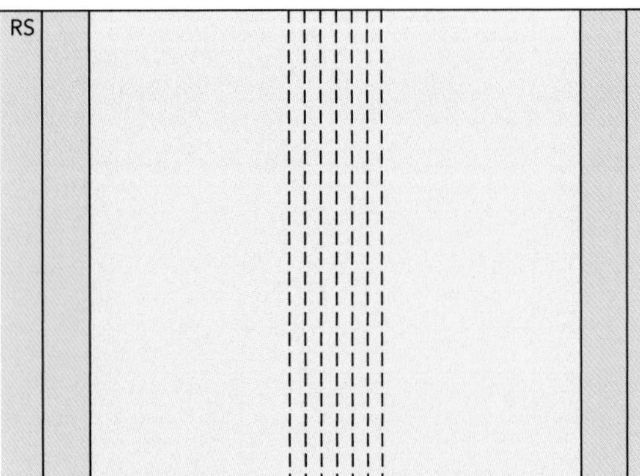

Fig 12b

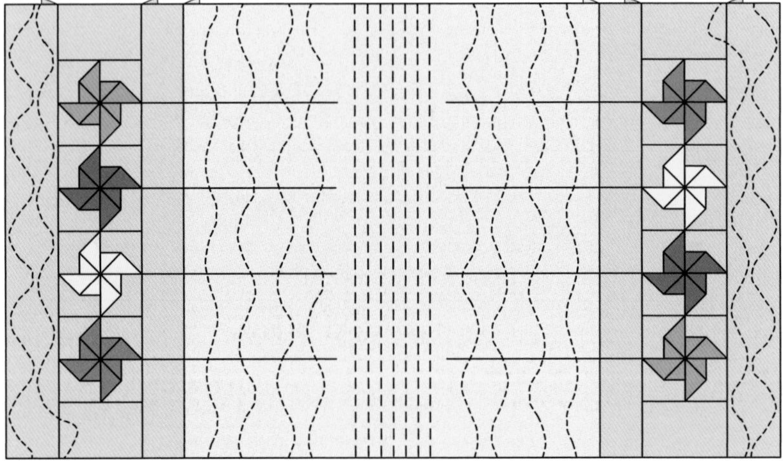

Assembling the Bag

9 Trim the quilted layers to 16½in × 28½in (42cm × 72.4cm). Fold the rectangle in half across the quilted base with right sides together. Make a mark a generous ¼in (6mm) from either side on the top edge, and 1½in (3.8cm) from either side at the bottom folded edge. Join these points with a marking pencil to show the seamline (Fig 13). Pin or tack along the lines so that you can turn the bag to the right side and check that the seams between the sea and the sand exactly match before stitching along the drawn lines firmly through all the layers.

Fig 13

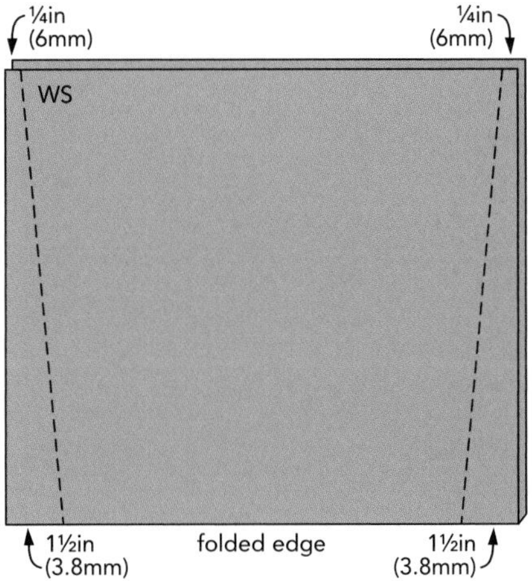

10 Trim the seams to a ¼in (6mm) seam allowance. Either zigzag the raw edges by machine to neaten them or bind them with a folded strip of lining fabric.

11 Still keeping the bag wrong side outwards, match the side seams at the top of the bag and flatten the bottom to make a triangular shape (Fig 14).

Fig 14

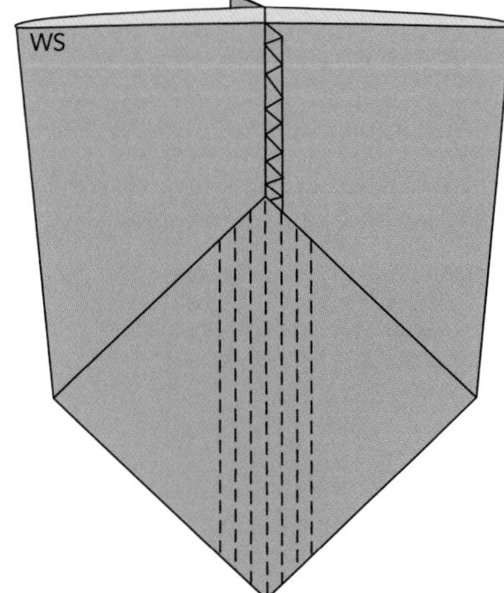

12 Mark a line across each of the two quilted triangular points 1½in (3.8cm) from the corner and stitch through all layers (Fig 15) – this makes the flat base of the bag. Trim each triangular stitched corner ¼in (6mm) beyond the stitching. Neaten the raw edges of the seams as before.

Fig 15

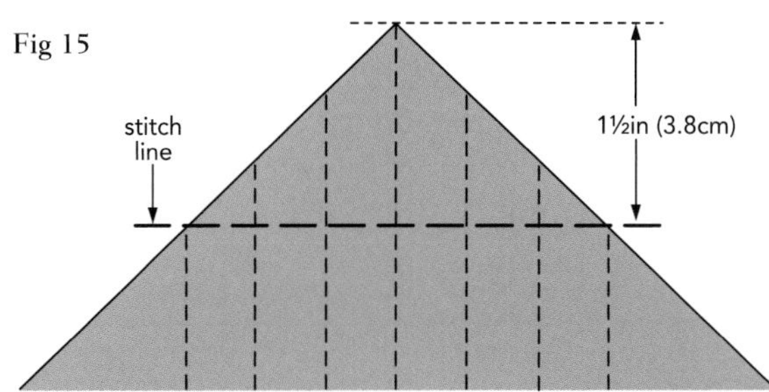

Making the Handles

13 From the sky fabric cut four strips each 2in × 30in (5.1cm × 76.2cm). Cut two strips of wadding with the same measurements.

14 Place two fabric strips together with right sides facing. Lay them on a strip of wadding and pin the three layers together. Machine a ¼in (6mm) seam along each of the two long sides (Fig 16). Repeat this with the other two strips of fabric and the wadding strip.

Fig 16

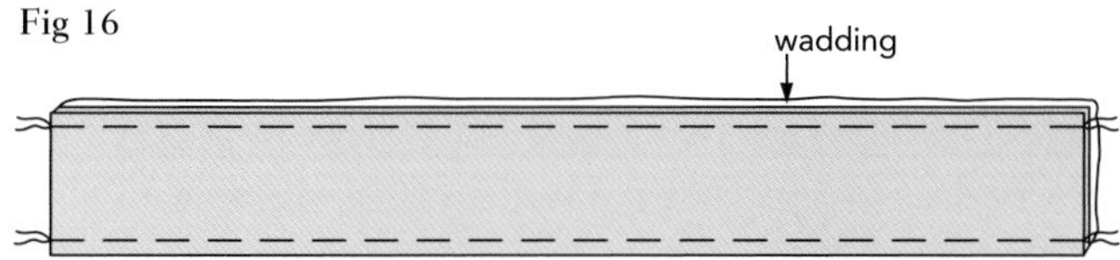

15 Turn each handle through to the right side and press firmly. Topstitch along each of the two long sides.

Making the Ties

16 From the sky fabric cut two strips each 1½in × 10½in (3.8cm × 26.7cm). Press over a ¼in (6mm) turning on each of the long sides (Fig 17a). Fold each strip in half lengthwise with wrong sides facing and press (Fig 17b). Topstitch along each of the long sides on both folded strips.

Fig 17a

Fig 17b

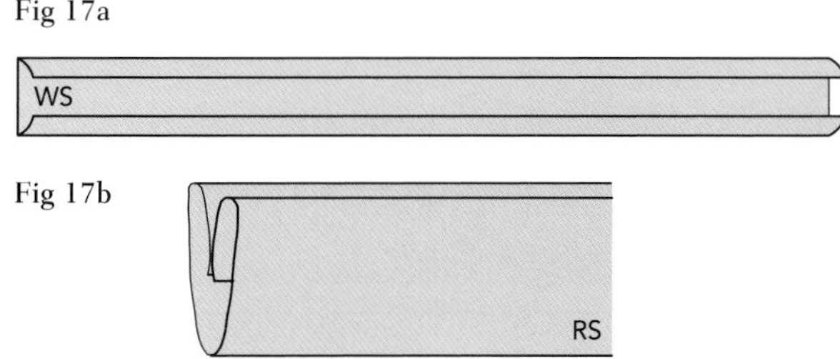

17 Cut four squares of fabric each 1½in × 1½in (3.8cm × 3.8cm) from any of the windmill fabrics – these may be all the same fabric or four different ones. Iron a ¼in (6mm) turning to the wrong side of the fabric on one side of each square (Fig 18a). Pin two squares right sides facing with the turnings matching and stitch around the other three sides with a ¼in (6mm) seam as in Fig 18b. Trim the corners to reduce bulk and turn the squares right side out. Slip one end of a tie strip into the stitched square and slipstitch along the top edges to secure the tie strip. Repeat this with the other tie strip.

Fig 18a

Fig 18b

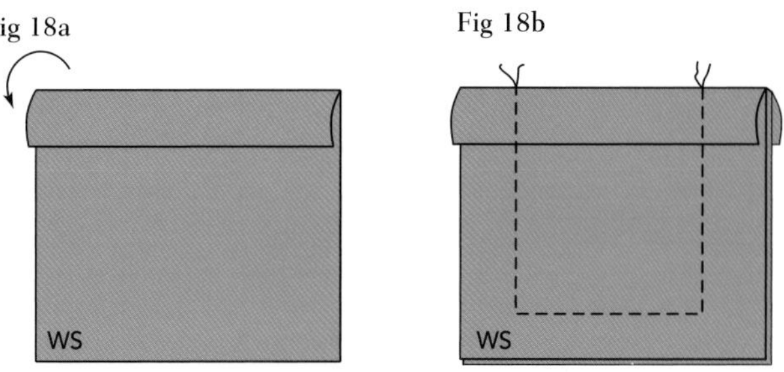

Finishing the Bag Top

18 Pin the raw end of each tie to the top edge of the bag, right sides facing, positioning each tie exactly midway between the two side seams and matching the raw edges. Position and pin each end of one handle as in Fig 19. The ends of the handle should be 2½in (6.4cm) from the pinned tie on either side. Repeat this with the second handle on either side of the other tie strip.

Fig 19

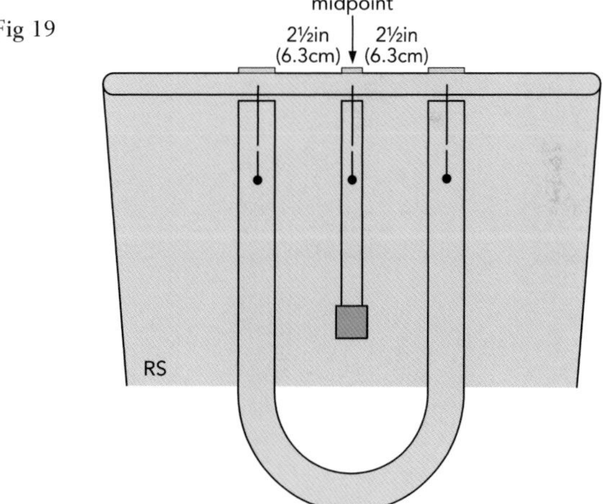

19 From the lining fabric cut a strip 2½in × 32½in (6.4cm × 82.6cm) – the strip may be joined if necessary. Stitch the short sides together to make a circle.

20 Pin the lining strip to the outside of the top edge of the bag, right sides facing. Stitch along the top edge, stitching through all the layers of the bag and the handles and ties. Fold the lining strip over to the inside of the bag along the stitched seam. Finger-press a ¼in (6mm) turning on the bottom edge of the lining strip and pin this edge in place on the lining of the bag. Slipstitch it into place by hand.

21 Finally, topstitch along the top edge of the bag to give a firm finish.

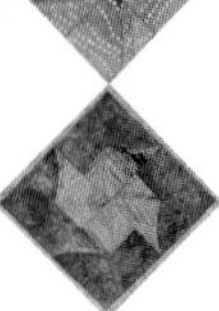

Christmas Windmills

The bright wall hanging below by Avril Ellis in festive greens and reds is an interesting design, which combines several of the techniques described in this second section of the book. Her Folded Windmill block is in a larger 6in (15.2cm) size. The alternating Folded Flower block comes as a block measuring 5½in x 5½in (14cm x 14cm), and it's not easy to change this sizing, so to make it compatible with the Windmill block, Avril added a narrow frame of background fabric to bring it up to size. The deep green border is 2½in (6.4cm) wide, so she incorporated a small square of One-square Folded Cathedral Window in each corner in this size.

Windmills Baby Quilt

Chris Laudrum made the delightful baby quilt shown opposite for her grandson Tom. It uses just the Folded Windmill block in six shades of marbled fabrics, varying the colours for each windmill and background. Each block is bordered with a frame ½in (1.3cm) finished width in the same fabric as the windmill. The 2in (5.1cm) finished width sashing highlights the blocks beautifully. This quilt is only about a year old, but the constant use and washing has faded it delightfully so that it already looks like an antique. The greatest compliment for a quilt is that it is much used, much loved and finally worn out.

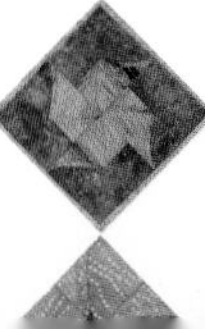

Finishing Techniques

Traditionally, Cathedral Window has no borders, no backing and no layering with wadding. This, I suspect, was part of its attraction in the Depression years, when a large, warm and heavy quilt could be made with fabrics that were to hand without any outlay for extra lengths of backing fabric and filling. When I first learned Cathedral Window I planned a design of a cushion with a surrounding border to enhance the classic Cathedral Window design. This presented a problem, as the finished blocks of Cathedral Window did not have raw edges that could be stitched to the border strips of fabric in the usual way. There were no books to tell me how to do this (because no one ever had!), so I just had to invent my own method of attaching the borders.

Borders for Cathedral Window

Since that first cushion design, most of my pieces have had borders around them, which have been important elements in the final design. I often use silk as it adds richness and links up with the windows, which are also silk. This is what Janet Covell used in her Rose Window wall hanging (right), which is a very effective design using three fabrics for the background Cathedral Window folded squares with a design of silk windows and a final frame also in silk. The border is the only area where there is obvious quilting, following the diagonal lines of the folded squares.

In her piece, Sun Arise (opposite), Kate Badrick chose a cotton fabric that shaded from pale to very dark grey for the borders of her quilt and arranged the border strips so that the colour deepened from top to bottom.

Because the borders need to be brought up to the same thickness as the folded blocks, I back them with lightweight wadding (batting). This then has to be covered on the reverse side, and the simplest way to do this is to back the entire quilt.

Janet Covell's lovely Rose Window wall hanging (see page 32) uses beautifully coloured silk fabrics and a final framing border of silk.

If you do choose to add a border, this can be an area that can complement the Cathedral Window in design. In my piece Dawn to Dusk (see page 80), the colours shade gently from silvery-blue in the centre and bottom-right corner up to dark blue night-sky colours in the top left. I have toned the hand stitching on the border strips in the same way, using long and short backstitches rather than the expected quilting stitch. The fabric is a matt textured silk/linen, and I have varied the stitching, using a collection of decorative threads and changing the shading from silvers in the lighter areas to greys and black in the dark top-left corner. I also added chunky French knots and even little stitched silver stars to the quilting to add interest and texture.

In my smaller wall hanging Fronds (see page 84), the main design had silk in the windows, but I felt a matt border of linen would be more appropriate than silk (see page 133). I textured the linen by going over it lightly with a large brush and some brown stencil cream, and then stitched it by hand using long and short backstitches with gold and bronze decorative threads and occasional French knots to give texture. I added more stitched lines on the left side of the quilt where the design is denser and stronger.

Kate Badrick stitched broken lines of quilting horizontally on the border of her Sun Arise quilt, using silver and glittery black threads to enhance the horizontal shading of the fabric (see picture below).

In adding borders to Cathedral Window I broke with tradition completely – I don't think I even knew there was a tradition to break at the time. After all these years I find myself now wanting to return to the traditional un-backed version, simply because I am using so many different fabrics to create the background folded shapes that the back has become as interesting as the front. This discovery has spurred me on to find efficient ways and strategies for joining the folded squares together by machine, which gives a much cleaner look to the seams on the reverse of the quilt than the traditional hand oversewing does.

Kate Badrick's piece, Sun Arise (see page 83), cleverly shades cotton fabrics in the blocks and also in the borders (see border detail below).

Adding Borders

Only when the quilt is approaching completion should you think about possible borders. It is tempting to plan the whole thing as you begin, especially when you are calculating fabric quantities, but it is only when the quilt is finally together that you can decide on the best frame for the design.

As you select possible fabrics for the border, try pinning a strip around the quilt to get the effect and to make the final decision on the width of the border. The border strips need a backing layer of fine wadding (batting) to give them a weight and thickness similar to the main Cathedral Window units that make up the centre of the quilt design. I prefer to mitre the corners of the borders as this echoes the diagonal elements in Cathedral Window.

Neatly mitred corners always look elegant, especially on a cushion.

Adding a Mitred Border

1 Press the quilt from the back to pull it out into a regular shape. Keep the folded blocks as level as possible on the outer edges of the design – do not let the corners of each block lose their sharpness when you press. Turn the quilt to the right side after the first pressing and iron around the outer edges, pressing the corners of each folded block again to keep them as sharp as possible.

2 For the two side border strips, measure the quilt from top to bottom down the centre and in another two places down it. Hopefully, after the pressing these measurements will be more or less the same. Do not measure along the outer side edges as these always spread a little.

3 The width of the cut border strips is determined by first deciding how wide you want the finished border to be. Remember that the outer edge of the border will be bound, so take that into consideration when you calculate. Add a ¼in (6mm) wide seam allowance to each side of the desired finished border width.

4 The length of each side strip will be the measurement of the quilt taken in step 2 *plus twice* the cut width of the border strip. For example, if the border strips are 3in (7.6cm) cut width, add 6in (15.2cm) to the quilt measurement. Cut two strips in the border fabric in this length. These will be the side borders. Many quiltmakers prefer to add an extra ½in (1.3cm) or so to the length of each strip, just to be safe, and trim away excess after stitching the mitred corners.

5 Measure the quilt from side to side in several places as before. Follow step 4 to cut the border strips for the top and bottom borders.

6 Mark the exact quilt measurement on the wrong side of each border strip, using a sharp marking pencil and leaving an equal amount at either end for the mitring (Fig 1).

Fig 1

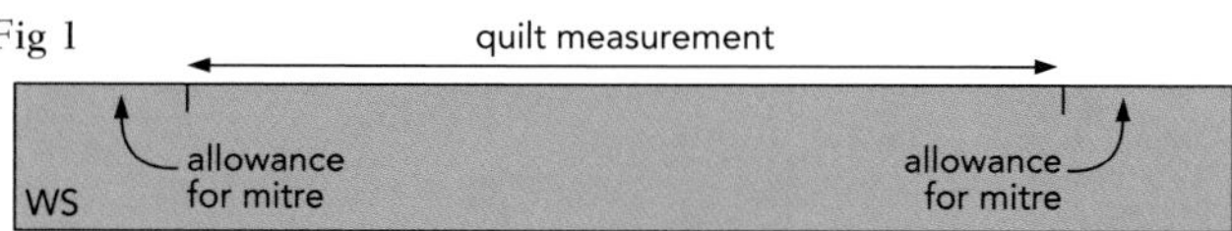

7 Cut a piece of thin, firm wadding t o match each of the four cut strips of border fabric (I use Hobb's Thermore, but any thin, firm wadding will do).

8 Lay a strip of fabric right side up on a cut strip of wadding and pin it in place. Machine stitch through both layers along one long edge of the layered strip ¼in (6mm) from the edge (Fig 2). This edge will be joined to the edge of the quilt.

Fig 2

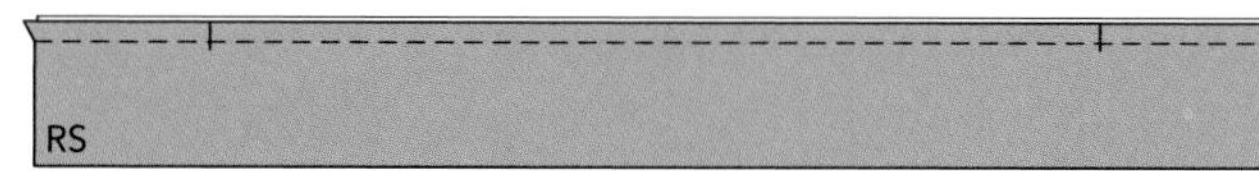

9 Turn the strip to the wrong side. Use a marking pencil to draw a line 45° from the marked points at the stitching line out to the other long edge on the wadding. I use the 45° line on my rotary ruler to do this. Note that the 45° line begins on the line of machine stitches where the drawn mark meets those stitches (Fig 3).

Fig 3

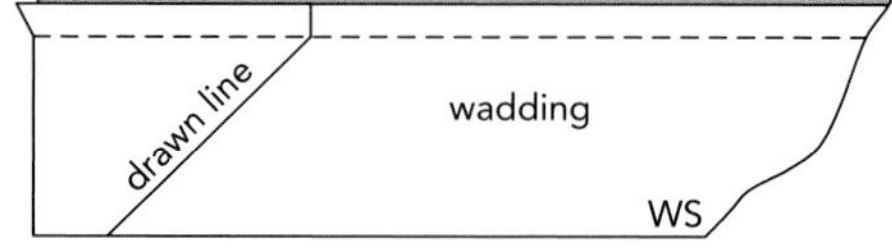

10 Trim the wadding in the seam allowance back as close to the stitching as is safe to reduce the bulk.

11 Repeat steps 8–10 with each of the other three border strips.

Attaching the Strips to the Quilt

12 On each border strip, fold the seam allowance over the wadding so the machine stitches lie along the fold (Fig 4).

Fig 4

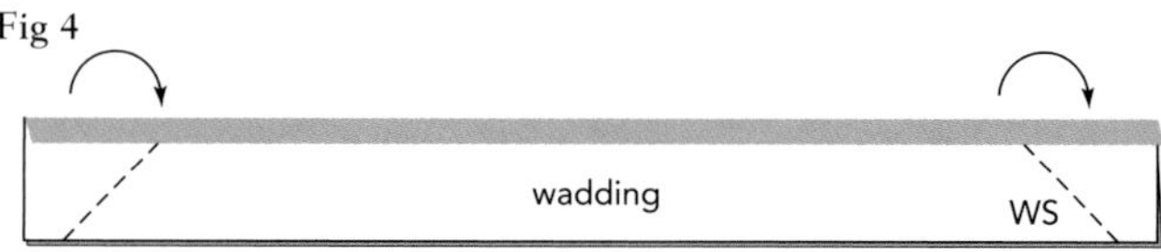

13 Pin one strip to the edge of the quilt with right sides facing, matching the marked points on the strip to the corners of the quilt. You may well have to ease in a little fullness in the Cathedral Window edges to fit the border strip. Distribute any fullness evenly and pin along the length (Fig 5).

Fig 5

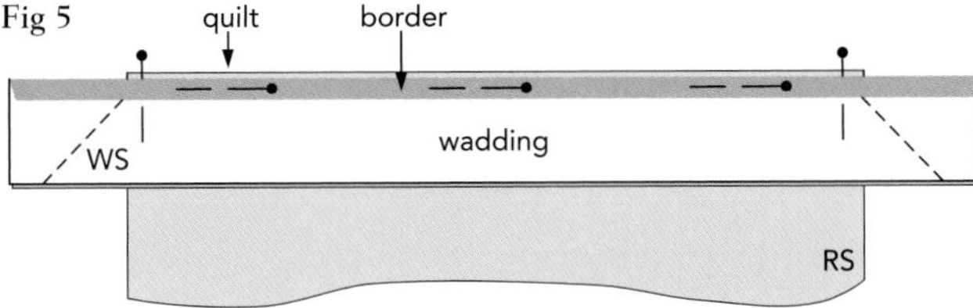

Fig 6

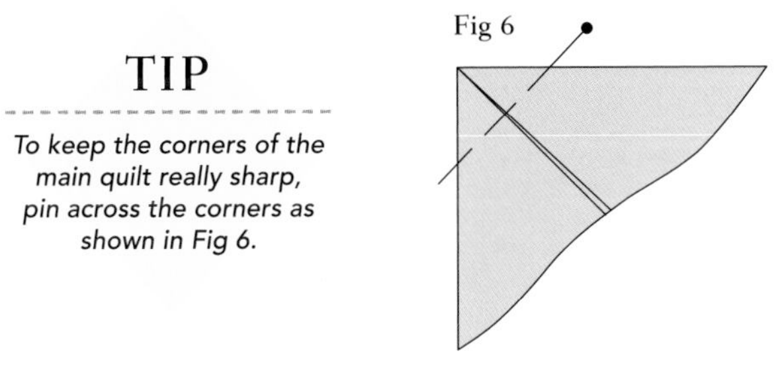

TIP

To keep the corners of the main quilt really sharp, pin across the corners as shown in Fig 6.

14 Oversew the edges together in the same way as the Cathedral Window folded squares were stitched together to make the main quilt.

15 Repeat this process with all four border strips to attach them to the main design. Now move on to Mitring the Corners, right.

Attaching the Strips by Machine

16 If you have been joining the folded squares of your design by machine you will probably want to attach the border strips in the same way. If so, complete the design but leave the blocks around the edge of the design with their outer points left unfolded (Fig 7). Cut the four border strips as described above in steps 2–7. Place each strip of fabric right side up on a piece of wadding. Pin or tack the layers together – do not machine them together.

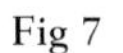

Fig 7

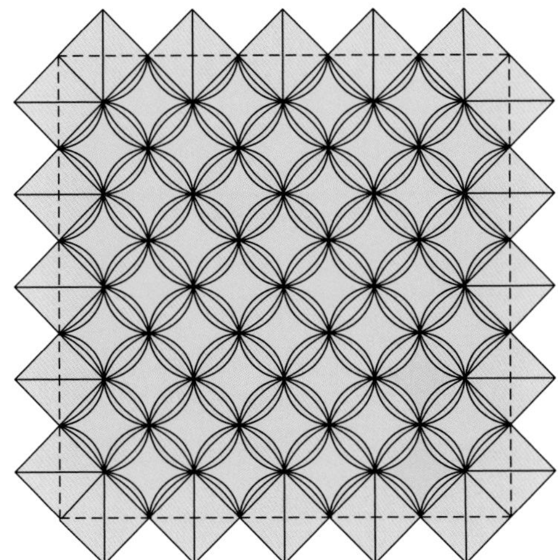

17 Place a border strip right side up on a flat surface. Place the quilt on to it right side up and position it so that the drawn lines on the Cathedral Window blocks overlap the fabric strip by ¼in (6mm) (Fig 8). The marked lines on the border strip should exactly match the end of the drawn lines on the Cathedral Window squares – ease the blocks in a little if necessary to make them fit the border strip between the two drawn marks. Pin into position.

Fig 8

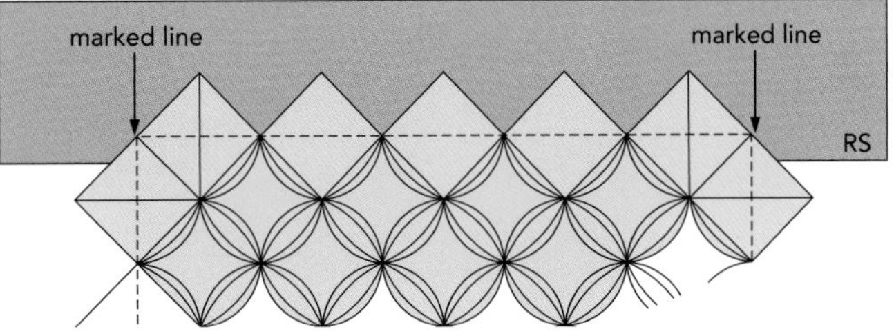

18 Stitch by machine through the drawn lines on the Cathedral Window blocks to join the border strip to the design. Start and finish stitching ¼in (6mm) from the ends of the stitching lines as usual (see step 8 Machining the Blocks Together on page 21).

19 Press the corners of the Cathedral Window blocks to the centre and stitch into position to complete the centre design. Repeat this to attach all four border strips to the quilt.

Mitring the Corners

Fig 9

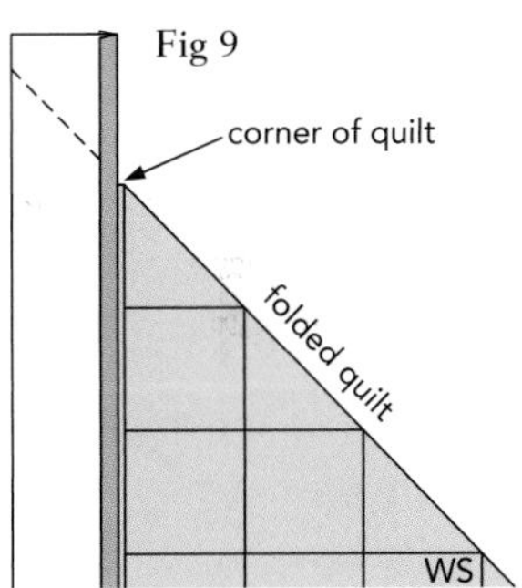

20 Fold the quilt diagonally with right sides together at one corner, so that the two border strips are lying on top of each other (Fig 9).

21 Pushing the seam allowance towards the quilt, position the two drawn lines on top of each other and pin. Stitch along these lines by machine through all the layers of fabric and wadding – use a walking foot on the machine to do this (Fig 10).

Fig 10

22 Open out the mitred corner and check that it is truly square on the corner with a square ruler. Trim the wadding as close to the stitching as possible. Trim the excess fabric in the seam allowance down to a ¼in (6mm) and finger-press it open. Light pressing is possible on the right side of the border with a cool iron, taking care not to let the iron come in contact with the wadding. Continue on, repeating the process of mitring on all four corners of the quilt.

Backing the Quilt

To back a bordered design, cut a piece of fabric about 1in (2.5cm) larger than the quilt in both directions. Place the backing fabric right side down on a flat surface with the quilt centred on it right side up. As the Cathedral Window design needs to be held in position on the backing but is too thick to quilt comfortably, I find tying or knotting the layers is the best solution.

Knotting or Tying a Quilt

Tying or knotting the layers of a quilt together with small knots is an efficient way of holding the layers in place instead of quilting. I have always made a double reef knot (thanks to my Girl Guide training), but have discovered a slip knot used in Amish quilts which is quick, easy and really secure.

1 Mark the position of each knot to be made with a glass-headed pin – they don't get buried in the layers of folded squares as easily as normal pins. Pin at regular intervals at junctions of the folded Cathedral Window squares about 3in–4in (7.6–10.2cm) apart. If you remove the pins one by one as you make each knot you will know which ones still need to be processed. Knots can be made on the back or the front, but for Cathedral Window pieces they should be as invisible as possible, so make the knots on the back and use thread that matches the front, changing colour where necessary. The small bar stitch on the front will be scarcely noticeable.

2 To make a knot, use a double thickness of normal sewing thread. I often use thicker embroidery thread to knot conventional quilts, but thinner thread is best here. Working from the back, push the needle straight through all the quilt layers. Pull the needle through, leaving about 2in (5cm) of thread on the surface of the back of the quilt. Turn the quilt over to the front and position the needle back into the quilt to make a tiny but secure stitch at the junction of blocks. The needle should be pushed straight back through the quilt about 1/8in (3mm) from the point where it came through (Fig 1a).

Fig 1a

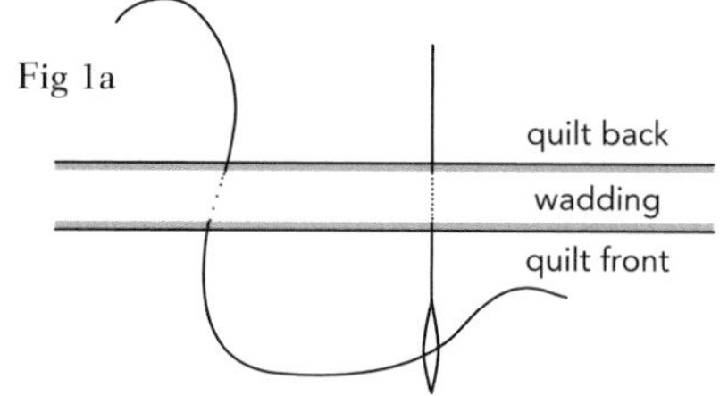

3 Hold the 2in (5cm) length of thread straight. Take the needle behind it to the left, then across the front to the right (Fig 1b). Bring the needle up through the loop to form a slip knot (Fig 1c). Now pull the needle until the knot begins to tighten (Fig 1d).

Fig 1b

Fig 1c

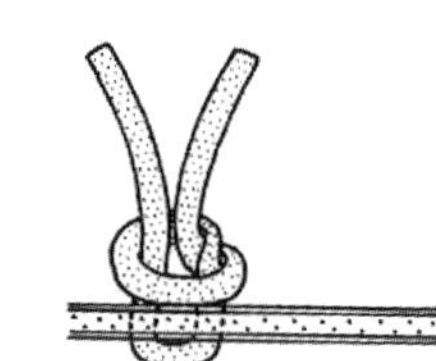

Fig 1d

4 Finally, pull both ends of the thread to tighten the knot. Trim both threads to about 3/8in (9mm) to give a tufted effect or run them into the layers of the quilt so that there are no thread ends showing.

Backs of quilts do not have to be plain. This is part of the reverse side of my quilt, Dawning Rose (see page 65). The fabric is a block-printed batik and gives an unexpected bonus when the viewer lifts a corner to see the label.

Quilting the Border

The borders of Cathedral Window quilts may be quilted or left plain. I usually quilt wider borders and try to add some originality to the quilting to reflect the design of the main quilt. I like to quilt by machine in the seamline where the borders have been joined to the main quilt, as this helps to hold the quilt top in place on the backing, especially if the piece is a large wall hanging, which may be heavy and might sag in time without this extra stitching. Finally, the outer edges of the borders are bound in the usual way.

For Fronds (right and see also page 84), the border of linen fabric was textured with stencil crèmes and stitched in a variety of decorative threads including irregular backstitch and French knots.

Binding the Quilt

I have given two methods for binding a quilt; one that uses four strips of binding with squared corners, which is suitable for designs with a horizontal and vertical emphasis such as sashed quilts, and one that uses continuous binding with mitred corners.

Before adding the final binding, check that the quilt lies flat and the corners are really square. Tacking or basting with small stitches near to the edge of the quilt will help keep the quilt flat and avoid wavy edges. Trim the wadding (batting) and backing fabric down to a scant ¼in (6mm) beyond the quilt top (Fig 1).

Fig 1

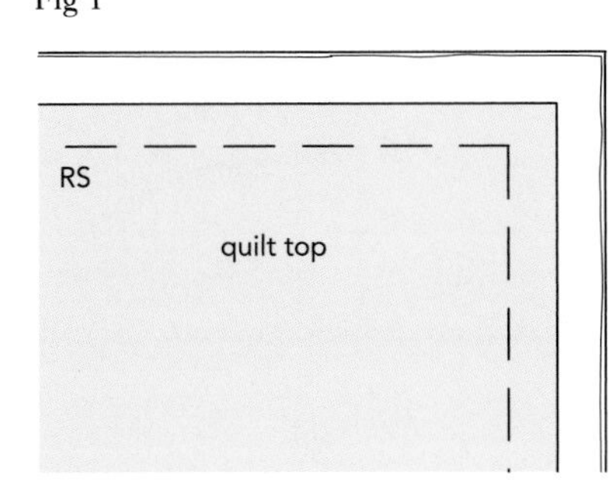

It is quite likely that the strips for the binding will have to be joined to make the lengths needed for the quilt. You may even want to add to the overall design with a multi-fabric binding where many short lengths have been joined. The binding will lie flatter and be easier to handle if the joins are made on the bias, making a 45° angle with the long edges of the strip. When stitching the binding to the quilt, use a walking foot on your machine so that all the layers are fed through the machine evenly.

Joining the Strips

1 Cut all strips for the binding 2½in (6.3cm) wide. Trim the ends of each strip at an angle of 45° as in Fig 2. To do this, position the 45° on a rotary ruler along the top of the strip and cut along the ruler's edge (Fig 3).

Fig 2

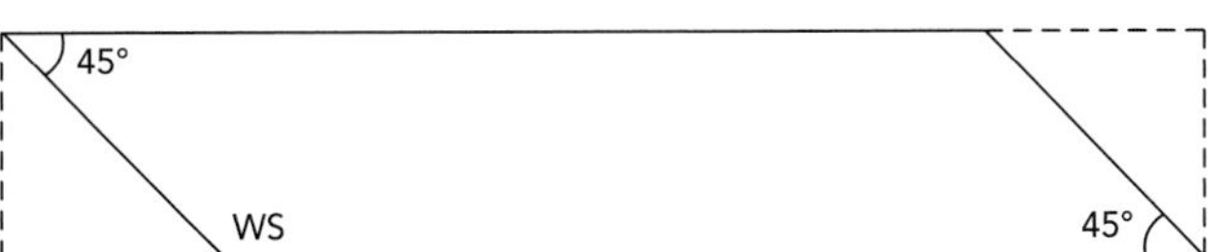

Fig 3

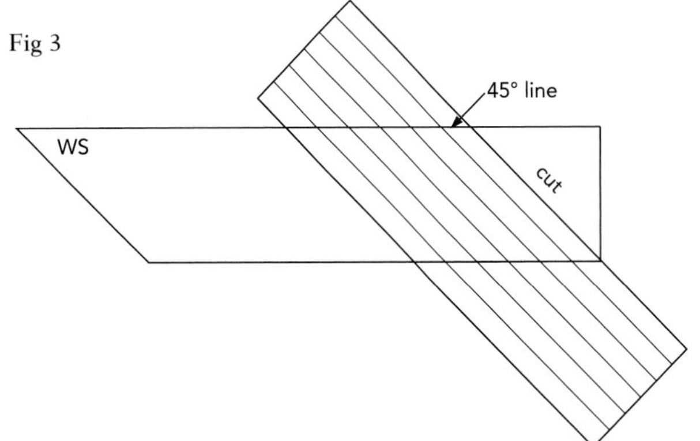

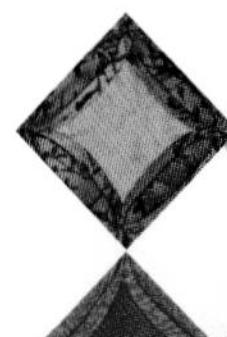

2 To join the strips, place two strips as in Fig 4 with right sides facing. Stitch a ¼in (6mm) seam as shown. Press the diagonal seam open.

Fig 4

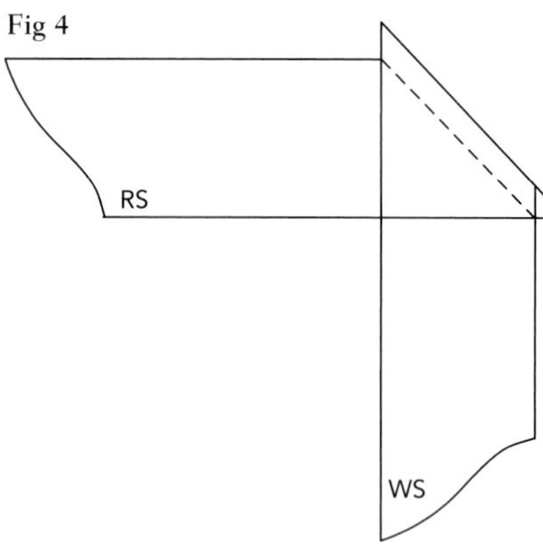

Square-cornered Binding

1 Cut four strips of fabric for the binding, each 2½in (6.3cm) wide. The two side strips should measure the length of the quilt from top to bottom. The two strips for the top and bottom edges should measure the width of the quilt from side to side plus 1½in (3.8cm). Shorter lengths can be joined if you do not have enough fabric.

2 Take each side binding strip and fold it in half, right side *outwards*, without pressing. Pin a folded strip to one side of the quilt, matching the edges of the binding with the edge of the quilt top (Fig 5). Stitch a seam ¼in (6mm) from the edge of the quilt top through all the layers (Fig 6). Repeat this with the second strip on the other side of the quilt.

Fig 5

Fig 6

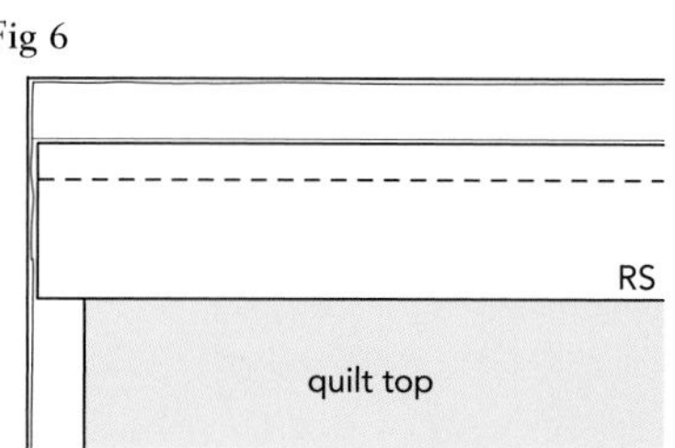

3 Bring the folded edge of the binding over to the back and stitch by hand, just covering the line of machine stitches (Fig 7).

Fig 7

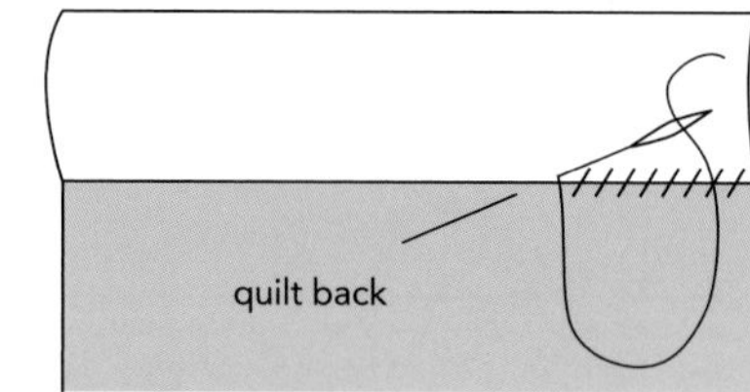

4 Pin and stitch the folded binding to the top and bottom of the quilt in the same way, leaving about ¾in (1.9cm) of binding extending beyond the quilt at each end (Fig 8). Trim this back to about ½in (1.3cm) and fold in over the quilt edge (Fig 9). Fold the binding over to the back of the quilt and slipstitch in place (Fig 10). Make sure that the corners are really square before you stitch them.

Fig 8

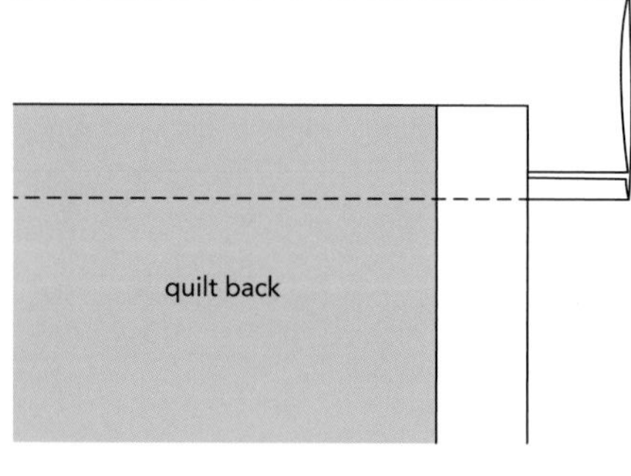

Fig 9

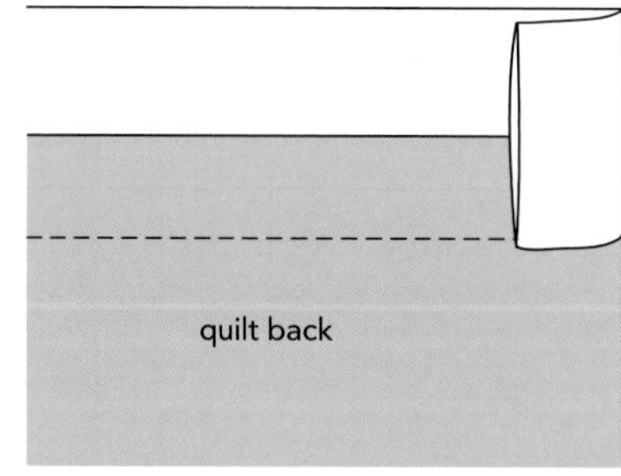

Fig 10

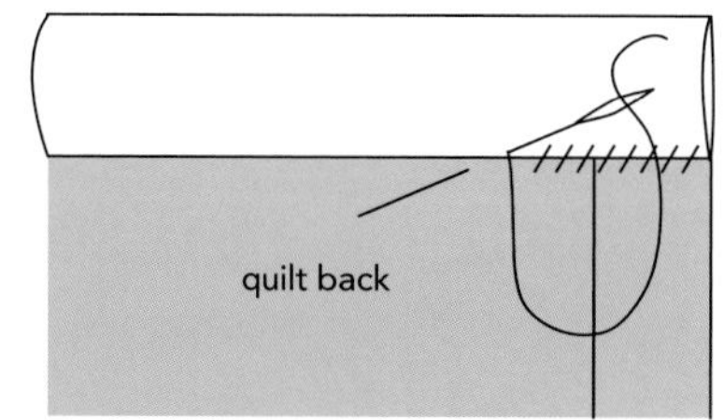

Continuous Binding with Mitred Corners

1 Make a length of binding strip 2½in (6.3cm) wide and long enough to go right round the quilt, plus about 11in (28cm) to allow for turning the corners and overlapping at the start and finish. Both ends of the binding should be trimmed on the diagonal as in Fig 2 (page 133).

2 Fold the binding in half lengthwise, right side *outwards*, and press the entire length. Fold and press a ¼in (6mm) seam to the wrong side of one diagonal end of the length of binding (Fig 11).

Fig 11

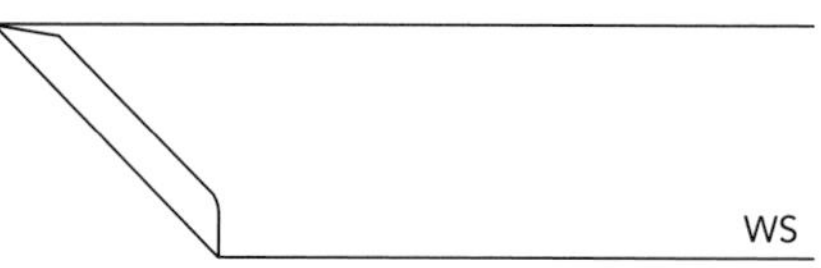

3 Starting with this folded end, pin the folded binding strip along one side of the quilt, matching the edges of the binding with the edge of the quilt top. Do not begin at a corner of the quilt. Instead, make the start and finish of the binding some way down one side where it will be less obvious (Fig 12). Pin to exactly ¼in (6mm) from the nearest corner of the quilt top. Mark this point on the binding with a dot (Fig 13).

Fig 12

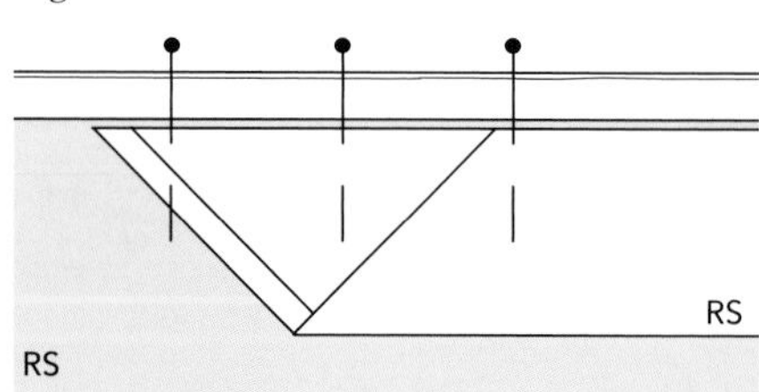

Fig 13

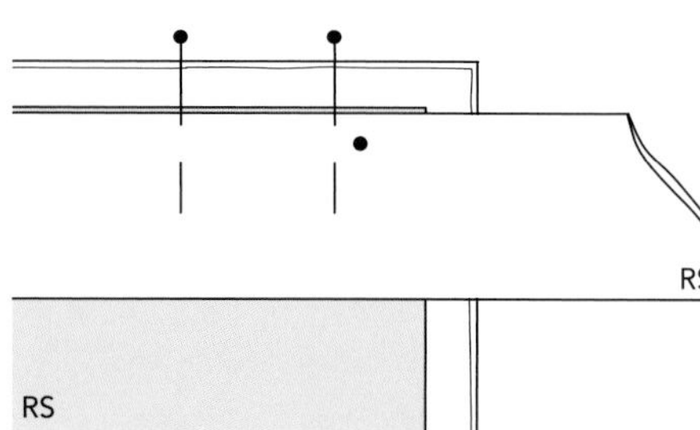

4 Begin stitching about 4in–5in (10cm–12.5cm) from the start of the pinned binding, using a ¼in (6mm) seam allowance. Finish exactly on the marked dot, backstitching to secure the seam.

5 Remove the quilt from the machine and place it on a flat surface ready for pinning the next side. Fold the binding back at right angles from the stitched side (Fig 14).

Fig 14

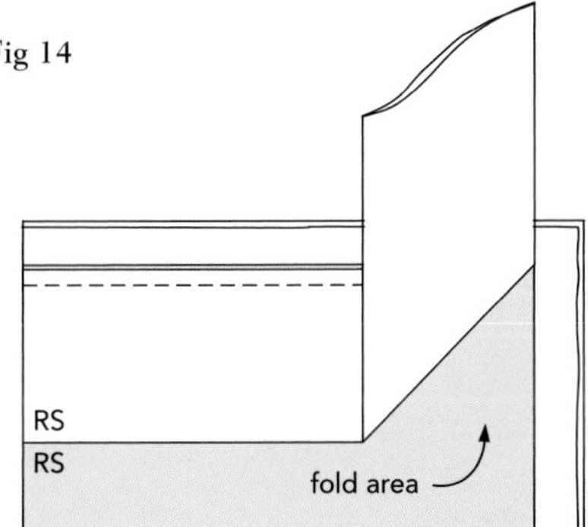

6 Fold the binding down again with the top fold level with the edge of the wadding and backing and the raw edges level with the edge of the quilt top (Fig 15).

Fig 15

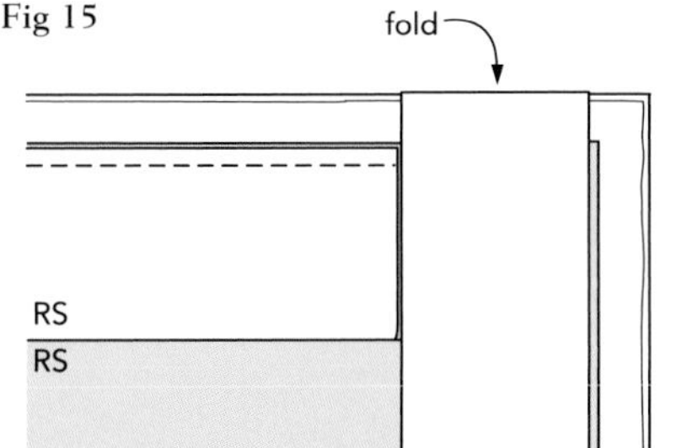

7 Pin the folded layers in place and continue to pin the binding to the side of the quilt until it reaches the next corner. Mark the turning corner ¼in (6mm) from the edge of the quilt top with a dot as before.

8 Stitch the pinned binding with the usual ¼in (6mm) seam, starting at the edge of the quilt (Fig 16) and continuing to the marked dot. Backstitch to secure the seam at the dot.

Fig 16

9 Continue to pin and stitch the binding to the quilt, one side at a time, using the method above for turning each corner. On the final side where the binding starts and finishes, slip the finishing end of the strip between the layers of the other end of the binding. Trim it so that the folded edge of the beginning section overlaps the end piece by about ½in (1.3cm) (Fig 17). Pin the overlapping sections and stitch.

Fig 17

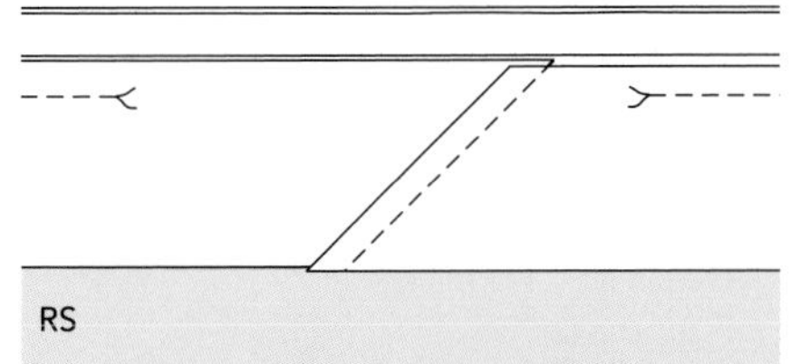

10 Fold the binding over to the back of the quilt and stitch it in place by hand in the same way as the square-cornered binding. The front corners will form a neat mitre which can then be tweaked into place and left unstitched as a diagonal fold (Fig 18). The diagonal overlap, where the two ends of binding meet, can be left unstitched or made more secure by neat hand stitching in a matching thread.

The corners on the back of the quilt should be arranged into a mitre by folding one side down and then the other side. Arrange the fold in the opposite direction to the fold on the front to distribute the layers evenly and make a flat corner.

Fig 18

A Final Thought…

Once the binding on the quilt is done, it's finished, apart from a label. I have to admit that I have not got round to labelling several of my recent quilts and it really won't do. Just a simple name and date is enough, but without it the quilt has no permanent identity. Good thing too you may say, but I would disagree. Future generations need to know some background to the quilt, even if they have rescued it from some junk shop. Everyone likes a good story, so an informative label will help them to fill in the missing details. You can write it with a fabric pen, embroider it or type out a whole history on to fabric via your computer – just do it!

About the Author

Lynne Edwards teaches and demonstrates a wide range of patchwork and quilting techniques, both hand and machine. She has written several textbooks that are considered to be definitive works. Her previous books for David & Charles are: *The Sampler Quilt Book* (1996), *The New Sampler Quilt Book* (2000), *Making Scrap Quilts to Use It Up* (2003) and *Stash-Buster Quilts* (2006).

In 1992 Lynne was awarded the Jewel Pearce Patterson Scholarship for International Quilt Teachers. This was in recognition of her outstanding qualities as a teacher and included a trip to the Houston Quilt Market and Festival. The award led to invitations to teach as part of the Houston Faculty in 1993 and 1995 and at the Symposium of the Australasian Quilters' Guild in Brisbane in 1993. International teaching trips followed, including venues in Europe, in Missouri, USA and the National Quilt Show in South Africa. In 2000, teaching commitments included Durban in South Africa and the National Canadian Festival, Canada in 2000. Since then international trips have included venues in Europe, USA, Canada and South Africa, and in 2007 New Zealand, Singapore and Dubai.

Lynne's long association with the quilting movement, both locally and nationally, has involved her in the organization of quilt shows – from local village halls to the Quilters' Guild National Exhibitions. She has served on selection committees and is an experienced judge of National Quilt Shows. She was Senior Judge at the South African Quilt Show in 1998, her first experience of judging overseas. In 2000, Lynne was given honorary lifetime membership of the Quilters' Guild of the British Isles, and in 2002 was awarded the Amy Emms Memorial Trophy for services to quilting.

In the New Year Honours of 2008, Lynne was awarded an MBE (Member of the Order of the British Empire) for her services to arts and crafts.

Dedications

This book is dedicated to the memory of Anna Wilson, a wonderful embroiderer and teacher who first introduced me to Cathedral Window many years ago and never told me it was always done with scraps and calico and that it could be difficult, so I flew with it right from the start.

Also to the memory of Tess Simpson and Marian Edwards, two of my Wednesday East Bergholt girls, and also Val Wakefield a Monday girl, all of whom are much missed by us all.

To my family, now expanded to include daughter-in-law Vicky and the Cowan family, who all feel as though they have been part of the family for ever.

And finally, to all those quilters who have been kind or polite enough to ask for this book on my favourite technique and especially to Michael Sarjent from the Home Workshop who has nagged me for years to do it. At last, Michael, at last...

Acknowledgments

My thanks go to the following people. To the amazing Tony Collins, who with the aid of his fiendish computer has patiently transformed my hand-drawn diagrams into the technical wonders that appear in the book. Also to his wife Linda who, as the resident quilter, was constantly on hand to explain what on earth it was all about.

To Cheryl Brown and Jane Trollope at David & Charles who allowed me to indulge in my specialist subject for this book. To Lin Clements, without whose diligent and thorough editing skills I would be lost. To Sue Cleave for the book layout and such attention to detail.

To Creative Grids, with whom it is always a pleasure to work, who actually welcomed making a specialist ruler for cutting rectangular Cathedral Window units without questioning my sanity. Tel: 01455 828667. www.creativegrids.com

To all the contributors to this book, whose original pieces of work are an inspiration to me and, I am sure, to the readers of the book. Finally, my thanks to all those workers in Cathedral Window who have written to me with photographs of their designs, which are lovingly kept in a scrapbook to inspire those just beginning with this wonderful technique.

Index

Answer Booklet with Solution CD Resource
Volume 1 (Chapters 1–20, R)
for
Tipler and Mosca's
Physics for Scientists and Engineers
Sixth Edition

David Mills
Professor Emeritus
College of the Redwoods

W. H. Freeman and Company
New York

Printed in the United States of America

ISBN-13: 978-0-7167-8479-1 (Volume 1: Chapters 1–20, R)
ISBN-10: 0-7167-8479-3 (Volume 1: Chapters 1–20), R)

Third printing

W. H. Freeman and Company
41 Madison Avenue
New York, NY 10010
Houndmills, Basingstoke
RG21 6XS, England
www.whfreeman.com

CONTENTS

Chapter 1
Measurement and Vectors

1 (*c*)

2 (*d*)

3 (*c*)

4 (*d*)

5 30.48 cm/ft, 1.609×10^5 cm/ft

6 (*c*)

7 (*e*)

8 $\frac{\mathrm{M}}{\mathrm{LT}^2}, \frac{\mathrm{kg}}{\mathrm{m}\cdot\mathrm{s}^2}$

9 False

10 (*b*)

11

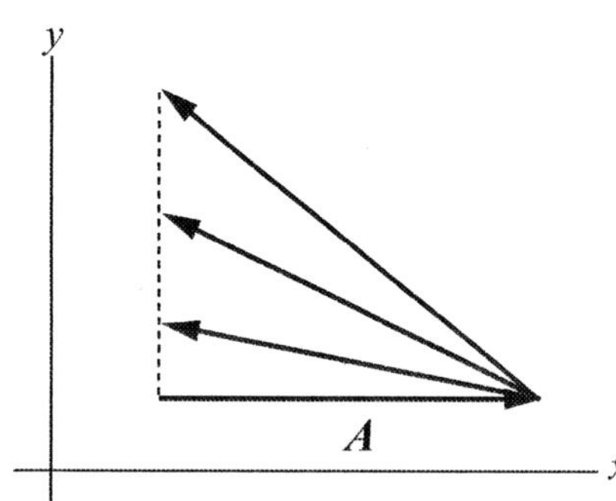

12

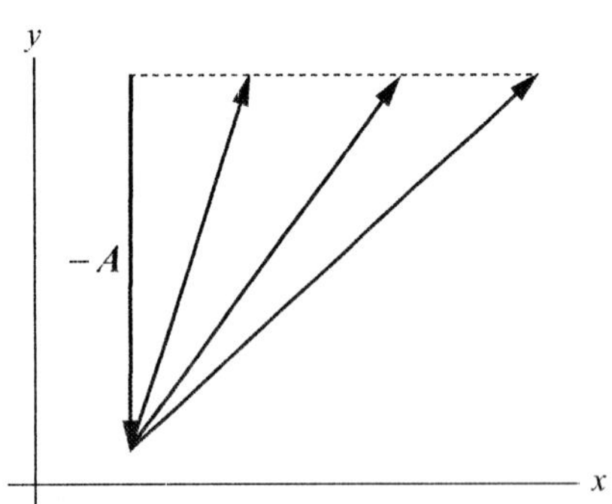

13

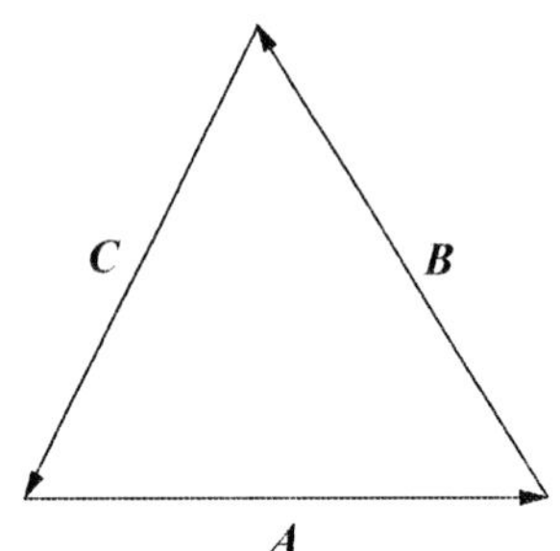

14 3.51×10^6 m

15 2.0×10^{27} molecules

16 3×10^6

17 (*a*) 1.1×10^{10} diapers (*b*) $5.5 \times 10^6\ \text{m}^3$ (*c*) $0.2\,\text{mi}^2$

18 (*a*) 2 billion dollars/d (*b*) 6×10^9 barrels/y , 2×10^7 barrels/d

19 (*a*) 50 MB (*b*) 7×10^2 novels

20 (*a*) 1 MW (*b*) 2 mg (*c*) 3 μm (*d*) 30 ks

21 (*a*) 0.000040 W (*b*) 0.000000004 s (*c*) 3,000,000 W (*d*) 25,000 m.

22 (*a*) 1 picoboo (*b*) 1 gigalow (*c*) 1 microphone (*d*) 1 attoboy (*e*) 1 megaphone (*f*) 1 nanogoat (*g*) 1 terabull

23 (*a*) C_1 is in m; C_2 is in m/s (*b*) C_1 is in m/s^2 (*c*) C_1 is in m/s^2
(*d*) C_1 is in m; C_2 is in s^{-1} (*e*) C_1 is in m/s; C_2 is in s^{-1}

24 (*a*) C_1 is in ft; C_2 is in ft/s (*b*) C_1 is in ft/s^2 (*c*) C_1 is in ft/s^2
(*d*) C_1 is in ft; C_2 is in s^{-1} (*e*) C_1 is in ft/s; C_2 is in s^{-1}

25 (*a*) 4×10^7 m (*b*) 6×10^6 m (*c*) 2×10^4 mi, 3.96×10^3 mi

26 2.47×10^3 km/h, 1.53×10^3 mi/h

27 210 cm

28 (*a*) 62.2 mi/h (*b*) 24 in (*c*) 91.4 m

29 1.28 km

30 1.61v km/h

31 (*a*) 36.00 km/h·s (*b*) 10.00 m/s^2 (*c*) 88 ft/s (*d*) 27 m/s

32 4045 m^2

33 (*a*) 1.3×10^4 lb (*b*) 4 cases

34 (*a*) 0.50 ft^3 (*b*) 0.014 m^3 (*c*) 14 L

35 (*a*) m/s^2 (*b*) s (*c*) m

36 (*a*) $L, \dfrac{\mathrm{L}}{\mathrm{T}}$ (*b*) $\dfrac{\mathrm{L}}{\mathrm{T}^2}$ (*c*) $\dfrac{\mathrm{L}}{\mathrm{T}^2}$ (*d*) $L, \dfrac{1}{\mathrm{T}}$ (*e*) $\dfrac{\mathrm{L}}{\mathrm{T}}, \dfrac{1}{\mathrm{T}}$

37 T^{-1}

38 $\dfrac{\mathrm{L}^3}{\mathrm{MT}^2}, \dfrac{\mathrm{m}^3}{\mathrm{kg}\cdot\mathrm{s}^2}$

39 (*a*) $\dfrac{\mathrm{M}}{\mathrm{T}^2}$ (*b*) $\dfrac{\mathrm{kg}\cdot\mathrm{m}^2}{\mathrm{s}^2}$

42 $[F][v]$

43 $\dfrac{\mathrm{M}}{\mathrm{L}^3}$

44 $\frac{C}{\sqrt{GM_S}} r^{3/2}$

45 (*a*) 30,000 (*b*) 0.0062 (*c*) 0.000004 (*d*) 217,000

46 (*a*) 1.3451×10^3 km (*b*) 1.2340×10^1 MW (*c*) 5.432×10^{-11} s (*d*) 3.0×10^3 mm

47 (*a*) 1.14×10^5 (*b*) 2.25×10^{-8} (*c*) 8.27×10^3 (*d*) 6.27×10^2

48 (*a*) 1.144×10^5 (*b*) 3.20×10^2 (*c*) 8.62×10^4 (*d*) 1.52×10^4

49 3.6×10^6

50 5.3×10^{-3} cm^2

51 (*a*) 26 mm^2 (*b*) 30 mm^2

52 (*a*)

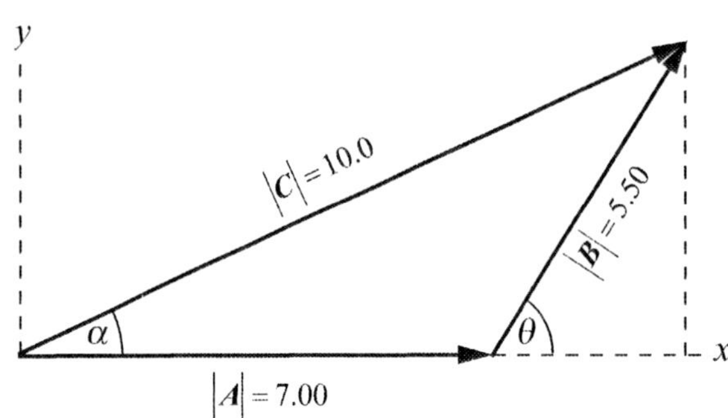

(*b*) 74.4°

53 (*a*) $A_x = 5.0$ m, $A_y = 8.7$ m (*b*) $v_x = -19$ m/s, $v_y = -16$ m/s (*c*) $F_x = 35$ lb, $F_y = 20$ lb

54 (*a*) 10 m, –33° = 327° (*b*) 83 m/s, 155° (*c*) –30 lb, 217°

55 You could have gone either 87 m north (60° north of east) or 87 m south (60° south of east)

56 The magnitude of the second leg of your journey is about 260 m at an angle of approximately 20° S of E. If you had initially walked into the southeast, the magnitude of the second leg of your journey would still be about 260 m but its direction would be approximately 20° N of E.

57 $(a)\ 40\hat{\boldsymbol{i}} - 50\hat{\boldsymbol{j}}$ $(b)\ -51°$

58 (*a*) The magnitude of $\vec{\boldsymbol{C}}$ is approximately 57 lb and the angle θ is approximately 68°.

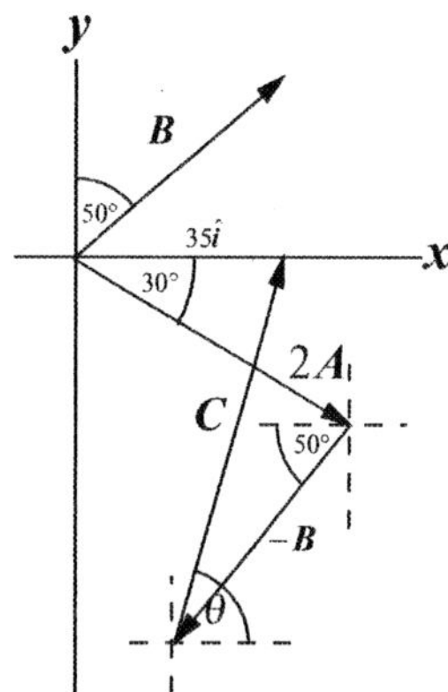

(*b*) 57 lb, 65°

59 $-0.59\hat{\boldsymbol{i}} - 0.81\hat{\boldsymbol{j}}$, $0.92\hat{\boldsymbol{i}} - 0.38\hat{\boldsymbol{j}}$, $-0.51\hat{\boldsymbol{i}} + 0.86\hat{\boldsymbol{j}}$

60 $(a)\ \hat{\boldsymbol{u}}_{\text{NE}} = 0.707\hat{\boldsymbol{i}} + 0.707\hat{\boldsymbol{j}}$ $(b)\ \hat{\boldsymbol{u}} = -0.940\hat{\boldsymbol{i}} - 0.342\hat{\boldsymbol{j}}$
$(c)\ \hat{\boldsymbol{u}}_{\text{SW}} = -0.707\hat{\boldsymbol{i}} - 0.707\hat{\boldsymbol{j}}$

61 3.32×10^{3} mi/h, 5.34×10^{3} km/h, 1.49×10^{3} m/s

62 62.2 mi/h

63 31.7 y

64 (*a*) 1.61 km/mi (*b*) 2.20 lb/kg

65 2.0×10^{23}

66 (*a*) 8.8×10^{6} in^{3} (*b*) 5.1×10^{3} ft^{3} (*c*) 1.4×10^{2} m^{3} (*d*) 1.4×10^{5} kg

67 (*a*) 1.4×10^{17} kg/m^{3} (*b*) 2.2×10^{2} m

68 (*a*) 6.3×10^{4} m^{3} (*b*) 1.8×10^{6} s or about 21 days!

69 (*a*) 4.848×10^{-6} parsec (*b*) 3.086×10^{16} m (*c*) 9.461×10^{15} m
(*d*) 6.324×10^{4} AU (*e*) $3.262\, c\cdot$y

70 (*a*) 7×10^3 electrons/m^3 (*b*) 4 protons/m^3

71

(*a*)

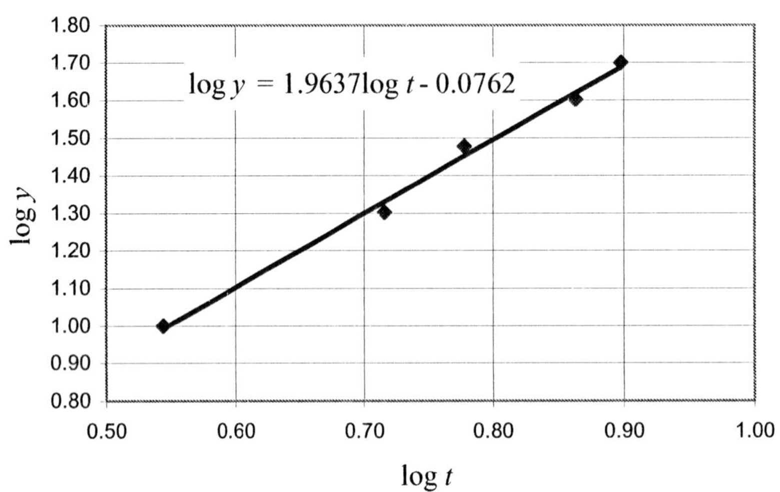

(*c*) $B = 0.84\ \text{m/s}^2$, $C = 2.0$ (*d*) 1.1 s (*e*) 1.7 m/s^2

72

(*a*)

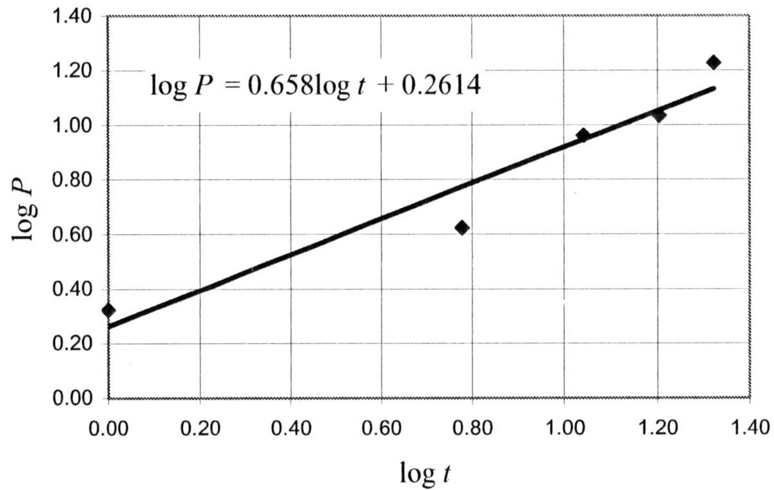

$B = \$1.83$, $C = 0.658$

(*b*) $P(20\ \text{y}) = \$13.14$

73 55.4×10^3 tons. The 50,000-ton claim is conservative. The actual weight is closer to 55,000 tons.

74 $h = 5.5\ \text{km}, L = 42\ \text{km}$

75

(*a*)

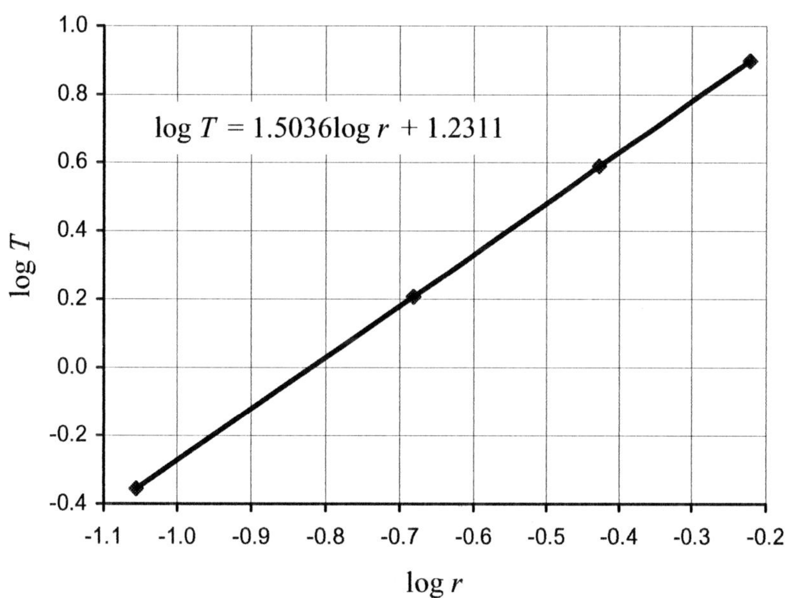

$n = 1.50, C = 17.0\ \text{y}/(\text{Gm})^{3/2}, T = \left(17.0\ \text{y}/(\text{Gm})^{3/2}\right) r^{1.50}$

(*b*) $r = 0.510\ \text{Gm}$

76 (*a*) $T = C\sqrt{\frac{L}{g}}$ (*b*) $T(1.0\ \text{m}) = 2.0\ \text{s}$, $T(0.50\ \text{m}) = 1.4\ \text{s}$ (*c*) $T = 2\pi\sqrt{\frac{L}{g}}$

77 (*a*) $\vec{F}_{\text{Paul}} = (35\ \text{lb})\hat{i} + (35\ \text{lb})\hat{j}$ $\vec{F}_{\text{Johnny}} = (-53\ \text{lb})\hat{i} + (-37\ \text{lb})\hat{j}$
(*b*) $\vec{F}_{\text{Connie}} = (18\ \text{lb})\hat{i} + (1.9\ \text{lb})\hat{j}, F_{\text{Connie}} = 18\ \text{lb}, \theta = 6.1°$ N of E

78 (*a*) 5.8 km (*b*) 59° E of N (*c*) $\vec{d} = (2.5\ \text{km})\hat{i} + (2.5\ \text{km})\hat{j} + (2.5\ \text{km})\hat{k}$
(*d*) $\phi = 60°$ above the horizon

Chapter 2
Motion in One Dimension

1 0

2 (*d*)

3 $v_{\text{av 1st half}} = \frac{2H}{T}$, $vel_{\text{av 2nd half}} = -\frac{2H}{T}$

4 (*a*) A car moving westward and slowing down.
(*b*) A car traveling northward and speeding up.

5 (*a*) Your speed increased from zero, stayed constant for a while, and then decreased.
(*b*) and (*c*)

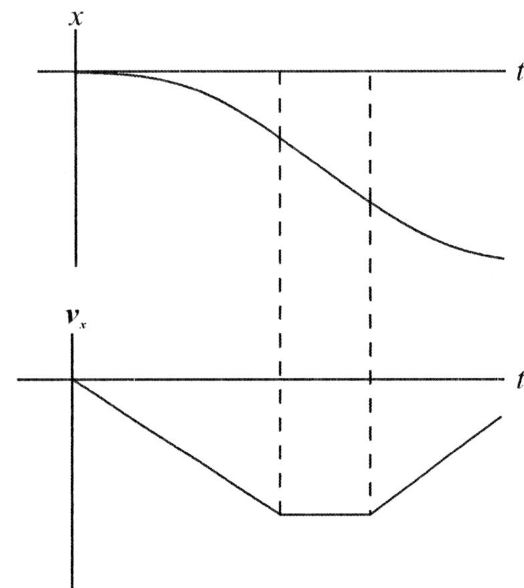

6 True

7 True

8

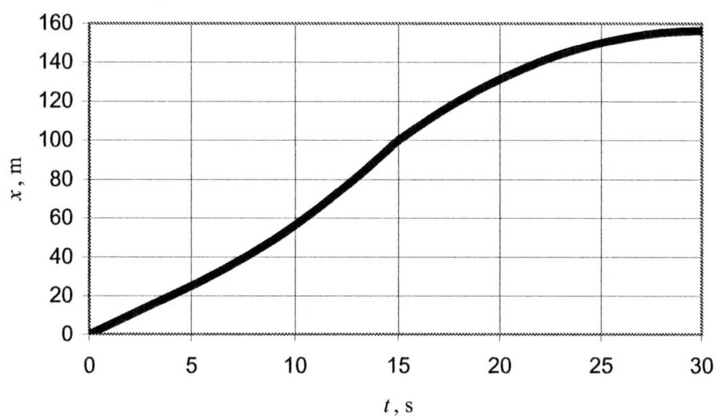

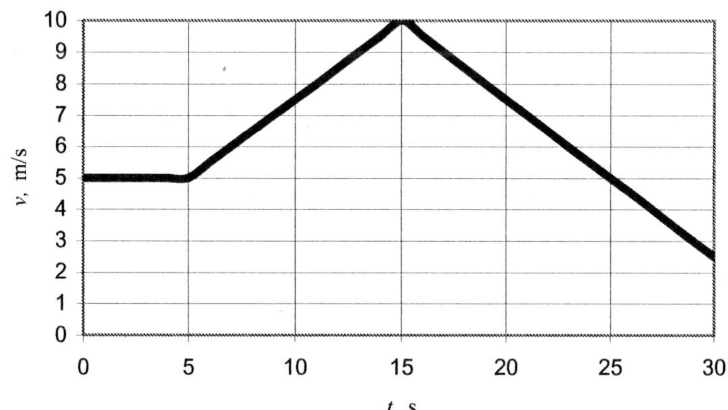

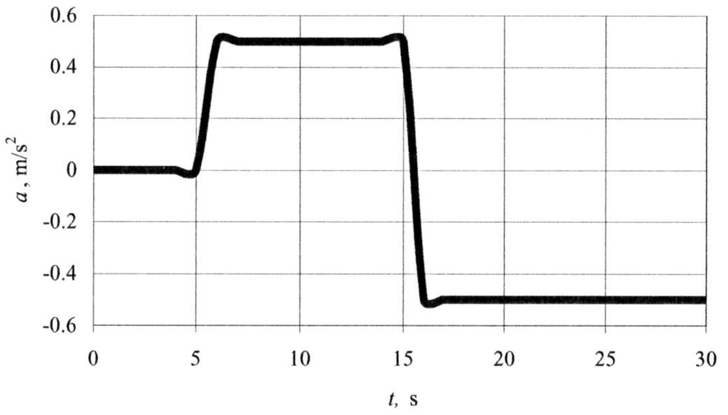

9 False

10 This can occur if the rocks have different initial speeds. Ignoring air resistance, the acceleration is constant. Choose a coordinate system in which the origin is at the point of release and upward is the positive direction. From the constant-acceleration equation $y = y_0 + v_0 t + \frac{1}{2}at^2$ we see that the only way two objects can have the same acceleration ($-g$ in this case) and cover the same distance, $\Delta y = y - y_0$, in different times would be if the initial velocities of the two rocks were different. Actually, the answer would be the same whether or not the acceleration is constant. It is just easier to see for the special case of constant acceleration.

11 (*a*)

12 (*a*) *d* (*b*) *b* (*c*) *e* (*d*) *a* and *c*

13 (*a*) *b* (*b*) *c* (*c*) *d* (*d*) *e*

14 (*a*) B (*b*) B and D (*c*) E (*d*) A

15 (*a*) B, D and E (*b*) A and D (*c*) C

16 (*a*)

curve *a*: $v(t_2) < v(t_1)$
curve *b*: $v(t_2) = v(t_1)$
curve *c*: $v(t_2) > v(t_1)$
curve *d*: $v(t_2) < v(t_1)$

(*b*)

curve *a*: $\text{speed}(t_2) < \text{speed}(t_1)$
curve *b*: $\text{speed}(t_2) = \text{speed}(t_1)$
curve *c*: $\text{speed}(t_2) < \text{speed}(t_1)$
curve *d*: $\text{speed}(t_2) > \text{speed}(t_1)$

17 (*a*) False (*b*) True (*c*) True

18 (*a*) velocity is to the right and constant; acceleration is zero
(*b*) velocity is zero; acceleration is to the left
(*c*) velocity is to the left and constant; acceleration is zero

19 (*a*) 0 (*b*) $-g$ (c) downward and greater than g in magnitude

20 (*a*) $2H/T$ (*b*) $\frac{1}{2}v_0$

21 (*a*) False (*b*) False (*c*) True

22 (*d*)

23 (*a*) *c*

(*b*)

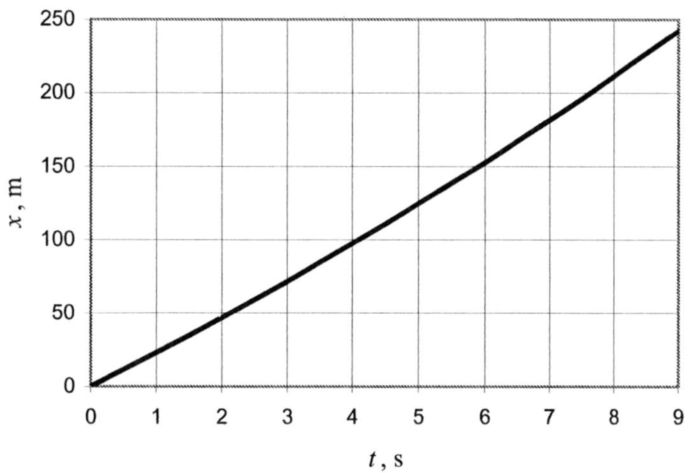

24 (*a*) 4*D* (*b*) 4*D*/*t* (*c*) *g*

25 B is passing A

26 (*a*) False (*b*) False (*c*) True

27 (*c*)

28 $\frac{t_2}{t_1} = \sqrt{2}$

29 (*a*) Yes, when the graphs intersect
(*b*) Yes, when the slopes of the curves have opposite signs
(*c*) Yes, when the curves have the same slope
(*d*) The two cars are farthest apart at the instant the two curves are farthest apart in the *x* direction.

30 The graph is a plot of velocity versus time. Thus, where the two curves cross, the truck and car are, at that instant, moving with equal velocities. The slope of a velocity versus time curve is equal to the instantaneous acceleration – thus, since the curve that represents the truck's velocity has a positive slope, and the car's curve has zero slope, the truck is accelerating at a higher rate than the car. Finally, the displacements of the two cars are determined by calculating the areas under the curves. In this instance, the curve representing the truck's velocity as a function of time encloses a triangular area that is exactly half that of the curve representing the car's velocity. Thus, at the instant represented by the point where the curves intersect, the truck has gone half as far as has the car.

31 $v_J = \frac{1}{2}v_{max}$

32 (*a*) *c* (*b*) *a* (*c*) *c, d* and *e* (*d*) *e*

33 (*a*) *d* (*b*) *b* (*c*) None (*d*) *c* and *d*

34

(*a*)

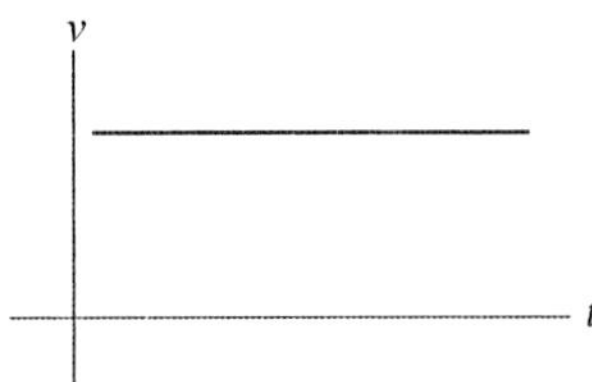

(*b*)

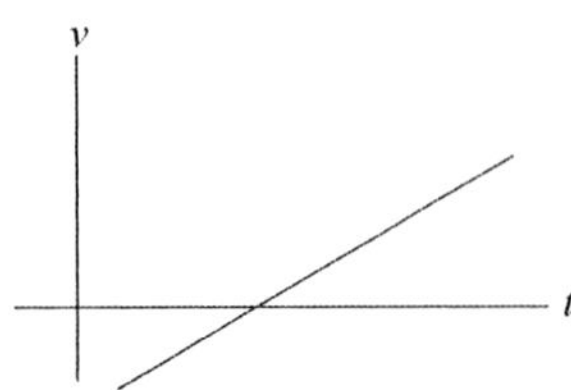

(*c*)

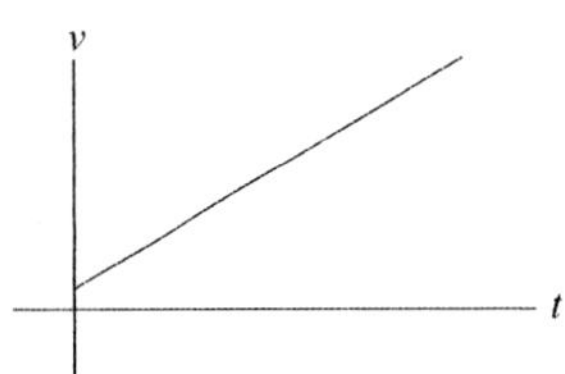

(*d*)

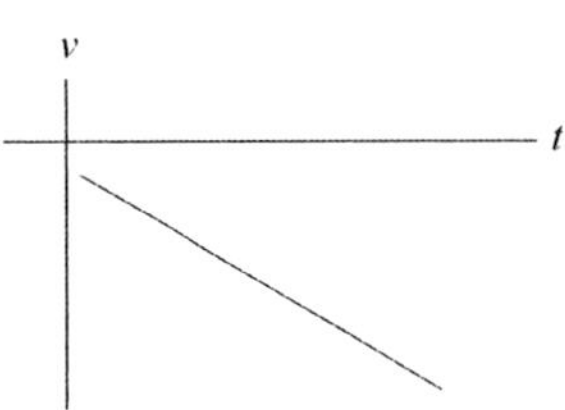

(*e*)

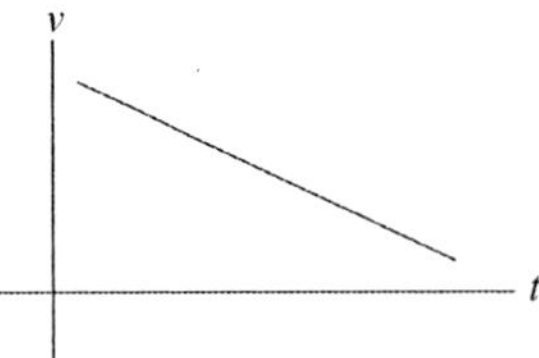

(*f*)

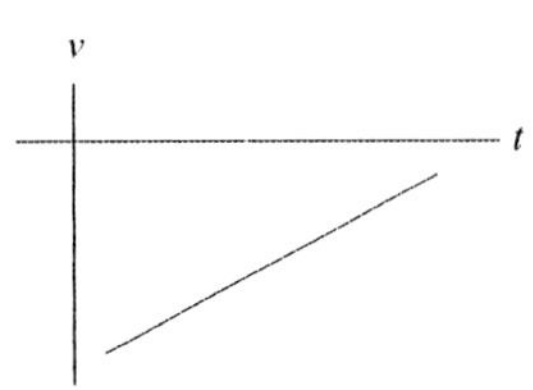

(*g*)

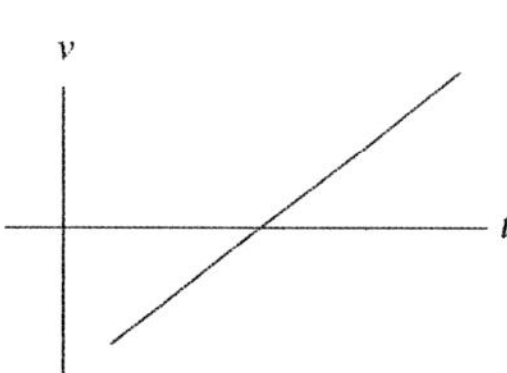

35 (*a*) *a, f* and *I* (*b*) *c* and *d* (*c*) *a, d, e, f, h* and *I* (*d*) *b, c* and g (*e*) *a* and *i, d* and *h, f* and *i*

36 33 m/s^2

37 -1.2×10^3 m/s^2

38 (*a*) 2.6 s, 32 m (*b*) 0.26 s, 32 cm (*c*) The analysis of the motion of a ping-pong ball requires the inclusion of air resistance for almost any situation, whereas the analysis of the motion of the sky diver doesn't require it until the fall distances and times are considerably longer.

39 4.03 m/s^2

40 (*a*) Because the ball is moving slowly its blur is relatively short (i.e., there is less blurring). (*b*) 3.9 m/s (*c*) 78 cm. If we assume that the juggler is approximately 6 ft (1.8 m) tall, then our calculated value for *h* seems to be a good approximation to the height shown in the photograph.

41 (*a*) 1.7 km $\approx$ 1 mi (*b*) You are probably lucky if the uncertainty in your time estimate is less than 1 s ($\pm$20%), so the uncertainty in the distance estimate is about 20% of 1.7 km or approximately 300 m. This is probably much greater than the error made by assuming *v* is constant.

42 (*a*) 4.0 ns (*b*) 67 min

43 (*a*) 0.28 km/min (*b*) −83 m/min (*c*) 0 (*d*) 0.13 km/min

44 (*a*) 2.6×10^5 m (*b*) 65 km/h

45 (*a*) 2.2 h (*b*) $\dfrac{t_{\text{supersonic}}}{t_{\text{subsonic}}} \approx 0.45$

46 (*a*) 8.3 min (*b*) 1.3 s

47 (*a*) 4.3 y (*b*) 4.3×10^6 y. Because 4.3×10^6 y >> 1000 y, Gregor does not have to pay.

48 67 km/h

49 23.5 s

50 (*a*) 6.0 m/s (*b*) 25 m

51 (*a*) 0 (*b*) 0.3 m/s (*c*) −2 m/s (*d*) 1 m/s

52 (*a*) 7.90×10^4 m/s (*b*) 3.16×10^7 m/s (*c*) 20×10^9 y

53 $v_{\text{av}} = 122$ km/h . $\text{Average}_{\text{three speeds}} = 1.04 v_{\text{av}}$. The average speed would be equal to one-third the sum of the three speeds if the three speeds were each maintained for the same length of time instead of for the same distance.

54 (*a*) 1.2×10^5 m (*b*) 0.24 km

55

(*a*)

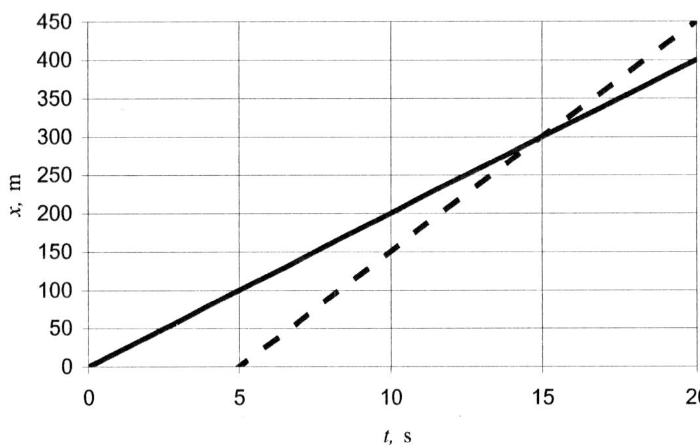

(*b*) 15 s (*c*) 300 m (*d*) 100 m

56 24 m

57 15 m/s

58 (*a*) 2.42 m/s^2 (*b*) 89.2 km/h

59 −2.0 m/s^2

60 (*a*) 8.0 m/s^2

(*b*)

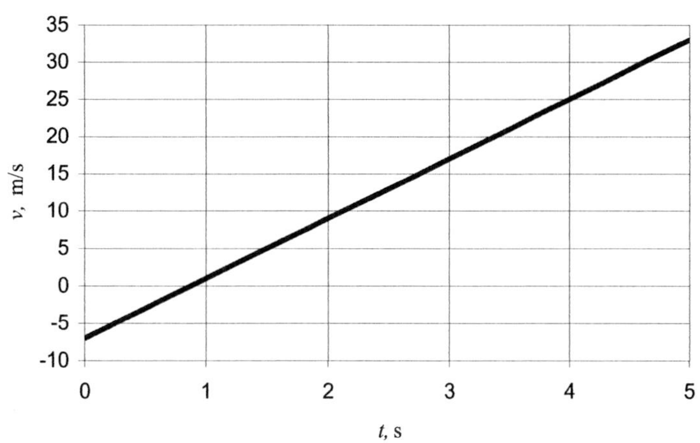

(*c*) These accelerations are the same.

61 (*a*) 2.0 m/s (*b*) $\Delta x = (2t-5)\Delta t + (\Delta t)^2$ (*c*) $v(t) = 2t - 5$

62 $v = (16\text{ m/s}^2)t - 6.0\text{ m/s}$, $a = 16\text{ m/s}^2$

63 (*a*) $v_{\text{av, AB}} = 3.3\text{ m/s}^2$, $a_{\text{av, BC}} = 0$, $a_{\text{avm CE}} = -7.5\text{ m/s}^2$ (*b*) 75 m
(*c*)

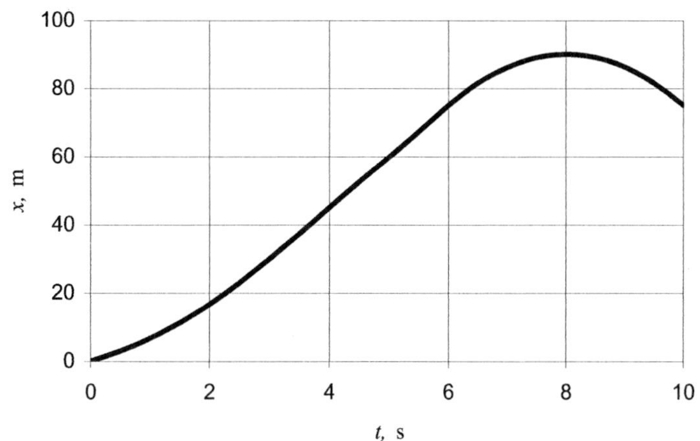

(*d*) At point D, $t = 8$ s, the graph crosses the time axis; therefore $v = 0$.

64 4*h*

65 (*a*) 80 m/s (*b*) 0.40 km (*c*) 40 m/s

66 50 m

67 16 m/s^2

68 3.0 m/s, 0.5 s

69 (*a*) 4.1 s (*b*) 20 m (*c*) 0.99 s and 3.1 s

70 (*a*) 9.68 s (*b*) 95.0 m/s (*c*) 168 s

71

(*a*)

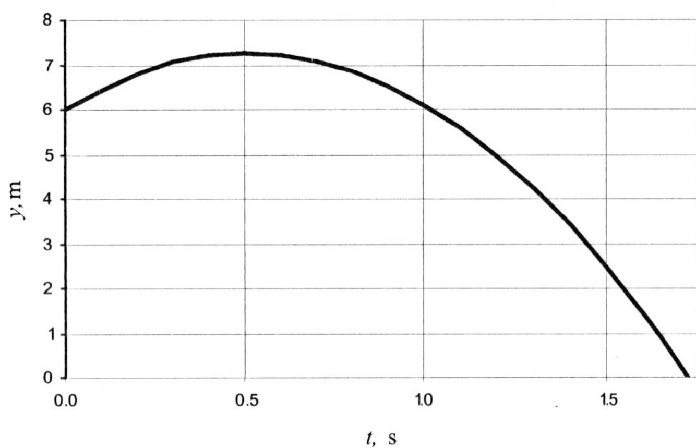

(*b*) 7.3 m (*c*) 1.7 s (*d*) 12 m/s

72 (*a*) 26 m (*b*) 23 m/s

73 44 m

74 94 m

75 68 m/s

76 7.77 m/s

77 (*a*) 0.67 km (*b*) 14 m/s

78 (*a*) 10 s (*b*) 27 s (*c*) 14 m

79 (*a*) You did not achieve your goal. To go higher, you can increase the acceleration value or the time of acceleration. (*b*) 1.4×10^2 s (*c*) 6.1×10^2 m/s

80 18 m

81 40 cm/s, -6.9 cm/s^2

82 146 m

83 (*a*) 11 mi/h (*b*) 0.60

84 (*a*) 17 m (*b*) 17 s

85 11 m

86 (*a*) 52 s (*b*) 61 mi/h

87 28 m

88 (*a*) 0.75 m/s^2 (*b*) 10 m/s (*c*) 0.52 km

89 (*a*) 2.4 m (*b*) 1.4 s

90 1.5 km

92 −64 m

93 (*a*) 2.1 d (*b*) 5.8 y

94 0.22 m/s^2, 0.022g

95 4.8 m/s

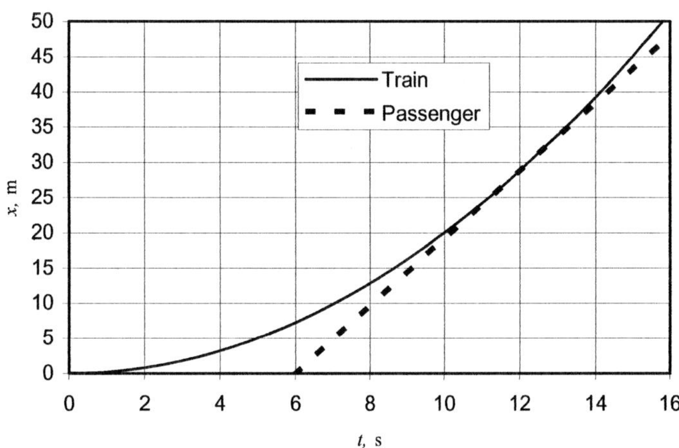

96 $2h/3$

97 $h/3$

98

(*a*)

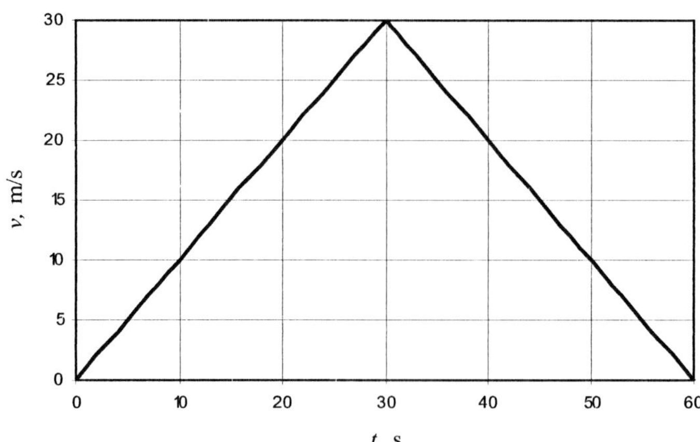
30
25
20
15
10
5
0
v, m/s
0
10
20
30
40
50
60
t, s

(*b*)

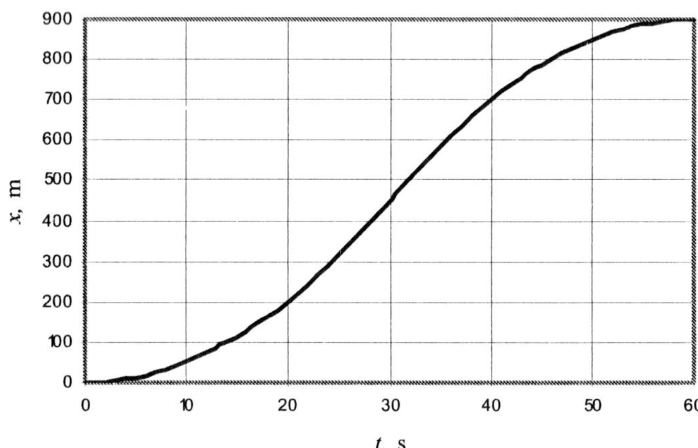
900
800
700
600
500
400
300
200
100
0
x, m
0
10
20
30
40
50
60
t, s

99 (*a*) 35 s (*b*) 1.2 km
(*c*)

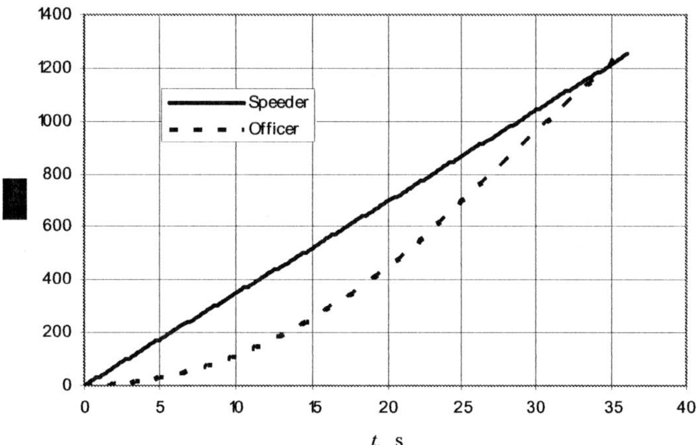

100 (*b*) 5.5 s (*c*) If you take the reaction time into account, the collision will occur sooner and be more severe.

101 (*a*) $2L/3$ (*b*) $\frac{2}{3}t_{\text{fin}}$ (*c*) $\sqrt{\dfrac{4aL}{5}}$

102
(*a*)

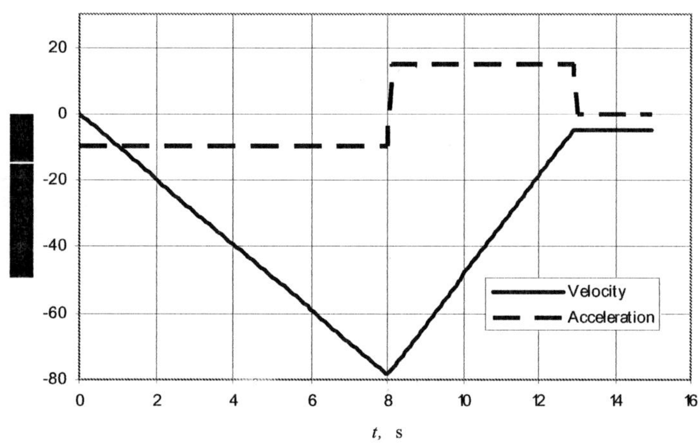

(*b*) 79 m/s (*c*) 4.9 s (*d*) 204 m (*e*) 24 s (*f*) –24 m/s

103 (*a*)

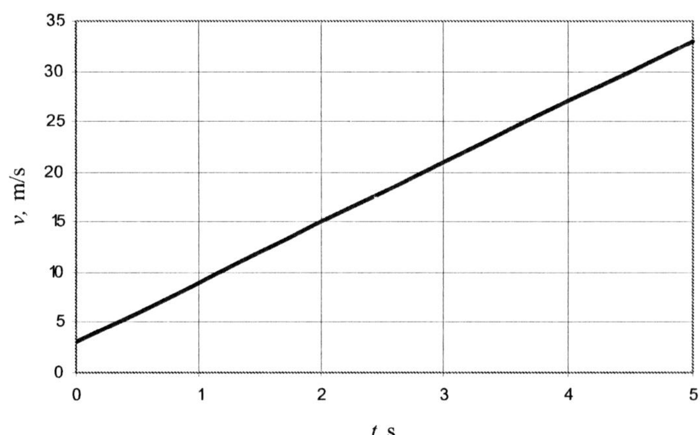

$$A_{\substack{\text{under}\\\text{curve}}} = 90\text{ m}$$

(*b*) $x(t) = (3.0\text{ m/s}^2)t^2 + (3.0\text{ m/s})t$, 90 m

104 (*a*) 1 m per box (*b*) 1.2 m, 3.2 m (*c*) 2.2 m/s (*d*) 4.3 m. This result is a little smaller than the sum of the displacements found in Part (*b*). The average of 2.5 m/s is not equal to the average velocity calculated above.

105 $x(t) = (2.3\text{ m/s}^3)t^3 - (5.0\text{ m/s})t$

106 $a_x = -10\text{ m/s}^2$, $v_x(t) = 50\text{ m/s} + (-10\text{ m/s}^2)t$, $x(t) = (50\text{ m/s})t - (5.0\text{ m/s}^2)t^2$

107 (*a*) 0.25 m/s per box (*b*) 0.93 m/s, 3.0 m/s, 6.0 m/s
(*c*)

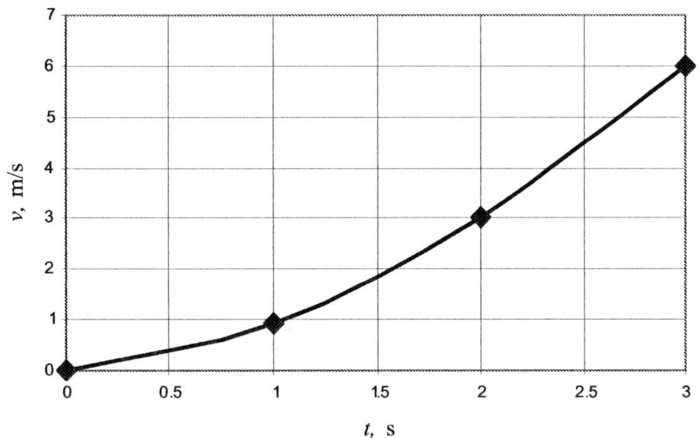

$$x(3\,\text{s}) = 6.5\,\text{m}$$

108 (*a*)

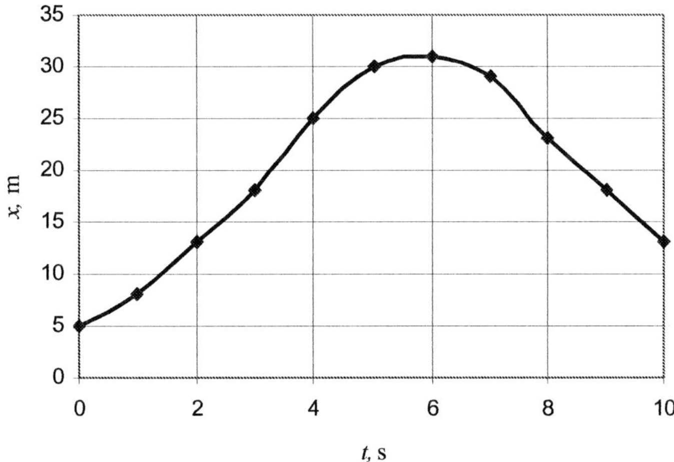

(*b*)

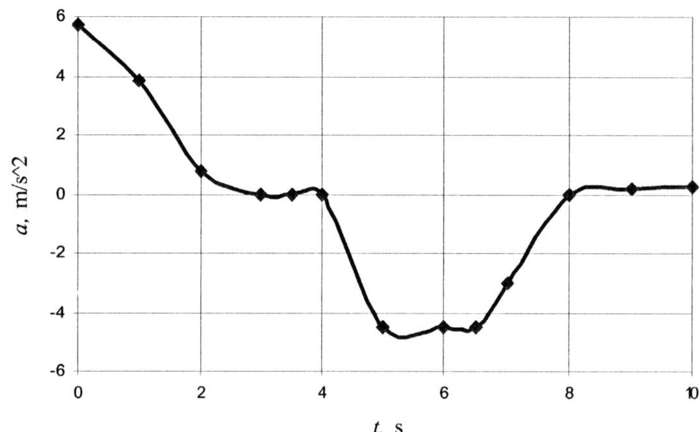

(*c*) $\Delta x_{3.0\,\text{s}\to 7.0\,\text{s}} = 11\,\text{m}$

109 (*a*)

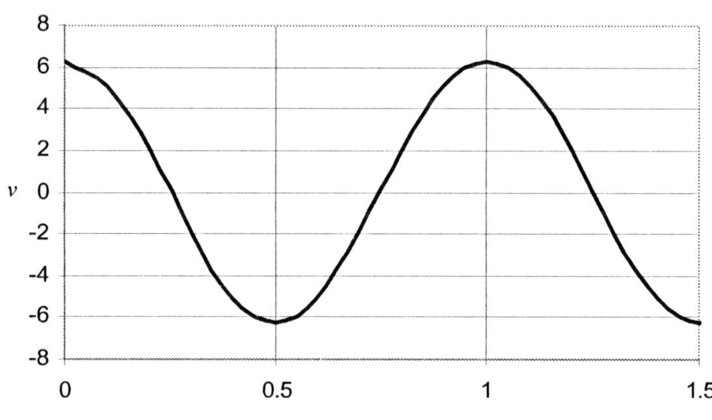

(*b*)

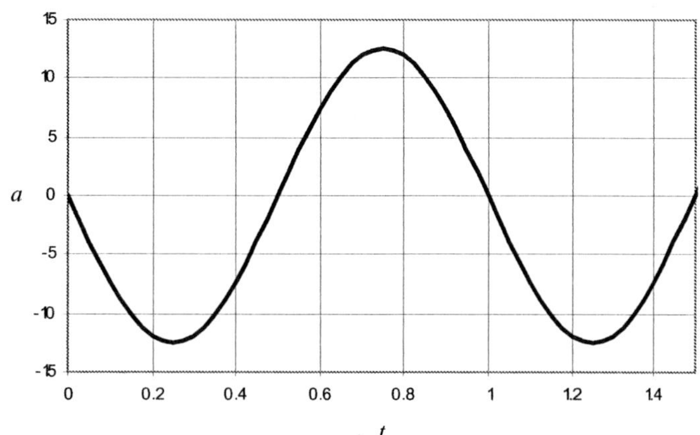

(*c*) The points at the greatest distances from the time axis correspond to turn-around points. The velocity of the body is zero at these points.

(*d*) The body is moving fastest as it goes through the origin. At these times the velocity is not changing and hence the acceleration is zero. The maximum acceleration occurs at the maximum distances where the velocity is zero but changing direction rapidly.

110 (*a*) $x(t)=\frac{1}{6}bt^3+v_{0x}+x_0$ (*b*) 38 m/s, 63 m (*c*) 38 m/s … in good agreement with the value found in Part (*b*).

111 (*a*) $v(t)=\left(0.10\text{ m/s}^3\right)t^2+9.5\text{ m/s}$
(*b*) $x(t)=\frac{1}{3}\left(0.20\text{ m/s}^3\right)t^3+\left(9.4\text{ m/s}\right)t^2-5.0\text{ m/s}$
(*c*) 13 m/s, 15 m/s. v_{av} is not the same as $\bar{v}$ because the velocity does not change linearly with time. The velocity does not change linearly with time because the acceleration is not constant.

112 (*a*) $v_x=v_{0x}+a_0t+\frac{1}{2}bt^2$ (*b*) $x=x_0+v_0t+\frac{1}{2}a_0t^2+\frac{1}{6}bt^3$ (*c*) $\bar{v}_x=v_{0x}+\frac{1}{2}a_0t+\frac{1}{6}bt^2$
(*d*) $v_{\text{av}}=v_{0x}+\frac{1}{2}a_0t+\frac{1}{4}bt^2$. $v_{\text{av},x}$ is not the same as $\bar{v}_x$ because the acceleration is not constant.

113 (*b*) 0.452 s (*c*) 12 m/s^2, 22%

114 (*a*)

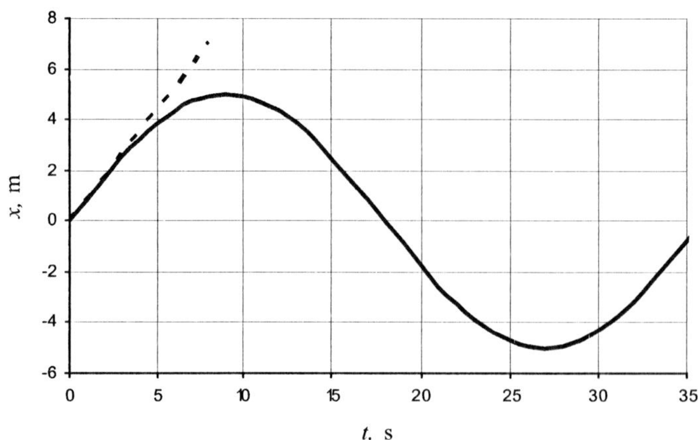

(*b*) 0.8 cm/s
(*c*)

t_0	t	Δt	x_0	x	Δx	$v_{av}=\Delta x/\Delta t$
(s)	(s)	(s)	(cm)	(cm)	(cm)	(m/s)
0	6	6	0	4.34	4.34	0.723
0	3	3	0	2.51	2.51	0.835
0	2	2	0	1.71	1.71	0.857
0	1	1	0	0.871	0.871	0.871
0	0.5	0.5	0	0.437	0.437	0.874
0	0.25	0.25	0	0.219	0.219	0.875

(*d*) 0.88 cm/s (*e*) As Δt, and thus Δx, becomes small, the value for the average velocity approaches that for the instantaneous velocity obtained in Part (*d*). For $\Delta t = 0.25$ s, they agree to three significant figures.

115 (*a*) The maximum value of the sine function (as in $v = v_{max}\sin(\omega t)$) is 1. Hence the coefficient B represents the maximum possible speed v_{max}. (*b*) $a = \omega v_{max}\cos(\omega t)$. Because a varies sinusoidally with time it is *not* constant.

(*c*) $|a_{max}| = \omega v_{max}$ (*d*) $x = x_0 + \frac{v_{max}}{\omega}[1-\cos(\omega t)]$

116 (*a*) 4.0 m/s (*b*) 1.2 s

117 (*a*) s^{-1} (*b*) $v_t = g/b$

118 $v = \frac{g}{b}\left(1-e^{-bt}\right)$, $y = v_t t - \frac{v_t}{b}\left(1-e^{-bt}\right)$

119 (*b*) 0.762

(*c*)

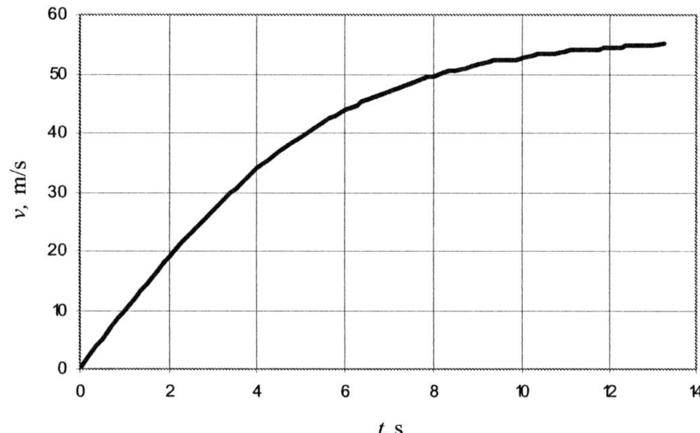

Note that the speed increases linearly over time (that is, with constant acceleration) for about time *T*, but then it approaches the terminal speed as the acceleration decreases.

120 41 m

121 25 m/s. Because 25 m/s is approximately 57 mi/h, you were approximately 32 mi/h over the speed limit! You would be foolish to contest your ticket.

122 2.06 km/s

Chapter 3
Motion in Two and Three Dimensions

1 No. Yes.

2 The displacement of an object is its final position vector minus its initial position vector ($\Delta\vec{r} = \vec{r}_f - \vec{r}_i$). The displacement can be less but never more than the distance traveled. Suppose the path is one complete trip around the earth at the equator. Then, the displacement is 0 but the distance traveled is $2\pi R_e$. No, the reverse cannot be true.

3 Zero

4 The angle between its velocity and acceleration vectors starts at 30° + 90° or 120° because the acceleration of the ball is straight down. At the peak of the flight of the ball the angle reduces to 90° because the ball's velocity vector is horizontal. When the ball reaches the same elevation that it started from the angle is 90° – 30° or 60°.

5 (*e*)

6 (*d*)

7 (*c*)

8 (*a*)

9 (*a*) The angle between its velocity and acceleration vectors starts at 30° + 90° or 120° because the acceleration of the ball is straight down. At the peak of the flight of the ball the angle reduces to 90° because the ball's velocity vector is horizontal. When the ball reaches the same elevation that it started from the angle is 90° – 30° or 60°.

(*b*)

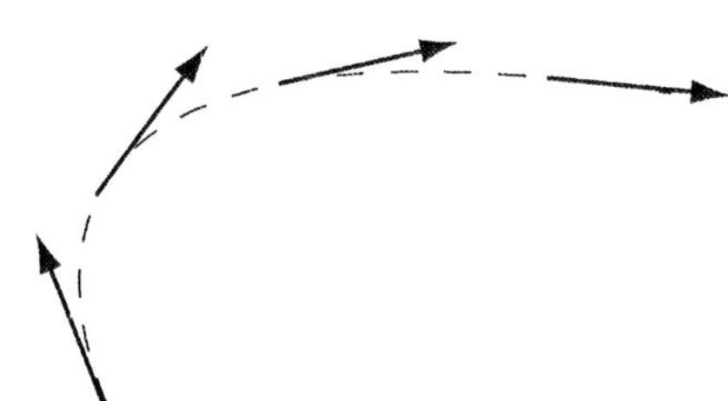

10 (*b*)

11 (*a*) A car moving along a straight road while braking.
(*b*) A car moving along a straight road while speeding up.
(*c*) A particle moving around a circular track at constant speed.

12 A particle moving at constant speed in a circular path is accelerating because the direction of its velocity vector is changing. If a particle is moving at constant velocity, it is not accelerating.

13 (*a*)

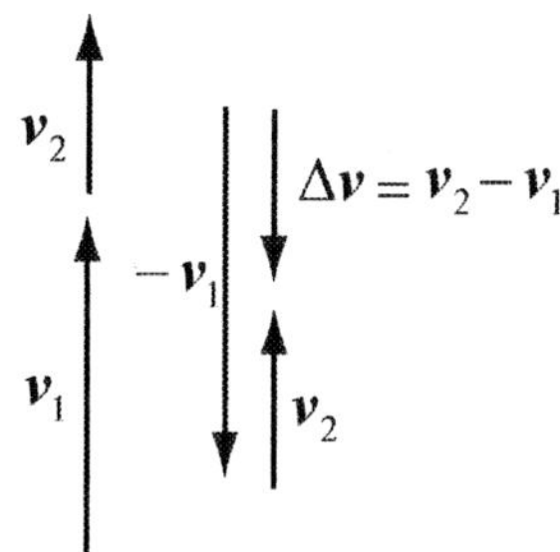

(*b*)

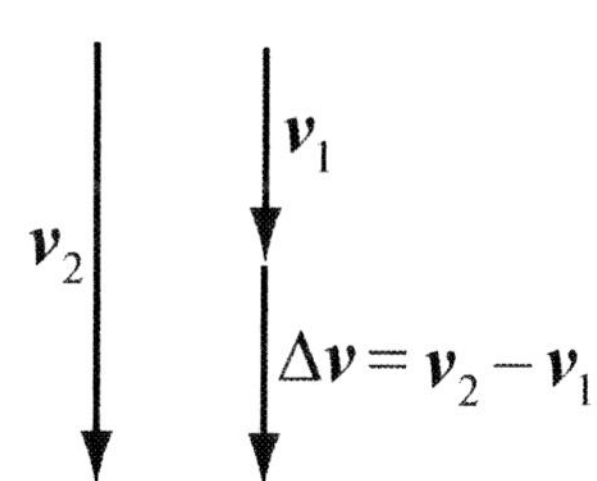

(*c*)

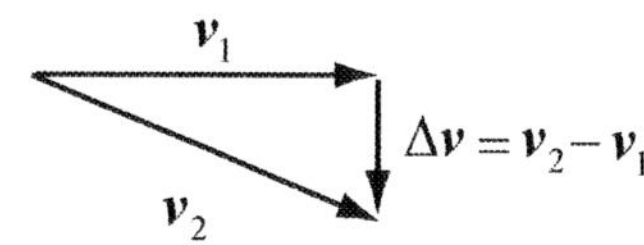

14

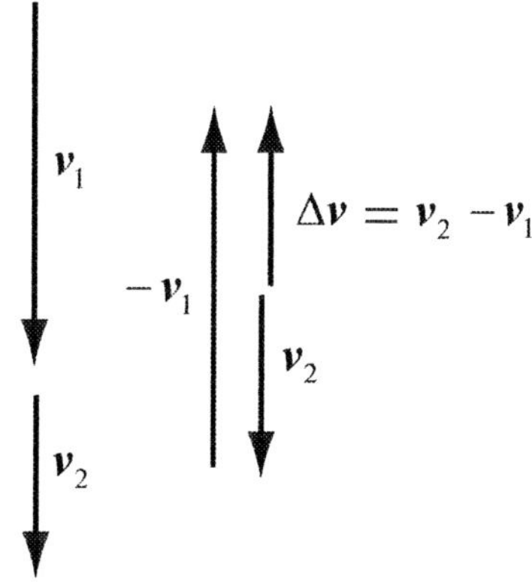

15

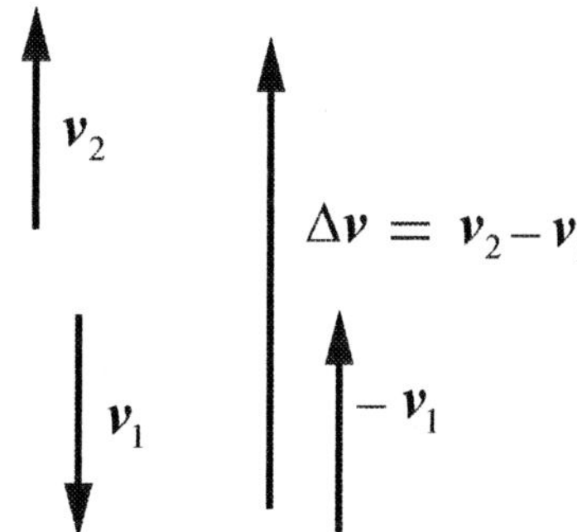

16 (*d*)

17 You must be walking west to make it appear to you that the rain is exactly vertical.

18 0.90 m/s

19 (*a*) True (*b*) True (*c*) True

20 (*e*)

21 (*a*)

22 (*b*)

23 (*d*)

24 (*a*) A and E (*b*) C (*c*) A and E. No. The horizontal components are equal at these points but the vertical components are oppositely directed.

25 (*a*) False (*b*) True (*c*) True (*d*) False (*e*) True

26

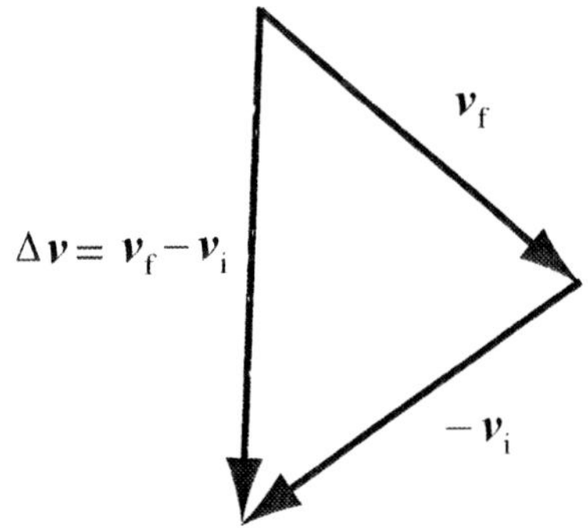

27 (*a*)

Path	Direction of velocity vector
AB	north
BC	northeast
CD	east
DE	southeast
EF	south

(*b*)

Path	Direction of acceleration vector
AB	north
BC	southeast
CD	0
DE	southwest
EF	north

(*c*) The magnitudes are comparable, but larger for DE because the radius of the path is smaller there.

28 If the guns are fired simultaneously, $t = t'$ and the balls are the same distance $\frac{1}{2}gt^2$ below the line of sight at all times. Therefore, they should fire the guns simultaneously.

29 The droplet leaving the bottle has the same horizontal velocity as the ship. During the time the droplet is in the air, it is also moving horizontally with the same velocity as the rest of the ship. Because of this, it falls into the vessel, which has the same horizontal velocity. Because you have the same horizontal velocity as the ship does, you see the same thing as if the ship were standing still.

30 (*a*) Because $\vec{A}$ and $\vec{D}$ are tangent to the path of the stone, either of them could represent the velocity of the stone.

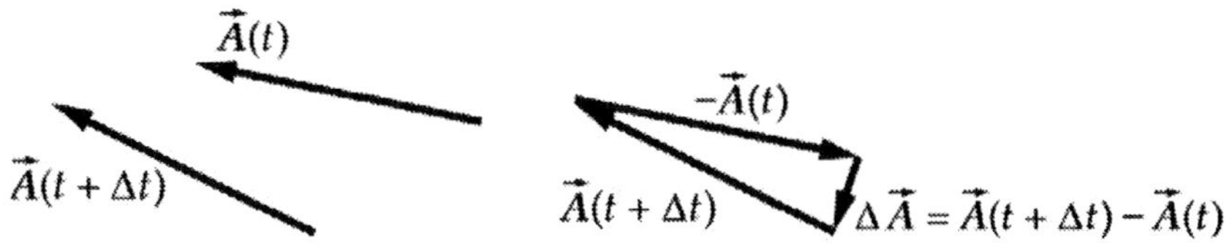

(*b*) Let the vectors $\vec{A}(t)$ and $\vec{A}(t + \Delta t)$ be of equal length but point in slightly different directions as the stone moves around the circle. These two vectors and $\Delta\vec{A}$ are shown in the diagram above. Note that $\Delta\vec{A}$ is nearly perpendicular to $\vec{A}(t)$. For very small time intervals, $\Delta\vec{A}$ and $\vec{A}(t)$ are perpendicular to one another. Therefore, $d\vec{A}/dt$ is perpendicular to $\vec{A}$ and only the vector $\vec{E}$ could represent the acceleration of the stone.

31 (*a*) True (*b*) False (*c*) False (*d*) True

32

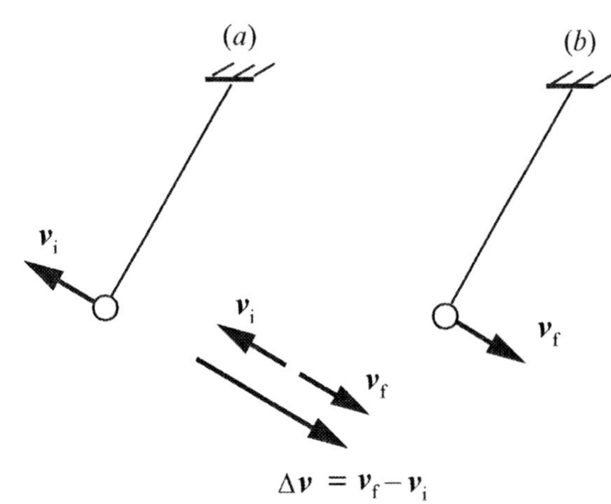

In the diagram, (*a*) shows the pendulum just before it reverses direction and (*b*) shows the pendulum just after it has reversed its direction. The acceleration of the bob is in the direction of the *change* in the velocity $\Delta\vec{v} = \vec{v}_f - \vec{v}_i$ and is tangent to the pendulum trajectory at the point of reversal of direction. This makes sense because, at an extremum of motion, $v = 0$, so there is no centripetal acceleration. However, because the velocity is reversing direction, the tangential acceleration is nonzero.

33

(*a*)

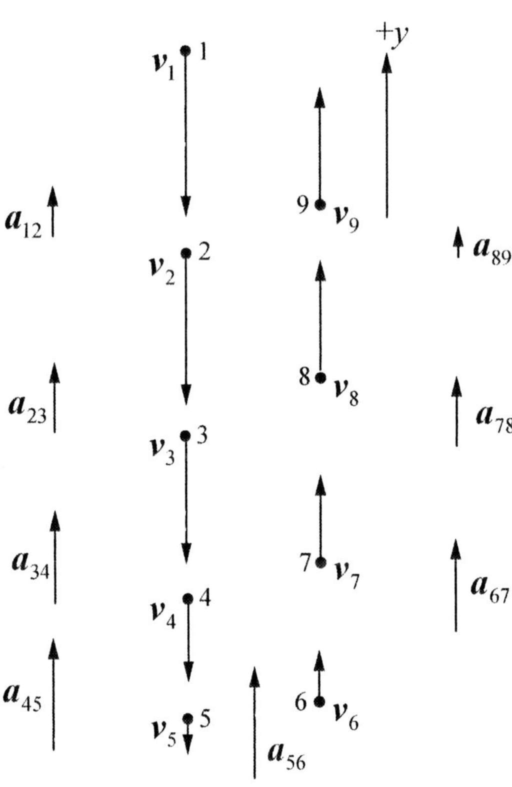

i	v (m/s)	Δv (m/s)	a_{ave} (m/s^2)
1	−0.78		
2	−0.69	0.09	1.8
3	−0.55	0.14	2.8
4	−0.35	0.20	4.0
5	−0.10	0.25	5.0
6	0.15	0.25	5.0
7	0.35	0.20	4.0
8	0.49	0.14	2.8
9	0.53	0.04	0.8

(*b*) The acceleration vector always points upward and so the sign of its *y* component does not change. The magnitude of the acceleration vector is greatest when the bungee cord has its maximum extension (your speed, the magnitude of your velocity, is least at this time and times near it) and is less than this maximum value when the bungee cord has less extension.

34 13 mi/h

35 7×10^4 m/s^2

36 (*a*) 17 m (*b*) 75 m (*c*) 45 m (*d*) 85 m

37 15 m/s

38 (1) $\vec{A} = (0.25\text{ m})\hat{j}$, $\vec{B} = (0.50\text{ m})\hat{j}$ (2) $\vec{A} = (0.25\text{ m})\hat{i}$, $\vec{B} = (0.50\text{ m})\hat{j}$
(3) $\vec{A} = -(0.25\text{ m})\hat{j}$, $\vec{B} = (0.50\text{ m})\hat{j}$ (4) $\vec{A} = -(0.25\text{ m})\hat{i}$, $\vec{B} = (0.50\text{ m})\hat{j}$

39 $\Delta\vec{B} = 0$, $\Delta\vec{A} = -(0.25\text{ m})\hat{i} - (0.25\text{ m})\hat{j}$

40 $\vec{D} = (0.25\text{ m})\hat{i} - (0.50\text{ m})\hat{j}$

41

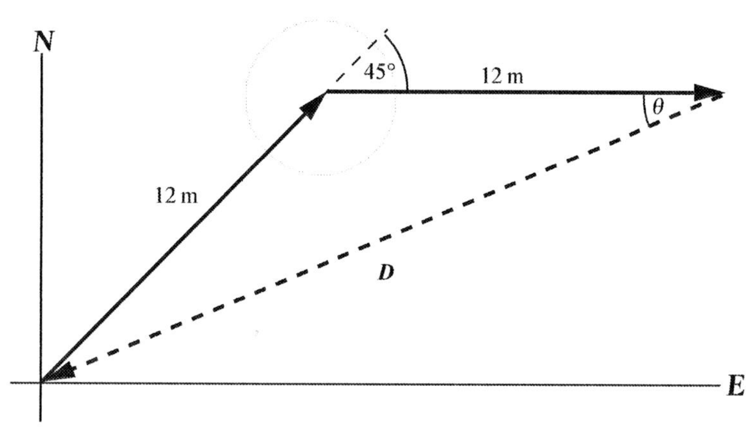

$D \approx 22$ m and $\theta \approx 23°$

42 (*a*) 0.9 km (*b*) 1 rad north of east (*c*) 1/7

43 (*a*) $\vec{D} = (3.0\text{ m})\hat{i} + (3.0\text{ m})\hat{j} + (3.0\text{ m})\hat{k}$ (*b*) 5.2 m

44 1.7×10^5 m

45 $\vec{v}_{\text{av}} = (14\text{ km/h})\hat{i} + (-4.1\text{ km/h})\hat{j}$

46 (*a*) 2.8 m/s @ 45° (*b*) 3.1 m/s @ 45°

47 7.2 m/s

48 (*a*) 36 m/s (*b*) 150° (*c*) 7.2 m/s² @ 34°

49 (*a*) $\vec{v}_{\text{av}} = (33\ \text{m/s})\hat{i} + (27\ \text{m/s})\hat{j}$ (*b*) $\vec{a}_{\text{av}} = (-3.0\ \text{m/s}^2)\hat{i} + (-1.8\ \text{m/s}^2)\hat{j}$

50 (*a*) $\vec{v}(2.0\ \text{s}) = (10\ \text{m/s})\hat{i} + (-3.0\ \text{m/s})\hat{j}$ (*b*) $\vec{r} = (44\ \text{m})\hat{i} + (-9.0\ \text{m})\hat{j}, r(4\ \text{s}) = 45\ \text{m}$, $\theta = -12°$

51 $\vec{v} = 30\hat{i} + (40 - 10t)\hat{j}$, $\vec{a} = (-10\ \text{m/s}^2)\hat{j}$

52 (*a*) $\vec{v} = [(6.0\ \text{m/s}^2)\hat{i} + (4.0\ \text{m/s}^2)\hat{j}]t$, $\vec{r} = [(10\ \text{m}) + (3.0\ \text{m/s}^2)t^2]\hat{i} + [(2.0\ \text{m/s}^2)t^2]\hat{j}$
(*b*) $y = \frac{2}{3}x - \frac{20}{3}\ \text{m}$

53 (*a*) $\vec{v}_{\text{av}} = (20\ \text{m/s})(-\hat{i} + \hat{j})$ (*b*) $\vec{a}_{\text{av}} = (-2.0\ \text{m/s}^2)\hat{i}$ (*c*) $\Delta\vec{r} = (600\ \text{m})(-\hat{i} + \hat{j})$

54 (*a*) $\vec{v}_{\text{av}} = (6.56\ \text{m/s})\hat{i} + (4.10\ \text{m/s})\hat{j}$. Because the final and initial velocities are both zero, the average acceleration is zero. (*b*) $\Delta\vec{r}_{\text{AC}} = (50.0\ \text{m})\hat{i} + (125\ \text{m})\hat{j}$
(*c*) $d_{\text{tot}} = 304$ m

55 (*a*) 16° west of north (*b*) 280 km/s

56 (*a*) 0.80 m/s (*b*) 1.8 m/s (*c*) 26°

57 8.5°, 2.57 h

58 5.2 km/h

59 Because $t_{\text{roundtrip, EW}} < t_{\text{roundtrip, NS}}$, you should fly your plane across the wind.

60 (*a*) AZ = (012°) (*b*) 1.5 × 10² kt

61 (*a*) $\vec{r}_{\text{BA}}(6.0\ \text{s}) = (-1.2\times10^2\ \text{m})\hat{i} + (4.0\ \text{m})\hat{j}$ (*b*) $\vec{v}_{\text{BA}}(6.0\ \text{s}) = (-20\ \text{m/s})\hat{i} - (12\ \text{m/s})\hat{j}$
(*c*) $(-2.0\ \text{m/s}^2)\hat{j}$

62 1.2 m/s

63 (*a*) $\vec{v}_{\text{rel}} = (0.80\ \text{m/s})\hat{i} - (1.2\ \text{m/s})\hat{j}$, 1.4 m/s (*b*) 56° below the horizontal

64 (*a*) 1.00 (*b*) $\Delta\vec{y}_{\text{BT}} = (1.22\ \text{m})\hat{j}$ (*c*) 20.6 m/s (*d*) 13.8°

65 1.5×10^{-6} m/s², 1.55×10^{-7}

66 (*a*) 3.7×10^{-6} m/s^2 (*b*) 3.1 m/s^2

67 (*a*) 463 m/s, 3.37 cm/s^2 (*b*) 0.343% (*c*) 380 m/s, 2.76 cm/s^2 (*d*) The plane of the person's path is parallel to the plane of the equator – the acceleration vector is in the plane – so that it is perpendicular to Earth's axis, pointing at the center of the person's revolution, rather than the center of Earth.

68 $2.78 \times 10^{-4}\,g$

69 (*a*) 1.8 m/s, 14 s (*b*) 0.89 m/s, 0.40 m/s^2

70 (*a*) 5.4×10^{8} m/s^2 (*b*) -3.0×10^{-5} m/s^2

71 (*a*) 15 cm (*b*) 1300*g* to 2700*g*

72 1.1 m

73 $h = \dfrac{(v_0 \sin\theta_0)^2}{2g}$

74 42 m/s

75 34 m/s

76 76°

77 20.3 m/s, 36.1°

78 $v^2 = v_0^2 - 2gh$

79 69.3°

80 (*a*) 49 s (*b*) 12 km (*c*) 12 km

81 (*a*) 18 m/s (*b*) 13°

82 (*a*) 2.3 km (*b*) 43 s (*c*) 9.2 km

83 (*a*) 8.1 m/s (*b*) 23 m/s

84 0.41 km

85 –63.4°

86 (*a*) 2.8 m/s (*b*) The droplet is falling faster when it hits the spider.

87 (*a*) No (*b*) 0.34 m (*c*) 5.2 m

88 (*a*) 82 m (*b*) 0.10 km

89 (*a*) 0.97 s (*b*) 4.2 m (*c*) 13 m/s 70° below the horizontal

91 (*a*) 485 km (*b*) 1.70 km/s

92 (*a*) 194 m (*c*) 159 m, 22%

93 (*a*) 17 m (*b*) 46 m (*c*) 87 m

94 (*b*) 402 ft

95 (*b*) 80 m (*c*) 88 m. The approximate solution is smaller. The estimate ignores higher order terms and they are important when the differences are not small.

96 (*a*) 121 m/s (*b*) 150 m/s (*c*) 742 m (*d*) 168 m/s, 63.3° with the vertical

99 (*a*) 11 m/s (*b*) 3.1 s (*c*) $\vec{v} = (6.5\text{ m/s})\hat{i} + (-22\text{ m/s})\hat{j}$

100 (*a*) 18 m (*b*) 0.40 s (*c*) 5.2 m (*d*) 1.8 s

101 (*a*) 21.5 m/s (*b*) 3.53 s (*c*) 19.3 m/s

102 (*a*) 1.9° (*b*) 38 m/s

103 (*a*) 7.41 m/s (*b*) 0.756 s (*c*) 15.9 m/s, 17.5 m/s, 25.0°

104 (*a*) He should apply the brakes. (*b*) 14 m/s ≈ 50 km/h

105 (*a*) 0.785 m (*b*) 105 m

106 (*a*) 1.2 s (*b*) 4.3 m

107 (*a*) 1.1 m (*b*) 3.9 m

108 20.5 m/s

109 (*a*) 15 km (*b*) 54 s

110 (*a*) $\vec{\boldsymbol{v}}_{\text{t}} = (1.0\text{ m/s})\hat{\boldsymbol{i}} + (1.0\text{ m/s})\hat{\boldsymbol{j}}$ (*b*) $\vec{\boldsymbol{a}} = (2.0\text{ m/s}^2)\hat{\boldsymbol{i}} + (-3.5\text{ m/s}^2)\hat{\boldsymbol{j}}$
(*c*) $\vec{\boldsymbol{v}}(t) = [(1.0\text{ m/s}) + (2.0\text{ m/s})t]\hat{\boldsymbol{i}} + [(1.0\text{ m/s}) + (-3.5\text{ m/s}^2)t^2]\hat{\boldsymbol{j}}$
(*d*) $\vec{\boldsymbol{r}}(t) = [(4.0\text{ m}) + (1.0\text{ m/s})t + (1.0\text{ m/s}^2)t^2]\hat{\boldsymbol{i}} + [(3.0\text{ m}) + (1.0\text{ m/s})t + (-1.8\text{ m/s}^2)t^2]\hat{\boldsymbol{j}}$

111 $\vec{\boldsymbol{v}}_{\text{BA}} = (-400\text{ mi/h})\hat{\boldsymbol{i}} + (700\text{ mi/h})\hat{\boldsymbol{j}}$

112 (*a*) 2.47 s (*b*) 15.3 m

113 4th step

114 (*a*) 1.41*L* (*b*) 1.73*L* (*c*) 1.62*L*

115 (*a*) $v_{\text{min}} > \dfrac{x}{\cos\theta}\sqrt{\dfrac{g}{2(x\tan\theta - h)}}$ (*b*) $v_{\text{min}} > 26\ \text{m/s}$ or $58\ \text{mi/h}$

116 (*a*) 0.98 km/h at $\theta = 241°$ (*b*) 39.6° west of north (*c*) 3.3 h ≈ 3 h 18 min

119 (*a*) 26 m/s (*b*) 7.8°

120 $v_{x,\text{Bug}} = -36\ \text{cm/s}$, $v_{y,\text{Bug}} = -66\ \text{cm/s}$

121 52.9 km, 52.8° east of north

122 42 s

Chapter 4
Newton's Laws

1 Yes, there are forces acting on it. They are the same as those that would act on it if it was sitting on your table at home.

2 You are in a non-inertial frame that is accelerating to the east, opposite the other car's apparent acceleration.

3 In the limo you hold one end of the string and suspend the object from the other end. If the string remains vertical, the reference frame of the limo is an inertial reference frame.

4 Yes, the object must have an acceleration relative to the inertial frame of reference. According to Newton's first and second laws, an object must accelerate, relative to any inertial reference frame, in the direction of the net force. If there is "only a single nonzero force," then this force is the net force.

Yes, the object's velocity may be momentarily zero in some inertial reference frame and not in another. During the period in which the force is acting, the object may be momentarily at rest, but its velocity cannot remain zero because it must continue to accelerate. Thus, its velocity is always changing.

5 No. Predicting the direction of the subsequent motion correctly requires additional information.

6 (*c*)

7 The mass of the probe is constant. However, the solar system will attract the probe with a gravitational force.

8 You could use a calibrated spring (a spring with a known stiffness constant) to pull on each astronaut and measure their resulting acceleration. Then you could use Newton's second law to calculate their mass.

9 Your apparent weight is the reading of a scale. If the acceleration of the elevator (and you) is directed upward, the normal force exerted by the scale on you is greater than your weight. You could be moving down but slowing or moving up and speeding up. In both cases your acceleration is upward.

10 Because you are moving with constant velocity, your frame of reference is an inertial reference frame. In an inertial reference frame there are no fictitious forces. Thus moving or not moving, the ball will follow the same trajectory in your reference frame. The net force on the ball is the same, so its acceleration is the same.

11 The most significant force in our everyday world is gravity. It literally keeps us on or near the ground. The other most common force is the electromagnetic force. It provides the "glue" to hold solids together and make them rigid. It is of great importance in electric circuits.

12 (*a*) Any object for which the vector sum of the three forces doesn't add to zero. For example, a sled on a frictionless surface pulled horizontally. The normal force plus the weight plus the pulling force do not add to zero, so the sled accelerates.

(*b*) Pulling a fish vertically upward at constant velocity while it is still in the water. The forces acting on the fish are the pull, the weight of the fish, and water drag forces. These forces add up to zero.

(*c*) The three forces need to add vectorially to zero. An example is a picture hung by two wires.

13 (*a*) Normal force, contact, (*b*) Normal force, contact, (*c*) Normal force, contact, (*d*) Normal force, contact, (*e*) Gravitational force, action-at-a-distance

The two normal forces that the two blocks exert on each other and the two normal forces that the table and the bottom block exert on each other

14

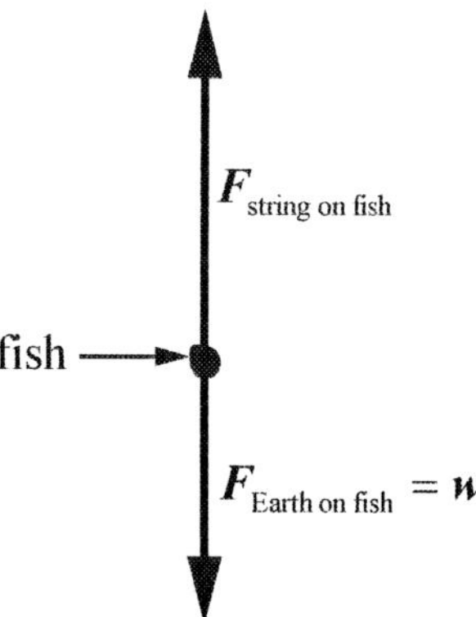

Force	Type	Category
$\vec{F}_{\text{string on fish}}$	Tension	Contact
$\vec{F}_{\text{Earth on fish}}$	Gravity	Action-at-a-distance

Because the fish accelerates upward, the tension force must be greater in magnitude than the gravitational force acting on the fish.

15 When the plate is sitting on the table, the normal force F_{n} acting upward on it is exerted by the table and is the same size as the gravitational force F_g acting on the plate. Hence, the plate does not accelerate. However, to slow the plate down as it hits the table requires that $F_{\text{n}} > F_g$ (or $F_{\text{n}} >> F_g$ if the table is hard and the plate slows quickly). A large normal force exerted on delicate china can easily break it.

16 (*a*) You produce this force. It acts on the briefcase. It acts upward. The reaction force is the force the briefcase exerts on your hand.
(*b*) The floor produces this force. It acts on your feet. It acts upward. The reaction force is the force your feet exert on the floor.
(*c*) Earth produces this force. It acts on you. It acts downward. The reaction force is the gravitational force you exert on Earth.
(*d*) The bat produces this force. It acts on the ball. It acts horizontally. The reaction force is the force the ball exerts on the bat.

17 (*a*) The normal force of the block on the sprinter, in the forward direction.
(*b*) The frictional force by the ice on the puck, in the opposite direction to the velocity.
(*c*) The gravitation force by Earth on the ball, in the downward direction.
(*d*) The force exerted by the bungee cord on the jumper, in the upward direction.

18 (*a*) True. By definition, third law pairs cannot act on the same object.
(*b*) False. Action and reaction forces are equal independently of any motion of the involved objects.

19 (*a*) (2) 100 N, (*b*) Their accelerations will be the same. (*c*) The directions of their acceleration are the same.

20 (*a*) False. If the rock is accelerating, the force the girl exerts must be greater than the weight of the stone.
(*b*) False. The reaction force to the pull of gravity is the force the rock exerts on Earth.
(*c*) True. These forces constitute a Newton's third law pair.
(*d*) False. If she moves the stone downward at a constant speed, the net force acting on the stone must be zero.
(*e*) False. If she is slowing the stone, it is experiencing acceleration and the net force acting on it can not be zero. The force of her hand on the stone, which has the same magnitude as the force of the stone on her hand, is greater than the force of gravity on the stone.

21

(*a*)

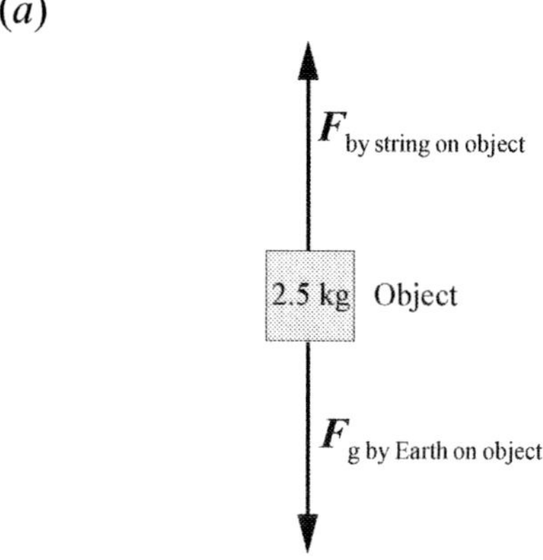

Force	Third-Law Pair
$\vec{F}_{\text{by string on object}}$	$\vec{F}_{\text{by object on string}}$
$\vec{F}_{\text{g by Earth on object}}$	$\vec{F}_{\text{by object on Earth}}$

(*b*)

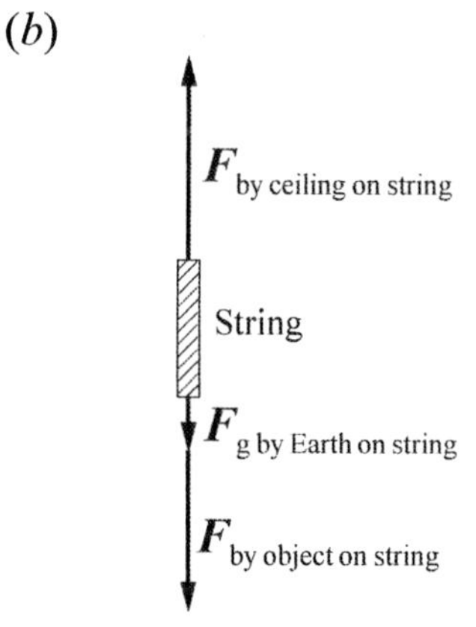

Force	Third-Law Pair
$\vec{F}_{\text{by ceiling on string}}$	$\vec{F}_{\text{by string on ceiling}}$
$\vec{F}_{\text{by Earth on string}}$	$\vec{F}_{\text{by string on Earth}}$
$\vec{F}_{\text{by object on string}}$	$\vec{F}_{\text{by string on object}}$

22 (*a*) (*c*)

(*b*)

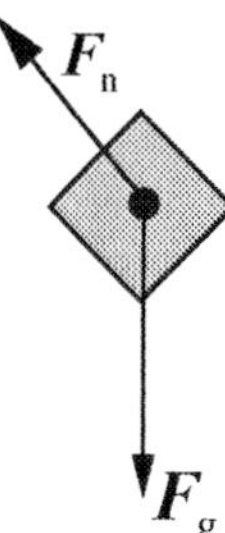

Because the incline is frictionless, the force $\vec{F}_n$ the incline exerts on the block must be normal to the surface and is a contact force. The second object capable of exerting a force on the block is the earth and its force; the gravitational force $\vec{F}_g$ acting on the block acts directly downward and is an action-at-a-distance force. The magnitude of the normal force is less than that of the weight because it supports only a portion of the weight.

(*c*) The reaction to the normal force is the force the block exerts perpendicularly on the surface of the incline. The reaction to the gravitational force is the upward force the block exerts on Earth.

23 (*a*)

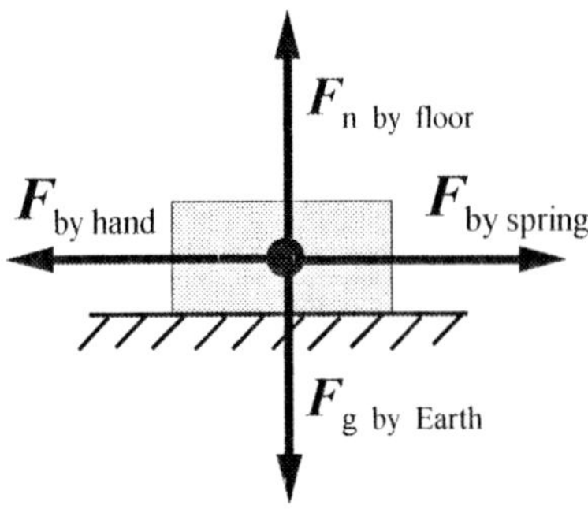

(*b*)

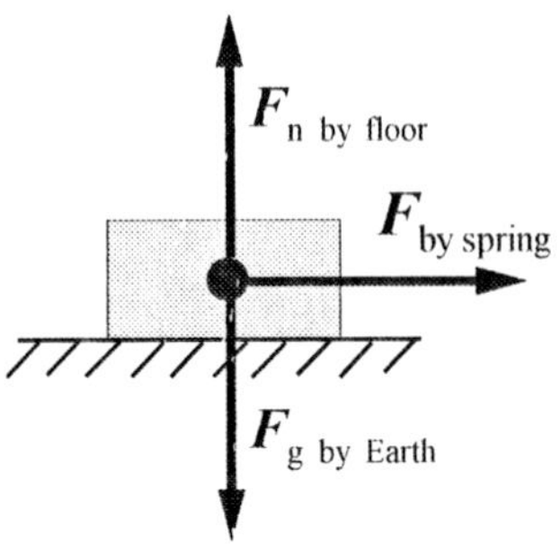

(*c*)

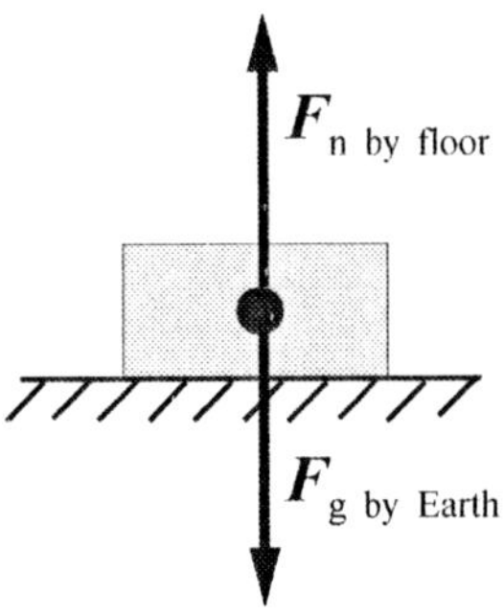

24

(*a*) Newton's third law accounts for this as follows. When you push with your hands against the desk, the desk pushes back on your hands with a force of the same magnitude but opposite direction. This force accelerates you backward.

(*b*) The reaction force to the force that caused your acceleration is the force that you exerted on the desk.

(*c*) When you pushed on the desk, you did not apply sufficient force to overcome the force of friction between the desk and the floor. In terms of forces on the desk, you applied a force, and the floor applied a friction force that, when added as vectors, cancelled. The desk, therefore, did not accelerate and Newton's third law is not violated.

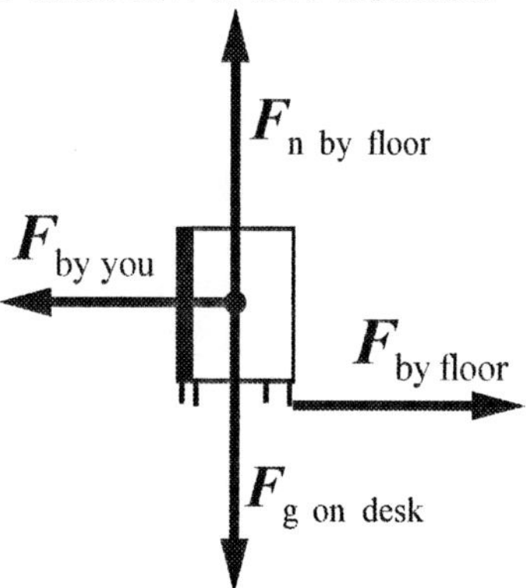

25 (*a*) m_2/m_1 (*b*) m_2/m_1 (*c*) $\Delta x = \frac{1}{2}F\left(\frac{1}{m_2} - \frac{1}{m_1}\right)(\Delta t)^2$. Because $m_1 > m_2$, the object whose mass is m_2 is ahead.

26 150 N/cm

27 3.6 kN

28 1.4 kN

29 −17 kN

30 (*a*) Opposite the original velocity (*b*) 5.00 s (*c*) 3.00 kg

31 (*a*) 6.0 m/s^2 (*b*) 1/3 (*c*) 2.3 m/s^2

32 $F_2 = 3F_1$

33 12 kg

34 $\vec{a} = (4.0\,\text{m/s}^2)\,\hat{\imath} - (2.0\,\text{m/s}^2)\hat{\jmath}$

35 (*a*) −3.8 kN (*b*) 3.00 cm

36 (*a*) 0.0514 N (*b*) 6.49 s

37 (*a*) 4.2 m/s^2 @ 45° from each force (*b*) 8.4 m/s^2 @ 15° from $2\vec{F}$

38 (*a*) −0.30 m/s (*b*) 0.38 m/s

39 (*a*) 4.0 m/s^2 (*b*) 2.4 m/s^2

40

(*a*)

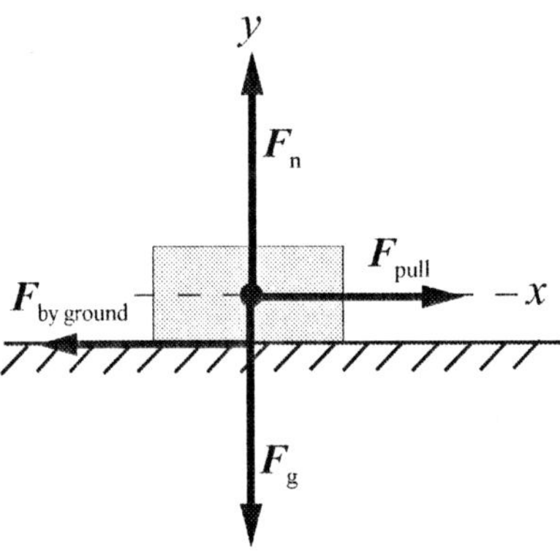

(*b*) 259 N
(*c*) 736 N
(*d*) 400 N

41 (*a*) $\vec{a} = (1.5\,\text{m/s}^2)\hat{\imath} + (-3.5\,\text{m/s}^2)\hat{\jmath}$ (*b*) $\vec{v}(3.0\,\text{s}) = (4.5\,\text{m/s})\hat{\imath} + (-11\,\text{m/s})\hat{\jmath}$
(*c*) $\vec{r}(3.0\,\text{s}) = (6.8\,\text{m})\hat{\imath} + (-16\,\text{m})\hat{\jmath}$

42 (*c*)

43 (*a*) 5.3×10^2 N (*b*) 1.2×10^2 lb

44 74.8 kg

45 (*a*) 2.45 kN (*b*) 409 N (*c*) 2.04 kN

46

(*a*) 0.67 kg

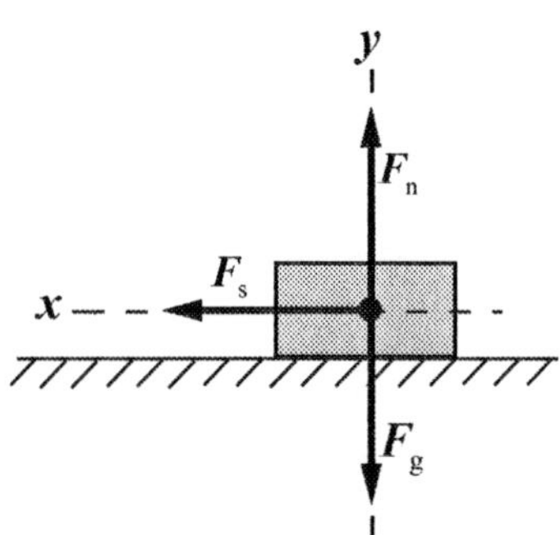

(*b*) Because the object's mass is the same on the moon as on Earth and the force exerted by the spring is the same, its acceleration on the moon would be same as on Earth.

47

(*a*)

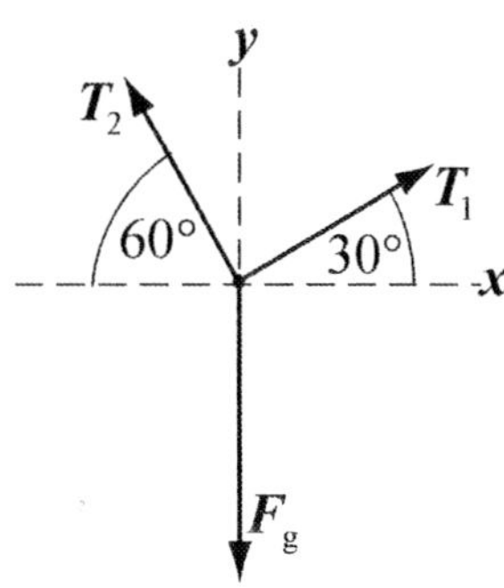

(*b*) T_2 is greater than T_1

48 (*b*)

49 (*a*) 37° (*b*) 4.1 N (*c*) $T_1 = 3.4$ N, $\boldsymbol{T}_2 = 2.4\,\text{N}$, $\boldsymbol{T}_3 = 3.4\,\text{N}$

50 $T_{\text{hor}} = 100$ N, $T_{45} = 141$ N

51 $\vec{\boldsymbol{F}}_3 = (-5.0\,\text{N})\hat{\boldsymbol{i}} + (-26\,\text{N})\hat{\boldsymbol{j}}$

52 (*a*) $T_1 = 60$ N, $T_2 = 52$ N, $m = 5.3$ kg
(*b*) $T_1 = 46$ N, $T_2 = 46$ N, $m = 4.7$ kg
(*c*) $T_1 = 34$ N, $T_2 = 59$ N, $T_3 = 34$ N, $m = 3.5$ kg

53 (*a*) 3.82 kN (*b*) 4.30 kN

55

(*a*)

Cell	Content/Formula	Algebraic Form
C9	($B$2-2*B9)/(2*$B$4)	$(N-2\mathrm{i})\dfrac{F}{2T_{\mathrm{H}}}$
D9	SIN(ATAN(C9))	$\sin\left(\tan^{-1}\theta_{\mathrm{i}}\right)$
E9	COS(ATAN(C9))	$\cos\left(\tan^{-1}\theta_{\mathrm{i}}\right)$
F9	0.000	0
G9	0.000	0
F10	F9+$B$1/($B$2+1)*E9	$x_{\mathrm{i}-1}+\dfrac{L}{N+1}\cos\theta_{\mathrm{i}-1}$
G10	G9+$B$1/($B$2+1)*D9	$y_{\mathrm{i}-1}+\dfrac{L}{N+1}\cos\theta_{\mathrm{i}-1}$

	A	B	C	D	E	F	G
1	$L=$	10	m				
2	$N=$	10					
3	$F=$	1	N				
4	$T_{\mathrm{H}}=$	3.72	N				
5							
6							
7							
8		i	$\tan(\theta_{\mathrm{i}})$	$\sin(\theta_{\mathrm{i}})$	$\cos(\theta_{\mathrm{i}})$	x_{i}	y_{i}
9		0	1.344	0.802	0.597	0.000	0.000
10		1	1.075	0.732	0.681	0.543	0.729
11		2	0.806	0.628	0.778	1.162	1.395
12		3	0.538	0.474	0.881	1.869	1.966
13		4	0.269	0.260	0.966	2.670	2.396
14		5	0.000	0.000	1.000	3.548	2.632
15		6	−0.269	−0.260	0.966	4.457	2.632
16		7	−0.538	−0.474	0.881	5.335	2.396
17		8	−0.806	−0.628	0.778	6.136	1.966
18		9	−1.075	−0.732	0.681	6.843	1.395
19		10	−1.344	−0.802	0.597	7.462	0.729
20		11				8.005	0.000

(*b*) A horizontal component of tension 3.72 N gives a spacing of 8 m. At this spacing, the arch is 2.63 m high, tall enough for someone to walk through.

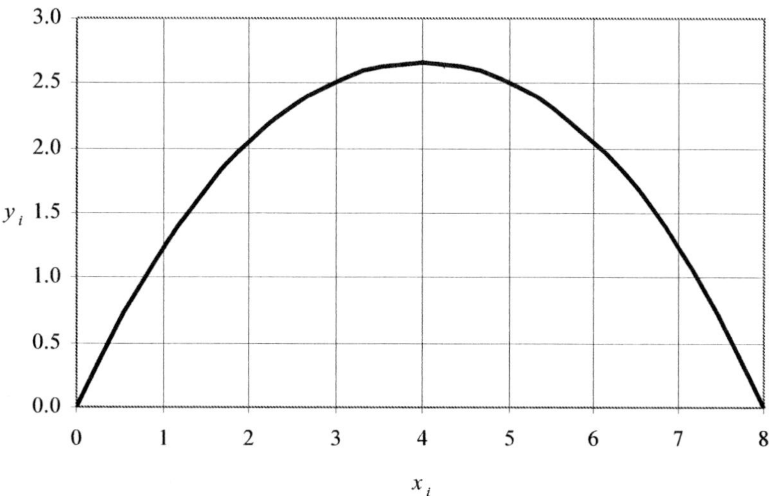

The spreadsheet graph shown below shows that changing the horizontal component of tension to 5 N broadens the arch and decreases its height as predicted by our mathematical model.

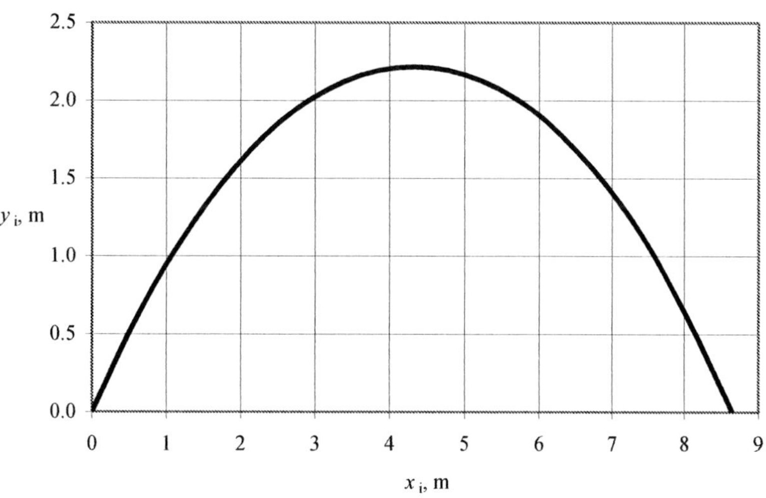

56

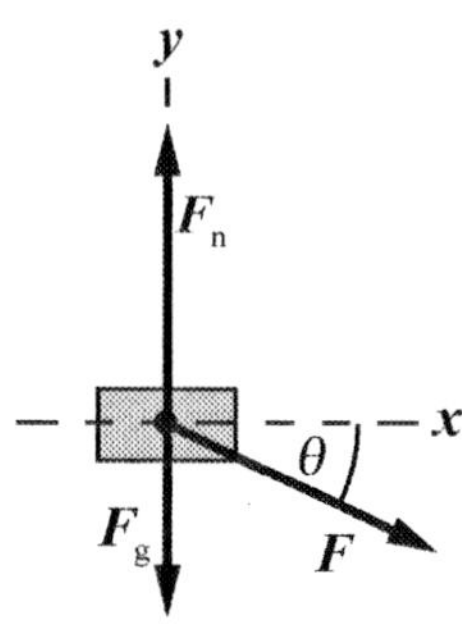

$$a = 10.2 \text{ m/s}^2$$

57 56.0 N

58 (*a*) 98 N (*b*) 98 N (*c*) 49 N (*d*) 98 N

59 (*a*) $T = 0.43$ kN, $F_n = 0.25$ kN (*b*) $T = mg\sin\theta$

60 (*a*) 1.5×10^2 N (*b*) $a = 3.4$ m/s^2

61 0.55 kN

62 $h = \dfrac{v_0^2}{2g}$

63

(*a*)

(*b*)

(*c*) No, there is no difference.

64 5.19 m/s^2

65 (*a*) 20 N (*b*) 20 N (*c*) 26 N (*d*) $\boldsymbol{T}_{0\to 5.0\text{s}} = 20\,\text{N}$, $\boldsymbol{T}_{5\text{s}\to 9\text{s}} = 15\,\text{N}$

66

(*a*)

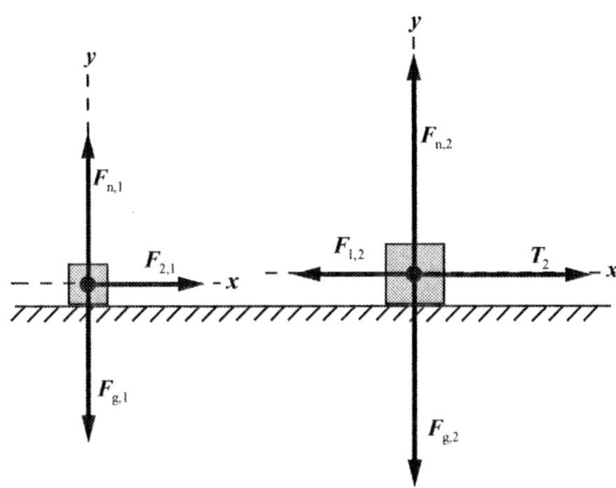

67 (*a*) 1.3 m/s^2 (*b*) $T_1 = 17$ N, $T_2 = 21$ N

68 (*a*) $a = \dfrac{F}{m_1 + m_2}$, $F_{1,2} = \dfrac{Fm_2}{m_1 + m_2}$ (*b*) 0.40 m/s^2, 2.4 N

69 (*a*) $a = \dfrac{F}{m_1 + m_2}$, $F_{2,1} = \dfrac{Fm_1}{m_1 + m_2}$ (*b*) 0.40 m/s^2, 0.8 N

70 $F = 202$ N, $F_{2,1} = 100$ N, $F_{3,2} = 101$ N, $F_{4,3} = 201$ N

72 (*a*) 6.2 N (*b*) 0.25 N (*c*) $F_2 = 4.9$ N, $F_3 = 3.7$ N, $F_4 = 2.5$ N, $F_5 = 1.2$ N

73

(*a*)

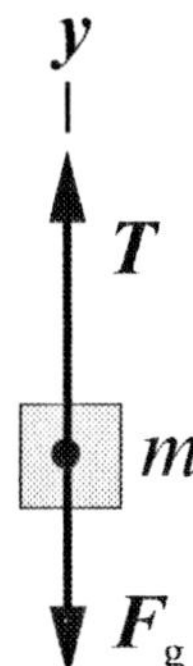

(*b*) 592 N

74

(*a*)

(*b*) 47.2 kN (*c*) 224 kN

75 (*a*) $a = \dfrac{g(m_2 - m_1 \sin\theta)}{m_1 + m_2}$, $T = \dfrac{g m_1 m_2 (1 + \sin\theta)}{m_1 + m_2}$ (*b*) 2.5 m/s2, 37 N

76 (*a*) 48 kg (*b*) 0.42 kN

77 (*a*) 1.4 m/s^2, 61 N (*b*) $\dfrac{m_1}{m_2} = 1.19$

78 (*a*) 10 m/s^2 (*b*) $T = 60\,\text{N} + (8.0\,\text{N/m})x$

79 (*a*) 0.40 kN (*b*) 0.37 kN

80 $a_{10} = 1.1$ m/s^2, $a_{20} = -1.1$ m/s^2, $T = 45$ N

81 (*a*) 5.0 cm (*b*) $a_{20} = 2.5$ m/s^2, $a_5 = 4.9$ m/s^2, $T = 25$ N

82

(*a*)

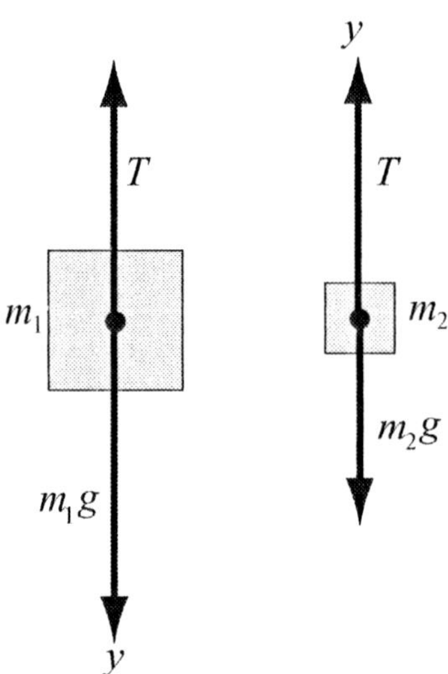

83 $m_{\text{2nd mass}} = 1.4\,\text{kg or } 1.1\,\text{kg}$

84 (*a*) $g = \frac{2L}{t^2}\left(\frac{m_1 + m_2}{m_1 - m_2}\right)$

85 $F_{\text{on } m_2} = \left(\frac{2mm_1}{m + m_1 + m_2}\right)g$

86 (*b*) The suspended object will be positioned below and ahead (by 9.3°) of point *P* during the braking.

87 $T_{\text{B}} = 305\,\text{N}$, $F_{\text{mast on the deck}} = 1.55\,\text{kN}$

88 (*a*) 0.49 kN (*b*) 0.59 kN (*c*) 0.69 kN

89 (*a*) -0.10 km/s^2 (*b*) 15 cm (*c*) 55 ms

90

(*a*)

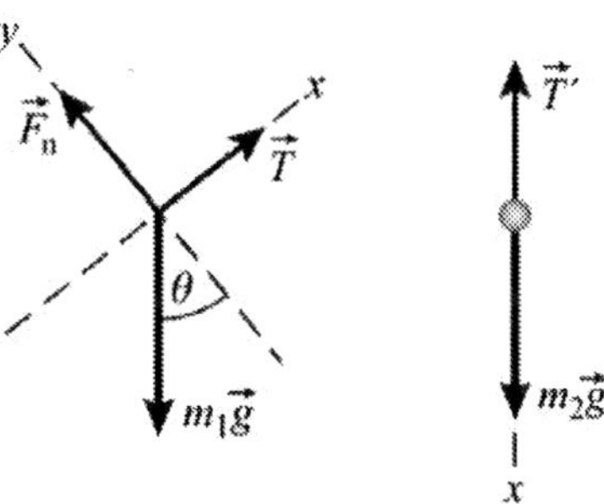

(*b*) -1.71 m/s^2, 0.864 N (*c*) 1.08 s Because the block is released from rest and its acceleration is negative, it will slide down the incline.

91 (*a*) $a = \frac{F}{m_1 + m_2}$ (*b*) $F_{\text{net}} = \frac{m_2}{m_1 + m_2}F$ (*c*) $T = \frac{m_1}{m_1 + m_2}F$

92

(*a*) 17 m/s^2

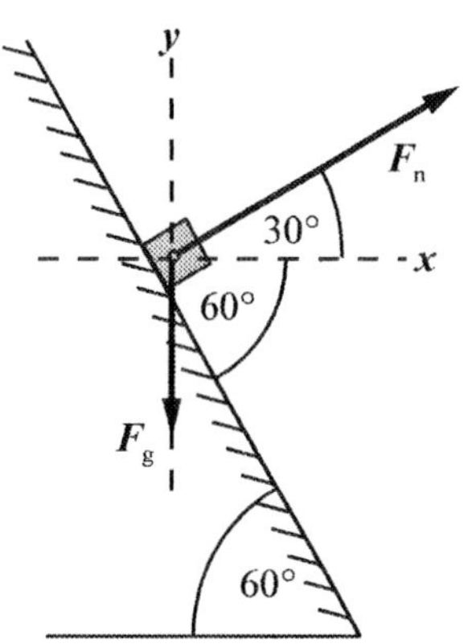

(*b*) Under this condition, there would be a net force in the *y* direction and the block would accelerate up the wedge.

93 (*a*) 55.0 g (*b*) 2.45 m/s^2, 2.03 N

94 3

95 (*a*) $T = \frac{1}{3}(F_2 + 2F_1)$ (*b*) $t_0 = \dfrac{3T_0}{4C}$

96 (*a*) 115 kg (*b*) 115 kg (*c*) 3.75 m/s^2 (*d*) $g_{\text{Pluto}} = 0.30 g_{\text{Moon}}$

97 (*a*) You should throw your boot in the direction away from the closest shore. (*b*) 420 N (*c*) 7.52 s

98 $a_2 = \dfrac{(m_1 - m_2)g + 2m_1 a}{m_1 + m_2}$, $a_1 = \dfrac{(m_2 - m_1)g + 2m_2 a}{m_1 + m_2}$, $T = \dfrac{2m_1 m_2}{m_1 + m_2} g$

99

(*a*)

Cell	Content/Formula	Algebraic Form
C1	650	m
D5	(B5–B4)/2	$\frac{1}{2}\Delta t$
E5	(C5–C4)/D5	$\dfrac{\Delta v}{\Delta t}$
F5	$D$1*E5	ma
F10	(F5+F6+F7+F8+F9)/5	F_{ave}

	A	B	C	D	E	F
1			*m*=	650	kg	
2						
3		*t* (s)	*v* (m/s)	t_{midpt} (s)	*a* (m/s^2)	*F*=*ma* (N)
4		0.0	0			
5		1.8	10	0.90	5.56	3611
6		2.8	20	2.30	10.00	6500
7		3.6	30	3.20	12.50	8125
8		4.9	40	4.25	7.69	5000
9		6.5	50	5.70	6.25	4063
10						5460
11						

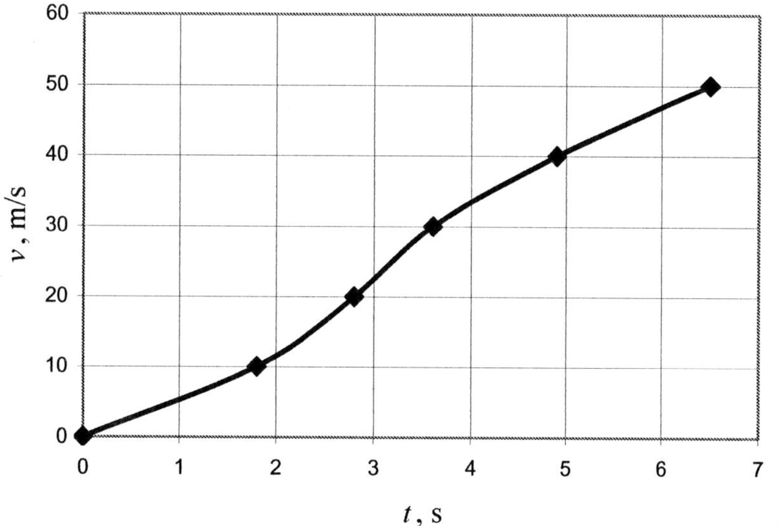

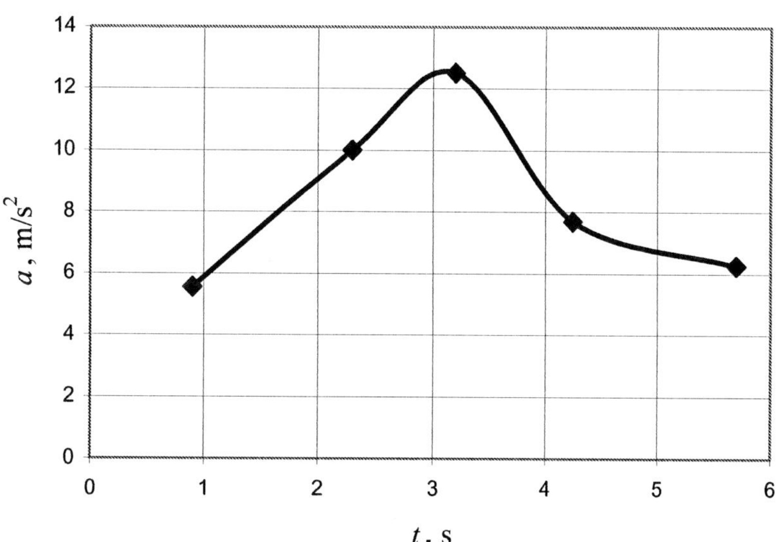

(*b*) 2.8 s to 3.6 s.
(*c*) 5500 N
(*d*) 160 m

Chapter 5
Additional Applications of Newton's Laws

1 Static and kinetic frictional forces are responsible for the accelerations. If the coefficient of static friction between the truck bed and the object is sufficiently large, then the object will not slip on the truck bed. The larger the acceleration of the truck, the larger the coefficient of static friction that is needed to prevent slipping.

2 Because a_x is independent of m and F_g, the critical accelerations are the same.

3 (*d*)

4 (*d*)

5 (*c*)

6

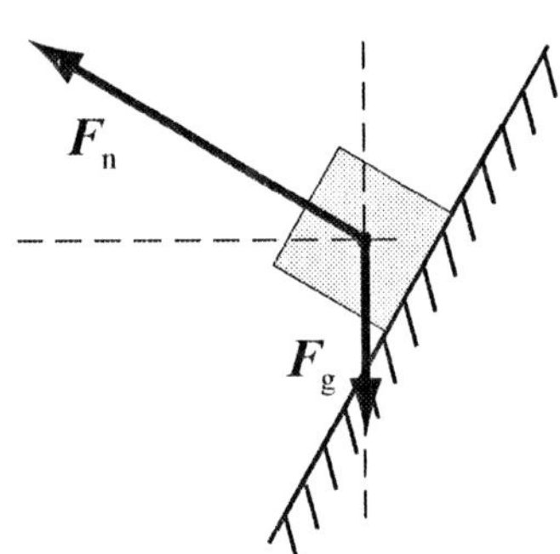

The horizontal component of $\vec{F}_n$ is responsible for the centripetal force on the block.

7 As the spring is extended, the force exerted by the spring on the block increases. Once that force exceeds the maximum value of the force of static friction, the block will slip. As it does, it will shorten the length of the spring, decreasing the force that the spring exerts. The force of kinetic friction then slows the block to a stop, which starts the cycle over again.

8 (*a*) True (*b*) False (*c*) False

9 (*a*), (*b*), and (*c*)

10

(*a*) Demonstration 1:

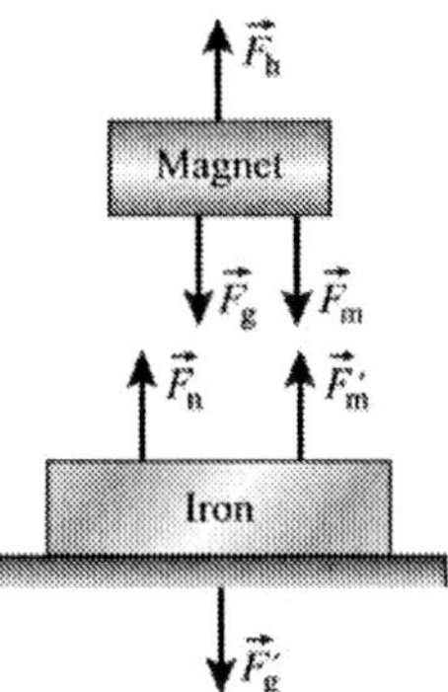

Demonstration 2:

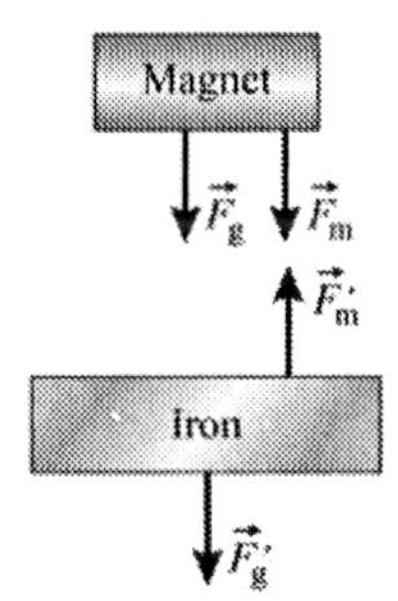

(*b*) Because the magnet doesn't lift the iron in the first demonstration, the force exerted on the iron must be less than its (the iron's) weight. This is still true when the two are falling, but the motion of the iron is not restrained by the table, and the motion of the magnet is not restrained by the hand. Looking at the second diagram, the net force pulling the magnet down is greater than its weight, implying that its acceleration is greater than g. The opposite is true for the iron: the magnetic force acts upwards, slowing it down, so its acceleration will be less than g. Because of this, the magnet will catch up to the iron piece as they fall.

11 Block 1 will hit the pulley before block 2 hits the wall.

12 Air drag depends on the frontal area presented. Reducing it by crumpling the paper makes the force of air drag a lot less so that gravity is the most important force. The paper will thus accelerate at approximately g (until speeds are high enough for drag forces to come back into play in spite of the reduced area).

13 Air drag is proportional to the density of air and to the cross-sectional area of the object. On a warm day the air is less dense. The air is also less dense at high altitudes. Pointing his hands results in less area being presented to air drag forces and, hence, reduces them. Rounded and sleek clothing has the same effect as pointing his hands.

14 In your frame of reference (the accelerating reference frame of the car), the direction of the force must point toward the center of the circular path along which you are traveling; that is, in the direction of the centripetal force that keeps you moving in a circle. The friction between you and the seat you are sitting on supplies this force. The reason you seem to be "pushed" to the outside of the curve is that your body's inertia "wants", in accordance with Newton's first law (the law of inertia), to keep it moving in a straight line–that is, tangent to the curve.

15 (*c*)

16 Point A: Free-body diagram 3
Point B: Free-body diagram 4
Point C: Free-body diagram 5
Point D: Free-body diagram 2

17 (*a*) The drag force is proportional to the area presented and some power of the speed. The drag force on the feather is larger because the feather presents a larger area than does the rock. As the rock gains speed, the drag force on it increases. The drag force on the rock eventually exceeds the drag force on the feather because the drag force on the feather cannot exceed the gravitational force on the feather.

(*b*) Terminal speed is much higher for the rock than for the feather. The acceleration of the rock will remain high until its speed approaches its terminal speed.

18 (*b*)

19 The acceleration of m_1 is greater.

20 There is only one force that can cause the car to move forward–the friction of the road! The car's engine causes the tires to rotate, but if the road were frictionless (as is closely approximated by icy conditions) the wheels would simply spin without the car moving anywhere. Because of friction, the car's tire pushes backwards against the road–from Newton's third law, the frictional force acting on the tire must then push it forward. This may seem odd, as we tend to think of friction as being a retarding force only, but it is true.

21 The friction of the road on the tire causes the car to slow down.

22 (*a*) A solid spherical shell, or donut, or tire
(*b*) A solid hemispherical shell
(*c*) Any sphere with one side a different density than the other, or a density variation that isn't radially symmetric

(*d*) Any stick with a non-uniform and non-symmetric density variation. A baseball bat is a good example of such a stick

23 The center of mass moves downward.

24 The spacecraft speed increased toward the moon. The speed of the third-stage booster decreased, but the booster continued to move away from Earth and toward the moon. Right after the explosion, the center of mass velocity was the same as before. After a while, however, the backward pull of gravity of Earth will cause it to decrease because the speeds of both the lunar ship and the booster decrease.

25 The acceleration of the center of mass is zero.

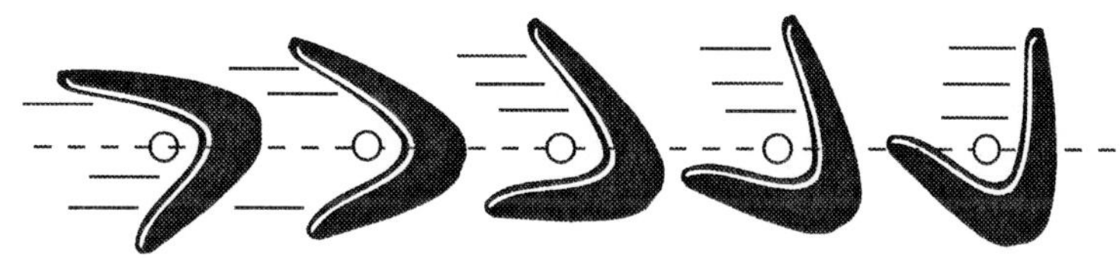

26 (*a*) 0.58 kN (*b*) 0.20 kN, 0.38 kN (*c*) 0.50

27 (*a*) M/T, kg/s (*b*) M/L, kg/m (*c*) ML/T^2 (*d*) 57 m/s (*e*) 87 m/s

28 $v_{t,r} = 3.3\,m/s$ and $v_{t,h} = 20\,m/s$

29 $\mu_s \approx 1.4$ This is probably not such a good idea. Tires on asphalt or concrete have a maximum coefficient of static friction of about 1.

30 The angle between your legs is about 28°.

31 (*b*)

32 (*e*)

33 (*a*) 15 N (*b*) 12 N

34 (*b*)

35 500 N

36 0.417

37 (*a*) 5.9 m/s^2 (*b*) 76 m

38 (*a*) Because $\mu_s > \mu_k$, *f* will be greater if the wheels do not slip. (*b*) 0.42

39 (*a*) 49.1 N (*b*) 123 N

40 (*a*) 2000 N, 0.102 (*b*) 772 m, 94.7 m (c) 0.830. Although 0.830 is a rather high value for a coefficient of static friction, it is possible that a car, equipped with good tires, could safely navigate this curve at the given speed.

41 (*a*) 4.6° (*b*) 4.6°

42 (*a*) Method 2 is preferable because it reduces F_n and, therefore, f_s.
(*b*) $F_1(30°) = 0.52\,\text{kN}$, $F_2(30°) = 0.25\,\text{kN}$, $F_1(0°) = 0.29\,\text{kN}$, $F_1(0°) = 0.29\,\text{kN}$

43 84 cm/s

44 (*a*) $0.61\text{kg} \le m_2 \le 3.4\text{kg}$ (*b*) 9.8 N

45 2.4 m/s^2, 37 N

46 0.21

47 (*a*) 4.0 m (*b*) 0.47

48 (*a*) 49 m (*b*) 0.11 km

49 (*a*) 2.7 m/s^2 (*b*) 10 s

50 (*a*) 16 m/s^2 (*b*) 20 N (*c*) 20 N (*d*) Because $a_{min} = g/\mu_s$, the box will not fall if $a \ge g/\mu_s$

51 (*a*) 0.96 m/s^2 (*b*) 0.18 N

52 (*a*) $a = g\left(\sin\theta - \frac{\mu_1 m_1 + \mu_2 m_2}{m_1 + m_2}\cos\theta\right)$ (*b*) $T = \left(\frac{m_1 m_2}{m_1 + m_2}\right)(\mu_1 - \mu_2)g\cos\theta$
If $\mu_1 = \mu_2$, $T = 0$ and the blocks move down the incline with the same acceleration of $g(\sin\theta - \mu\cos\theta)$. Inserting a stick between them can't change this; therefore, the stick must exert no force on either block.

53 (*a*) The static-friction force opposes the motion of the object, and the maximum value of the static-friction force is proportional to the normal force F_N. The normal force is equal to the weight minus the vertical component F_V of the force F. Keeping the magnitude F constant while increasing θ from zero results in a decrease in F_V and thus a corresponding decrease in the maximum static-frictional force f_{max}. The object will begin to move if the horizontal component F_H of the force F exceeds f_{max}. An increase in θ results in a decrease in F_H. As θ increases from 0, the decrease in F_N is larger than the decrease in F_H, so the object is more and more likely to slip. However, as θ approaches 90°, F_H approaches zero and no movement will be initiated. If F is large enough and if θ increases from 0, then at some value of θ the block will start to move.

(*b*)

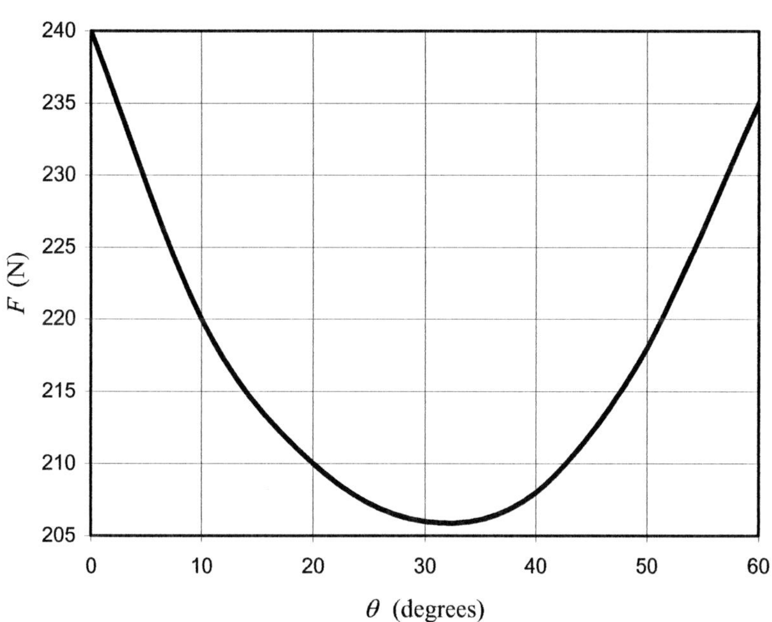

From the graph, we can see that the minimum value for F occurs when $\theta \approx 32°$.

54 (*c*) Once the block is moving, the coefficient of friction will decrease, so the angle can be decreased.

56 (*a*) 80.0 N (*b*)$F_{net} = 600$ N, $F = 680$ N (*c*) 6.80 m/s^2

57 (*a*) 0.24 (*b*) 1.4 m/s^2

58 (*a*) 6.1 m/s^2 (*b*) $-10\,\text{m/s}^2$

59 (*a*) 18 N (*b*) 1.5 m/s^2, 2.9 N (*c*) $a_1 = 2.0\,\text{m/s}^2$, $a_2 = 7.8\,\text{m/s}^2$

60 (*a*) 24 N (*b*) 1.6 m/s^2

61 (*a*) 5.7° (*b*) 1.9 m/s

62 (*a*) $0 \le m \le 12$ kg (*b*) 50 kg $\le m \le$ 69 kg

63 (*a*) $F_{\min} = -1.6\,\text{kg}$, $F_{\max} = 84\text{ N}$ (*b*) $F_{\min} = 5.8\,\text{N}$ and $F_{\max} = 37\,\text{N}$ (The $+x$ direction is to the right.)

64

Cell	Formula/Content	Algebraic Form
C9	C8+$B$6	$t + \Delta t$
D9	D8+F9*$B$6	$v + a\Delta t$
E9	$B$5–($B$3)*($B$2)*$B$5/ (1+$B$4*D9^2)^2	$F - \dfrac{\mu_k mg}{\left(1+2.34\times10^{-4}v^2\right)^2}$
F9	E10/$B$5	F_{net}/m
G9	G9+D10*$B$6	$x + v\Delta t$
K9	0.5*5.922*I10^2	$\frac{1}{2}at^2$
L9	J10-K10	$x - x_2$

	A	B	C	D	E	F	G	H	I	J
1	g=	9.81	m/s^2							
2	$Coeff_1$=	0.11								
3	$Coeff_2$=	2.30E–04								
4	m=	10	kg							
5	$F_{applied}$=	70	N							
6	Δt=	0.05	s				t	x	x_2	$x-x_2$
7										
8										
9	t	v	F_{net}	a	x			μ=variable	μ=constant	
10	0.00	0.00			0.00		0.00	0.00	0.00	0.00
11	0.05	0.30	59.22	5.92	0.01		0.05	0.01	0.01	0.01
12	0.10	0.59	59.22	5.92	0.04		0.10	0.04	0.03	0.01
13	0.15	0.89	59.22	5.92	0.09		0.15	0.09	0.07	0.02
14	0.20	1.18	59.22	5.92	0.15		0.20	0.15	0.12	0.03
15	0.25	1.48	59.23	5.92	0.22		0.25	0.22	0.19	0.04
205	9.75	61.06	66.84	6.68	292.37		9.75	292.37	281.48	10.89
206	9.80	61.40	66.88	6.69	295.44		9.80	295.44	284.37	11.07
207	9.85	61.73	66.91	6.69	298.53		9.85	298.53	287.28	11.25
208	9.90	62.07	66.94	6.69	301.63		9.90	301.63	290.21	11.42
209	9.95	62.40	66.97	6.70	304.75		9.95	304.75	293.15	11.61
210	10.00	62.74	67.00	6.70	307.89		10.00	307.89	296.10	11.79

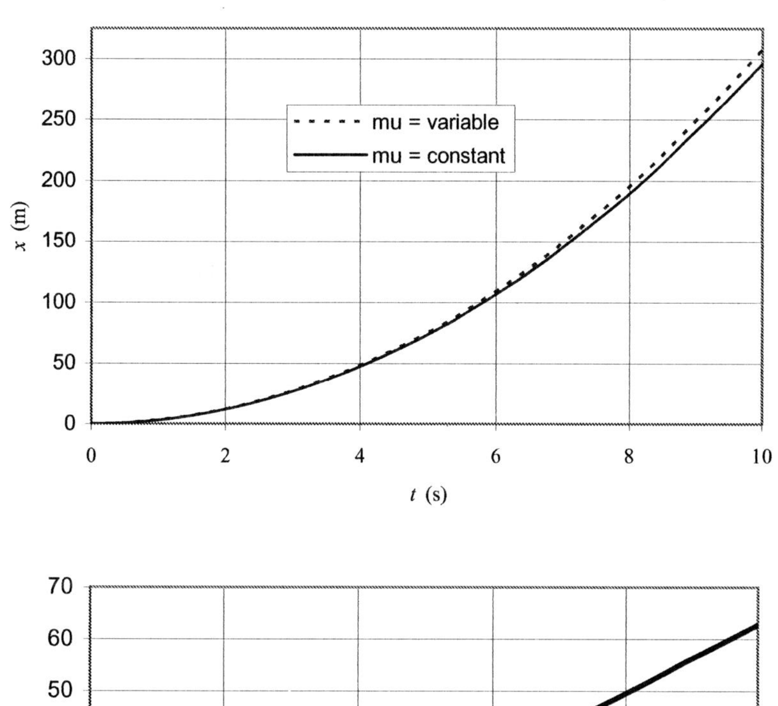

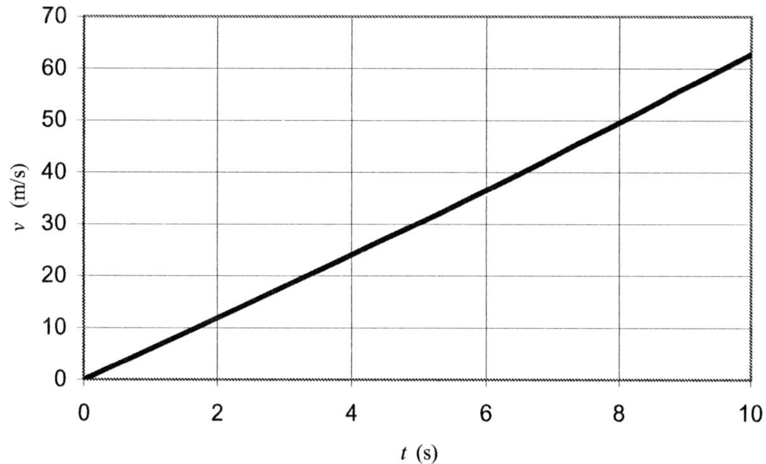

65 (*b*) 0.30 (*c*) 2.8 m/s

66

(*b*)

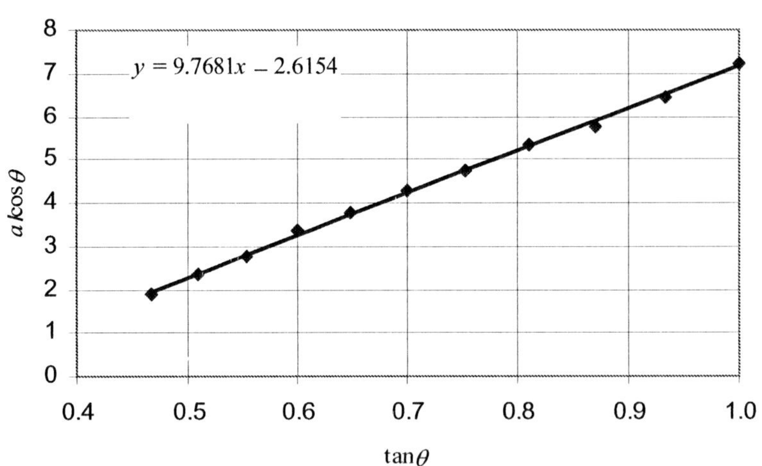

The percentage error in g from the commonly accepted value of 9.81 m/s^2 is 0.408%.

67 2.8×10^{-4} kg/m

68 3.3×10^{-9} kg/s

69 $d_{n\text{ filters}} = \sqrt{n}\, d_{1\text{ filter}}$

70 (*a*) 0.59 kN (*b*) 0.94 kg/m (c) 4.41 m/s^2, downward

71 25 m/s

72 (*a*) 2.42 cm/s (*b*) 1.15 h

73 (*a*) About 38 ms (*b*) With the drag force in Problem 72 it takes about 86 times longer than it does using the centrifuge.

74 6.2 m/s

75 25°

76 4.5 m/s

77 (*a*) 1.4 m/s (*b*) 8.5 N

78 (*a*) $\dfrac{F_n}{mg} = 4.5$ (*b*) An observer in an inertial reference frame would see the pilot's blood continue to flow in a straight line tangent to the circle at the lowest point of the arc. The pilot accelerates upward away from this lowest point ant therefore it appears, from the reference frame of the plane, as though the blood accelerates downward.

79 (*a*) 8.33 m/s^2, upward (*b*) 667 N, upward (*c*) 1.45 kN, upward

80 $r = \dfrac{m_2 g T^2}{4\pi^2 m_1}$

81 $T_1 = [m_2(L_1 + L_2) + m_1 L_1](2\pi/T)^2$, $T_1 = m_2(L_1 + L_2)(2\pi/T)^2$

82

(*a*) and (*b*)

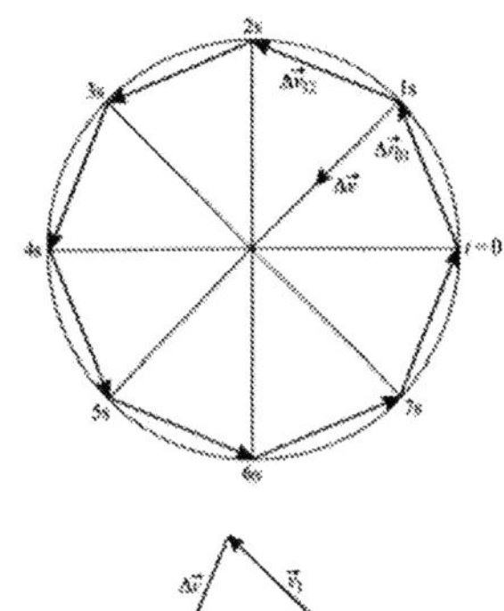

(*c*) $a = 2.3$ cm/s^2, $a_c = 2.5$ cm/s^2, $a_c = 1.1a$

83 (*a*) 53° above horizontal, 0.41 kN (*b*) 53° below horizontal

84 (*a*) 9.6° (*b*) 0.58 s

85 (*a*) 0.40 N (*b*) 0.644

86 (*a*) 2.6 N (*b*) 1.2 m/s

87 52°

88 15.9 m/s

89 12.8 m/s and 8.4 m/s

90 (*a*) 500 N, 0.0255 (*b*) 3.09 km, 108 m (*c*) 0.730

91 (*a*) 7.3 m/s (*b*) 0.54

92 2.2 km

93 22°

94 (*a*) 8.3 kN (*b*) 1.6 kN (*c*) 0.19

95 (*a*) 7.8 kN (*b*) −0.78 kN

96 0.18 km

97 20 km/h $\le v \le$ 56 m/h

98 The speed of the ball after 10 s is approximately 41.4 s. The uncertainty in this result is about 0.02%.

99 (*a*) About 60.4 m. (*b*) About 60.6 m (*c*) About 3.3 s (*d*) About 3.7 s (*e*) Less than

100 0.200 s, 2.44 m/s at that time, about 1.2%.

101 (0.23 cm, 0)

102 79 cm

103 (2.0 m, 1.4 m)

104 (0, 0.29*a*)

105 (1.5 m, 1.4 m)

106 (*a*) $x_{\text{cm}} = \frac{H}{2}\left(\frac{1+\left(\frac{x}{H}\right)^2}{1+\frac{x}{H}}\right)$ (*b*) $x_{\text{cm}}\big|_{x=H(\sqrt{2}-1)} = H\left(\sqrt{2}-1\right)$

107 $\left(\frac{1}{4}L, \frac{1}{4}L\right)$

108 $\left(\frac{1}{4}L(1+\cos\theta), \frac{1}{4}L\sin\theta\right)$

110 (24 cm, 0)

112 (*a*) At the end, the density has to be positive, so $A - cL > 0$ or $A > cL$.

(*b*) $\left(\dfrac{L}{2}\left(\dfrac{1-\dfrac{2cL}{3A}}{1-\dfrac{cL}{2A}}\right), 0\right)$ Because $A > cL$, both the numerator and denominator are positive. Because the denominator is always larger than the numerator, it follows that $x_{\text{cm}} < \frac{1}{2}L$. This makes physical sense because the mass of the rod decreases with distance and so most of it is to the left of the midpoint of the rod. Note also, that if $c = 0$, our result predicts a uniform density (of A) and the center of mass is at the midpoint of the rod (as it should be).

113 $\vec{v}_{\text{cm}} = (3.0\,\text{m/s})\hat{i} - (1.5\,\text{m/s})\hat{j}$

114 $\vec{v}_{\text{cm}} = (4.00\,\text{m/s})\,\hat{i}$

115 $\vec{a}_{\text{cm}} = (2.4\,\text{m/s}^2)\hat{i}$

116 (*a*) Yes; initially the scale reads $(M + m)g$; while the object whose mass is m is in free fall, the reading is Mg. (*b*) $\vec{a}_{\text{cm}} = -\dfrac{mg}{M+m}\hat{j}$ (*c*) Mg

117

(*a*)

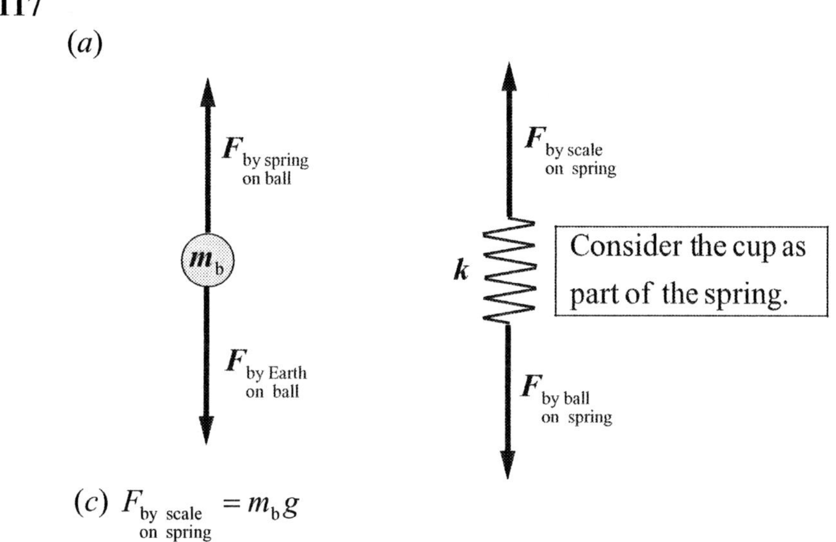

(*c*) $F_{\substack{\text{by scale}\\ \text{on spring}}} = m_{\text{b}}g$

118 (*a*) $a_{\text{cm}} = \dfrac{(m_1 - m_2)^2}{(m_1 + m_2)(m_1 + m_2 + m_{\text{c}})}g$ (*b*) $F = \left[\dfrac{4m_1m_2}{m_1 + m_2} + m_{\text{c}}\right]g$

(*c*) $F = 2T + m_{\text{c}}g$

119

(*a*)

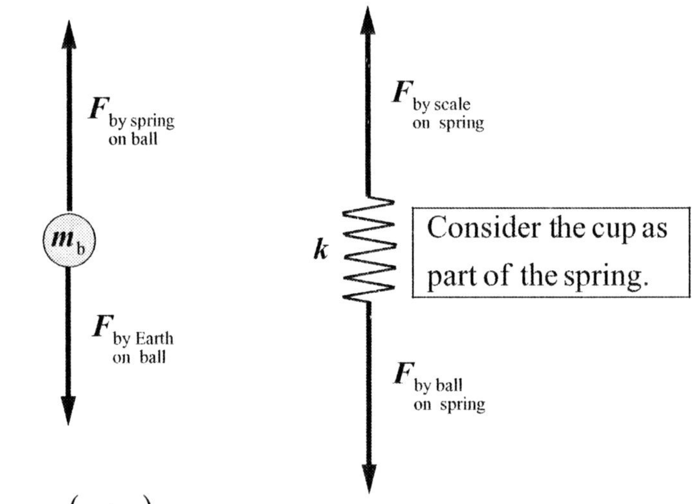

(*b*) $d' = \dfrac{m_b(g+a)}{k}$

(*c*) $F_{\substack{\text{by scale}\\ \text{on spring}}} = m_b(a+g)$

120 0.50

121 0.51

122 (*a*) 10.7 m/s (*b*) 8.10 N

123 1.49 kN

124 (*a*) $\dfrac{F_1}{\sin\theta_{23}} = \dfrac{F_2}{\sin\theta_{13}} = \dfrac{F_3}{\sin\theta_{12}}$

125 (*a*) 49 m/s^2 (*b*) 13 rev/min

126 $T = (m_1 + m_2)g\mu_s \cos\theta$

127 (*a*) 0.19 kN (*b*) 52 N (*c*) 35 N (*d*) 0.24 (*e*) 0.58 kN

128 (*c*) 1.4 rev/min

129 0.43

130 (*d*) $F_{\text{net}} = 13\pi^2$ N

131

(*a*)

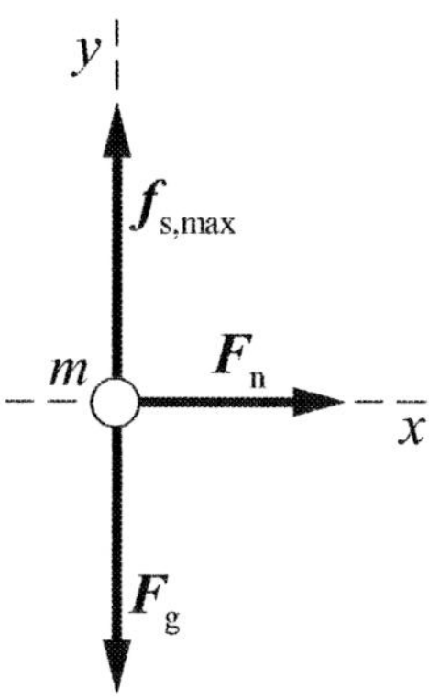

(*b*) 0.74 kN

(*c*) 20 rev/min . Because your mass does not appear in the expression for *N,* this result holds for all patrons, regardless of their mass.

132 1.2 kg, 0.67

133 Yes, Sally's claim seems to be supported by Liz's calculation.

134 (*a*) 9*g* (*b*) Because this acceleration exceed the safe acceleration by 4*g,* this is not a safe practice.

135 4.67×10^6 m. It is inside the surface of Earth.

136 $y_{\text{cm}} = \frac{1}{6}r$

137 (*a*) 35 cm (*b*) 4.7 m/s downward (*c*) 14.2 kN, 9.81 m/s^2, downward

138 (*a*) 4.5 m (*b*) 4.5 m (*c*) 2.5 m

139 (*a*) 4.91 m/s (*b*) 1.64 m/s downward (*c*) 1.09 m/s^2 downward

Chapter 6
Work and Kinetic Energy

1 (*a*) True (*b*) True (*c*) False (*d*) True (*e*) True

2 The normal and gravitational forces do zero work because they act at right angles to the box's direction of motion. You do positive work on the box and friction does negative work. Overall the net work is zero because its kinetic energy doesn't change (zero to zero).

3 (*a*) False (*b*) False (*c*) False (*d*) True

4 2

5 An object moving along a circular path at constant speed has constant kinetic energy but is accelerating (because its velocity is continually changing). No, because if the object is not accelerating, the net force acting on it must be zero and, consequently, its kinetic energy must be constant.

6 (*b*)

7 The work required to stretch a spring 2.0 cm is greater than the work required to stretch it 1.0 cm by a factor of 4.

8 3 times greater

9 (*d*)

11 (*a*) False (*b*) False (*c*) False (*d*) False

13 (*a*) False (*b*) False (*c*) True (*d*) True

14 (*a*) Yes. Any unit vectors that are not perpendicular to each other (as are $\hat{\boldsymbol{i}}$, $\hat{\boldsymbol{j}}$, and $\hat{\boldsymbol{k}}$) will have a scalar product different from zero.

(*b*) $\sqrt{\vec{\boldsymbol{v}}\cdot\vec{\boldsymbol{v}}} = \sqrt{v^2\cos 0^\circ} = v$ is the object's speed.

(*c*) Zero, because at the instant the ball leaves the horizontal table, $\vec{\boldsymbol{v}}$ and $\vec{\boldsymbol{a}}(=\vec{\boldsymbol{g}})$ are perpendicular.

(*d*) Positive, because the final velocity of the ball has a downward component in the direction of the acceleration.

15 $2\Delta t$

16 No, the laser power may only last for a short time interval.

17 The only external force (neglecting air resistance) that does center-of-mass work on the car is the static friction force $\vec{f}_s$ exerted by the road on the tires. The positive center-of-mass work this friction force does is translated into a gain of kinetic energy.

18 (*a*) -2.1×10^5 J (*b*) 2.1×10^5 J (*c*) 3.4 kW

19 (*a*) 4.5×10^{18} J (*b*) 1% (*c*) 1.4×10^{11} W

20 $K_{\text{orbital}} = 2$ TJ, $W_{\text{by gravity}} = 2$ TJ

21 21 kJ

22 (*a*) 11 kJ (*b*) 2.7 kJ (*c*) 43 kJ

23 (*a*) 147 J (*b*) 266 J

24 (*a*) 0.24 kJ (*b*) −0.18 kJ (*c*) 0.06 kJ

25 11 kJ, 3.5 kW

26 54 kg

27 (*a*) 6.0 J (*b*) 12 J (*c*) 3.5 m/s

28 (*a*) 2.8 J (*b*) 11 J (*c*) 2.8 m/s (*d*) 3.3 J (*e*) 2.8 m/s

30 (*a*) N/m^3 (*b*) 9.5 J (*c*) 13 m/s

31 (*a*) $m(y) = 20.0\,\text{kg} - \left(2.5\dfrac{\text{kg}}{\text{m}}\right)y$ (*b*) 0.59 kJ

32

(*a*) 76 J, 0

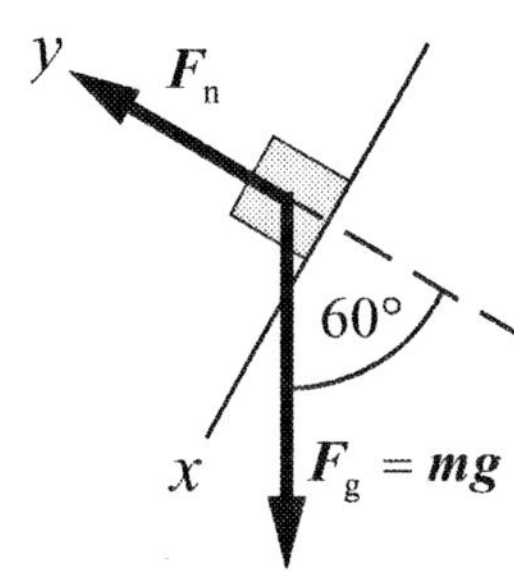

(*b*) 76 J (*c*) 5.0 m/s (*d*) 5.4 m/s

33

(*a*)

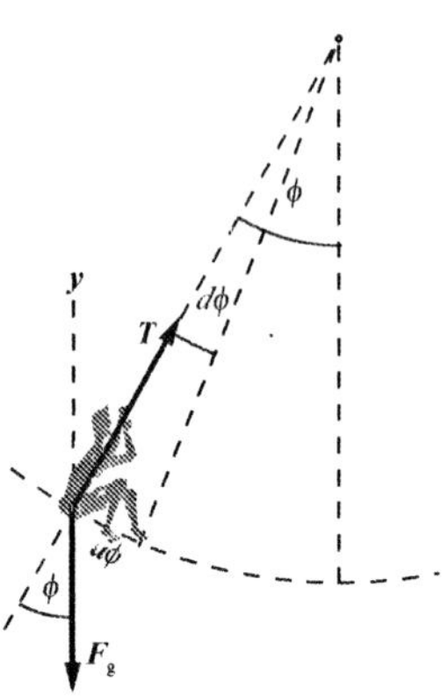

(*b*) $dW_{F_g} = -mg\ell \sin\phi \, d\phi$ (*c*) 2.5 kJ, 7.0 m/s

35 $W_{x_0 \to x} = \frac{A}{x_0} - \frac{A}{x}$, $K_{x \to \infty} = \frac{A}{x_0}$, $v_{x \to \infty} = \sqrt{\frac{2A}{mx_0}}$

36 (*a*) 2*h* (*b*) *wh* (*c*) *wh* (*d*) 2

37 180°

38 18 m^2

39 (*a*) −24 (*b*) −10 (*c*) 0

40 (*a*) 143° (*b*) 108° (*c*) 90°

41 (*a*) 1.0 J (*b*) 0.21 N

42 (*a*) $\hat{\boldsymbol{u}}_A = 0.82\hat{\boldsymbol{i}} - 0.41\hat{\boldsymbol{j}} - 0.41\hat{\boldsymbol{k}}$ (*b*) 0.40

43 (*b*) $\vec{\boldsymbol{B}} = \pm 6\hat{\boldsymbol{i}} \pm 8\hat{\boldsymbol{j}}$ No.

44 (*a*) $A_x = \cos\theta_1$, $A_y = \sin\theta_1$ and $B_x = \cos\theta_2$, $B_y = \sin\theta_2$

45 (*b*) $\vec{\boldsymbol{p}} = (34\ \text{kg}\cdot\text{m/s})\hat{\boldsymbol{i}} + (-16\ \text{kg}\cdot\text{m/s})\hat{\boldsymbol{j}}$ (*c*) 0.28 kJ, 0.28 kJ

46 (*b*) $m = 2/3$, $b = -1/3$

48 Force B

49 (*a*) $P(t) = (3.1\text{ W/s})t$ (*b*) 9.4 W

50 (*a*) 24 W (*b*) –50 W (*c*) 24 W

54 (*a*) 0.15 kW, (*b*) 0.46 kW

55 (*a*) 0.381 kg/m (*b*) 148 mi/h

56 At the time you applied your brakes, which occurred as you passed the 50 mi/h sign, you were doing 6 mi/h under the limit. Your explanation should convince the judge to void the ticket.

57 3.2×10^5 m

58 (*a*) 706 MJ (*b*) 59 MW

59 50 kW

60 (*a*) 1.60 μW (*b*) 1.07 fN (*c*) 1.39×10^6 m/s

61 (*a*) 405 N
(*b*) 19.9 N

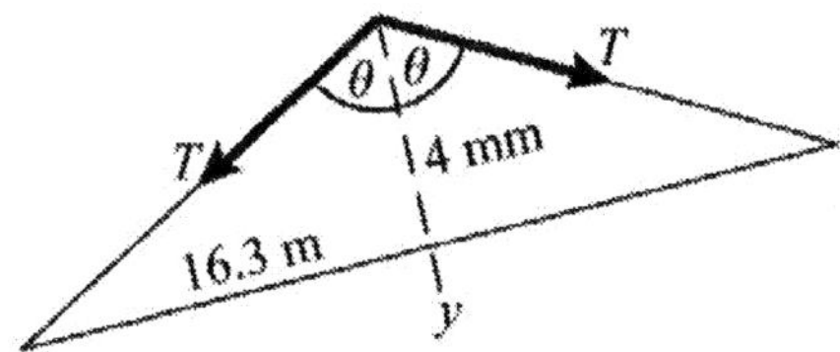

(*c*) 39.7 mJ

62 (*a*) $K_f = \frac{1}{3}bL^3$ (*b*) $v_f = \sqrt{\dfrac{2bL^3}{3m}}$

63 (*a*) $F(x) = mC^2x$ (*b*) $W = \frac{1}{2}mC^2x_1^2$

64 (*a*) 0, 0 (*b*) 78 J, $v_f = \sqrt{\dfrac{156\text{ J}}{m}}$

65 (*a*) $v = (6t^2 - 8t)$, $a = (12t - 8)$ (*b*) $P = 8mt(9t^2 - 18t + 8)$
(*c*) $W = 2mt_1^2(3t_1 - 4)^2$

66 (*a*) 5.7 J (*b*) –17 W

67 (*a*) 208 kW (*b*) 5.74 km

68

(*a*)

x, m	−4.00	−3.00	−2.00	−1.00	1.00	2.00	3.00	4.00
W, J	−11	−10	−7.0	−3.0	1.0	0	−2.0	−3.0

(*b*) 2.50 m

69

(*a*)

x	W
(m)	(J)
−4.00	6
−3.00	4
−2.00	2
−1.00	0.5
0	0
1.00	0.5
2.00	1.5
3.00	2.5
4.00	3

(*b*) 28.0 J

70 (*a*) $W_{\text{by }T} = Tx$ (*b*) $v_\text{f} = \sqrt{2\left(\frac{T}{M} - g\sin\theta\right)x}$ (*c*) $P = T\sqrt{2\left(\frac{T}{M} - g\sin\theta\right)x}$

71 (*b*) $W_{1\,\text{rev, cw}} = (10\pi\,\text{m})F_0, W_{1\,\text{rev, ccw}} = (-10\pi\,\text{m})F_0$

72 (*b*) −0.90 J (*c*) No work is done because the force is perpendicular to the velocity.

73 (*a*) $F_x = -kx\left(1 - \frac{y_0}{\sqrt{x^2 + y_0^2}}\right)$ (*c*) $v_\text{f} = \frac{L^2}{2y_0}\sqrt{\frac{k}{m}}$

74 (*a*) 7.7 kJ (*b*) 0.32 kN

Chapter 7
The Conservation of Energy

1 (*d*)

2 (*c*)

3 (*a*) False (*b*) False (*c*) False (*d*) False

4 The boards do not do any work on you. Your loss of kinetic energy is converted into thermal energy of your body.

5 (*a*) True (*b*) True (*c*) True (*d*) True (*e*) False

6 (*c*)

7 (*a*) False (*b*) False (*c*) False (*d*) False (*e*) True

8 (*a*)

Point	dU/dx	F_x
A	+	−
B	0	0
C	−	+
D	0	0
E	+	−
F	0	0

(*b*) $|F_x|$ is greatest at point C (*c*) The equilibrium is stable at point D

9 (*d*)

10 No.

11 (*a*) Yes (*b*) No (*c*) No

12 (*a*) 245 kJ (*b*) 687 N (*c*) 1.36 kW

13 (*a*) 25 cm (*b*) −0.12 kJ

14 (*a*) 17 MJ, 0.19 kW (*b*) 3.9 Mcal/d (*c*) Approximately 23 kcal/lb is higher than the estimate given in the statement of the problem. However, by adjusting the day's activities, the metabolic rate can vary by more than a factor of 2.

15 (*a*) 16 s (*b*) 6.8 min

16 (*a*) 1.1×10^{-17} kg (*b*) (*c*) 1.1×10^{-6} kg

17 3%

18 2.6×10^{11} m^2, 88%

19 2.4×10^5 L/s

20 0.88 GW

21 (*a*) 0.39 kJ (*b*) 2.5 m, 4.9 m/s (*c*) 24 J, 0.37 kJ (*d*) 0.39 kJ, 20 m/s

22 (*a*) $U(x) = -(6.0\,\text{N})(x - x_0)$ (*b*) $U(x) = 24\,\text{J} - (6.0\,\text{N})x$
(*c*) $U(x) = 50\,\text{J} - (6.0\,\text{N})x$

23 (*a*) 10 cm (*b*) 14 cm

24 (*a*) $-Ax^3$ (*b*) 0

25 (*a*) C/x^2, and $\vec{F} = F_x\hat{i}$
(*b*) If $x > 0$, F_x is positive and $\vec{F}$ points away from the origin. If $x < 0$, $\vec{F}$ points toward the origin.
(*c*) Decrease
(*d*) If $x > 0$, $\vec{F}$ points toward the origin. If $x < 0$, $\vec{F}$ points away from the origin.

26

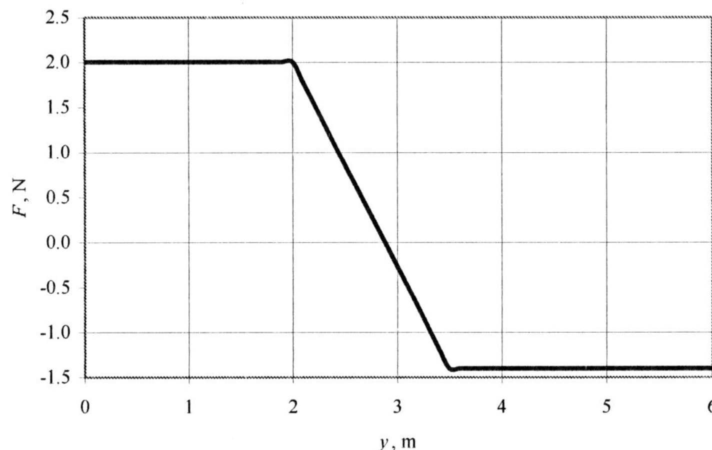

27 $U(x) = \dfrac{-625\,\text{N}\cdot\text{m}^2}{x} + 303\,\text{J}$

28 (*a*) $F_x = 6x(x-1)$ (*b*) $x = 0$ and $x = 1$ m (*c*) Stable equilibrium at $x = 0$, unstable equilibrium at $x = 1$ m

29 (*a*) $F_x = 4x(x+2)(x-2)$ (*b*) $x = -2$ m and $x = 2$ m (*c*) Unstable equilibrium at $x = -2$ m, stable equilibrium at $x = 0$, unstable equilibrium at $x = 2$ m

30 $x = -2$ m, 0, and 2 m

x, mm	$F_{x-1\,\text{mm}}$	$F_{x+1\,\text{mm}}$	Equilibrium
−200	<0	<0	Unstable
0	>0	<0	Stable
200	>0	>0	Unstable

31 (*a*) $x = 0$ and $x = 2.0$ m

(*b*)

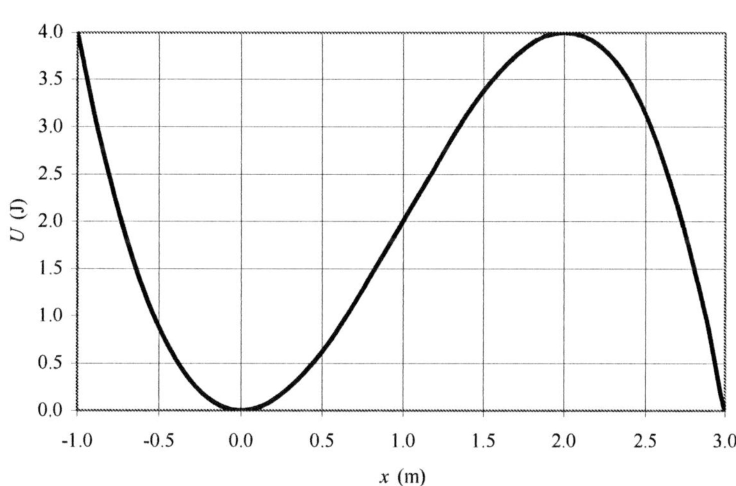

(*c*) Stable equilibrium at $x = 0$, unstable equilibrium at $x - 2.0$ m (*d*) 2.0 m/s

32 (*a*) U decreases as x increases (*b*) $U(x) = \frac{4.0}{x^2}\,\text{N}\cdot\text{m}^3$

(*c*)

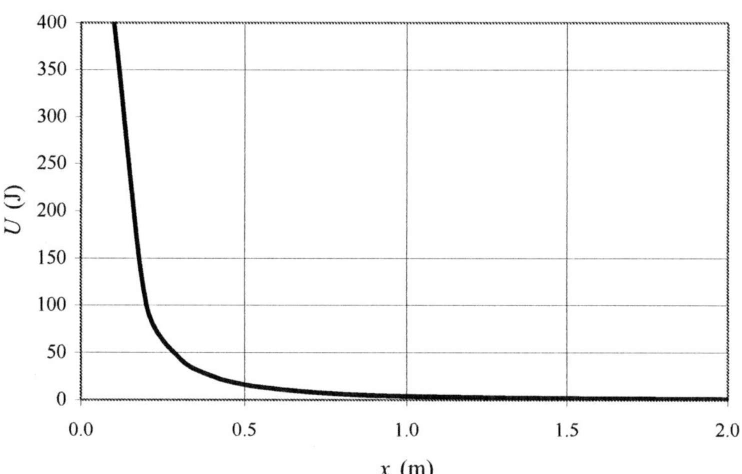

33 (*a*) $U(\theta) = (m_2\ell_2 - m_1\ell_1)g\sin\theta$
(*b*) U is a minimum at $\theta = -\pi/2$, U is a maximum at $\theta = \pi/2$

34 $m_1 = 5.7$ kg, $m_2 = 4.3$ kg

35 (*a*) $U(y) = -mgy - 2Mg\left(L - \sqrt{y^2 + d^2}\right)$ (*b*) $y = d\sqrt{\dfrac{m^2}{4M^2 - m^2}}$

(*c*) $\dfrac{m}{2M} = \dfrac{y}{\sqrt{y^2 + d^2}}$ (*d*) This is a point of stable equilibrium.

36 $x_2 = 6x_1$

37 $v = \sqrt{\dfrac{gL}{2}}$

38 3.9 m

39 (*a*) 0.858 m (*b*) The block will retrace its path, rising to a height of 5.00 m.

40 9.95 m/s. The initial speed of the ball is fast enough to warrant the use of goggles, 5.05 m

41 26°

42 1.4 m/s

43 $U = \dfrac{[mg(\sin\theta + \mu_s \cos\theta)]^2}{2k}$

44 10.0 m/s

45 $6mg$

46 $2mg$

47 16.7 kN

48 (*a*) 9.4 m/s (*b*) No.

49 $6mg$

50 27 m/s

51 (*a*) 31 m (*b*) 34 m/s

52 (*a*) 60° (*b*) 51° No.

53 (*a*) 0.15 km (*b*) 45 m/s

54 (*a*) 3.5 m/s (*b*) 7.9 J (*c*) 25 N (*d*) 49°

55 (*a*) $K_{max} = \frac{5}{2}mgL$ (*b*) $6mg$

56 8.9 m/s

57 (*a*) 20° (*b*) 5.4 m/s

58 $v_2 = L\theta\sqrt{\frac{k}{m} + \frac{g}{L}}$

59 $v_2 = L\sqrt{2\frac{g}{L}(1-\cos\theta) + \frac{k}{m}\left(\sqrt{\frac{13}{4} - 3\cos\theta} - \frac{1}{2}\right)^2}$

60 (*a*) 3.14×10^{16} J (*b*) 7.5 Mton TNT

61 (*a*) 82 kJ (*b*) The energy comes from the internal chemical energy of your body. (*c*) 328 kJ (*d*) −0.410 MJ.

62 (*a*) 6.3×10^4 J (*b*) 0.53

63 (*a*) 0.10 kJ (*b*) 70 J (*c*) 34 J (*d*) 2.9 m/s

64 (*a*) 6.1 m/s (*b*) 2.2 m

65 (*a*) 7.7 m/s (*b*) 59 J (*c*) 0.33

66 (*a*) 0.61 kJ (*b*) 0.35

67 (*a*) (14 N)y (*b*) −(14 N)y (*c*) 2.0 m/s

68 (*a*) $\Delta E_{\text{therm}} = \frac{3}{8}mv_0^2$ (*b*) $\mu_{\text{k}} = \frac{3v_0^2}{16\pi gr}$ (*c*) Because it lost $\frac{3}{4}K_{\text{i}}$ in one revolution, it will only require another 1/3 revolution to lose the remaining $\frac{1}{4}K_{\text{i}}$.

69 0.87 m, 2.7 m/s

70 (*a*) $d = \frac{mg}{k}(\sin\theta + \mu_{\text{s}}\cos\theta)$ (*b*) $\mu_{\text{k}} = \frac{1}{2}(\tan\theta - \mu_{\text{s}})$

71 (*a*) 9.0×10^{13} J (*b*) \$$2.5 \times 10^6$ (*c*) 2.8×10^4 y

72 6×10^{-5} kg No, not noticeable! The mass change, compared to the mass of the bomb, is negligible.

73 (*a*) 3.9×10^{31} MeV (*b*) 4.2×10^8 m/s. As expected, this result (4.2×10^8 m/s) is greater than the speed of light (and thus incorrect). Use of the nonrelativistic expression for kinetic energy is not justified.

74 4×10^{16} kg/s

75 1.1×10^5 reactions/s

76 22.1 MeV

77 0.782 MeV

78 (*a*) 3.82×10^{-12} J (*b*) 2.62×10^{14} reactions/s

79 (*a*) 1.1 kg (*b*) 2.7×10^{9} kg

80 (*a*) 6.0×10^{33} (*b*) 8.3×10^{-34} J . A microscopic oscillator would certainly not exhibit any obvious movement.

81 (*a*) 6 (*b*) 0.21 eV

82 $W_{\text{tension force}} = mgL\sin\theta + \frac{1}{2}mv^2$

83 $\Delta E_{\text{therm}} = -mgv\Delta t\sin\theta$

84

(*a*) In the following graph, α was set equal to 1 and k was set equal to 5.

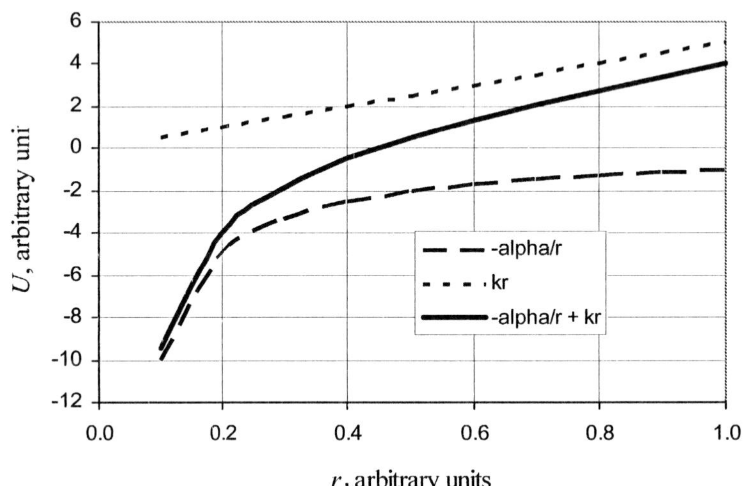

(*b*) $F = -\frac{\alpha}{r^2} + k$

(*c*) $F_{r>>1} \to k$, $F_{r<<1} \to -\frac{\alpha}{r^2}$

85 12 m^2

86 (*a*) 2.8×10^{21} s^{-1} (*b*) 28 m^2 (*c*) 2.5×10^3 m^2

87 (*a*) 0.208 (*b*) 2.5 MJ

88 70 kW

89 (*a*) $x_{1,-} = \frac{2\mu_k mg}{k} - x_i$ (*b*) $v_0 = \sqrt{\frac{k}{m}x_0^2 - 2\mu_k g x_0}$ (*c*) $\mu_k = \frac{kx_i}{2mg}$

90 (*a*) 45 kW (*b*) \$7.24

91 (*a*) 11 kW (*b*) $-6.8\,\text{kW}$ (*c*) \$1.81, \$5.43

92 4.42×10^3 kN/m

93 (*a*) 1.61 kJ (*b*) 0.6 kJ (*c*) 23 m/s

94 $x = \frac{mg}{k}\sin\theta + \sqrt{\left(\frac{mg}{k}\right)^2 \sin^2\theta + \frac{2mg\ell}{k}\sin\theta}$

96 (*a*) $W_s = \frac{1}{2}mv_0^2$ (*b*) $k = \frac{mv_0^2}{d^2}$ (*c*) $\Delta E_{\text{therm}} = \frac{1}{2}mv_0^2 - mgh$

97 (*a*) 17 m (*b*) 4.91 kN (*c*) 4.9 m/s^2 (*d*) 13 kN, upward (*e*) 5.5 kN, 64° (*f*) 1.4 kN

98 (*a*) 29 kW (*b*) 5.2 m

99 (*a*) $F_{20} = 491$ N, $F_{30} = 981$ N (*b*) $P_{20} = 9.8$ kW, $P_{30} = 29$ kW (*c*) 8.8° (*d*) 6.36 km/L

100 (*a*) 0.12 MJ (*b*) 90.0 kJ (*c*) 2.0

102 (*a*) 11.4 m/s (*b*) 13.0 m/s

103 (*a*) $v = \sqrt{\frac{2mgY}{M+m}}$ (*b*) Same as in (*a*)

104 2.7 kW

107 (*a*)

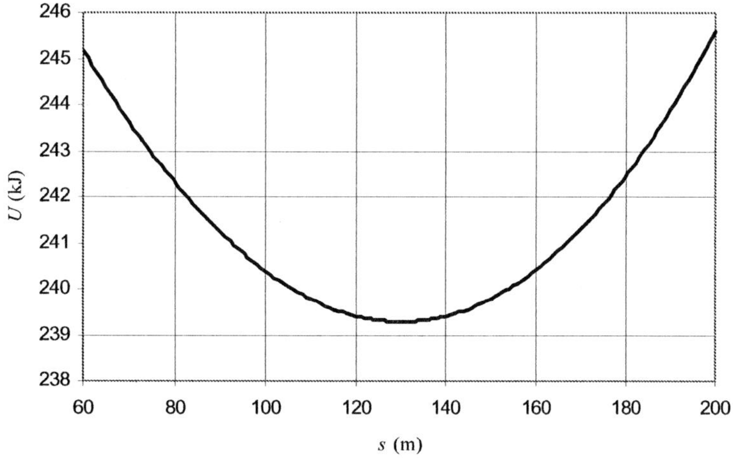

(*b*) 5.4 kJ

108 (*a*) $\Delta U = k\left(\sqrt{L^2 + x^2} - L\right)^2$ (*b*) $F_{\text{restoring}} = 2kx\left(1 - \frac{L}{\sqrt{L^2 + x^2}}\right)$

(*c*)

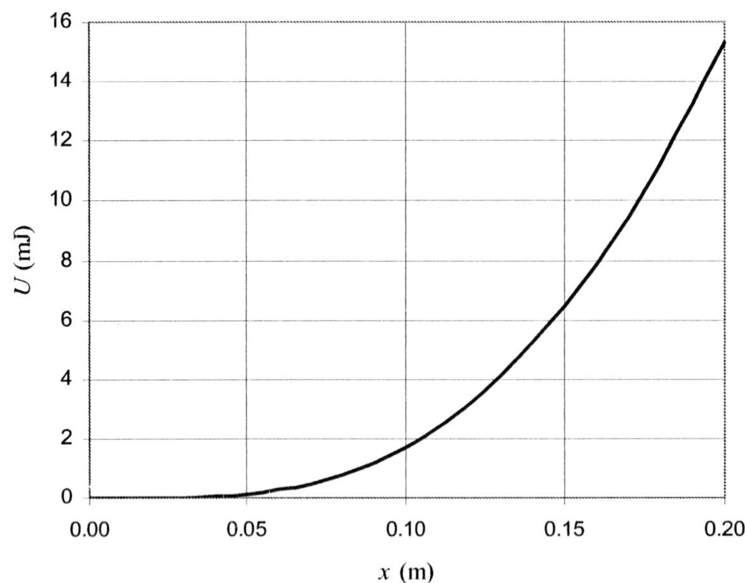

(*d*) 5.9 cm/s

Chapter 8
Conservation of Linear Momentum

2 1

4 (*a*) True (*b*) False (*c*) True

5 The momentum of the bullet-gun system is initially zero. After firing, the bullet's momentum is directed west. Momentum conservation requires that the system's total momentum does not change, so the gun's momentum must be directed east.

6 When she jumps from a boat to a dock, she must, in order for momentum to be conserved, give the boat a recoil momentum, that is, her forward momentum must be the same as the boat's backward momentum. When she jumps through an identical displacement from a boulder to a tree stump, the mass of the boulder plus Earth is so large that the momentum she imparts to them is essentially zero.

7 In a way, the rocket does need something to push upon. It pushes the exhaust in one direction, and the exhaust pushes it in the opposite direction. However, the rocket does not push against the air.

8 The kinetic energy of the sliding ball is $\frac{1}{2}mv_{\text{cm}}^2$. The kinetic energy of the rolling ball is $\frac{1}{2}mv_{\text{cm}}^2 + K_{\text{rel}}$, where K_{rel} is its kinetic energy relative to its center of mass. Because the bowling balls are identical and have the same velocity, the rolling ball has more kinetic energy. There is no problem here because the relationship $K = p^2/2m$ is between the center of mass kinetic energy of the ball and its linear momentum.

9 Think of someone pushing a box across a floor. Her push on the box is equal but opposite to the push of the box on her, but the action and reaction forces act on *different objects*. Newton's second law is that the sum of the forces acting on the box equals the rate of change of momentum of the box. This sum does not include the force of the box on her.

10 It's not possible for both to remain at rest after the collision, as that wouldn't satisfy the requirement that momentum is conserved. It is possible for one to remain at rest: This is what happens for a one-dimensional collision of two identical particles colliding elastically.

11 Hovering in midair while tossing objects violates the conservation of linear momentum! To throw something forward requires being pushed backward. Superheroes are not depicted as experiencing this backward motion that is predicted by conservation of linear momentum. This action does not violate the conservation of energy.

12 There is only one force that can cause the car to move forward–the friction of the road! The car's engine causes the tires to rotate, but if the road were frictionless (as is closely approximated by icy conditions) the wheels would simply spin without the car moving anywhere. Because of friction, the car's tire pushes backwards against the road and the frictional force acting on the tire pushes it forward. This may seem odd, as we tend to think of friction as being a retarding force only, but it is true.

13 The road. (The frictional force by the road on the tire against the road causes the car to slow down.)

14 Because $\Delta p = F\Delta t$ is constant, the safety net reduces the force acting on the performer by increasing the time Δt during which the slowing force acts.

15 About 10^4

16 In both (*a*) and (*b*), longer impulse times (Impulse = $F_{av}\Delta t$) are the result of collisions with a carpet and bails of hay. The average force on a glass or a car is reduced (nothing can be done about the impulse, or change in linear momentum, during a collision but increasing the impulse time decreases the average force acting on an object) and the likelihood of breakage, damage or injury is reduced.

17 (*a*) False (*b*) True (*c*) True (*d*) True

18 If the collision is perfectly inelastic, the bodies stick together and neither will be moving after the collision. Therefore, the final kinetic energy will be zero and all of it will have been lost (that is, transformed into some other form of energy). Momentum is conserved because in an isolated system the net external force is zero.

19 (*a*) The loss of kinetic energy is the same in both cases.
(*b*) The situation in which the two objects have oppositely directed velocities.

20 Pea A will travel farther. Both peas are acted on by the same force, but pea A is acted on by that force for a longer time. By the impulse-momentum theorem, its momentum (and, hence, speed) will be higher than pea B's speed on leaving the shooter.

21 (*b*)

22 You only used conservation of linear momentum for the few fractions of a second of actual contact between the cars. Over that short time, friction and other external forces can be neglected. In the long run, over the duration of the accident, they cannot.

23 The water is changing direction when it rounds the corner in the nozzle. Therefore, the nozzle must exert a force on the stream of water to change its momentum, and from Newton's third law, the water exerts an equal but opposite force on the nozzle. This requires a net force in the direction of the momentum change.

24 In the center-of-mass reference frame the two objects approach with equal but opposite momenta and remain at rest after the collision.

25 In the center-of-mass frame the two velocities are equal and opposite, both before and after the collision. In addition, the speed of each puck is the same before and after the collision. The direction of the velocity of each puck changes by some angle during the collision.

26 (*a*) In the center-of-mass frame of the ground, the center of mass moves in a parabolic arc. (*b*) Relative to the center of mass, each end of the baton would describe a circular path. The more massive end of the baton would travel in the circle with the smaller radius because it is closer to the location of the center of mass.

27 The downward force of lunar gravity and the upward thrust provided by the rocket combustion products.

28 (*a*) Yes, the car should slow down. An easy way of seeing this is to imagine a "packet" of grain being dumped into the car all at once: This is a completely inelastic collision, with the packet having an initial horizontal velocity of 0. After the collision, it is moving with the same horizontal velocity that the car does, so the car must slow down. (*b*) When the packet of grain lands in the car, it initially has a horizontal velocity of 0, so it must be accelerated to come to the same speed as the car of the train. Therefore, the train must exert a force on it to accelerate it. By Newton's third law, the grain exerts an equal but opposite force on the car, slowing it down. In general, this is a frictional force which causes the grain to come to the same speed as the car. (*c*) No, the car does not speed up. Imagine a packet of grain being "dumped" out of the railroad car. This can be treated as a collision, too. It has the same horizontal speed as the railroad car when it leaks out, so the train car doesn't have to speed up or slow down to conserve momentum.

29 Think of the sail facing the fan (like the sail on a square rigger might), and think of the stream of air molecules hitting the sail. Imagine that they bounce off the sail elastically–their net change in momentum is then roughly twice the change in momentum that they experienced going through the fan. Thus the change in momentum of the air is backward, so to conserve momentum of the air-fan-boat system, the change in momentum of the fan-boat system will be forward.

30 (*a*) 0.12 s (*b*) 4.2×10^5 N

31 (*a*) 2.33 s (*b*) 6.7 m/s

32 (*a*) $\vec{v}_{\text{p}} = -\dfrac{m_{\text{b}}}{m_{\text{p}}} v_{\text{b}} \hat{i}$ (*b*) 0 (*c*) $\Delta s = \dfrac{m_{\text{b}}}{m_{\text{p}} + m_{\text{b}}} L$

33 5.5 m/s

34 $\vec{v}_{\text{woman}} = (3.7\text{ m/s})\hat{i}$

35 4.0 m/s to the right

36 (*c*)

37 $\vec{v}' = 2v\hat{i} - v\hat{j}$

38 (*a*) $X_1 = 1.00$ m, $X_2 = 1.15$ m (*b*) 0

39 0.084

40 (*a*) $v_{\text{w}} = \sqrt{\dfrac{2ghm^2}{M(M+m)}}$ (*b*) These results are exactly what we would expect in this case: The physics is that of a block sliding down a fixed wedge incline with no movement of the incline.

41 (*a*) 44 J (*b*) $\vec{v}_{\text{cm}} = (1.5\text{ m/s})\hat{i}$ (*c*) $\vec{v}_{1,\text{rel}} = (3.5\text{ m/s})\hat{i}$, $\vec{v}_{2,\text{rel}} = (-3.5\text{ m/s})\hat{i}$ (*d*) 37 J

42 (*a*) 60 J (*b*) $\vec{v}_{\text{cm}} = (3.8\text{ m/s})\hat{i}$ (*c*) $\vec{v}_{1,\text{rel}} = (1.3\text{ m/s})\hat{i}$, $\vec{v}_{2,\text{rel}} = (-0.8\text{ m/s})\hat{i}$ (*d*) 4 J

43 (*a*) 11 N·s (*b*) 1.3 kN

44 (*a*) 3.8 N·s (*b*) 2.9 kN

45 1.81 MN·s, 0.60 MN

46 (*a*) 6.0 N·s (*b*) 4.6 kN

47 0.23 kN

48 (*a*) 50 ms (*b*) 84 N Because the weight of the ball is less than 2% of the average force exerted on the ball, it is reasonable to have neglected its weight.

49 (*a*) 1.1 N·s directed into the wall (*b*) 0.36 kN, into the wall
(*c*) 0.48 N·s, away from the wall (*d*) 3.8 N, away from the wall

50 (*a*) 1.3 ms (*b*) 6.7 kN

51 (*a*) 0.20 s (*b*) 27 ms (*c*) Because the collision time is much shorter for the sawdust landing, the average force exerted on the vaulter by the airbag is much less than the average force the sawdust exerts on him.

52 (*a*) 50 μN (*b*) 6

53 (*a*) 20 m/s (*b*) Twenty percent of the initial kinetic energy is transformed into thermal energy, acoustic energy, and the deformation of metal

54 3.1 m/s

55 (*a*) –2.0 m/s (*b*) The collision was not elastic.

56 $3v$

57 $v_{p,f} = -254$ m/s, $v_{nuc,f} = 46$ m/s

58 $v_{2f} = 4.8$ m/s, $v_{3f} = 0.8$ m/s. Because $K_i = K_f$, we can conclude that the values obtained for v_{2f} and v_{3f} are consistent with the collision having been elastic.

59 (*a*) $\vec{v}_{cm} = (5.0\ \text{m/s})\hat{i}$ (*b*) 0.25 m (*c*) $\vec{v}_{1f} = 0$ and $\vec{v}_{2f} = (7.0\ \text{m/s})\hat{i}$

60 (*a*) $v_m = \sqrt{2gh}$, $v_M = \sqrt{2gH}$ (*b*) $v_{mi} = \sqrt{2gh} + \frac{M}{m}\sqrt{2gH}$

(*c*) $E_i = mg\left[h + \frac{2M}{m}\sqrt{hH} + \left(\frac{M}{m}\right)^2 H\right]$, $E_f = g(mh + MH)$

(*d*) $W_{\text{friction}} = gMH\left[2\sqrt{\frac{h}{H}} + \frac{M}{m} - 1\right]$

61 (*a*) $0.2v_0$ (*b*) $0.4v_0$

62 0.217%

63 0.45 km/s

66 $v = 2\left(1+\dfrac{m_2}{m_1}\right)\sqrt{gL}$

67 $h = \dfrac{2m_1^2v^2}{9m_2^2g}$

68 13.0 cm

69 0.0529

70 3.9 m

71 (*a*) The meteorite should impact Earth along a line exactly opposite Earth's orbital velocity vector. (*b*) 2.71×10^{-15}% (*c*) 1.00×10^{23} kg

72 101 g

73 1.5×10^6 m/s

74 $v_{\rm p} = 1.74\times10^7$ m/s, $v_\alpha = 4.34\times10^6$ m/s

75 (*a*) $\vec{v}_1 = (312\,\text{m/s})\hat{i} + (66.6\,\text{m/s})\hat{j}$ (*b*) 5.6 km (*c*) 35.8 kJ

76 $v_\alpha = 1.4 \times 10^6$ m/s, ±121°

77 0.91

78 $0.825 \le e \le 0.849$

79 (*a*) 20% (*b*) 0.89

80 (*a*) 3.5 m/s (*b*) 11 J (*c*) 0.75

81 (*a*) 1.7 m/s (*b*) 0.83

82 (*a*) 0.35 (*b*) 32 m. Because home runs must travel at least 100 m in modern major league ballparks, this is a "dead" ball and should be tossed out.

83 (*a*) At room-temperature rubber will bounce more when it hits a stick than it will at freezing temperatures. (*b*) 3.8 cm

85 (*a*) 60° (*b*) $v_{\text{cf}} = 2.50\,\text{m/s}$, $v_8 = 4.33\,\text{m/s}$

86 (*a*) $\vec{v}_{1\text{f}} = \frac{1}{2}v_0\hat{i} + v_0\hat{j}$ (*b*) $\Delta E = \frac{1}{16}mv_0^2$. Because $\Delta E \neq 0$, the collision is inelastic.

87 (*a*) $v_1 = 1.7\,\text{m/s}$ and $v_2 = 1.0\,\text{m/s}$ (*b*) Because the angle between $\vec{v}_1$ and $\vec{v}_2$ is 90°, the collision was elastic.

88 (*a*) $\theta_2 = 45.0°$, $v_2 = \sqrt{2}v_0$

89 5.3 m/s, 29°

91 $$K_{\text{i}} = K_{\text{f}} = \frac{p_1^2}{2}\left[\frac{m_1^2 + 6m_1m_2 + m_2^2}{m_1^2m_2 + m_1m_2^2}\right] = \frac{p_1'^2}{2}\left[\frac{m_1^2 + 6m_1m_2 + m_2^2}{m_1^2m_2 + m_1m_2^2}\right]$$
$p_1' = \pm p_1$. If $p_1' = +p_1$, the particles do not collide.

92 (*a*) $\vec{v}_{\text{cm}} = (-3.0\,\text{m/s})\hat{i}$ (*b*) $\vec{u}_3 = (-2.0\,\text{m/s})\hat{i}$, $\vec{u}_1 = (6.0\,\text{m/s})\hat{i}$
(*c*) $\vec{u}_3' = (2.0\,\text{m/s})\hat{i}$, $\vec{u}_1' = (-6.0\,\text{m/s})\hat{i}$ (*d*) $\vec{v}_3' = (-1.0\,\text{m/s})\hat{i}$, $\vec{v}_1' = (-9.0\,\text{m/s})\hat{i}$
(*e*) $K_{\text{i}} = K_{\text{f}} = 42$ J

93 (*a*) $\vec{v}_{\text{cm}} = 0$ (*b*) $\vec{u}_3 = (-5.0\,\text{m/s})\hat{i}$, $\vec{u}_5 = (3.0\,\text{m/s})\hat{i}$
(*c*) $\vec{u}_3' = (5.0\,\text{m/s})\hat{i}$, $\vec{u}_5' = (-3.0\,\text{m/s})\hat{i}$ (*d*) $\vec{v}_3' = (5.0\,\text{m/s})\hat{i}$, $\vec{v}_5' = (-3.0\,\text{m/s})\hat{i}$
(*e*) $K_{\text{i}} = K_{\text{f}} = 60$ J

94 1.20 MN

95 (*a*) 360 kN (*b*) 120 s (*c*) 1.72 km/s

96 (*c*) 25 s

97 (*d*) 28

98 (*a*) 1.09 km (*b*) 29.8 s (*c*) Because this burn time is approximately one-fifth of the total flight time, we cannot expect the answer we obtained in Part (*b*) to be very accurate. It should, however, be good to about 30% accuracy, as the maximum distance the model rocket could possibly move in this time is $\frac{1}{2}vt_{\text{b}} = 243\,\text{m}$, assuming constant acceleration until burnout.

99 0.19 m/s, $K_{\text{i}} = 31$ mJ, $K_{\text{f}} = 12$ mJ

100 (*a*) 33 mJ (*b*) 0.31 m/s, –0.19 m/s, 19 mJ (*c*) 12 mJ

101 (*a*) $\vec{p} = -(1.1\times10^5\ \text{kg}\cdot\text{km/h})\,\hat{i} + (1.1\times10^5\ \text{kg}\cdot\text{km/h})\hat{j}$ (*b*) 43 km/h. The direction of the wreckage is 46° west of north.

102 (*a*) 2.5 m (*b*) 0.18 kJ, 0.27 kJ (*c*) All the kinetic energy derives from the chemical energy of the woman and, assuming she stops via static friction, the kinetic energy is transformed into her internal energy. (*d*) After the shot leaves the woman's hand, the raft-woman system constitutes an inertial reference frame. In that frame the shot has the same initial velocity as did the shot that had a range of 6 m in the reference frame of the land. Thus, in the raft-woman frame, the shot also has a range of 6 m and lands at the front of the raft.

103 (*a*) 6.3 m/s (*b*) 20 m

104 (*a*) No. The vertical reaction force of the rails is an external force, so the momentum of the system will not be conserved. (*b*) 4.3 m/s (*c*) −569 J

105 (*a*) The velocity of the basketball will be equal in magnitude but opposite in direction to the velocity of the baseball. (*b*) 0 (*c*) $2v$

106 (*a*) $\frac{1}{2}$ (*b*) $\frac{7}{3}v$

107 (*a*) 30 km/s (*b*) 8.1. The energy comes from an immeasurably small slowing of Saturn.

108 36 m/s

109 The driver was not telling the truth.

110 0.50 kg or 0.32 kg

111 8.9 kg

113 (*b*) 55

114 (*a*) 19 (*b*) 158

115 (*a*) $v_{2\text{f}} = \left(\dfrac{m_\text{b}}{m_2 + m_\text{b}}\right)\left(1 + \dfrac{m_1}{m_1 + m_\text{b}}\right)v$, $v_{1\text{f}} = -\dfrac{m_2 m_\text{b}(2m_1 + m_\text{b})}{(m_1 + m_\text{b})^2(m_2 + m_\text{b})}v$

(*b*) $\Delta K = \frac{1}{2}\dfrac{m_2 m_\text{b}^2(2m_1 + m_\text{b})^2}{(m_2 + m_\text{b})^2(m_1 + m_\text{b})^2}\left(1 + \dfrac{m_1 m_2}{(m_1 + m_\text{b})^2}\right)v^2$. This additional energy came from chemical energy in the astronaut's bodies.

116 32 g

117 1.70 m/s

Chapter 9
Rotation

1 (*a*) The point on the rim. (*b*) Both turn through the same angle. (*c*) The point on the rim. (*d*) Both have the same angular velocity. (*e*) Both have zero tangential acceleration. (*f*) Both have zero angular acceleration. (*g*) The point on the rim.

2 (*a*) False (*b*) True (*c*) True (*d*) False

3 (*c*)

4 Because the merry-go-round is slowing, the sign of its angular acceleration is negative.

5 (*a*) Tara (*b*) Tara (*c*) Neither

6 Disk B has the larger moment of inertia about its center. It has the same total mass but, on average, it is further from its center.

7 By choking up, you are rotating the bat about an axis closer to the center of mass, thus reducing the bat's moment of inertia. The smaller the moment of inertia the larger the angular acceleration (a quicker bat) for the same torque.

8 (*a*) No. If the object is slowing down, they are oppositely directed.
(*b*) The angular speed of the object will decrease.
(*c*) Yes. At the instant the object is stopping and turning around (angularly), such as a pendulum at its turnaround (highest) point, the net torque is not zero and the angular velocity is zero.

9 (*b*)

10 (*d*)

11 (*b*)

12 (*c*)

13 One reason is to maximize the moment arm about the line through the hinge pins for the force exerted by someone pulling or pushing on the knob.

14 (*c*)

15 (*b*)

16 You could spin the pipes about their center. The one which is easier to spin has its mass concentrated closer to the center of mass and, hence, has a smaller moment of inertia.

17 (*b*)

18 (*c*)

19 (*a*)

22 You are finding positions at which gravity exerts no torque on the object, so the gravitational force (weight) passes through the center of mass. Thus you are triangulating, and in theory, two such lines should intersect at the center of mass. In practice, several lines do a better and more accurate job.

23 12 rev

25 10%

26 The orientation of the slice of toast will be at angles of 203° and 275° with respect to the ground; that is, with the jelly-side down.

27 Approximately 6.

28 (*a*) 0.28 rad/s (*b*) 1.3 rev

29 (*a*) 16 rad/s (*b*) 47 rad (*c*) 7.4 rev (*d*) 4.7 m/s and 73 m/s^2

30 (*a*) 0.13 rad/s^2 (*b*) 1.7 rad/s (*c*) 7.2 rev

31 (*a*) 40 rad/s (*b*) $a_t = 0.96$ m/s^2, $a_t = 0.19$ km/s^2

32 (*a*) 0.23 rad/s (*b*) 2.8 m/s, 0.65 m/s^2

33 (*a*) 0.59 rad/s^2 (*b*) 4.7 rad/s

34 73 μrad/s

35 3.6 rad/s

36 1.3 rad/s^2

37 1.0 rad/s, 9.9 rev/min

38 (a) 30 rad/s^2, -1.2×10^2 rad/s^2 (b) 28 rad/s (c) 4.0

39 (a) 3.34 rad or 2.94 rad (b) 780 d

40 4.7×10^{-5} kg·m^2

41 56 kg·m^2

42 28 kg·m^2

43 (a) 28 kg·m^2 (b) 28 kg·m^2

44 $I = \frac{7}{5}MR^2$

45 2.6 kg·m^2

46 (a) $I = m_1x^2 + m_2(L - x)^2$

47 (b) $I_{\text{cm}} = \frac{1}{12}m(a^2 + b^2)$

48 (a) $I_{\text{app}} = 0.0400$ kg·m^2, $I = 0.0415$ kg·m^2, $I_{\text{app}}/I = 0.964$ (b) The rotational inertia would increase because I_{cm} of a hollow sphere is greater than I_{cm} of a solid sphere.

49 5.4×10^{-47} kg·m^2

51 0.045 kg·m^2

52 Because its moment of inertia is smaller that that of the less massive rug beater, the more massive rug beater will be easier to use.

54 (a) $C = 0.508\frac{M}{R^3}$ (b) $I = 0.329MR^2$

55 $I = \frac{3}{10}MR^2$

56 $I = \frac{1}{4}MR^2$

57 $I_x = 3M\left(\frac{H^2}{5} + \frac{R^2}{20}\right)$

58 (a) -2.45 rad/s^2 (b) 0.0133 N·m

59 (*a*) 1.9 N·m (*b*) 1.2 × 10^2 rad/s^2 (*c*) 62 rad/s
60 (*a*) 19.1 kg·m^2 (*b*) –10.0 N·m

61 (*a*) $a_t = g\sin\theta$ (*b*) $mgL\sin\theta$

62 (*b*) $F_P = F_0\left(\frac{3x}{2L} - 1\right)$

63 (*a*) $d\tau_f = \frac{2\mu_k M g}{R^2} r^2 dr$ (*b*) $\tau_f = \frac{2}{3} MR\mu_k g$ (*c*) $\Delta t = \frac{3R\omega}{4\mu_k g}$

64 (*a*) 1.1 J (*b*) 1.1 J

65 (*a*) 85 mJ (*b*) 72 rev/min

66 $K_{rot} = 2.6 \times 10^{29}$ J, 10^4

67 (*a*) 19.6 kN (*b*) 5.9 kN·m (*c*) 0.27 rad/s (*d*) 1.6 kW

68 (*a*) $\omega_f = \sqrt{\frac{8mg}{R(2m + M)}}$ (*b*) $F = mg\left(1 + \frac{8m}{2m + M}\right)$

69 (*a*) 3.6 rad/s (*b*) 3.6 rad/s

70 (*a*) $\omega = \sqrt{\frac{84mg}{(27m + M)L}}$ (*b*) $\omega \approx \sqrt{\frac{28g}{9L}}$

71 3.1 m/s^2, T_1 = 12 N, T_2 = 13 N

72 (*a*) 3.9 m/s (*b*) 49 rad/s

73 30°

74 1.6 m/s^2 , 16 N, 17 N

75 8.21 m/s

76 (*a*) 2.7 m/s (*b*) 27 rad/s (*c*) 0.23 kN, 0.24 kN (*d*) 1.5 s

77 (*a*) $a = \frac{g}{1 + \frac{2M}{5m}}$ (*b*) $T = \frac{2mMg}{5m + 2M}$

78 (*a*) 9.48 cm/s^2 (*b*) T_1 = 4.95 N, T_2 = 4.96 N, ΔT = 0.01 N (*c*) 9.71 cm/s^2,

$T_1 = T_2 = 4.95$ N

79 (*a*) 72 kg (*b*) 1.4 rad/s^2, 0.29 kN, 0.75 kN

80 (*a*) *Mg* (*b*) 2*g*/*R* (*c*) 2*g*

81 (*a*) $a = \dfrac{g\sin\theta}{1+\dfrac{m_1}{2m_2}}$ (*b*) $T = \dfrac{\frac{1}{2}m_1 g\sin\theta}{1+\dfrac{m_1}{2m_2}}$ (*c*) $v = \sqrt{\dfrac{2gh}{1+\dfrac{m_1}{2m_2}}}$

(*d*) $a = g$, $T = 0$ and $v = \sqrt{2gh}$

82 (*a*) 1.2 kg·m^2(*b*) $I_{tot} = 3.1$ kg·m^2, $I = 1.9$ kg·m^2

83 10 kJ

84 (*a*) 71.4% (*b*) 66.7% (*c*) 50.0%

85 3.1 m/s

86 (*b*) $T = \frac{1}{3}Mg$

87 (*a*) 0.19 m/s^2 (*b*) 0.96 N

88 16°

89 20°

90 (*a*) $a = \frac{3}{5}g\sin\theta$ (*b*) $f_s = \frac{2}{5}mg\sin\theta$ (*c*) $\theta_{max} = \tan^{-1}\left(\frac{5}{2}\mu_s\right)$

91 (*a*) $a = \frac{2}{3}g\sin\theta$ (*b*) $f_s = \frac{1}{3}mg\sin\theta$ (*c*) $\theta_{max} = \tan^{-1}\left(3\mu_s\right)$

92 1.09

93 $v' = \sqrt{\dfrac{4}{3}}v$

94 0.058°

95 0.22 kJ

96 $a_B = \dfrac{3F}{M+3m}$

97 (*a*) $\alpha = \frac{2F}{R(M+3m)}$, counterclockwise (*b*) $a_C = \frac{F}{M+3m}$, in direction of $\vec{F}$

(*c*) $a_{CB} = -\frac{2F}{M+3m}$, opposite to direction of $\vec{F}$

98 (*a*) $K_B = \frac{mFd}{m+\frac{1}{3}M}$ (*b*) $K_{cyl} = \frac{MFd}{3m+M}$

99 (*a*) 0.40 rad/s^2, 0.20 rad/s^2 (*b*) 4.0 N, clockwise

100 (*a*) $h = 2.7R - 1.7r$ (*b*) 76 cm wide by 44 cm high

101 (*a*) $s_1 = \frac{12}{49}\frac{v_0^2}{\mu_k g}$, $t_1 = \frac{2}{7}\frac{v_0}{\mu_k g}$, and $v_1 = \frac{5}{7}v_0$ (*b*) 5/7 (*c*) $s_1 = 27$ m, $t_1 = 3.9$ s, and $v_1 = 5.7$ m/s

102 30 rad/s

103 $v = \frac{2r\omega_0}{7}$

104 (*a*) 2.0 × 10^2 m/s (*b*) 8.0 × 10^3 rad/s (*c*) 2.6 × 10^2 m/s (*d*) 3.0 km

105 (*a*) 0.19 s (*b*) 0.67 m (*c*) 2.9 m/s

106 (*a*) $\omega_0 = \frac{5v_0(h-R)}{2R^2}$ (*b*) $v = \frac{5}{21}v_0$ (*c*) $K_i = \frac{19}{18}mv_0^2$

107 (*a*) and (*b*) $\Delta t = \frac{4}{7}\frac{v_0}{\mu_k g}$ and $v = \frac{11}{7}v_0$ (*c*) $\Delta x = \frac{36}{49}\frac{v_0^2}{\mu_k g}$

108 (*a*) 0.087 rad/s^2 (*b*) 0.57 kN·m (*c*) 6.6 × 10^3 kg·m^2

109 13 cm

110 (*a*) 2.4 N·m (*b*) 67 rad/s^2 (*c*) 3.3 × 10^2 rad/s (*d*) 2.0 kJ (*e*) 8.3 × 10^2 rad

111 (*a*) 7.4 m/s^2 (*b*) 15 m/s^2 (*c*) 2.4 m/s

112 $\frac{1}{7}(5h_1 + 2R)$

113 (*a*) 7.8 × 10^2 kJ (*b*) 90 N·m, 0.15 kN (*c*) 1.4 × 10^3 rev

114 (*a*) 0.12 m (*b*) 0.43 m/s^2 (*c*) 3.0 J (*d*) 12 J

115 (*a*) 15 m (*b*) 15 rad/s

116 (*a*) 9.6 rad/s^2 (*b*) 4.4 rad/s

117 (*a*) $\omega = \sqrt{\dfrac{4g}{3r}}$ (*b*) $F = \frac{7}{3}Mg$

118 (*a*) 0.14 rad/s^2 (*b*) 57 cm/s^2 (*c*) 51 cm/s^2 (*d*) 1.83 rad/s

119 (*a*) 32.2 rad/s (*b*) 23° (*c*) 24 rad/s^2

120 (*a*) 0.23 kN/m (*b*) 0.16 kJ

121 (*a*) 14.7 m/s^2 (*b*) 66.7 cm

122 0.75 *mg*, 0.50 *mg*, 0.25 *mg*, 0

123 42 J

124 (*b*) $f = F/3$ in the $+x$ direction.

125

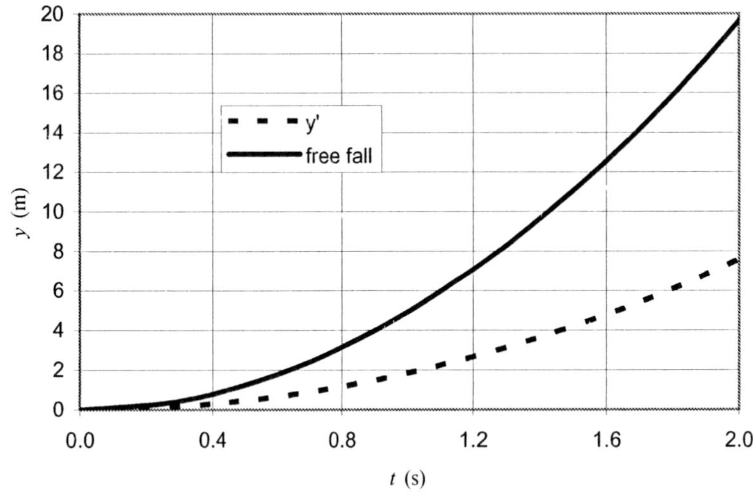

126 $\theta = \cos^{-1}\left(\dfrac{r}{R}\right)$

127 (*a*) 26 N (*b*) 1.1 m/s^2 (*c*) 3.2 kg

128 (*a*) $f = \frac{T}{3}\left(\frac{2r}{R} - 1\right)$ (*b*) $a = -\frac{2T}{3m}\left(1 + \frac{r}{R}\right)$ (*c*) $r > 0.5R$ (*d*) $f > 0$, in the direction of $\vec{T}$

Chapter 10
Angular Momentum

1 (*a*) True (*b*) False (*c*) False

2 (*b*)

3 90°

4 (*b*)

5 (*a*) doubling $\vec{p}$ doubles $\vec{L}$ (*b*) doubling $\vec{r}$ doubles $\vec{L}$

6 $\vec{L}$ is constant

7 False. A high diver going from a tucked to a layout position.

8 (*a*) Increase (*b*) Increases (*c*) Decreases (*d*) Stays the same

9 (*e*)

10 (*b*)

11 The hardboiled egg is solid inside, so everything rotates with a uniform angular speed. By contrast, when you start an uncooked egg spinning, the yolk will not immediately spin with the shell, and when you stop it from spinning the yolk will continue to spin for a while.

12 The purpose of the second smaller rotor is to prevent the body of the helicopter from rotating. If the rear rotor fails, the body of the helicopter will tend to rotate on the main axis due to angular momentum being conserved.

13 (*a*)

14 (*d*)

15 (*a*) To the right (*b*) Down

16 If $\vec{L}$ points up and the car travels over a hill or through a valley, the force on the wheels on one side (or the other) will increase and car will tend to tip. If $\vec{L}$ points forward and car turns left or right, the front (or rear) of the car will tend to lift. These problems can be averted by having two identical flywheels that rotate on the same shaft in opposite directions.

17 (*a*) Your kinetic energy decreases. Increasing your moment of inertia I while conserving your angular momentum L decreases you kinetic energy $K = \frac{L^2}{2I}$. (*b*) Extending your arms out to the side increases your moment of inertia, decreases your angular speed. The angular momentum of the system is unchanged.

18 The center of mass of the rod-and-putty system moves in a straight line, and the system rotates about its center of mass.

19 4 rev/s

20 5

21 (*a*) 33 (*b*) 33 (*c*) 8 (*d*) 14

22 0.55 s

23 (*a*) $2.4\times10^{-8}\ \text{kg}\cdot\text{m}^2/\text{s}$ (*b*) $\ell(\ell+1)=5.2\times10^{52}$, $\ell\approx2.3\times10^{26}$ (*c*) $\Delta\ell=2.3\times10^{18}$. The quantization of angular momentum is not noticed in macroscopic physics because no experiment can detect a fractional change in ℓ of 10^{-6}%.

24 (*a*) 2.9×10^{7} rev/d. (*b*) The rotational kinetic energy *increases* by a factor of approximately 7×10^{8}. The additional rotational kinetic energy comes at the expense of gravitational potential energy, which decreases as the sun gets smaller.

25 (*a*) 0.331 (*b*) Because experimentally $C < 0.4$, the mass density must be greater near the center of Earth.

26 4.9 m/s, 36 rad/s, 18 rad/s, $24\ \text{kg}\cdot\text{m}^2/\text{s}$

27 $\vec{\tau} = FR\hat{k}$

28 $\vec{\tau} = -mgx\hat{k}$

29 (*a*) $24\hat{k}$ (*b*) $-24\hat{j}$ (*c*) $-5\hat{k}$

30 While none of these sets of vectors are perpendicular, those in (*a*) and (*b*) are the closest, with $\phi = 45°$, to being perpendicular.

33 $\vec{B} = 4\hat{j} + 3\hat{k}$

34 $\vec{B} = 4\hat{i} + 3\hat{j}$

37 (*a*) $54\,\mathrm{kg\cdot m^2/s}$, upward (*b*) $54\,\mathrm{kg\cdot m^2/s}$, downward (*c*) 0

38 (*a*) $28\,\mathrm{kg\cdot m^2/s}$, away from you (*b*) $32\,\mathrm{kg\cdot m^2}$ (*c*) $0.88\,\mathrm{rad/s^2}$

39 (*b*) Downward

41 (*a*) $1.3\times10^{-5}\,\mathrm{kg\cdot m^2/s}$, away from you (*b*) $1.3\times10^{-5}\,\mathrm{kg\cdot m^2/s}$, away from you (*c*) $1.3\times10^{-5}\,\mathrm{kg\cdot m^2/s}$, away from you (*d*) $8.8\times10^{-5}\,\mathrm{kg\cdot m^2/s}$, pointing toward you

42 (*a*) 0 (*b*) If the forces are not along the same line, there will be a net torque (but still no net force) acting on the system. This net torque would cause the system to accelerate angularly, contrary to observation, and hence makes no sense physically.

43 (*a*) –4.9 N·m. Note that, because *L* decreases as the particle rotates clockwise, the angular acceleration and the net torque are both upward. (*b*) $\omega_{\text{orbital}} = 0.48\text{ rad/s} - \left(0.19\text{ rad/s}^2\right)t$, downward.

44 (*a*) $3.8\times10^2\,\mathrm{kg\cdot m^2/s}$ (*b*) $15\,\mathrm{kg\cdot m^2/s^2}$ (*c*) $15\,\mathrm{kg\cdot m^2/s^2}$ (*d*) 38 N

45 (*a*) $\tau_{\text{net}} = Rg\left(m_2\sin\theta - m_1\right)$ (*b*) $L = vR\left(\dfrac{I}{R^2} + m_1 + m_2\right)$

(*c*) $a = \dfrac{g\left(m_2\sin\theta - m_1\right)}{\dfrac{I}{R^2} + m_1 + m_2}$

46 2.6×10^2 s

48 (*a*) 0 (*b*) $\dfrac{v_1}{v_2} = \dfrac{r_2}{r_1}$

49 (*a*) 5.0 rev/s (*b*) 0.62 kJ (*c*) Because no external agent does work on the system, the energy comes from your internal energy.

50 (*a*) $\omega_{\text{f}} = \dfrac{1}{1+\dfrac{mR^2}{I_0}}\omega_{\text{i}}$ (*b*) $\omega' = \omega_{\text{f}}$.

51 10 mm/s

52 (*a*) $\omega_f = \frac{3}{5}\omega_0$ (*b*) $\Delta K = -\frac{16}{25}K_i$. The frictional force between the surfaces is responsible for some of the initial kinetic energy being converted to thermal energy as the two disks come together.

53 (*a*) $r_0 m v_0$ (*b*) $\frac{1}{2}mv_0^2$ (*c*) $m\dfrac{v_0^2}{r_0}, \frac{3}{2}mv_0^2$

54 (*a*) $v_B = 2.4$ m/s, $v_C = 4.0$ m/s (*b*) 3 N/m

55 125°

57 (*a*) $3.46\times10^{-47}\ \text{kg}\cdot\text{m}^2$ (*b*) 1.00 meV, 2.01 meV, 6.02 meV

58 (*a*) $1.41\times10^{-46}\ \text{kg}\cdot\text{m}^2$ (*b*) 0.247 meV, 0.495 meV, 1.48 meV (*c*) The energy (0.99 meV) is too low to produce visible radiation.

59 (*a*) No. None of the allowed values of E_ℓ are equal to E_{0r}. (*b*) 2.5

60 14 J·s

61 $\vec{v}_{cm} = \dfrac{m}{M+m}\vec{v}$, $\omega = \left(\dfrac{mMd}{\frac{1}{12}ML^2(M+m)+Mmd^2}\right)v$

62 4/7

63 $v = \sqrt{\dfrac{(0.5M+0.8m)\left(\frac{1}{3}ML^2+0.64mL^2\right)g}{0.32Lm^2}}$

64 7.7 m/s

65 (*a*) $v_{cm} = J/M$ (*b*) $V = 4J/M$ (*c*) $V = -2J/M$ (*d*) Yes, one point remains motionless, but only for a very brief time.

66 (*a*) $L_0 = m_p v_0 b$ (*b*) $\omega = \dfrac{2m_p v_0 b}{(M+2m_p)R^2}$ (*c*) $K_f = \dfrac{(m_p v_0 b)^2}{(M+2m_p)R^2}$

(*d*) $\Delta E = \frac{1}{2}m_p v_0^2\left[1-\dfrac{2m_p b^2}{(M+2m_p)R^2}\right]$

67 0.39

68 (*a*) 1.2 kg (*b*) 7.5 J

69 (*a*) 18 J·s (*b*) 0.41 rad/s (*c*) 15 s (*d*) 0.079 J·s

70 (*a*) 3.3 rad/s (*b*) 16 cm/s (*c*) 54 cm/s^2 (*d*) 1.3 N

71 (*a*) $\vec{L} = -(48\,\text{kg}\cdot\text{m}^2/\text{s})\hat{k}$ (*b*) $\vec{\tau} = (21\,\text{N}\cdot\text{m})\hat{k}$

72 $\vec{L} = (72t\,\text{J}\cdot\text{s})\hat{k}$, $\vec{\tau} = (72\,\text{N}\cdot\text{m})\hat{k}$

73 (*a*) $0.24\,\text{kJ}\cdot\text{s}$ (*b*) 0.31 kJ

74 (*a*) $\vec{L}_{\text{hor}} = (5.4\,\text{J}\cdot\text{s})\cos\omega t\,\hat{i} + (5.4\,\text{J}\cdot\text{s})\sin\omega t\,\hat{j}$, $\vec{L}_{\text{vertical}} = (3.1\,\text{J}\cdot\text{s})\hat{k}$
(*b*) 15 N·m,

75 (*a*) Because $\tau_{\text{net}} \neq 0$, angular momentum is not conserved. (*b*) Because, in this frictionless environment, the net external force acting on the object is the tension force and it acts at right angles to the object's velocity, the energy of the object is conserved. (*c*) $v' = v_0$

76 $\omega_{\text{f}} = \dfrac{ML^2 + 5m(r^2 + \ell^2)}{ML^2 + 5m(r^2 + L^2)}\omega$, $K_{\text{i}} = \left[\frac{1}{20}ML^2 + \frac{1}{4}m(r^2 + \ell^2)\right]\omega^2$,

$$K_{\text{f}} = \frac{1}{20}\left[\frac{\left[ML^2 + 5m(r^2 + \ell^2)\right]^2}{ML^2 + 5m(r^2 + L^2)}\right]\omega^2$$

77 Yes. The solution depends only upon conservation of angular momentum of the system, so it depends only upon the initial and final moments of inertia.

78 $\omega = 30$ rad/s, $\omega_{\text{f}} = 11\,\text{rad/s}$, $K_{\text{i}} = 0.18\,\text{kJ}$, $K_{\text{f}} = 62\,\text{J}$

80 (*a*) $\omega_{\text{f}} = \dfrac{M}{M + 2m}\omega_{\text{i}}$ (*b*) $\omega_{\text{f}} = \dfrac{M}{M + 2m}\omega_{\text{i}} - 2\left(\dfrac{m}{M}\right)\dfrac{v}{R}$

81 (*a*) 0.228 rad/s (*b*) 0.192 rad/s

82 (*c*) 2.18 km

83 $4.47 \times 10^{22}\,\text{N}\cdot\text{m}$

84 (*a*) 1.44×10^{32} rad/s (*b*) 1.44×10^{14} m/s. Given that our model predicts a value for the speed of a point on the "equator" of a spinning electron that is greater than the speed of light, the idea that the spin angular momentum of an electron is analogous to that of a spinning sphere with spatial extent lacks credibility.

85 −79.9 cm

86 (*a*) 27 rad/s (*b*) $L = (0.30\,\mathrm{kg \cdot m^2/s})e^{(1.41\,\mathrm{s}^{-1})t}$

Chapter R
Relativity

1 In the reference frame of the car both events occur at the same location (the location of the car). Thus, your friend's watch measures the proper time between the two events.

2 (*a*) Because the door is at rest in the reference frame of the car, its width in that frame is its proper width. If your friend measures this width, say by placing a meter stick against the door, than he will measure the proper width of the door.
(*b*) In the reference frame in which you are at rest, the door is moving, so its width is less than its proper width. To measure this width would be challenging. (You could measure the width by measuring the time for the door to go by. The width of the door is the product of the speed of the car and the time.)

3 Yes. Let the initial frame of reference be frame 1. In frame 1 let L be the distance between the events, let T be the time between the events, and let the $+x$ direction be the direction of event B relative to event A. Next, calculate the value of L/T. If L/T is less than c, then consider the two events in a reference frame 2, a frame moving at speed $v = L/T$ in the $+x$ direction. In frame 2 both events occur at the same location.

4 Yes.

5 Yes.

6 We will refer to the two events as event A and event B. Assume that in the reference frame of the first observer there is a stationary clock at the location of each event, with clock A at the location of event A and clock B at the location of event B, and that the two clocks are synchronized. Because the two events are simultaneous in this frame, the readings of the two clocks at the time the events occur are the same. Also, event A and the reading of clock A at the time of event A are a spacetime coincidence, so all observers must agree with that clock reading. In like manner, event B and the reading of clock B at the time of event B are a spacetime coincidence. If observer B is moving parallel with the line joining the two clocks then the clocks readings will differ by Lv/c^2 in the reference frame of B, where L is the distance between the clocks in the reference frame of observer A. This means that observer B will agree that the two clock readings at the times of the events are the same, but will not agree that the events occurred at the

same time unless $L = 0$.Let the two events A and B be separated by a distance $\Delta x = x_B - x_A$ and a time $\Delta t = t_B - t_A$ in frame S. Then, in a frame S' that is moving with speed v relative to S, the time separation is $t_B' - t_A' = \gamma(\Delta t - v\Delta x/c^2)$. If the observers agree on the simultaneity of the two events, then $t_B' - t_A' = \Delta t = 0$ and, since v is not zero, Δx must be zero. Thus, they will agree only if the two events occur at the same point in space.

7 (*a*)

8 (*a*) True (*b*) True (*c*) False (*d*) True (*e*) True (*f*) False (*g*) True

10 (*a*)

11 (*a*)

12 (*a*) The linear momentum of the electron-positron pair was zero just before the emission of the photons and therefore must be zero after their emission. (*b*) (3)

13 5.9 ns

14 (*a*) 0.97*c* (*b*) 10.2 y

15 (*a*) 5×10^{-13}% (*b*) 1.000 000 000 000 005 (*c*) 7.5×10^{-13}%

16 (*a*) 4.9×10^{-8} s (*b*) 13 m (*c*) 6.6 m

17 6.6 m

18 (*a*) 49 μs (*b*) 15 km

19 659 m

20 1.58×10^{8} m/s

21 (*a*) 1.3×10^{2} y (*b*) 88 y

22 2.8×10^{8} m/s

23 (*a*) 60 cm (*b*) 2.5 ns

24 85.2 m

25 0.80*c*

26 39 m, 92 m

27 (*a*) $4.50 \times 10^{-10}\%$ (*b*) 2.37 μmin

28 (*a*) 8.5% (*b*) 8.5%, a result that agrees, to two significant figures, with the result obtained in (*a*).

29 45 min

30 (*a*) 40.0 $c \cdot$min (*b*) 25.0 $c \cdot$min (*c*) 15.0 $c \cdot$min

31 25 min, 25 min

33 60 min

34 ratio = 1

35 $0.400c$, event B can precede event A provided $v > 0.400c$

36 4.39 μs

37 (*a*) 14 y (*b*) 40 y

38 (*a*) 50.0 y^{-1} (*b*) 533 (*c*) 1.07×10^3 (*d*) 50.0 y^{-1} (*e*) 267 (*f*) 1.33×10^3 (*g*) Al is 2.67 y younger than Bert.

39 (*a*) 1.01 (*b*) 1.15 (*c*) 1.67 (*d*) 7.09

40 (*a*) $0.742c$ (*b*) 1.04 GeV/c

41 (*a*) 0.155 mc^2 (*b*) 1.29 mc^2 (*c*) 6.09 mc^2

42 50%. Because $\sqrt{1 - v^2/c^2} < 1$, the non-relativistic expression is always low compared to the relativistically correct expression for momentum.

43 2.97 GeV

44

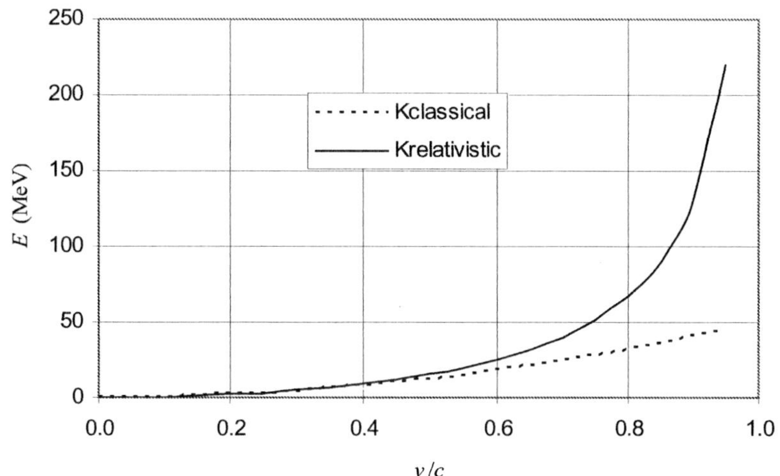

The relativistic formula, represented by the dashed curve, begins to deviate from the non-relativistic curve around $v/c \approx 0.4$

45 (*b*) 0.866*c* (*c*) 0.999*c*

48 (*a*) 1.62 GeV/*c* (*b*) 0.866*c*

49 (*a*) 0.75% (*b*) 69%

50 (*a*) 5.3 y (*b*) 3.5 y

51 (*a*) 0.943

52 (*a*) 12 min (*b*) 27 min

53 In 100 lifetimes $d \approx 6600$ km or approximately one Earth radius. This relatively short distance should convince your classmate that the origin of the muons that are observed on Earth is within our atmosphere, and that they certainly are not from the Sun.

54 (*a*) 1.2 km (*b*) 4.2 μs (*c*) 30 μs

55 (*a*) 4.50 km/s (*b*) 0.334 μs

56 (*a*) 4.61% (*b*) 6.22×10^{10} m (*c*) 0.016%

57 (*a*) 0.75*c* (*b*) 5.0 ft (*c*) No. In your rest frame, the back end of the ladder will clear the door before the front end hits the wall of the shed, while in Ernie's rest frame, the front end will hit the wall of the shed while the back end has yet to clear the other door.

Chapter 11
Gravity

1 (*a*) False (*b*) True (*c*) True (*d*) False

2 (*c*)

3 Earth is closest to the Sun during winter in the northern hemisphere. This is the time of fastest orbital speed. Summer would be the time for minimum orbital speed.

4 Haley's comet was traveling at its fastest orbital speed in 1987 and at its slowest orbital speed 38 years previously in 1949.

5 To obtain the mass M of Venus you need to measure the period T and semi-major axis a of the orbit of one of the satellites, substitute the measured values into $\frac{T^2}{a^3}=\frac{4\pi^2}{GM}$ (Kepler's third law) and solve for M.

6 No. As described by Kepler's third law, the asteroids closer to the Sun have a shorter "year" and are orbiting faster.

7 (*d*)

8 (*c*)

9 (*b*)

10 Between Earth and the moon, the gravitational pulls on the spaceship are oppositely directed. Because of the moon's relatively small mass compared to the mass of Earth, the location where the gravitational forces cancel (thus producing no net gravitational force, a weightless condition) is considerably closer to the moon.

11 (*b*)

12 You could take careful measurements of its position as a function of time in order to determine whether its trajectory is an ellipse, a hyperbola, or a parabola. If the path is an ellipse, it will return; if its path is hyperbolic or parabolic, it will not return. Alternatively, by measuring its distance from the Sun, you can estimate the gravitational potential energy (per kg of its mass, and neglecting the planets) of the object, and by determining its position on several successive nights, the speed of the object can be determined. From this, its kinetic energy (per kg) can be determined. The sum of these two gives the comet's total energy (per kg) and if it is positive, it will likely swing once around the Sun and then leave the Solar System forever.

13 You should fire the rocket in a direction to oppose the orbital motion of the satellite. As the satellite gets closer to Earth after the burn, the potential energy will decrease. However, the total mechanical energy will decrease due to the frictional drag forces transforming mechanical energy into thermal energy. The kinetic energy will increase until the satellite enters the atmosphere where the drag forces slow its motion.

14 Near the moon you would fire the rockets to accelerate the spacecraft with the thrust acting in the direction of your ship's velocity at the time. When the rockets have shut down, as you leave the moon, your kinetic energy will initially decrease (the moon's gravitational pull exceeds that of Earth), and your potential energy will increase. After a certain point, Earth's gravitational attraction would begin accelerating the ship and the kinetic energy would increase at the expense of the gravitational potential energy of the spacecraft-Earth-moon system. The spacecraft will enter Earth's atmosphere with its maximum kinetic energy. Eventually, landing in the ocean, the kinetic energy would be zero, the gravitational potential energy a minimum, and the total mechanical energy of the ship will have been dramatically reduced due to air drag forces producing heat and light during re-entry.

15 At a point inside the sphere a distance *r* from its center, the gravitational field strength is directly proportional to the amount of mass within a distance *r* from the center, and inversely proportional to the square of the distance *r* from the center. The mass within a distance *r* from the center is proportional to the cube of *r*. Thus, the gravitational field strength is directly proportional to *r*.

16 The pictorial representation shows the point of interest *P* and the gravitational fields $\vec{g}_{\text{rod}}$ and $\vec{g}_{\text{sphere}}$ due to the rod and the sphere as well as the resultant field $\vec{g}_{\text{net}}$. Note that the net field (the sum of $\vec{g}_{\text{rod}}$ and $\vec{g}_{\text{sphere}}$) points slightly toward the habitat end of the ship. At very large distances, the rod+sphere mass distribution looks like a point mass, so the field's distance dependence is an inverse square dependence.

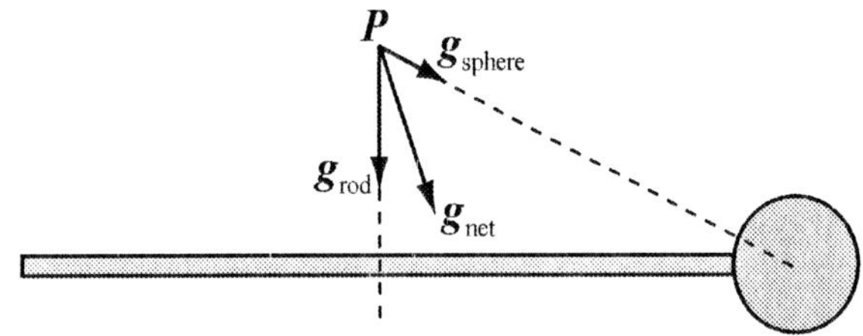

17 $M_{\text{galaxy}} \approx 1.1 \times 10^{11}\ M_S$

18 $a_{g,\text{cheese}} = 0.39\ \text{m/s}^2$, $a_{g,\text{cheese}} \approx 0.24 a_{g,\text{moon}}$

19 3.0 km

20 (*a*) 1.33 AU (*b*) 12.3 M_J

21 (*a*) 6.28×10^{-4} rad/s, 2.78 h (*b*) $L_J = 1.93 \times 10^{43}\ \text{kg} \cdot \text{m}^2/\text{s}$, $L_S = 7.85 \times 10^{42}\ \text{kg} \cdot \text{m}^2/\text{s}$, 0.70% (*c*) $T_{\text{Sun}} = 3.64$ h, $T_{\text{Sun}} = 1.31 T_{\max}$

22 50.5 AU

23 84.0 y

24 11.7 y

25 $4.90 \times 10^{11}\ \text{m} = 3.27$ AU

26 1.42×10^5 km

27 (*a*) 1.6×10^{11} m (*b*) 2.7×10^{10} m, 2.9×10^{11} m

28 258 d. In order for bones and muscles to maintain their health, they need to be under compression as they are on Earth. Due to the long duration (well over a year) of the round trip, you would want to design an exercise program that would maintain the strength of their bones and muscles.

29 (*a*) 90°(*b*) 0.73 AU (*c*) 0.63 y

30 $v_p = 1.09$ km/s, $v_a = 959$ m/s

31 (*a*) 1.90×10^{27} kg

32 (*a*) 8.71 m/s^2 (*b*) In orbit, the astronauts experience only one (the gravitational force) of the two forces (the second being the normal force-a compressive force—exerted by Earth) that normally act on them. Lacking this compressive force, their bones and muscles, in the absence of an exercise program, will weaken. In orbit, the astronauts are not weightless—they are normal-forceless.

33 (*a*) 22.7 h (*b*) 1.22×10^{9} m

34 6.02×10^{24} kg

35 $w' = 10w$

36 39.2 m/s^2

37 2.27×10^{4} m/s

38 1.93×10^{12} m/s^2

39 (*a*) 1.4 (*b*) It is farther from the Sun than Earth. Kepler's third law [$T^2 = Cr_{av}^3$] tells us that longer orbital periods together with larger orbital radii means slower orbital speeds, so the speed of objects orbiting the Sun decreases with distance from the Sun. The average orbital speed of Earth, given by $v = 2\pi r_{ES}/T_{ES}$ is approximately 30 km/s. Because the given maximum speed of the asteroid is only 20 m/s, the asteroid is farther from the Sun.

40 (*a*) 37.6 N (*b*) 2.66 km/s (*c*) 37.0 h

41 (*a*) 7.37 m (*b*) 31.9 μm

42 $T = \frac{2\pi}{\sqrt{KM}} r$

43 0.605

44 (*a*) 5.77 kg (*b*) Because this result is determined by the effect on m_2 of Earth's gravitational field, it is the *gravitational mass* of m_2.

45 10^{9} m

46 (*a*) -6.25×10^{9} J (*b*) -3.12×10^{9} J (*c*) 7.90 km/s

47 2.38 km/s

48 15.8 km/s

49 (*a*) 8.7 kW·h (*b*) $500

51 6.9 km/s

52 9.4×10^5 m

53 19.4 km/s

55 13.8 km/s

57 (*a*) 7.31 h (*b*) 1.04 GJ (*c*) 8.72×10^{12} J·s

58 3.38×10^5, 1.50%, In this analysis we've neglected gravitational forces from other planets and the Sun.

59 11.1 GJ

60 (*a*) 7.65 km/s (*b*) 3.2 km/s (*c*) 5.0 d

61 $(4.0\,\text{N/kg})\hat{\boldsymbol{i}}$

62 $(1.0\times10^{-8}\,\text{N})\hat{\boldsymbol{j}}$

63 (*a*) Along a line at 45° above the +*x* axis. (*b*) $|\vec{g}| = \sqrt{2}\dfrac{Gm}{L^2}$

64 (*a*) $\vec{F} = 0\hat{\boldsymbol{i}} + (9.7\times10^{-8}\,\text{N})\hat{\boldsymbol{j}}$ (*b*) $\vec{g} = (4.8\times10^{-8}\,\text{N/kg})\hat{\boldsymbol{j}}$

65 (*a*) $(-1.7\times10^{-11}\,\text{N/kg})\hat{\boldsymbol{i}}$ (*b*) $(-8.3\times10^{-12}\,\text{N/kg})\hat{\boldsymbol{i}}$ (*c*) 2.5 m

67 (*a*) $\frac{1}{2}CL^2$ (*b*) $\vec{g} = \dfrac{2GM}{L^2}\left[\ln\left(\dfrac{x_0}{x_0-L}\right)-\left(\dfrac{L}{x_0-L}\right)\right]\hat{\boldsymbol{i}}$

68 (*b*) $\vec{g}_x = -\dfrac{GM}{x_0(x_0-L)}\hat{\boldsymbol{i}}$ (*c*) $\vec{F} = -\dfrac{GMm_0}{x_0(x_0-L)}\hat{\boldsymbol{i}}$

69 (*a*) 0 (*b*) 0 (*c*) 3.2×10^{-9} N/kg

70 The gravitational attraction force is zero. The gravitational field inside the 2.00 m shell due to that shell is zero; therefore, it exerts no force on the 1 m-shell, and, by Newton's third law, that shell exerts no force on the larger shell.

71 $g_1 = g_2$

72 $g_2 = \frac{R_1^2}{R_2^2} g_1$

73 (*a*) $F(r = 3a) = \frac{Gm(M_1 + M_2)}{9a^2}$ (*b*) $F(r = 1.9a) = \frac{GmM_1}{3.61a^2}$ (*c*) $F(r = 0.9a) = 0$

74 (*a*) $F(x = 3a) = \frac{Gm}{a^2}\left(\frac{M_1}{9} + \frac{M_2}{4.84}\right)$ (*b*) $F(x = 1.9a) = \frac{GmM_2}{1.21a^2}$

(*c*) $F(x = 0.9a) = 0$

76 $\Delta w = 1.88\,\text{N}$. If Earth's crustal density actually increased with depth, this increase with depth would partially compensate for the decrease in the fraction of Earth's mass between a descending team member and the center of Earth; with the result that the loss in weight would be lower than the actual experimental result.

77 $g(x) = G\left(\frac{4\pi\rho_0 R^3}{3}\right)\left[\frac{1}{x^2} - \frac{1}{8(x - \frac{1}{2}R)^2}\right]$

78 $|\vec{g}| = \frac{2\pi\rho_0 GR}{3}$

79 $\omega = \sqrt{\frac{4\pi\rho_0 G}{3}}$

80 (*a*) 6.4×10^8 kg/m^2 (*b*) $g(r > 5.0\,\text{m}) = \frac{6.7\,\text{N}\cdot\text{m}^2/\text{kg}}{r^2}$,

$g(r < 5.0\,\text{m}) = 0.27\,\text{N/kg}$

81 1.0 m/s

82 3.56×10^{-5}

83 (*a*) $\vec{F} = -\frac{GMm}{d^2}\left[1 - \frac{\frac{d^3}{4}}{\left\{d^2 + \frac{R^2}{4}\right\}^{3/2}}\right]\hat{i}$ (*b*) $\vec{F}(R) = -0.821\frac{GMm}{R^2}\hat{i}$

85 249 y

86 5.97×10^{24} kg

87 (*a*) $W = GM_E m\left(\frac{1}{r_1} - \frac{1}{r_2}\right)$

88 1 h 48 min

89 (*a*) 3.36×10^9 (*b*) 241

90 (*a*) 5.43×10^6 m/s (*b*) 2.25×10^6 m/s, 201

91 1.70 Mm

92 (*b*) 29.5 km

94 $v_2 = \sqrt{\frac{2Gm_1^2}{r(m_1 + m_2)}}$, $v_1 = \sqrt{\frac{2Gm_2^2}{r(m_1 + m_2)}}$

95 1.60×10^{-4}

96 $3.7 \times 10^6\ M_{\text{Sun}}$

97 $v = 1.16\sqrt{\frac{GM}{a}}$

98 (*a*) $\frac{1}{2}gmR_E$ (*b*) $\sqrt{gR_E}$ (*c*) $\sqrt{3gR_E}$

99 $g(r > R_2) = \dfrac{GM}{r^2}$, $g(r) = \dfrac{GM\left(r^3 - R_1^3\right)}{r^2\left(R_2^3 - R_1^3\right)}$

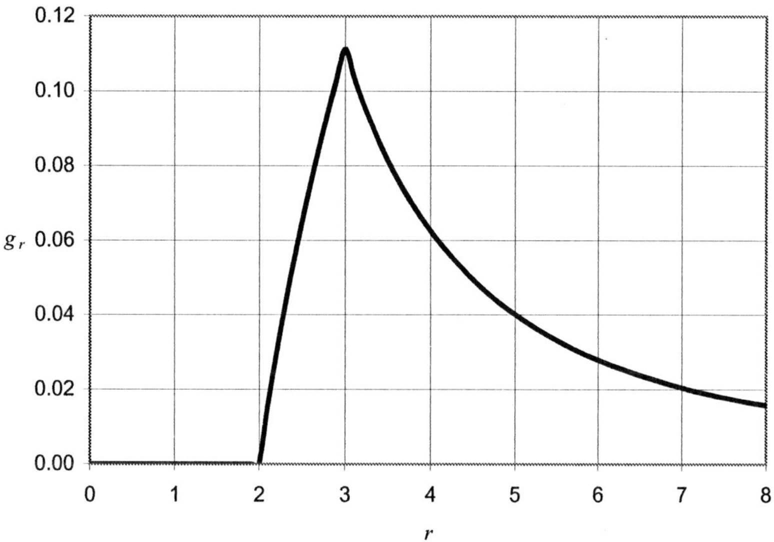

100 (*a*) $g(x) = \dfrac{GM}{\left(R^2 + x^2\right)^{3/2}} x$

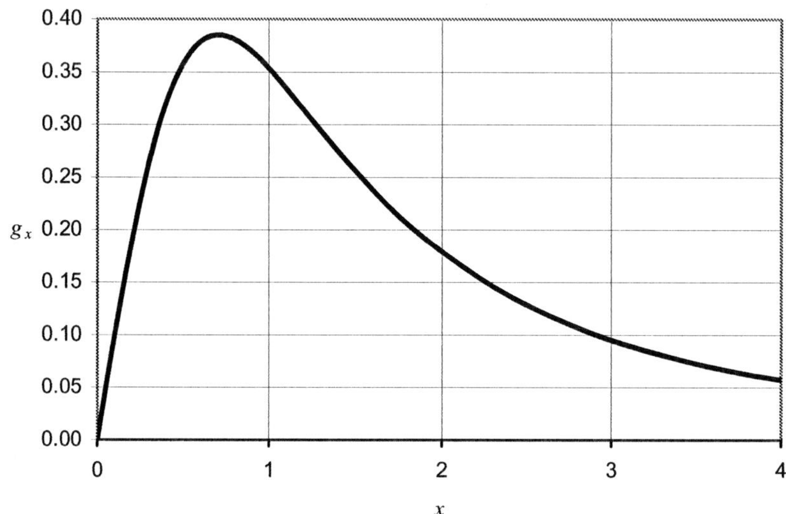

(*b*) $x = \pm \dfrac{R}{\sqrt{2}}$

101 $g = \dfrac{2G\lambda}{r}$

103 (*b*) $U = -\frac{GMm_0}{L}\ln\left(\frac{x_0 + L/2}{x_0 - L/2}\right)$ (*c*) $F(x_0) = -\frac{Gmm_0}{x^2 - L^2/4}$. This answer and the answer given in Example 11-8 are the same.

104 $F = \frac{GMm}{a(a+L)}$

105 34 pN

106 (*a*) 177 (*c*) 0.454. Because the ratio of the forces is less than one, the moon is the main cause of the tidal stretching of the oceans on Earth.

107 (*a*) The gravitational force is greater on the lower robot, so if it were not for the cable its acceleration would be greater than that of the upper robot and they would separate. In opposing this separation, the cable is stressed.
(*b*) 2.2×10^5 m

Chapter 12
Static Equilibrium and Elasticity

1 (*a*) False (*b*) True (*c*) True (*d*) False

2 (*a*) False (*b*) False (*c*) True (*d*) True

3 (*b*)

4 You cannot stand up because your body's center of gravity must be above your feet.

5 The higher the sign, the greater the torque about the horizontal axis through the lowest extremes of the posts for a given wind speed. In addition, the deeper the post holes the greater the maximum opposing torque about the same axis for a given consistency of the dirt. Thus, higher signs require deeper holes for the signposts.

6 $V = \dfrac{m}{M}v$

7 The main reason this is done is to lower the center of gravity of the mug. The lower the center of gravity the more stable the mug is.

8 Dynamically the boats are in equilibrium along their line of motion, but in the plane of their sail and the sailors, they are in static equilibrium. The torque on the boat, applied by the wind acting on the sail, has a tendency to tip the boat. The rudder counteracts that tendency to some degree, but in particularly strong winds, when the boat is sailing at particular angles with respect to the wind, the sailors need to "hike out" to apply some torque (due to the gravitational force of Earth on the sailors) by leaning outward on the beam of the boat. If the wind strengthens, they need to extend their bodies further over the side and may need to get into a contraption called a "trapeze" that enables the sailor to have his or her entire body outside the boat.

9 (*b*)

10 55 cm

11 (*b*) 2.0 N/cm

12 170 lb, 400 lb

13 (*b*) Taking long strides requires a large coefficient of static friction because θ is large for long strides. (*c*) If μ_s is small, that is, there is ice on the surface, θ must be small to avoid slipping.

14 (*a*) $\frac{3}{4}Mg$, $\frac{1}{4}Mg$ (*b*) $m = \frac{1}{2}M$

15 84 cm

17 692 N, 2.54 kN

18 4.2 m

19 0.728 m

20 (*a*) 0.181 kN (*b*) 0.46 kN

21 $\frac{1}{2}W$, $\frac{\sqrt{3}}{2}W$

22 44 N, 44 N

23 (*a*) $\vec{F} = (30\,\mathrm{N})\hat{i} + (30\,\mathrm{N})\hat{j}$ (*b*) $\vec{F} = (35\,\mathrm{N})\hat{i} + (45\,\mathrm{N})\hat{j}$

24 $x < 2.3$ m

25 (*a*) $F_n = Mg - F\sqrt{\dfrac{2R-h}{h}}$ (*b*) $F_{c,h} = F$ (*c*) $F_{c,v} = F\sqrt{\dfrac{2R-h}{h}}$

26 $F = Mg\sqrt{\dfrac{h}{2R-h}}$

27 (*a*) 6.87 N (*b*) 1.7 N·m (*c*) 8.3 N, 15 N

28 (*a*) 149 N (*b*) 133 N (*c*) 133 N

29 (*a*) 71 N (*b*) 3.5 m (*c*) 0.50 kN

30 0.23

31 (*b*) *a*/3 (*c*) *Mg*/2

32 $D = \frac{1}{2}\left(\sqrt{3}b - a\right)$

33 $h = \mu_s L \tan\theta \sin\theta$

34 $0.85L$

35 $\mu_s = \dfrac{2h}{L\tan\theta\sin\theta}$

36 (*a*) 450 N (*b*) 0.24 kN (*c*) *T* will decrease.

37 59°

38 0.63 kN, 22°

39 62°

40 0.98 mm

41 (*a*) 42 N (*b*) 0.14%

42 0.83 mm

43 5.0°

44 1.81 mm

46 (*a*) 34.7 cm (*b*) 0.08 J

47 (*a*) 1.4×10^6 N/m^2 (*b*) 7 mJ (*c*) 28 mJ. There is about 4 times as much energy stored in the rubber when 0.30 kg are hung from it. That is because the stored energy increases quadratically with an increase in the mass.

48 7.2 mm

49 0.69

50 56 N, 0.28 mm

51 Because $\text{Stress}_{\text{failing}} < \text{Stress}_{\text{cable}}$, the cable will not support the elevator.

54 (*a*) $0.316r_0$ (*b*) $T = \dfrac{9\pi r_0^2 Y}{10}$

55 1.5 kN

56 99 cm

57 $m_1 = 0.15$ kg, $m_2 = 0.71$ kg, $m_3 = 0.36$ kg

58 (*a*) 0.75 (*b*) 1.1 kN

59 1.8 kg

60 (*a*) 3

61 0.15

62 0.58

63 $\mu_s < 0.50$

64 1.15 kg

65 $\mu_s = \frac{1}{2}(\cot\theta - 1)$

66 83 cm

67 (*a*) 0.15 kN (*b*) 3.8 m

68 (*a*) 10 kN, 6.9 kN, 41° below the horizontal (*b*) 5.3 kN, 15° above the horizontal.

69 $\mu_s < 0.50$

70 4.0 g

71

(*c*)

Cell	Formula/Content	Algebraic Form
B5	B4+1	$i+1$
C5	C4+$B$1/(2*B5)	$d_i + \frac{L}{2i}$

	A	B	C	D
1	*L*=	0.20	m	
2				
3		*i*	offset	
4		1	0.100	
5		2	0.150	
6		3	0.183	
7		4	0.208	
8		5	0.228	
9		6	0.245	
10		7	0.259	
11		8	0.272	
12		9	0.283	
13		10	0.293	
98		95	0.514	
99		96	0.515	
100		97	0.516	
101		98	0.517	
102		99	0.518	
103		100	0.519	

$d_5 = 15$ cm, $d_{10} = 26$ cm, and $d_{100} = 52$ cm

(*d*) No

72 (*a*) 7.9 N (*b*) 29 N (*c*) 7.9 N

73 566 N

74 $\mu_{\text{s,beam-floor}} = 0.58$, $\mu_{\text{s,cylinder-floor}} = 0.14$

75 $F_{\text{n}} = 2mg,\ F = mg\frac{r}{\sqrt{R(2r-R)}},\ F_{\text{W}} = mg\frac{R-r}{\sqrt{R(2r-R)}}$

76 1

Chapter 13
Fluids

1 (*e*)

2 (*c*)

3 (*c*)

4 True. This is a special case. Because the volumes are equal, the average density is the average of the two densities. ***This is not a general result.***

5 Pressure increases approximately 1 atm every 10 m in fresh water. To breathe requires creating a pressure of less than 1 atm in your lungs. At the surface you can do this easily, but not at a depth of 10 m.

6 Yes. Because the volumes of the two objects are equal, the downward force on each side is reduced by the same amount (the buoyant force acting on them) when they are submerged, . The buoyant force is independent of their masses. That is, if $m_1L_1 = m_2L_2$ and $L_1 \neq L_2$, then $(m_1 - c)L_1 \neq (m_2 - c)L_2$.

7 (*b*)

8 (*c*)

9 False. The buoyant force on a submerged object depends on the weight of the displaced fluid which, in turn, depends on the volume of the displaced fluid. Because the bricks have the same volume, they will displace the same volume of water.

10 (*a*) When the bottle is squeezed, the force is transmitted equally through the fluid, leading to a pressure increase on the air bubble in the diver. The air bubble shrinks, and the loss in buoyancy is enough to sink the diver.

(*b*) As water enters its tanks, the average density of the submarine increases and, because it is displacing less water, the buoyant force on it decreases. Thus the submarine will start to sink.

(*c*) Breathing in lowers one's average density and breathing out increases one's average density. Because denser objects float lower on the surface than do less dense objects, a floating person will oscillate up and down on the water surface as he or she breathes in and out.

11 Because the pressure increases with depth, the object will be compressed and its density will increase as its volume decreases. Thus, the object will sink to the bottom.

12 The acceleration-producing force acting on the fluid is the product of the difference in pressure between the wide and narrow parts of the pipe and the area of the narrow part of the pipe.

13

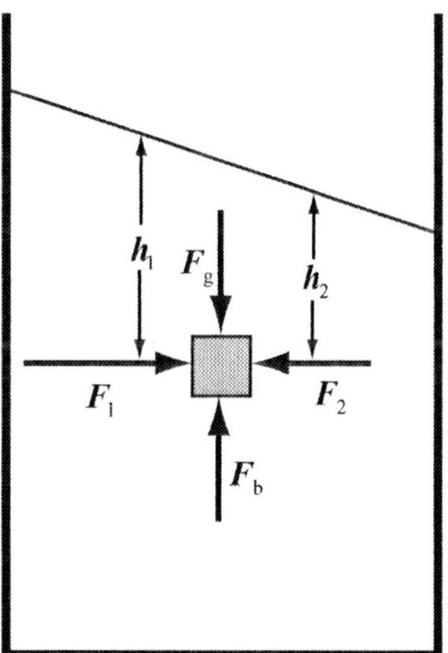

The pictorial representation shows the glass and an element of water in the middle of the glass. As is readily established by a simple demonstration, the surface of the water is not level while the glass is accelerated, showing that there is a pressure gradient (a difference in pressure) due to the differing depths ($h_1 > h_2$ and hence $F_1 > F_2$) of water on the two sides of the element of water. This pressure gradient results in a net force on the element as shown in the figure. The upward buoyant force is equal in magnitude to the downward gravitational force.

14 The water level in the pond will fall slightly. When the anchor is in the boat, the boat displaces enough water so that the buoyant force on it equals the sum of the weight of the boat, your weight, and the weight of the anchor. When you drop the anchor into the water, it displaces just its volume of water (rather than its weight as it did while in the boat). The total weight of the boat becomes less and the boat displaces less water as a consequence.

15 (*c*)

16 (*f*)

17 The mounding around entrance 1 will cause the streamlines to curve concave downward over the entrance. An upward pressure gradient produces the downward centripetal force. This means there is a lowering of the pressure at entrance 1. No such lowering occurs aver entrance 2, so the pressure there is higher than the pressure at entrance 1. The air circulates in entrance 2 and out entrance 1. It has been demonstrated that enough air will circulate inside the tunnel even with slightest breeze outside.

18 3.50 m

19 1.11 kg/m^3

20 0.379 kg

21 1.0×10^2 kg

22 2 Tg

23 0.748 g/cm^3

24 24.5 kg/m^3

25 0.773

26 1.7 μm

27 29.8 in of Hg

28 (*a*) 10.3 m (*b*) 75.7 cm

29 1.5 N

30 1.1 m

31 230 N

32 184 cm^2

33 197 atm. Because a depth of only 2 km is required to produce a one-percent compression, this does not occur in our oceans.

34 54.2 atm, $P_{\text{woman}} \approx 18\, P_{\text{elephant}}$

35 (*a*) 15 kN (*b*) 0.34 kg

36 16 cm

37 45 cm

39 1.4%

40 (*a*) 5.9 L, 58 N (*b*) 0.17 kN. This occurs in the same way that the force on Pascal's barrel is much greater than the weight of the water in the tube. The downward force on the base is also the result of the downward component of the force exerted by the slanting walls of the cone on the water.

41 4.36 N

42 3.0×10^3 kg/m^3

43 (*a*) 11×10^3 kg/m^3 (*b*) From Table 13-1, we see that the density of the unknown material is close to that of lead.

44 2.69×10^3 kg/m^3

45 800 kg/m^3, 1.11

46 7.0×10^3 kg/m^3

47 250 kg/m^3

48 183 m^3

49 3.9 kg

50 12.4 N, 36.7 N

51 4.9×10^5 N

52 (*a*) 45 m/s^2 (*b*) 7.3 m/s

53 2.5×10^7 kg

54 (*a*) 65 m/s (*b*) 22 atm

55 (*a*) 12.0 m/s (*b*) 133 kPa (*c*) The flow rates are the same.

56 1.68 cm

57 (*a*) 4.6 L/min (*b*) 7.6×10^{-2} m^2

58 (*a*) 4.9 m/s (*b*) $v(x) = \dfrac{0.304\,\text{m}^3/\text{s}}{(0.45\,\text{m} - 0.20x)^2}$

59 144 kPa

60 13.1 L/s

61 0.20 kPa. Because $\Delta P \propto I_V^2$ (ΔP as a function of I_V is a parabola that opens upward), this pressure difference is the minimum pressure difference.

64 $x = 2\sqrt{h(H - h)}$

65 (*b*) $P_{top} = P_{at} - \rho g d$

66 2.4×10^5 Pa

67 (*a*) 9.28 cm/s (*b*) 0.331 cm (*c*) 0.76 cm

68 40.4 L/s

69 (*a*) $x = 2\sqrt{h(H - h)}$ (*c*) $x_{max} = H$

70 1.47 kPa

71 1.43 mm

72 3.98 mPa·s

73 90 mi/h. Because most major league pitchers can throw a fastball in the low-to-mid90s, this drag crisis may very well play a role in the game.

74 11 m/s, 17 m/s

75 2.91 L/s

76 0.33 m/s, 0.45 s

77 2

78 1.9 cm

79 36 kg/m^3

80 5.0×10^3 kg/m^3

81 0.71 kg

82 40 g

83 11.8 cm

84 64 g

85 1 m is a plausible diameter for such a pipe.

86 12.6 m, 7.63 m

87 29 s

88 22 cm, 37 cm

89 (*a*) 70 m^3 (*b*) 5.2 m/s^2

90 $9\rho_0$

91 (*b*) 0.13 km^{-1}

92 (*a*) 2.44% (*b*) 60 m^3

93 39 cm^3

Chapter 14
Oscillations

1 (*a*) False (*b*) True (*c*) True

2 The energy of a simple harmonic oscillator varies as the square of the amplitude of its motion. Hence, tripling the amplitude increases the energy by a factor of 9.

3 (*a*)

4 (*b*)

5 (*c*)

6 (*b*)

7 (*c*)

8 (*d*)

9 Neglecting the mass of the spring results in your using a value for the mass of the oscillating system that is smaller than its actual value. Hence, your calculated value for the period will be smaller than the actual period of the system and the calculated value for the frequency, which is the reciprocal of the period, will be higher than the actual value.

Because the total energy of the oscillating system depends solely on the amplitude of its motion and on the stiffness of the spring, it is independent of the mass of the system, and so neglecting the mass of the spring would have no effect on your calculation of the system's total energy.

10 (*a*)

11 (*d*)

12 (*d*)

13 (*b*)

14 The period of a simple pendulum depends on the square root of the length of the pendulum. Increasing the length of the pendulum will lengthen its period and, hence, the clock will run slow.

15 1 matches up with B, 2 matches up with D, and 3 matches up with A.

16 (*c*)

17 (*c*)

18 (*c*)

19 (*a*) True (*b*) False (*c*) True (*d*) False (*e*) True

20 (*a*)

21 (*b*)

22 (*c*)

23 (*b*)

24 (*c*)

25 About 5

26 About 1 Hz

27 8π

28 (*a*) Approximately 1.5 s (*b*) Approximately 2.0 s. From observation of people as they walk, these estimates seem reasonable.

29 (*a*) 3.00 Hz (*b*) 0.333 s (*c*) 7.0 cm (*d*) 0.0833 s in the $-x$ direction

30 (*a*) $\frac{\pi}{2}, \frac{3\pi}{2}$ (*b*) π (*c*) 0 (*d*) $\frac{\pi}{3}$

31 (*a*) $x = (0.25\,\text{m})\cos\left[\left(4.2\,\text{s}^{-1}\right)t\right]$ (*b*) $v = -(1.0\,\text{m/s})\sin\left[\left(4.2\,\text{s}^{-1}\right)t\right]$
(*c*) $a = -\left(4.4\,\text{m/s}^2\right)\cos\left[\left(4.2\,\text{s}^{-1}\right)t\right]$

32 (*a*) 1.3 m/s (*b*) 25 m/s^2 (*c*) 0.25 s.

33 (*a*) $x = (0.28\,\text{m})\cos\left[\left(4.2\,\text{s}^{-1}\right)t - 0.45\right]$ (*b*) $v = -(1.2\,\text{m/s})\sin\left[\left(4.2\,\text{s}^{-1}\right)t - 0.45\right]$
(*c*) $a = -\left(4.9\,\text{m/s}^2\right)\cos\left[\left(4.2\,\text{s}^{-1}\right)t - 0.45\right]$

34 (*a*) 12 cm (*b*) 12 cm (*c*) 8.5 cm (*d*) 3.5 cm

35 (*a*)

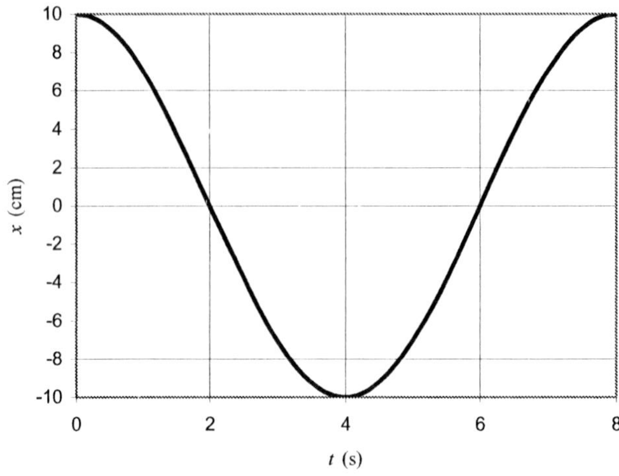

(*b*) 2.9 cm, 7.1 cm, 7.1 cm, 2.9 cm

36 13 Hz

37 (*a*) 7.9 m/s, 25 m/s^2 (*b*) 6.3 m/s, –15 m/s^2

38 (*b*) $x(0) = A_0 \cos\delta = A_c, v(0) = -\omega A_0 \sin\delta$

39 (*a*) 3.1 s, 0.32 Hz (*b*) $x = (40\,\text{cm})\cos\left[\left(2.0\,\text{s}^{-1}\right)t + \frac{\pi}{2}\right]$

40 (*a*) 31cm/s (*b*) $\frac{2\pi}{3}$ rad/s (*c*) $x = (15\,\text{cm})\cos\left[\left(\frac{2\pi}{3}\text{s}^{-1}\right)t + \pi\right]$

41 23 J

42 3.4 J

43 (*a*) 0.368 J (*b*) 3.83 cm

44 (*a*) 3.0 cm (*b*) 77 cm/s

45 1.4 kN/m

46 0.42 J

47 (*a*) 6.9 Hz (*b*) 0.15 s (*c*) 10 cm (*d*) 4.3 m/s (*e*) 1.9×10^2 m/s^2 (*f*) 36 ms, 0

48 (*a*) 1.88 Hz (*b*) 0.531 s (*c*) 8.00 cm (*d*) 0.947 m/s (*e*) 11.2 m/s^2 (*f*) 0.133 s, 0

49 (*a*) 0.68 kN/m (*b*) 0.42 s (*c*) 1.5 m/s (*d*) 23 m/s^2

50 0.601 Hz

51 (*a*) 3.08 kN/m (*b*) 4.16 Hz (*c*) 0.240 s

52 (*a*) 1.51 kg (*b*) 8.21 mm (*c*) $x = -(2.50\,\text{cm})\cos[(34.6\,\text{rad/s})t]$,
$v = (86.4\,\text{cm/s})\sin[(34.6\,\text{rad/s})t]$, $a = (29.9\,\text{m/s}^2)\cos[(34.6\,\text{rad/s})t]$

53 0.262 s

54 2.2 Hz

55 (*a*) 1.0 Hz (*b*) 0.50 s (*c*) 0.14 N

56 25 cm

57 (*a*) 6.7 cm (*b*) 0.26 s (*c*) Because $h < 8.0$ cm, the spring is never uncompressed. 77 cm/s

58 (*a*) 1.0 mm (*b*) 15 Hz

59 44 cm

60 6.2 m

61 12 s

62 9.79 m/s^2

63 11.7 s

65 $T = 2\pi\sqrt{\dfrac{L}{g\cos\theta}}$

66 (*a*) $v_{max} = \phi_0\sqrt{gL}$ (*b*) $v_{max} = \sqrt{2gL(1-\cos\phi_0)}$ (*d*) 1 mm/s (*e*) 0.2 m/s

67 1.1 s

68 2.0 s

69 0.50 $kg{\cdot}m^2$

70 The door's period, 0.64 s, is too short. The only way to increase it is to increase the height of the door.

71 21.1 cm from the center of the meter stick.

72 (*a*) 24 cm (*b*) $R/\sqrt{2}$, 2.1 s

74 (*c*) 0.00800%, 22.4 cm

75 (*a*) $d = 1.64$ (*b*) 2.31 cm

76 (*a*) 0.444 s (*b*) 0.180 J (*c*) 0.0450 kg/s

78 (*a*) 10.0% (*b*) 30.0 s (*c*) 62.8

79 (*a*) 0.31 (*b*) -3.1×10^{-2} %

80 (*a*) 3.6 cm, 2.2 cm (*b*) 38 J, 14 J

81 (*a*) 1.57% (*c*) $0.43E_0$

82 (*a*) 8.2 s (*b*) 26 s

83 (*a*) 5.51 Pa·s (*b*) 125

84 (*a*) 314 (*b*) 6.00 rad/s

85 (*a*) 1.0 Hz (*b*) 2 Hz (*c*) 0.35 Hz

86 (*a*) 19 (*b*) 180 (*c*) 3.50 rad/s

87 (*a*) 4.98 cm (*b*) 14.1 rad/s (*c*) 35.4 cm (*d*) 1.00 rad/s

88 (*a*) 34.5 cm (*b*) 1.81×10^{-4}

89 (*a*) 0.48 Hz, 2.1 s (*b*) $v = -(1.2\text{ m/s})\sin\left[(3.0\text{ rad/s})t + \frac{\pi}{4}\right]$ (*c*) 1.2 m/s

90 1.7×10^{25} kg

91 The error is greater if the clock is elevated.

92 (*a*) $T = \frac{2\pi}{\sqrt{\frac{k}{M} + \frac{g}{L}}}$ (*b*) 29.6 N/m

93 (*a*) $\mu_s = \frac{Ak}{(m_1 + m_2)g}$ (*b*) A is unchanged. E is unchanged. ω is reduced and T is increased.

94 (*a*) 2.46 m (*b*) 3.16 rad/s (*c*) 1.48 m

95 (*b*) 2.0 cm/s^2

96 (*b*) 24 ms

98 (*a*) 0.63 (*b*) 6.4 cm

100 13.1 N/m

101 6.44×10^{13} rad/s

102

(*c*)

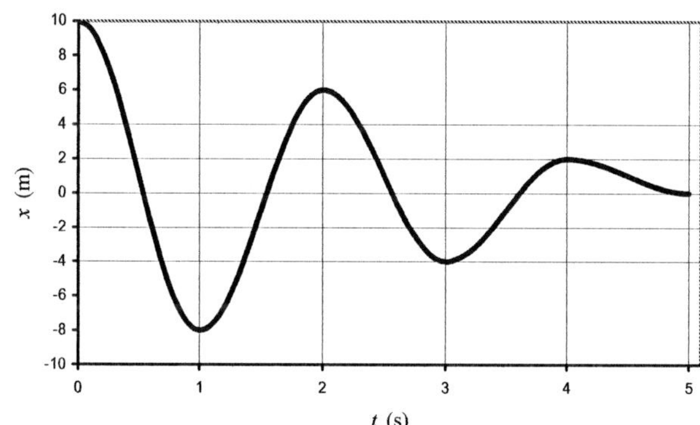

103 $T = 7.78\sqrt{\frac{R}{g}}$

104 (*c*) 84.4 min

107

(*a*)

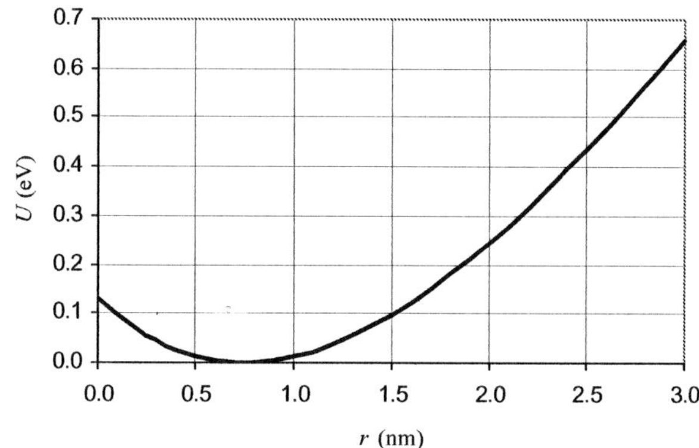

(*b*) $r = r_0$, $k = 2\beta^2 D$ (*c*) $\omega = 2\beta\sqrt{\frac{D}{m}}$

Chapter 15
Traveling Waves

1 The speed of a transverse wave on a uniform rope increases with increasing tension. The waves on the rope move faster as they move toward the ceiling because the tension increases due to the weight of the rope below the pulse.

2 (*b*)

3 (*b*)

4 (*c*)

5 The resonant (standing wave) frequencies on a string are inversely proportional to the square root of the linear density of the string $\left(f = \frac{1}{\lambda}\sqrt{\frac{F_T}{\mu}}\right)$. Thus, extremely high frequencies (which might otherwise require very long strings) can be accommodated on relatively short strings if the strings are linearly denser that the high frequency strings. High frequencies are not a problem as they utilize short strings anyway.

6 (*a*)

7 (*c*)

8 (*a*)

9 There was only one explosion. Sound travels faster in water than air. Abel heard the sound wave in the water first, then, surfacing, heard the sound wave traveling through the air, which took longer to reach him.

10 False

11 (*b*)

12 (*b*)

13 (*a*)

14 (*b*)

15 (*b*)

16 (*a*)

17 (*a*) False (*b*) True (*c*) True

18 (*a*) True (*b*) False

19 (*a*)

20 No. Because the wavelength of the radiation is small relative to the door, the diffraction effects are small and the waves do not spread out significantly as they pass through the door.

21 The light from the visible star will be shifted about its mean frequency periodically due to the relative approach toward and recession away from Earth as the star revolves about the common center of mass.

22

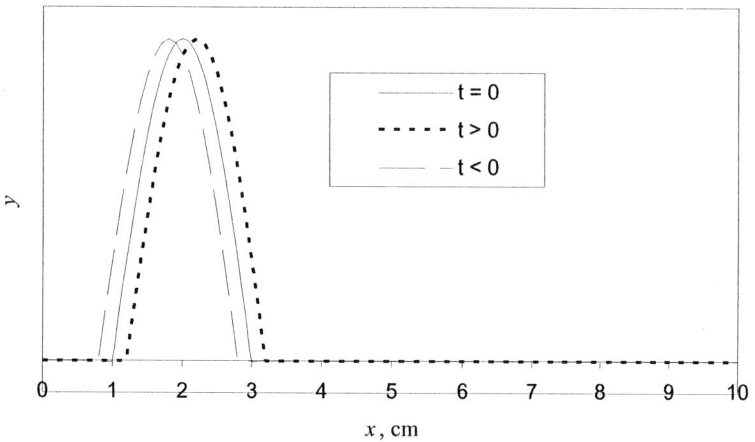

(*a*) One can see that at $t = 0$, the portion of the string between 1 cm and 2 cm is moving down, (*b*) the portion between 2 cm and 3 cm is moving up, and (*c*) the string at $x = 2$ cm is instantaneously at rest.

23

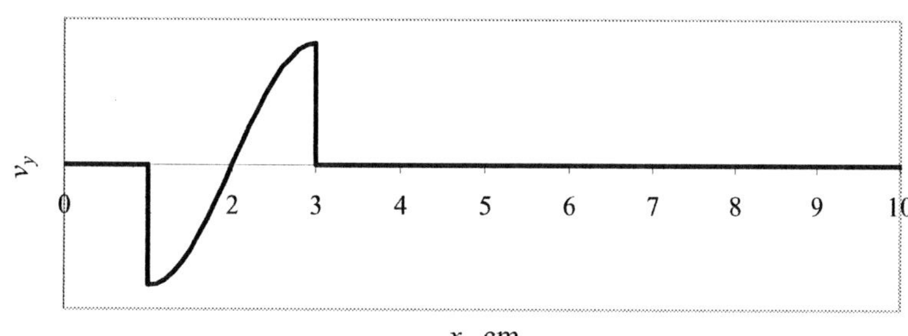

24 $t_{9m} = \frac{1}{3} t_m$

25 Path C. Because the wave speed is highest in the water and more of path C is underwater than are paths A or B, the sound wave will spend the least time on path C.

26 No. The term *Mach 2* means that the speed is twice the speed of sound at a given altitude. Because the speed of sound is lower at high altitudes than at ground level (due to lower density and colder temperature), *Mach 2* means less than twice the speed of sound at sea level.

27 11 ms

28 1.04 km/s

29 0.27 km/s, 21%

30 (*a*) 1.41 km/s (*b*) 2.70×10^{10} N/m^2

31 1.32 km/s

32 251 m/s

33 (*b*) 40 N (*c*) 40.8 N, 2%

34 (*b*) 5.0% (*c*) 347 m/s (*d*) 347 m/s

38 20 cm

39 9.9 W

40 171 Hz

41 (*a*) 5.00 m/s in the $-x$ direction. (*b*) 10.0 cm, 50.0 Hz, 0.0200 s (*c*) 0.314 m/s

42 (*a*) $y(x,t) = (0.025\,\text{m})\sin\left[(42\,\text{m}^{-1})x - (5.0\times10^{2}\,\text{s}^{-1})t\right]$ (*b*) 13 m/s (*c*) 6.3 km/s^2

43 (*a*) 6.8 J (*b*) 44 W

44 (*a*) $P(0) = \frac{1}{2}\mu\omega^2 A_0^2 v$ (*b*) $P(x) = \frac{1}{2}\mu\omega^2 A_0^2 v e^{-2bx}$

45 (*a*) 79 mW (*b*) The power can be increased by a factor of 100 by increasing either the frequency or the amplitude by a factor of 10, or by increasing the tension by a factor of 100.

47 (*a*) 0.75 Pa (*b*) 4.00 m (*c*) 85.8 Hz (*d*) 343 m/s

48 (*a*) 1.30 m (*b*) 0.649 m

49 (*a*) 36.4 μm (*b*) 83.4 mPa

50 (*a*) 20.9 μm (*b*) 10.4 μm

51 (*a*) If the pressure is a maximum at x_1 when $t = 0$, the displacement s is zero. (*b*) 3.64 μm

52 10

53 (*a*) 0.80 s (*b*) 30 m (*c*) 50.0 Hz, 6.86 m

54 (*a*) 100 m (*b*) 126 mW

55 (*a*) 50.3 W (*b*) 2.00 m (*c*) 4.44 mW/m^2

56 (*a*) 0.20 km (*b*) 6.2 m

57 (*a*) 20.0 dB (*b*) 100 dB

58 (*a*) 10^{-11} W/m^2 (*b*) 2×10^{-12} W/m^2

59 90 dB

60 99%

61 (*a*) 0.10 km (*b*) 0.13 W

62 3.2

63 (*a*) 80 dB (*b*) Eliminating the 70-dB and 73-dB sources does not reduce the intensity level significantly.

65 88 dB

66 5.1%

67 57 dB

68 $r = -0.20,\ \tau = 0.80$

72 (*a*) 1.72 m (*b*) 247 Hz

73 (*a*) 263 m/s (*b*) 1.32 m (*c*) 261 Hz

74 (a) 2.12 m (b) 162 Hz

75 153 Hz

76 (*a*) 23.6° (*b*) 11.5 km

77 2.254×10^8 m/s

78 79.1 km/h

79 174 mi/h

80 (*a*) 62 m (*b*) The sub is descending at 0.81 m/s.

81 (*a*) −7.78 kHz (*b*) −4.4 kHz

82 (*a*) Yes (*b*) 0.033 Hz

84 229 Hz

85 (*a*) 0.82 kHz (*b*) 0.85 kHz

86 (*a*) 90.6 km/h (*b*) 800 Hz (*c*) 926 Hz

87 714 Hz, 185 m

88 4.8 km

89 $\lambda_{max} = 500.02\ \text{nm}$, $\lambda_{min} = 499.98\ \text{nm}$

90 (*a*)

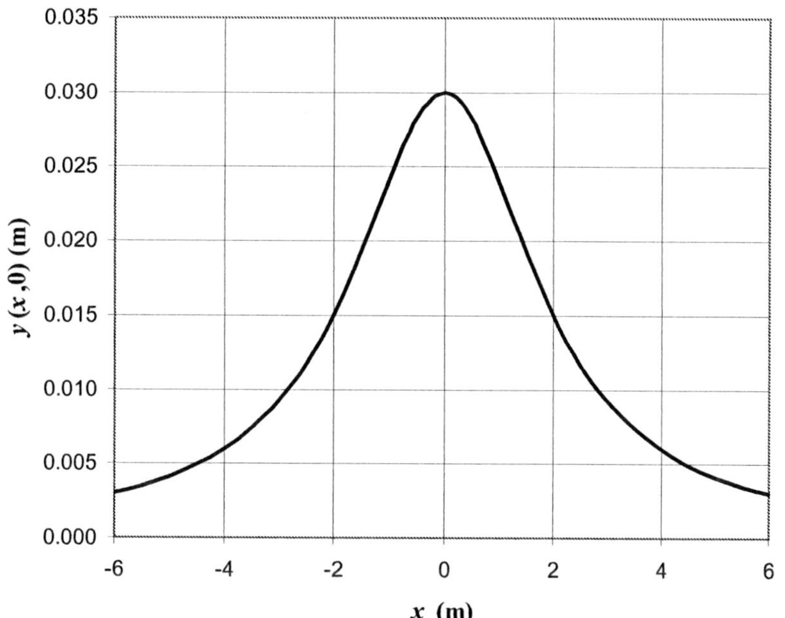

(*b*) $y(x,t) = \dfrac{0.120\,\text{m}^3}{(2.00\,\text{m})^2 + [x - (10.0\,\text{m/s})t]^2}$,

$y(x,t) = \dfrac{0.120\,\text{m}^3}{(2.00\,\text{m})^2 + [x + (10.0\,\text{m/s})t]^2}$

91 529 Hz, 474 Hz

92 (*a*) 0.593 Hz (*b*) 1.59 Hz

93 7.99 m from the left end of the wire.

94 65 km/h

95 (*a*) 55.6 N/m^2 (*b*) 3.49 W/m^2 (*c*) 0.110 W

96 1.07 kHz

97 77 kN

98 26.3 cm

99 206 m

100 11.7 ms

101 0.2 m

102 (*a*) 400 Hz, 2.5 ms (*b*) 0.32 km/s (*c*) 79 cm, 7.9 m^{-1}
(*d*) $y(x,t) = (0.50\,\text{mm})\sin\left[(7.9\,\text{m}^{-1})x - (2.51\times10^{3}\,\text{s}^{-1})t\right]$ (*e*) 1.3 m/s, 3.2 km/s^2
(*f*) 2.5 W

103 (*a*) 10.0 m/s (*b*) 2.00 m (*c*) $p_{\text{max}} = 1.26\times10^{-4}\,\text{kg}\cdot\text{m/s}$ (*d*) 3.95 mN

Chapter 16
Superposition and Standing Waves

1

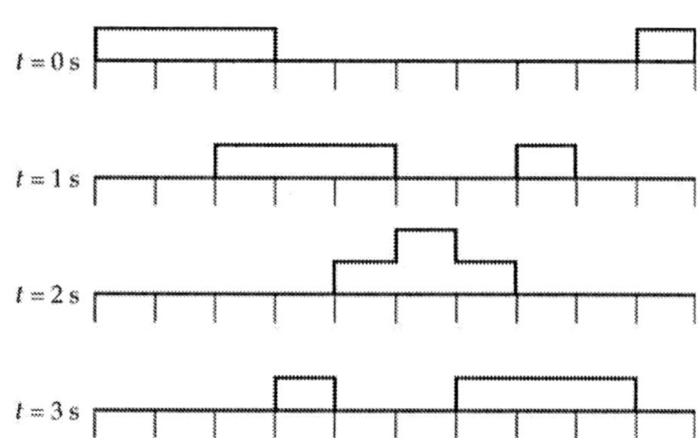

2

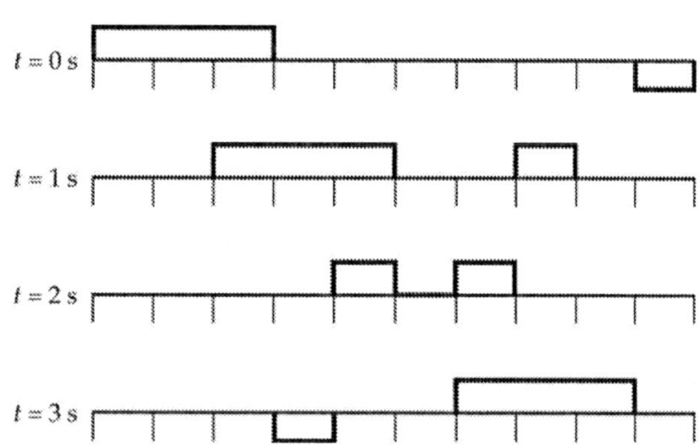

3 (*b*) and (*c*)

4 (*d*)

5 (*a*)

6 (*a*)

7 3.0 m

8 (*a*) True (*b*) True (*c*) True

9 (*b*)

10 (*a*) Decreases (*b*) Increases

11 (*a*)

12 (*c*)

13 You could measure the lowest resonant frequency f and the length L of the pipe. Assuming the end corrections are negligible, the wavelength equals $4L$ if the pipe is stopped at one end, and is $2L$ if the pipe is open at both ends. Then use $v = f\lambda$ to find the speed of sound at the ambient temperature. Finally, use $v = \sqrt{\gamma RT/M}$ (Equation 15-5),where $\gamma = 1.4$ for a diatomic gas such as air, M is the molar mass of air, R is the universal gas constant, and T is the absolute temperature, to estimate the temperature of the air.

14 The pipe will contract as the air in it becomes significantly colder, so the wavelength (equal to $4L$) will decrease as well. This effect, however, is negligible compared to the decrease in the speed of sound (recall that the speed of sound in a gas depends on the square root of the absolute temperature). Because $v = f\lambda$ and v decreases with λ remaining approximately constant, f must decrease.

15 (*a*) No (*b*) Yes

16 The light is being projected up from underneath the silk, so you will see light where there is a gap and darkness where two threads overlap. Because the two weaves have almost the same spatial period but not exactly identical (because the two are stretched unequally), there will be places where, for large sections of the cloth, the two weaves overlap in phase, leading to brightness, and large sections where the two overlap 90° out of phase (that is, thread on gap and vice versa) leading to darkness. This is exactly the same idea as in the interference of two waves.

17 Standing sound waves are produced in the air columns above the water. The resonance frequency of the air columns depends on the length of the air column, which depends on how much water is in the glass.

18 f will increase for each organ pipe. The effect will be even more pronounced.

19 The wavelength is determined mostly by the resonant cavity of the mouth; the frequency of sounds he makes is equal to the wave speed divided by the wavelength. Because $v_{\text{He}} > v_{\text{air}}$ (see Equation 15-5), the resonance frequency is higher if helium is the gas in the cavity.

20 1.1 kHz, 2 octaves

21 If you do not hear beats for the entire time the string and the tuning fork are vibrating, you can be sure that their frequencies, while not exactly the same, are very close. If the sounds of the vibrating string and the tuning fork last for 10 s, it follows that the beat frequency is less than 0.1 Hz. Hence, the frequencies of the vibrating string and the tuning fork are within 0.1 Hz of each other.

22 (*a*) 2.3 kHz (*b*) The eighth harmonic is within the range defined as audible. The ninth harmonic might be heard by a person with very good hearing.

23 3. The estimated frequencies agree with the observed frequencies to within 14%.

24 (*a*) 3.9 cm (*b*) 3.5 cm

25 7.1 cm

26 A

27 (*a*) 89° (*b*) 1.4A

28

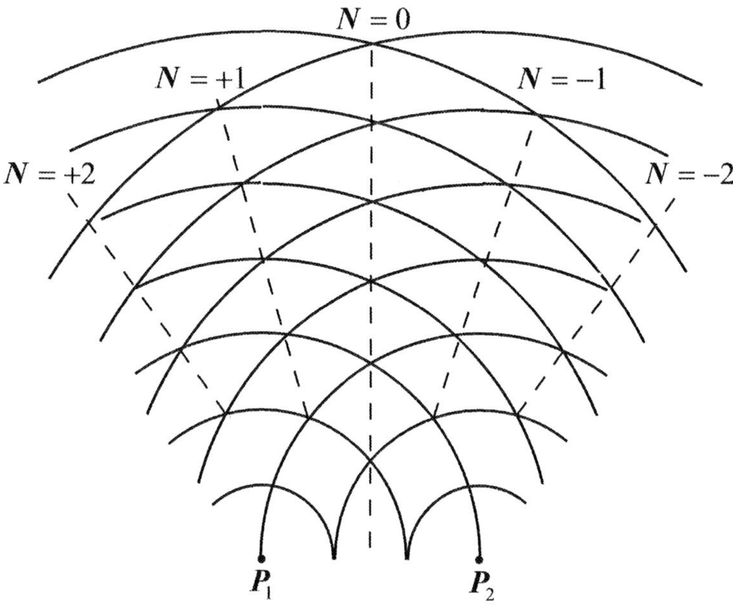

29 (*a*) 0 (*b*) $2I_0$ (*c*) $4I_0$

30 (*a*) $4I_0$ (*b*) $2I_0$ (*c*) 0

31 (*a*) 60.0 cm (*b*) $\frac{2\pi}{5}$ (*c*) 24.0 m/s

32 0.79π rad

33 $f_1 = 2$ kHz, $f_2 = 4$ kHz

34 $f_1 = 1$ kHz, $f_3 = 3$ kHz

35 (*b*)

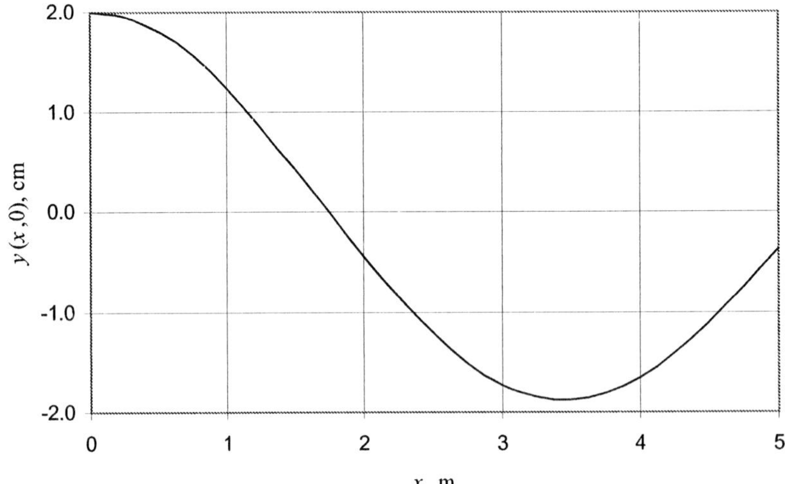

(*c*)

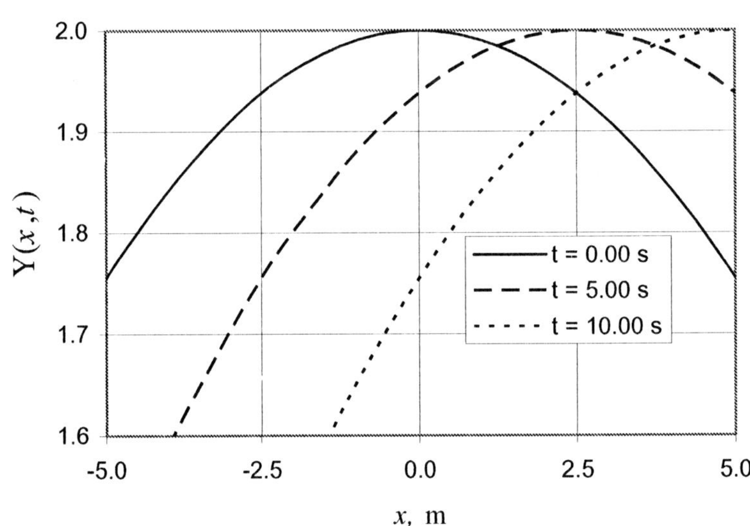

$v_{est} = 50$ cm/s, $v_{envelope} = 50$ cm/s

37 1.8 m, 51°

38 (*a*) 8.22° (*b*) 16.6° (*c*) 3

39 (*a*) 0.279 m (*b*) 1.23 kHz

(*c*)

m	θ_m (rad)
3	0.432
4	0.592
5	0.772
6	0.992
7	1.35
8	undefined

(*d*) 0.0698 rad

40 Constructive interference:

m	θ_c
1	7.01°
2	15.2°
3	23.6°
4	32.7°
5	42.8°

Destructive interference:

m	θ_d
1	3.00°
2	11.1°
3	19.3°
4	28.1°
5	37.6°

41 2.0 rad

42 (*a*) 504 Hz or 496 Hz (*b*) If the beat frequency is increased, then f_2 = 504 Hz; if it is diminished, f_2 = 496 Hz.

43 (*b*) 1.2 kHz (*c*) 15 Hz/mi/h

44 180 m/s

45 (*a*) 2.00 m, 2.50 Hz (*b*) $y_3(x,t) = (4.00\,\text{mm})\sin(\pi\ \text{m}^{-1})x\cos(50.0\pi\ \text{s}^{-1})t$

46 (*a*) 17 Hz (*b*) 8.6 Hz

47 (*a*) 521 m/s (*b*) 2.80 m, 186 Hz (*c*) 372 Hz and 558 Hz

48 (*a*) 1.25 Hz (*b*) Because the rope is fixed at just one end, the system does not support a second harmonic. (*c*) 3.75 Hz

49 141 Hz

50 (*a*) 4.3 m (*b*) 8.6 m

51 (*a*) 32.4 cm, 47.7 Hz (*b*) 15.0 m/s (*c*) 62.8 cm

52 (*a*) 200 m/s, 2.50 cm (*b*) 1.26 m (*c*) 1.26 m

53 (*a*) 71.5 Hz (*b*) 4.93 kHz (*c*) 35

54 (*a*) 345 m/s (*b*) 0.5 cm

55 452 Hz. Ideally, the pipe should expand so that *v*/*L*, where *L* is the length of the pipe, is independent of temperature.

56 66.7 cm, 63.8 cm, 57.4 cm

57 (*a*) 40.0 cm (*b*) 480 N (*c*) You should place your finger 9.2 cm from the scroll bridge.

58

Note	Frequency	$L(f')$	$x(f')$
	(Hz)	(cm)	(cm)
A	220	26.73	3.3
B	247	23.81	6.2
C	262	22.44	7.6
D	294	20.00	10

59 (*a*) 75 Hz (*b*) Fifth and sixth (*c*) 2.0 m

60 (*a*) Eighth and ninth (*b*) 2.2 m

61 (*a*) 0.574 g/m (*b*) $\mu_E = 1.29$ g/m, $\mu_A = 2.91$ g/m, $\mu_D = 2.91$ g/m, $\mu_G = 6.57$ g/m

62 One-fifth, one-third

63 (*a*) The two sounds produce a beat because the third harmonic of the A string equals the second harmonic of the E string, and the original frequency of the E string is slightly greater than 660 Hz. (*b*) 662 Hz

64 (*a*) $y_3(x,t) = (0.0300\,\text{m})\sin\left[\left(\frac{3\pi}{4}\,\text{m}^{-1}\right)x\right]\cos\left(200\pi\,\text{s}^{-1}\right)t$

(*b*) $dK = \frac{1}{2}\left[(6\pi\,\text{m/s})\sin\left[\left(\frac{3\pi}{4}\,\text{m}^{-1}\right)x\right]\sin\left(200\pi\,\text{s}^{-1}\right)t\right]^2 \mu dx$, 2.50 ms, 7.50 ms, … . The string is a straight line.
(*c*) (88.8 J/kg)m

65 (*a*) Because the frequency is fixed, the wavelength depends only on the tension on the string. This is true because the only parameter that can affect the wave speed on the string is the tension on the string. The tension on the string is provided by the weight hanging from its end. Given that the length of the string is fixed, only certain wavelengths can resonate on the string. Thus, because only certain wavelengths are allowed, only certain wave speeds will work. This, in turn, means that only certain tensions, and therefore weights, will work.

(*b*) Higher frequency modes on the same length of string results in shorter wavelengths. To accomplish this without changing frequency, you need to reduce the wave speed. This is accomplished by reducing the tension in the string. Because the tension is provided by the weight on the end of the string, you must reduce the weight.

(*d*) $w_1 = 19.2$ N, $w_2 = 4.80$ N, $w_3 = 2.13$ N

66 1 and 3

67 (*a*) $\Delta t = N/f_0$ (*b*) $\lambda \approx \Delta x/N$ (*c*) $k = 2\pi N/\Delta x$ (*d*) N is uncertain because the waveform dies out gradually, rather than stopping abruptly at some time; hence, where the pulse starts and stops is not well defined.

68 (*a*) $f_1 = 0.66$ Hz, $f_2 = 1.3$ Hz, $f_3 = 2.0$ Hz, $f_3 = 2.6$ Hz (*b*) $f_1 = 0.33$ Hz, $f_3 = 0.99$ Hz, $f_5 = 1.6$ Hz, $f_7 = 2.3$ Hz

69 6.74 m

70 (*a*) 4.00 m (*b*) $\frac{\pi}{2}\,\text{m}^{-1}$ (*c*) $800\pi\,\text{s}^{-1}$

(*d*) $y_5(x,t) = (0.0300\,\text{m})\sin\left[\left(\frac{\pi}{2}\,\text{m}^{-1}\right)x\right]\cos\left(800\pi\,\text{s}^{-1}\right)t$

71 (*a*) 1.9 cm, 3.6 m/s (*b*) 0, 0 (*c*) –1.2 cm, –2.2 m/s (*d*) 0, 0

72 (*a*) 5 (*b*) f_1 = 5.5 Hz, f_2 = 11 Hz, f_3 = 16 Hz

73 98.0 Hz

74 (*a*) 0.72 kN (*b*) F_2 = 2.9 kN, F_3 = 6.5 kN, F_4 = 12 kN,

75 (*a*) The pipe is closed at one end. (*b*) 262 Hz (*c*) 32.7 cm

76 (*a*) 2.47 kHz, 3.18 kHz (*b*) 353 Hz (*c*) 7th and 9th

77 (*a*) $y_1(x,t) = (0.010\,\text{m})\sin\left[\left(\frac{\pi}{2}\,\text{m}^{-1}\right)x - \left(40\pi\,\text{s}^{-1}\right)t\right]$,

$y_2(x,t) = (0.010\,\text{m})\sin\left[\left(\frac{\pi}{2}\,\text{m}^{-1}\right)x + \left(40\pi\,\text{s}^{-1}\right)t\right]$

(*b*) 2.00 m
(*c*) 2.5 m/s
(*d*) ±0.32 km/s^2

78 (*a*)

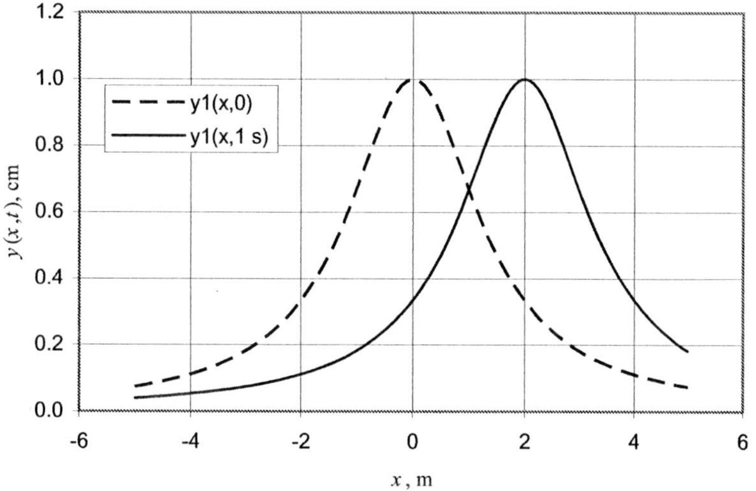
1.2
1.0
0.8
0.6
0.4
0.2
0.0
-6
-4
-2
0
2
4
6
y1(x,0)
y1(x,1 s)
y(x,t), cm
x, m

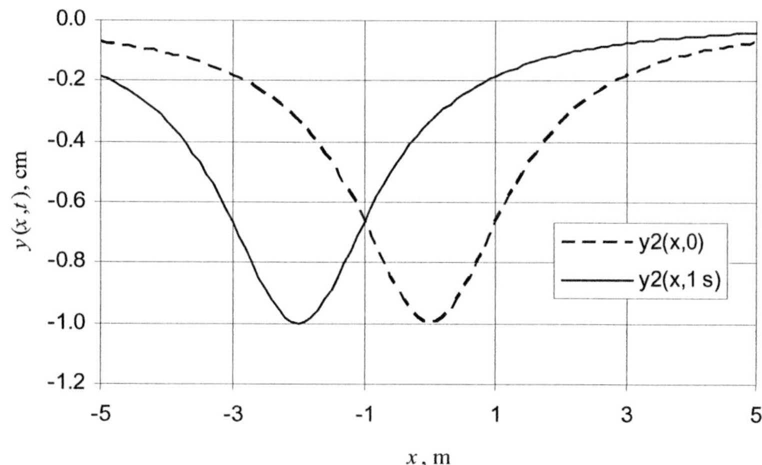
0.0
-0.2
-0.4
-0.6
-0.8
-1.0
-1.2
-5
-3
-1
1
3
5
y2(x,0)
y2(x,1 s)
y(x,t), cm
x, m

(*b*)

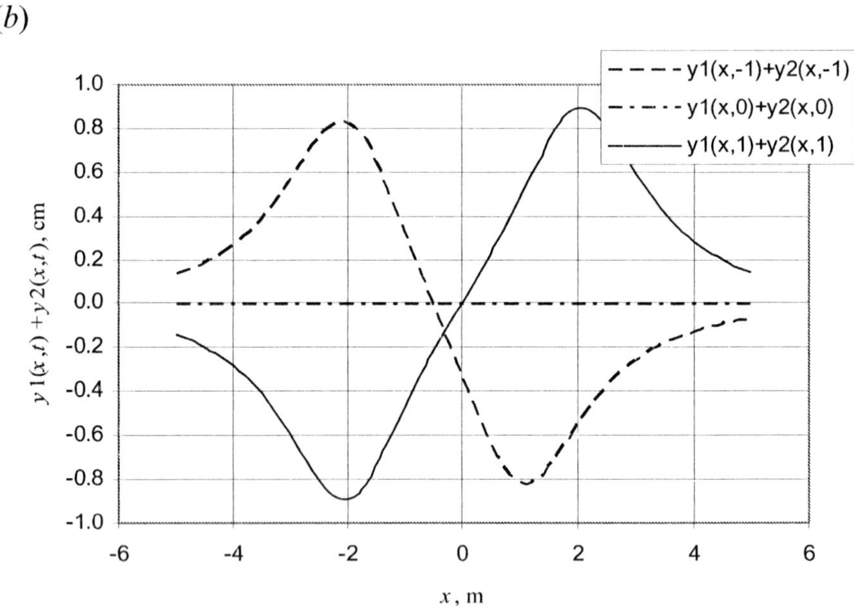

79 $y_{\text{res}}(x,t) = (10.0\text{ cm})\sin(kx - \omega t)$

81 (*b*) 203.4 Hz (*c*) 203.4 Hz

82 433 Hz

83 812 Hz

84 (*a*) 19.7 mJ (*b*) 0 (*c*) 1.00 m (*d*) At the midpoint of the wire

85 (*a*)

Cell	Content/Formula	Algebraic Form
A6	A5+0.1	$x + \Delta x$
B4	2*B3+1	$2n+1$
B5	(−1)^B$3*COS(B$4*$A5) /B$4*4/PI()	$\frac{4}{\pi}\sum_{n=0}^{\infty}\frac{(-1)^n\cos((2n+1)x)}{2n+1}$
C5	B5+(−1)^C$3*COS(C$4*$A5) /C$4*4/PI()	$\frac{4}{\pi}\sum_{n=0}^{\infty}\frac{(-1)^n\cos((2n+1)x)}{2n+1}$

	A	B	C	D		K	L
1							
2							
3		0	1	2		9	10
4		1	3	5		19	21
5	0.0	1.2732	0.8488	1.1035		0.9682	1.0289
6	0.1	1.2669	0.8614	1.0849		1.0134	0.9828

7	0.2	1.2479	0.8976	1.0352		1.0209	0.9912
8	0.3	1.2164	0.9526	0.9706		0.9680	1.0286
9	0.4	1.1727	1.0189	0.9130		1.0057	0.9742
10	0.5	1.1174	1.0874	0.8833		1.0298	1.0010
130	12.5	1.2704	0.8544	1.0952		0.9924	1.0031
131	12.6	1.2725	0.8503	1.1013		0.9752	1.0213
132	12.7	1.2619	0.8711	1.0710		1.0287	0.9714
133	12.8	1.2386	0.9143	1.0141		1.0009	1.0126
134	12.9	1.2030	0.9740	0.9493		0.9691	1.0146
135	13.0	1.1554	1.0422	0.8990		1.0261	0.9685

The solid curve is plotted from the data in columns A and B and is the graph of $f(x)$ for 1 term. The dashed curve is plotted from the data in columns A and F and is the graph of $f(x)$ for 5 terms. The dotted curve is plotted from the data in columns A and K and is the graph of $f(x)$ for 10 terms.

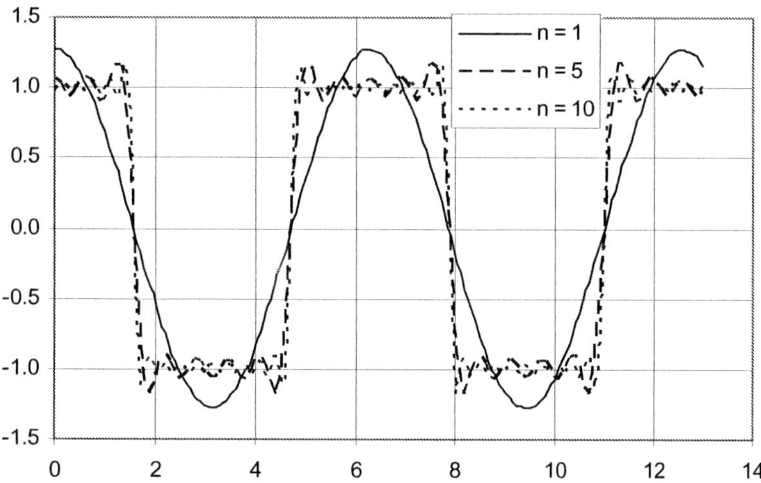

(*b*) It is equivalent to the Liebnitz formula.

86

Cell	Content/Formula	Algebraic Form
A6	A5+0.1	$x+\Delta x$
B4	2*B3+1	$2n+1$
B5	(−1)^\$B\$3*sin(\$B\$4*A5)/(\$B\$4)^2*4/PI()	$\frac{4}{\pi}\sum_{n}\frac{(-1)^n\sin(2n+1)x}{(2n+1)^2}$
C5	B5+((−1)^\$C\$3*sin(\$C\$4*A5)/(\$C\$4)^2*4/PI()	$\frac{4}{\pi}\sum_{n}\frac{(-1)^n\sin(2n+1)x}{(2n+1)^2}$

	A	B	C	D	K	L
1						
2						
3		0	1	2	9	10
4		1	3	5	19	21
5	0.0	0.0000	0.0000	0.0000	0.0000	0.0000
6	0.1	0.1271	0.0853	0.1097	0.0986	0.1011
7	0.2	0.2530	0.1731	0.2159	0.2012	0.1987
8	0.3	0.3763	0.2654	0.3163	0.3004	0.3005
9	0.4	0.4958	0.3640	0.4103	0.3983	0.4008
10	0.5	0.6104	0.4693	0.4998	0.5011	0.4985
72	6.7	0.5155	0.3812	0.4256	0.4153	0.4171
73	6.8	0.6291	0.4877	0.5146	0.5183	0.5154
74	6.9	0.7365	0.6005	0.6034	0.6171	0.6182
75	7.0	0.8365	0.7181	0.6963	0.7148	0.7166
76	7.1	0.9282	0.8380	0.7968	0.8183	0.8155

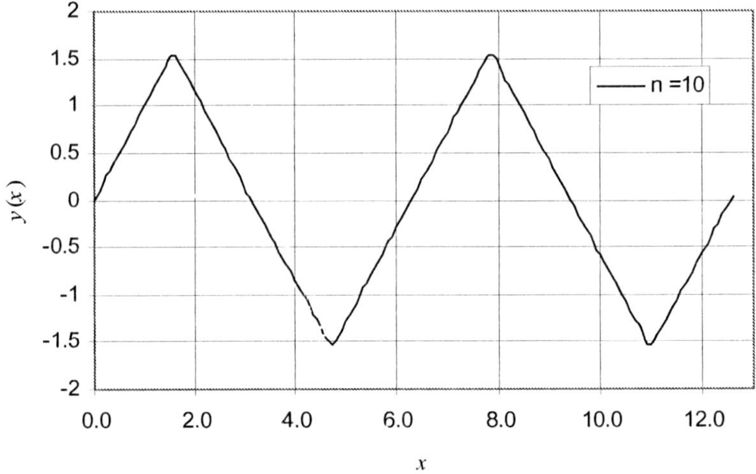

87

(*b*)

Cell	Content/Formula	Algebraic Form
B1	90	L
B2	1	r
B3	340	c
B8	B7+1	$n + 1$
C7	2/\$B\$3*((2*(B7−1) *\$B\$2)^2+\$B\$1^2)^0.5	Δt_n

	A	B	C	D
1	$L=$	90	m	
2	$r=$	1	m	
3	$c=$	343	m/s	
4				
5				
6		n	$t(n)$	delta $t(n)$
7		1	0.5248	0.0001
8		2	0.5249	0.0004
9		3	0.5253	0.0006
10		4	0.5259	0.0009
11		5	0.5269	0.0012
202		196	2.3338	0.0114
203		197	2.3452	0.0114
204		198	2.3566	0.0114
205		199	2.3679	0.0114
206		200	2.3793	0.0114

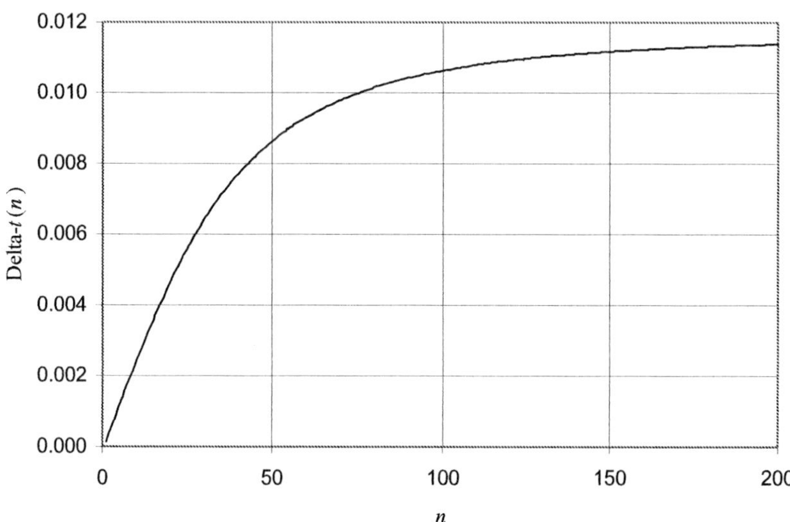

(c) The frequency heard at any time is $1/\Delta t_n$, so because Δt_n increases over time, the frequency of the culvert whistler decreases. $f_{\text{highest}} = 7.72$ kHz, $f_{\text{lowest}} = 85.5$ Hz

Chapter 17
Temperature and the Kinetic Theory of Gases

1 (*a*) False (*b*) False (*c*) True

2 Put each in thermal equilibrium with a third body; that is, a thermometer. If each body is in thermal equilibrium with the third, then they are in thermal equilibrium with each other.

3 Mert's room was colder.

4 (*a*)

5 From the ideal-gas law, the equation of the line from the origin to the point (T,V) is $V=\frac{nR}{P}T$. The slope of this line is nR/P. During the process A → B the slope of the line from the origin to (T,V) continuously decreases, so the pressure continuously increases.

6 From the ideal-gas law, the equation of the line from the origin to the point (T,P) is $P=\frac{nR}{V}T$. The slope of this line is nR/V. During the process A → B the slope of the line from the origin to (T,V) continuously increases, so the volume continuously decreases.

7 (*d*)

8 Because $v_{\text{rms}} \propto \sqrt{T}$, the temperature must be quadrupled in order to double the rms speed of the molecules.

9 The average kinetic energies are equal. The ratio of their rms speeds is equal to the square root of the reciprocal of the ratio of their molecular masses.

10 (*b*)

11 False.

12 For the Celsius scale, the ice point (0°C) and the boiling point of water at 1 atm (100°C) are more convenient than 273 K and 373 K; temperatures in roughly this range are normally encountered. On the Fahrenheit scale, the temperature of warm-blooded animals is roughly 100°F; this may be a more convenient reference than approximately 300 K. Throughout most of the world, the Celsius scale is the standard for nonscientific purposes.

13 It does not matter.

14 (*d*)

15 (*b*)

16 (*d*)

17 The rms speed is always somewhat greater than the speed of sound. However, it is only the component of the molecular velocities in the direction of propagation that is relevant to this issue. In addition, in a gas the mean free path is greater than the average intermolecular distance.

18 Because the rooms are connected by an open door, the air in each is at the same pressure. Because $P = NkT/V$, and the rooms have equal volumes, $N_A T_A = N_B T_B$ and the cooler room (A) has more air in it.

19 If the volume decreases the pressure increases because more molecules hit a unit of area of the walls in a given time. This happens because the number of molecules per unit volume increases as the volume decreases.

20 (*b*)

21 The average molecular speed of He gas at 300 K is about 1.4 km/s, so a significant fraction of He molecules have speeds in excess of Earth's escape velocity (11.2 km/s). Thus, they "leak" away into space. Over time, the He content of the atmosphere decreases to almost nothing.

22 3×10^{28}

23 1.2 kg/m^3

24 170 atm

25 (*a*) 3600 K (*b*) 230 K (*c*) Because hydrogen is lighter than air it rises to the top of the atmosphere. Because the temperature is high there, a greater fraction of the molecules reach escape speed. (*d*) 160 K, 10 K. Because g is less on the moon, the escape speed is lower. Thus, a larger percentage of the molecules are moving at escape speed.

26 (*a*) 1.84 km/s (*b*) 461 m/s (*c*) 393 m/s (*d*) Because v is greater than v_{rms} for CO_2 but less than v_{rms} for H_2, O_2 and CO_2, but not H_2 should be present.

27 (*a*) 1.23 km/s (*b*) 310 m/s (*c*) 264 m/s (*d*) Because v_e is greater than v_{rms} for O_2, CO_2, and H_2, all three gasses should be found on Jupiter.

28 0.1 Pa. $P_{av} \approx 10^{-6} P_{atm}$ and the average pressure from the ball is not significant compared to atmospheric pressure.

29 (*a*) 2 × 10^{11} atm (*b*) $v_{\text{rms, protons}} = 5 \times 10^5$ m/s, $v_{\text{rms, electrons}} = 2 \times 10^7$ m/s

30 20 mPa

31 0.01 g

32 10°F to 19°F

33 1063°C

34 27.0 F°

35 (*a*)

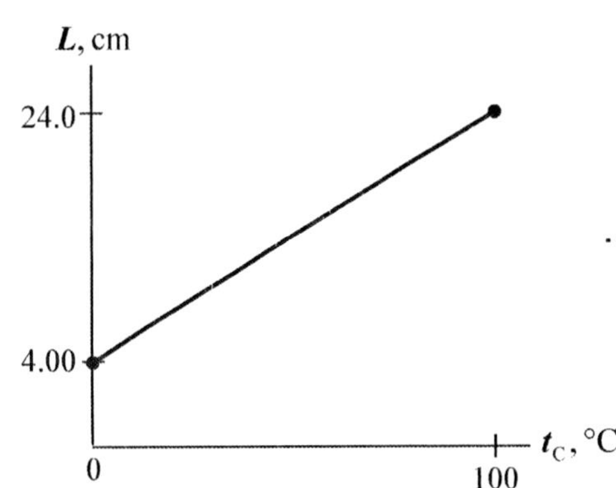

(*b*) 8.40 cm (*c*) 107°C

36 (*a*) 1.0 × 10^7 °C (*b*) 1.8 × 10^7 °F

37 −320°F

38

(*a*)

(*b*) – 205°C (*c*) 1.05 atm

39

(*a*)

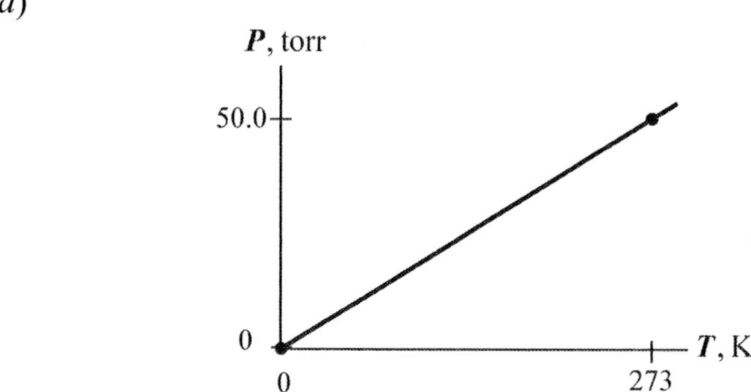

(*b*) 54.9 torr (*c*) 3.70×10^3 K

40

(*a*)

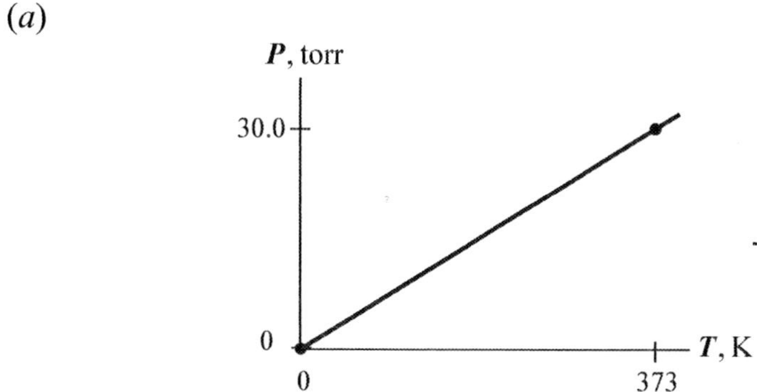

(*b*) 22.0 torr (*c*) 2.18 K

41 –40.0°C = –40.0°F

42 98°C, 208°F

43 −183°C, −297°F

44 $t_C = \frac{5}{4}t_R$, $t_F = \frac{9}{4}t_R + 32$

45 (*a*) $R_0 = 3.91 \times 10^{-3}$ K, $B = 3.94 \times 10^3$ K (*b*) 1.31 kΩ (*c*) –389 Ω/K , –4.33 Ω/K (*d*) The thermistor is more sensitive (has greater sensitivity) at lower temperatures.

46 1.15, or a 15% increase in volume.

47 1.79 mol, 1.08×10^{24} molecules

48 3.22×10^{24}

49 –83 *glips*

50 (*a*) 53°C (*b*) 76°C

51 (*a*) 3.7×10^3 mol (*b*) 60 mol

52 (*a*) 5.13 L (*b*) 60.1 L

53 11.1 atm

54 (*a*) 231 kPa (*b*) 201 kPa

55 (*a*) Air will be less dense when its water vapor content is higher. (*b*) 18 g

56 78 cm^3

57 1.1 kN

58 (*a*) 776 mol (*b*) 4.8 km (*c*) Because $F_{net} = 30$ N > 0, the balloon will rise higher than the altitude at which it is fully inflated. (*d*) 6.0 km

59 (*a*) 0.28 km/s (*b*) 0.87 km/s. The rms speed of argon atoms is slightly less than one-third the rms speed of helium atoms.

60 0.15 kJ

61 5.0×10^5 m/s, 2.1×10^{-16} J

62 162 m/s. Thermal speeds, even at temperatures as low as 4.20 K, are very large compared to most of the speeds we experience directly.

64 1.3×10^9 m, 9.7×10^5 s

65 $\frac{K}{\Delta U} = 7.9 \times 10^4$

68 $v_{av} = \frac{2}{\sqrt{\pi}}\sqrt{\frac{2kT}{m}}$

69 (*a*) $E_{peak} = \frac{1}{2}kT$, $E_{peak} = \frac{1}{3}E_{av}$

(*b*)

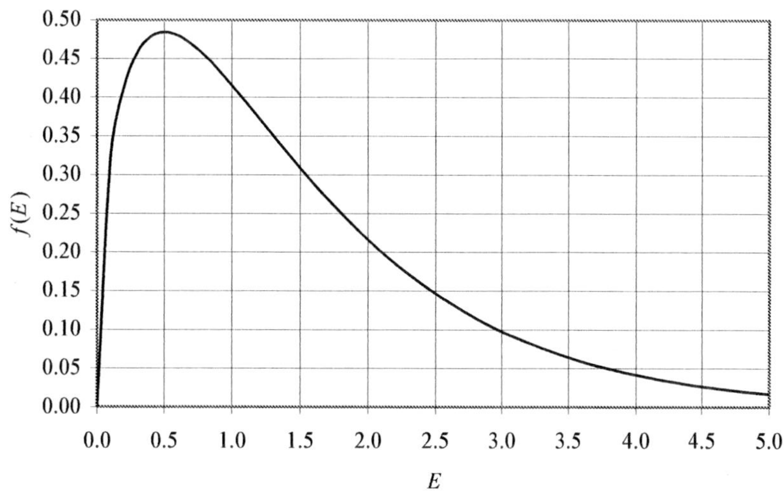

(*c*) The graph rises from zero to the peak much more rapidly than it falls off to the right of the peak. Because the distribution is so strongly skewed to the right of the peak, the outlying molecules with relatively high energies pull the average ($3kT/2$) far to the right of the most probable value ($kT/2$).

70 9.51 K

71 (*a*) 1.2×10^2 K (*b*) 2.4×10^2 K (*c*) 1.4 atm

72 (*a*) 3.99×10^{-26} m^3 (*b*) 3.42 nm (*c*) 0.375 nm

(*d*)

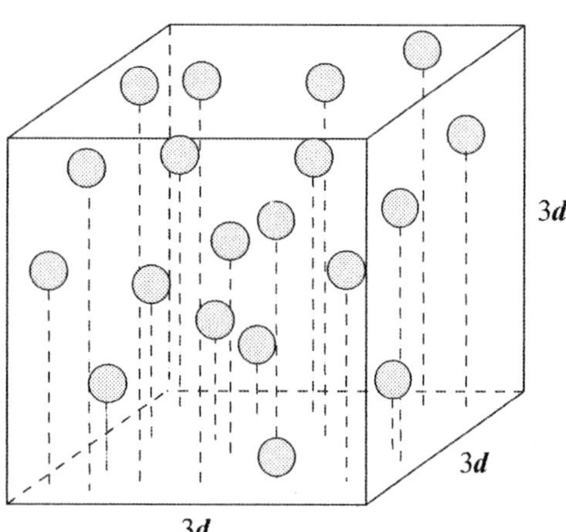

(*e*) If a particular molecule in the diagram is moving in a random direction, its chance of colliding with a neighbor is very small because it can miss in either of the two directions perpendicular to its motion. So the mean free path, or average distance between collisions, should be many times larger than the distance to the nearest neighbor.

73

(a) To escape from the surface of a droplet of water, molecules must have enough translational kinetic energy to overcome the attractive forces from their neighbors. Therefore, the molecules that escape will be those that are moving faster, leaving the slower molecules behind. The slower molecules have less kinetic energy, so the temperature of the droplet, which is proportional to the average kinetic energy per molecule, decreases.

(b) As long as the temperature is not too high, the molecules that evaporate from a surface will be only those with the most extreme speeds, at the high-energy "tail" of the Maxwell-Boltzmann distribution. Within this part of the distribution, increasing the temperature only slightly can greatly increase the percentage of molecules with speeds above a certain threshold. For example, suppose that we set an initial threshold at $E = 5kT_1$. Then imagine increasing the temperature by 10%, so $T_2 = 1.1T_1$. At the threshold, the ratio of the new energy distribution to the old one is

$$\frac{F(T_2)}{F(T_1)} = \left(\frac{T_1}{T_2}\right)^{\frac{3}{2}} e^{\frac{-E}{kT_2}} e^{\frac{+E}{kT_1}} = (1.1)^{\frac{-3}{2}} e^{\frac{-5}{1.1}} e^{5} = \frac{(0.867)(148.4)}{94.2} = 1.365$$

an increase of almost 37%.

74 5.4 kN

75 110 mol of H_2, 55 mol of O_2

76 3 cm. Because momentum must be conserved during this process and the center of mass moved to the right, the cylinder moved 3 cm to the left.

77 4m

78 0.605 nm

79 (a) 142 ms (b) 143 ms

80 (a) 2.1 m (b) 1.0 Hz

81

(*a*)

	A	B	C
1	*R*=	8.31	J/mol-K
2	*M*=	0.028	kg/mol
3	*T*=	300	K
4			
5	*v*	*f*(*v*)	sum *f*(*v*)*dv*
6	(m/s)	(s/m)	(unitless)
7	0	0.00E+00	0.00E+00
8	1	3.00E–08	3.00E–08
9	2	1.20E–07	1.50E–07
10	3	2.70E–07	4.20E–07
11	4	4.80E–07	9.01E–07
12	5	7.51E–07	1.65E–06

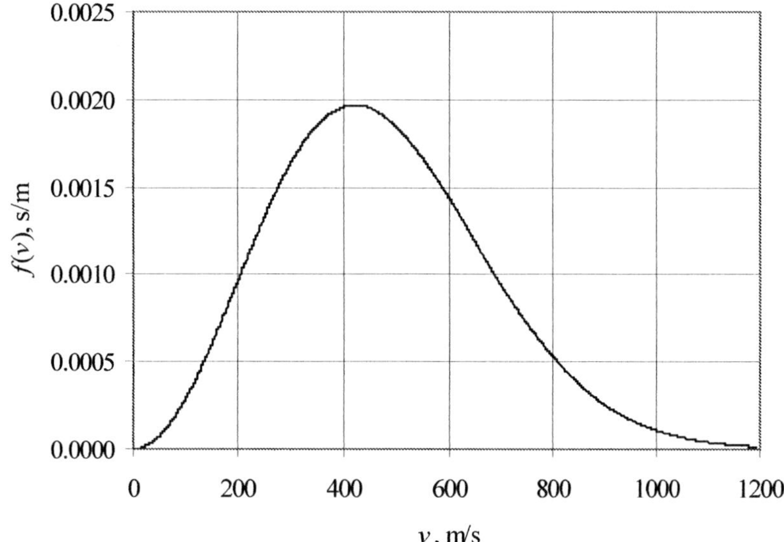

(*b*) As the temperature is increased, the graph spreads out horizontally and gets shorter vertically. More precisely, the horizontal position of the peak moves to the right in proportion to the square root of the temperature, while the height of the peak drops by the same factor, preserving the total area under the graph (which must be 1.0, the total probability of a molecule having any velocity between zero and infinity).

(*c*) A graph of $f(v)dv$ for nitrogen at 300 K follows. Each number in column C of the spreadsheet (shown in (*a*)) is approximately equal to the integral of *f*(*v*) from zero up to the corresponding *v* value. This integral represents the probability of a molecule having a speed or equal to this value of *v*.

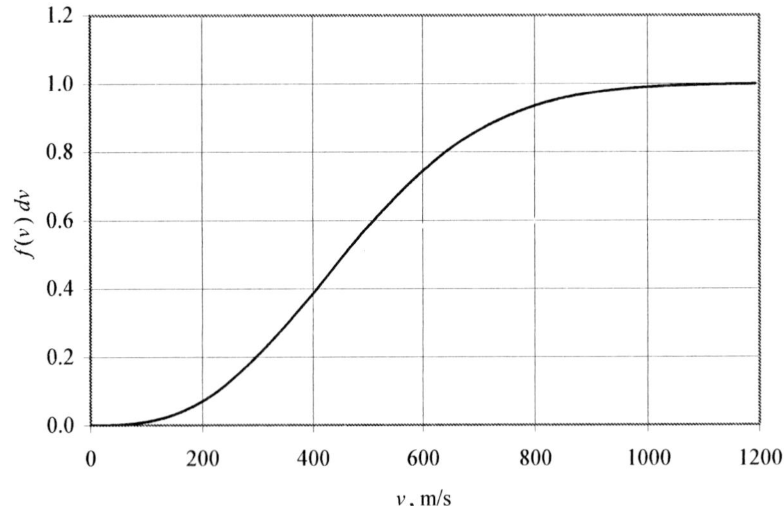

(*d*) About 7%. Note that this value is consistent with the graph of $f(v)$ shown immediately above.

(*e*) A little under 14%.

Chapter 18
Heat and the First Law of Thermodynamics

1 (*e*)

2 (*b*)

3 (*c*)

4 (*a*)

5 (*a*)

6 (*d*)

7 (*c*)

8 Some examples of systems in which internal energy is converted into mechanical energy are a steam turbine, an internal combustion engine, and a person performing mechanical work, e.g., climbing a hill. One example from everyday life is that of a hot gas that expands and does work–as in the piston of an engine. Another example is the gas escaping from a can of spray paint. As it escapes, it moves air molecules and, in the process, does work against atmospheric pressure.

9 Yes. $\Delta E_{\text{int}} = Q_{\text{in}} + W_{\text{on}}$. If the gas does work at the same rate that it absorbs heat, its internal energy will remain constant.

10 (*b*)

11 Particles that attract each other have more potential energy the farther apart they are. In a real gas the molecules exert weak attractive forces on each other. These forces increase the internal potential energy during an expansion. An increase in potential energy means a decrease in kinetic energy, and a decrease in kinetic energy means a decrease in translational kinetic energy. Thus, there is a decrease in temperature.

12 (*c*)

13 Particles that repel each other have more potential energy the closer together they are. The repulsive forces decrease the internal potential energy during an expansion. A decrease in potential energy means an increase in kinetic energy, and an increase in kinetic energy means an increase in translational kinetic energy. Thus, there is an increase in temperature.

14 The balloon that expands isothermally is larger when it reaches the surface. The balloon that expands adiabatically will be at a lower temperature than the one that expands isothermally. Because each balloon has the same number of gas molecules and is at the same pressure, the one with the higher temperature will be bigger.

15 (*a*)

16 (*b*)

17 (*a*) False (*b*) False (*c*) False (*d*) True (*e*) True (*f*) False (*g*) True

18 (*d*)

19 (*d*)

20

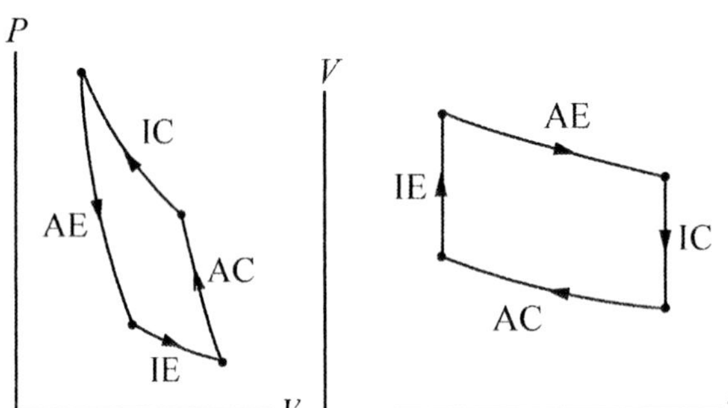

21 During a reversible adiabatic process, PV^{γ} is constant, where $\gamma < 1$ and during an isothermal processes PV is constant. Thus, the pressure rise during the compression is greater than the pressure drop during the expansion. The final process could be a constant volume process during which heat is absorbed from the system. A constant-volume cooling will decrease the pressure and return the gas to its original state.

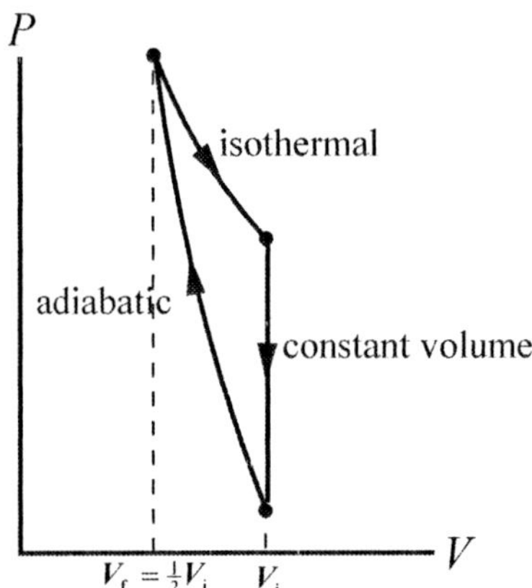

22 We can use the definition of heat capacity, the Dulong-Petit law, and the relationship between the mass of a substance and its molar mass to predict that $c_{Cu} > c_{Pb}$.

23 The temperature decreases.

24 5.7×10^4 kg/s

25 1.6 min, an elapsed time that seems to be consistent with experience.

26 3.69

27 1.2×10^{-3}%

28 500 kJ

29 31.3 kJ

30 311 kJ

31 48.8 g

32 60 kg

33 12.1°C

34 0.39 kJ/kg·K

35 4.5×10^2 kg

36 10.6°C

37 (*a*) 0°C (*b*) 125 g

38 0.17 kg

39 (*a*) 4.9°C (*b*) No ice is left.

40 (*a*) 298 K (*b*) Because the energy required to melt 500 g of ice is greater than the energy available, the final temperature will be 0°C.

41 (*a*) 5.26°C (*b*) 176 g (*c*) No

42 1.2 kJ/kg·K

43 618°C

44 (*a*) 28.5°C (*b*) 15.5°C

45 2.20 kJ

46 0.87 MJ

47 54 J

48 354 m/s

49 (*a*) 6.13 W (*b*) 38.1 min

50

(*a*)

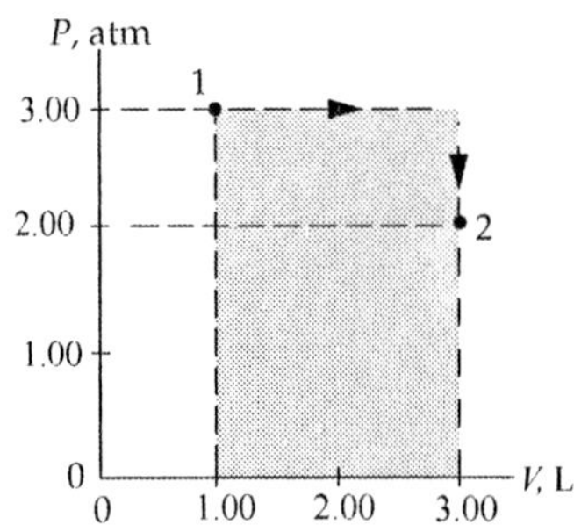

608 J

(*b*) 1.06 kJ

51

(*a*)

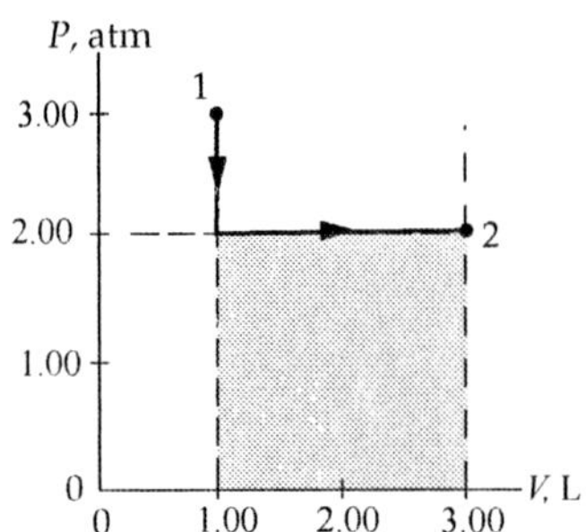

405 J

(*b*) 861 J

52

(*a*)

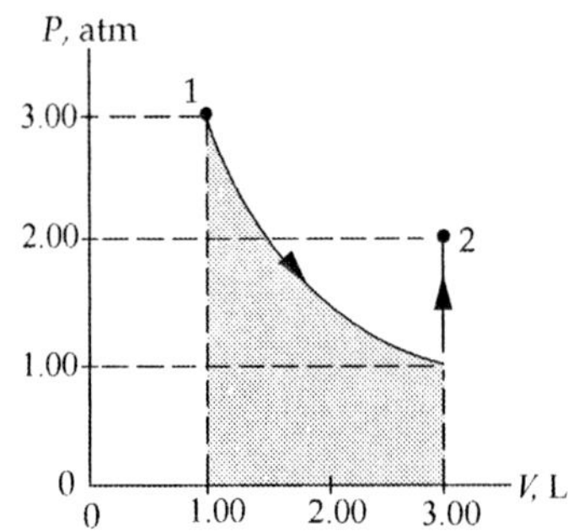

334 J

(*b*) 790 J

53
(*a*)

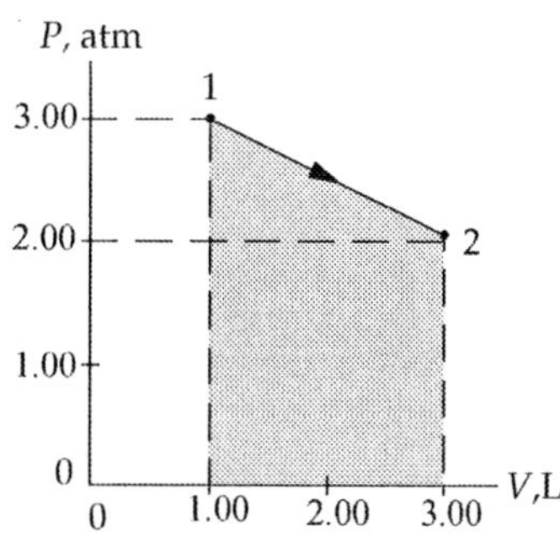

507 J
(*b*) 963 J

54

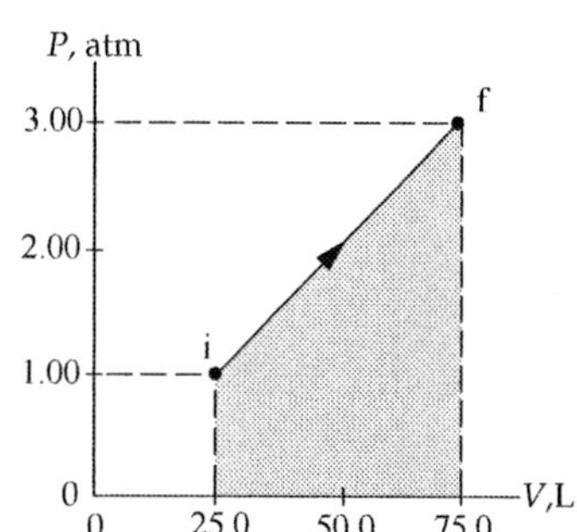

10.1 kJ

55 $W_{\text{by gas}} = \frac{3}{2} P_0 V_0$

56 (*a*) Because the volume of the can is fixed (constant), the heat all goes into increasing the internal energy of the gas and, thus, its temperature. At constant volume, the pressure rise is the maximum possible, threatening the structural integrity of the can, and possibly leading to a grenade-like shrapnel explosion.

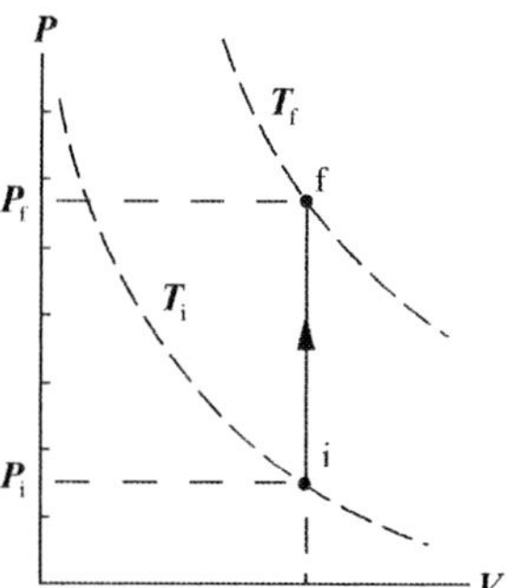

(*b*) 15.2 s

57 (*a*) 555 J (*b*) 555 J

58 (*a*) 3.99 mol (*b*) 14.9 kJ (*c*) 83.0 J/K

59 (*a*) 0.495 mol (*b*) 3.09 kJ (*c*) 20.8 J/mol·K (*d*) 10.3 J/K

60 (*a*) $c_V = 716 \dfrac{\text{J}}{\text{kg}\cdot\text{K}}$, $c_P = 1.00 \dfrac{\text{kJ}}{\text{kg}\cdot\text{K}}$ (*b*) 3%

61 (*a*) 6.24 kJ, 6.24 kJ (*b*) 6.24 kJ , 8.73 kJ, 2.49 kJ (*c*) 2.49 kJ

62 $5P_0V_0$

63 59.6 L

64 (*a*) 3.50 mol (*b*) $C_V = 43.6\,\text{J/K}$, $C_P = 72.7\,\text{J/K}$ (*c*) $C_V = 72.7\,\text{J/K}$, $C_P = 102\,\text{J/K}$

65 $\Delta C_P = -\frac{13}{2} Nk$

66 (*a*) $E_{\text{int,i}} = 3.40$ kJ (*b*) $E_{\text{int,f}} = 3.71$ kJ, $W_{\text{by gas}} = 0.19$ kJ (*c*) $E_{\text{int,f}} = 3.91$ kJ, $W_{\text{by gas}} = 0$

67 There are three translational degrees of freedom and three rotational degrees of freedom. In addition, each of the hydrogen atoms can vibrate against the oxygen atom, resulting in an additional 4 degrees of freedom (2 per atom). $C_{V,\text{water}} = 5Nk = 5nR$

68 (*a*) 55.7 g/mol (*b*) Fe

69 (*a*) 300 K, 7.80 L, 1.14 kJ, 1.14 kJ (*b*) 5.40 L, 208 K, 0, 574 J

70 (*a*) 300 K, 7.80 L, 1.14 kJ, 1.14 kJ (*b*) 6.00 L, 231 K, 0, 717 J

71 (*a*) 263 K (*b*) 10.8 L (*c*) 1.48 kJ (d) −1.48 kJ

72

(*a*)

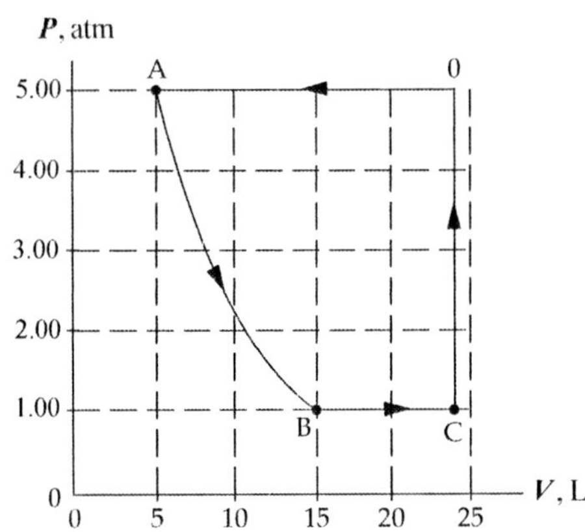

(*b*) −6.6 kJ (*c*) 6.6 kJ (*d*) −6.50 kJ

73 −0.14 kJ

74

(*a*)

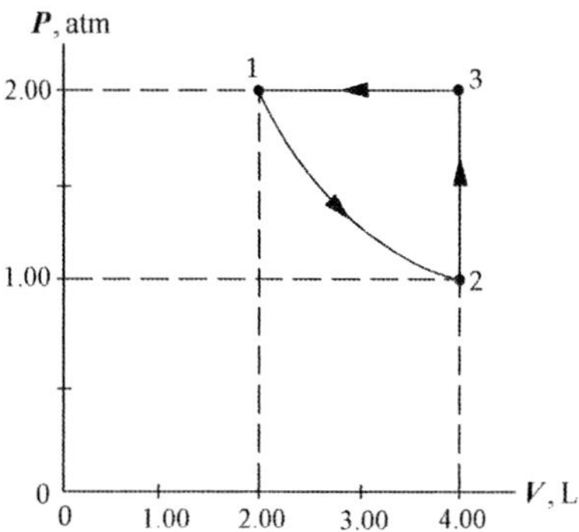

(*b*) $Q_{\text{in},1\to2} = 281\text{ J}$, $W_{2\to3} = 0$, $Q_{\text{in},2\to3} = 608\text{ J}$, $Q_{3\to1} = -1.01\text{ kJ}$, $W_{\text{by gas},3\to1} = 405\text{ J}$ (*c*) $T_1 = 24.4$ K, $T_2 = 24.4$ K, $T_3 = 48.7$ K

75

Process	Q_{in}	W_{on}	ΔE_{int}
	(kJ)	(kJ)	(kJ)
D→A	8.98	0	8.98
A→B	13.2	−13.2	0
B→C	−8.98	0	−8.98
C→D	−6.58	6.58	0

$W_{\text{by gas, tot}} = 6.6$ kJ

76

Process	Q_{in}	W_{on}	ΔE_{int}
	(kJ)	(kJ)	(kJ)
D→A	15.0	0	15.0
A→B	13.2	−13.2	0
B→C	−15.0	0	−15.0
C→D	−6.58	6.58	0

$W_{\text{by gas, tot}} = 6.6$ kJ

77
(*a*)

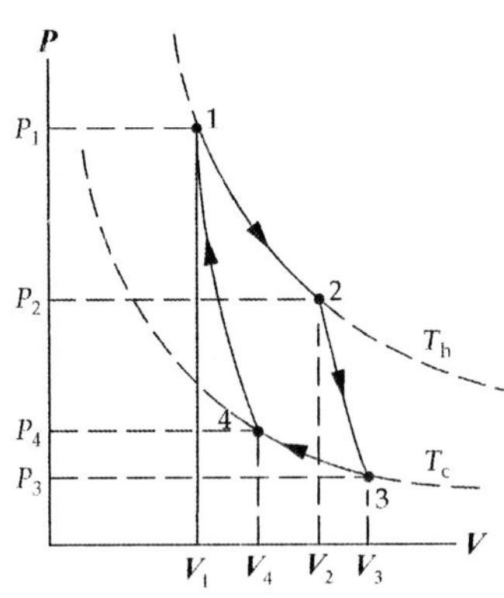

78 (*a*) 180 kJ (*b*) 45.9 mol

79 (*a*) 65 K, 81 K (*b*) 1.6 kJ (*c*) 2.2 kJ

80 (*a*) 65 K, 81 K (*b*) 3.2 kJ (*c*) 3.8 kJ

81 (*a*) 81 K, 81 K (*b*) 2.7 kJ (*c*) 3.3 kJ

82 $W_{ABC} = 4.2$ kJ, $Q_{ABC} = 4.8$ kJ

83 256 kcal

84 612°C → 843°C. Gasoline engines, with much lower compression ratios, would clearly have lower maximum operating temperatures and thus be subject to overall, average, lower temperatures and not require as extensive cooling systems.

85 (*a*) $c(4.00\,\mathrm{K}) = 9.20 \times 10^{-2}\,\frac{\mathrm{J}}{\mathrm{kg \cdot K}}$ (*b*) 0.0584 J/kg

86 (*a*) 3.91 kJ (*b*) 5.49 kJ

87 (*a*) 2.49 kJ (*b*) 3.26 kJ

88 (*a*) 2.74 kJ (*b*) 4.92 kJ

89 171 K

90 (*a*) $\Delta E_{int} = C_V \Delta T$ correctly gives the change in internal energy when the temperature changes and the volume is not constant because ΔE_{int} is the same for *all* gas processes that have the same ΔT. For an ideal gas, the internal energy is the sum of the kinetic energies of the gas molecules and this sum is proportional to kT. Any two processes that change the thermal energy of the gas by ΔE_{int} will cause the same temperature change ΔT. Consequently, ΔE_{int} is independent of the process that takes the gas from one state to another.

91

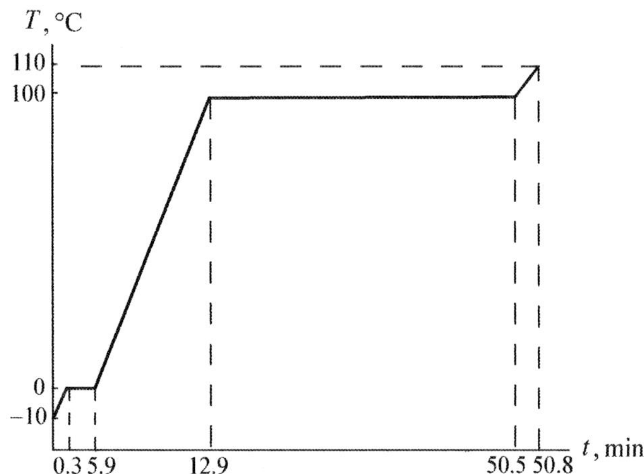

92 (*a*) 216 K (*b*) 160 K

93 396 K

95 (*b*) 4.62 kJ

96 $U_{300\text{ K}} = 795$ J, $U_{600\text{ K}} = 5.45$ kJ, $\Delta U = 4.65$ kJ. This result agrees with that of Problem 95 to within 1%.

97 (*a*) $P_2 = \frac{1}{2}P_0$ (*b*) The gas is diatomic. (*c*) During the isothermal process, *T* is constant and the translational kinetic energy is unchanged. During the adiabatic process, the translational kinetic energy increases by a factor of 1.32.

98 (*a*) $\tau = \frac{V}{A}\sqrt{\frac{m}{kT}}$ (*b*) 9 min

Chapter 19
The Second Law of Thermodynamics

1 (*c*)

2 (*a*)

3 (*a*)

4 The job of a refrigerator is to move heat from its cold interior to the warmer kitchen environment. This process moves heat in a direction that is opposite its "natural" direction of flow, analogous to the use of a water pump to pump water out of a boat. The term heat pumps is used to describe devices, such as air conditioners, that are used to cool living and working spaces in the summer and warm them in the winter.

5 The COP is defined so as to be a measure of the effectiveness of the device. For a refrigerator or air conditioner, the important quantity is the heat drawn from the already colder interior, Q_c. For a heat pump, the idea is to focus on the heat drawn into the warm interior of the house, Q_h.

6 As described by the second law of thermodynamics, more heat must be transmitted to the outside world than is removed by a refrigerator or air conditioner. The heating coils on a refrigerator are inside the room, so the refrigerator actually heats the room in which it is located. The heating coils on an air conditioner are outside one's living space, so the waste heat is vented to the outside.

7 Increasing the temperature of the steam increases its energy content. In addition, it increases the Carnot efficiency, and generally increases the efficiency of any heat engine.

8 (*c*)

9 A Carnot-cycle refrigerator is more efficient when the temperatures are close together because it requires less work to extract heat from an already cold interior if the temperature of the exterior is close to the temperature of the interior of the refrigerator. A Carnot-cycle heat engine is more efficient when the temperature difference is large because then more work is done by the engine for each unit of heat absorbed from the hot reservoir.

10 (*b*)

11 (*c*)

12 (*c*)

13 (*d*)

14 The processes A→B and C→D are adiabatic; the processes B→C and D→A are isothermal. The cycle is therefore the Carnot cycle shown in the adjacent *PV* diagram.

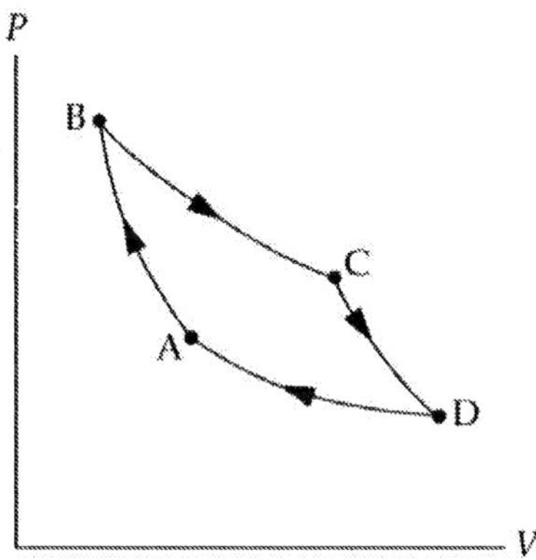

15 The cycle is that of the Otto engine (see Figure 19-3).

16

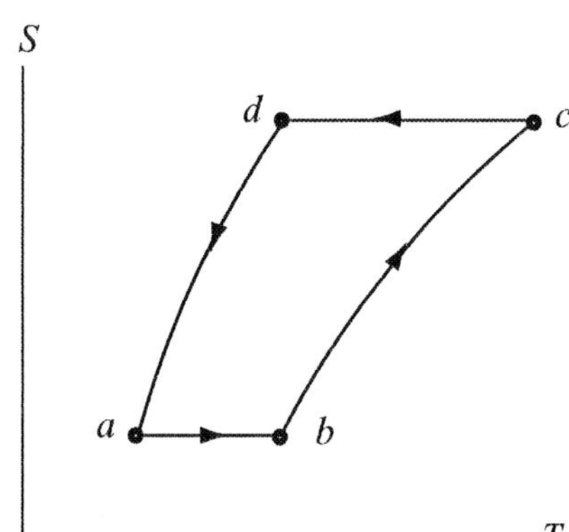

17

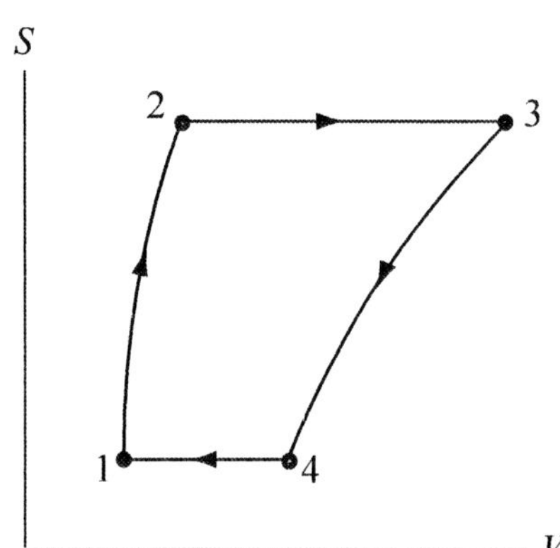

18

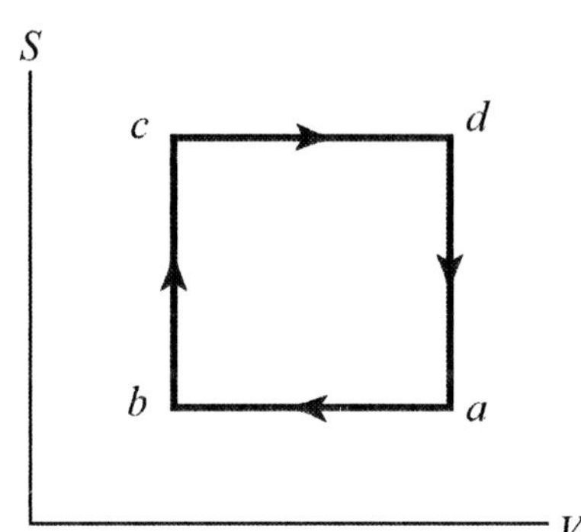

19

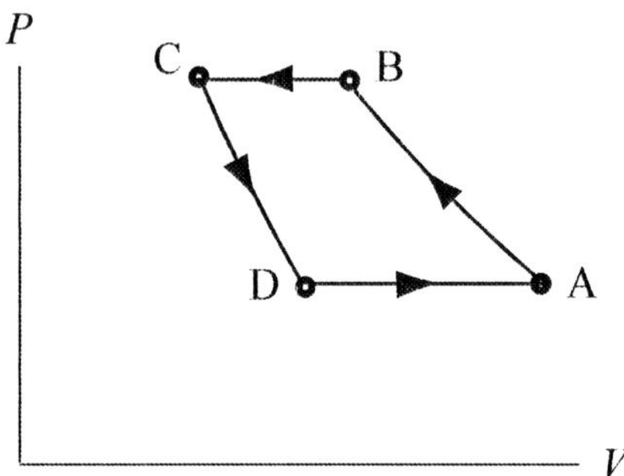

20 The son is out of line, here, but besides that, he's also wrong. While it is true that systems tend to degenerate to greater levels of disorder, it is not true that order cannot be brought forth from disorder. What is required is an agent doing work – for example, your friend – on the system in order to reduce the level of chaos and bring about order. His cleanup efforts will be rewarded with an orderly system after a sufficient time for him to complete the task. It is true that order will not come about from the disordered chaos of his room – unless he applies some elbow grease.

21 An increase of 47%

22 $10^{-10^{27}}$

23 56%

24 (*a*) 14 (*b*) 8.2 kW

25 (*a*) 1.75×10^{17} W (*b*) 6.02×10^{14} J/K·s

26 (*a*) 5 s (*b*) 2×10^{20} y (*c*) 2×10^{291} y (*d*) $10^{10^{23}}$ y (*e*) $10^{10^{7}}$ y, $10^{10^{7}}\, t_{\text{universe}}$

27 (*a*) 500 J (*b*) 400 J

28 (*a*) 30% (*b*) 280 J

29 (*a*) 40% (*b*) 80 W

30 (*a*) 1.7 (*b*) 38%

31

(*a*)

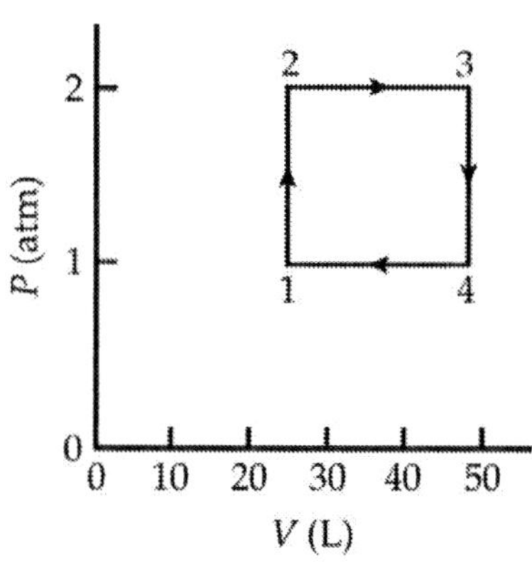

$W_{1\to2} = 0$, $Q_{1\to2} = 3.74\,\text{kJ}$, $\Delta E_{\text{int},1\to2} = 3.74\,\text{kJ}$, $W_{2\to3} = -4.99\,\text{kJ}$,
$Q_{2\to3} = 12.5\,\text{kJ}$, $\Delta E_{\text{int},2\to3} = 7.5\,\text{kJ}$, $W_{3\to4} = 0$,
$Q_{3\to4} = -7.48\,\text{kJ}$, $\Delta E_{\text{int},3\to4} = -7.48\,\text{kJ}$, $W_{4\to1} = 2.49\,\text{kJ}$, $Q_{4\to1} = -6.24\,\text{kJ}$,
$\Delta E_{\text{int},4\to1} = -3.75\,\text{kJ}$

(*b*) 15%

32 15%

33

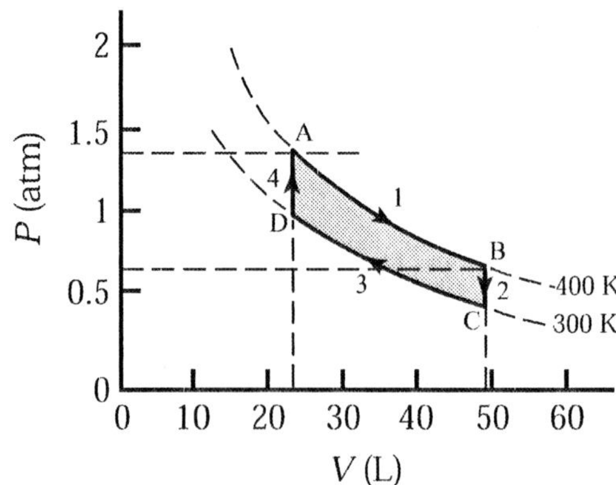

13.1%

34 (*a*) $T_1 = 301$ K, $T_2 = 601$ K (*b*) $Q_{1\to2} = 3.74$ kJ, $Q_{2\to3} = 3.46$ kJ, $Q_{3\to1} = -6.24$ kJ (*c*) 13%

35 (*a*) $T_2 = 600$ K, $T_3 = 1800$ K, $T_4 = 600$ K (*b*) 15%

36 (*a*)

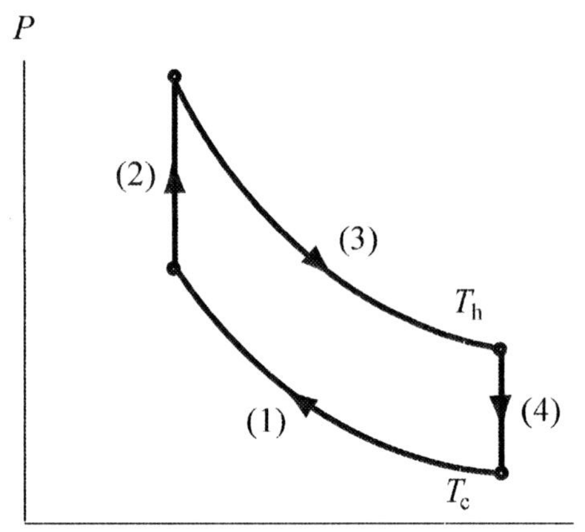

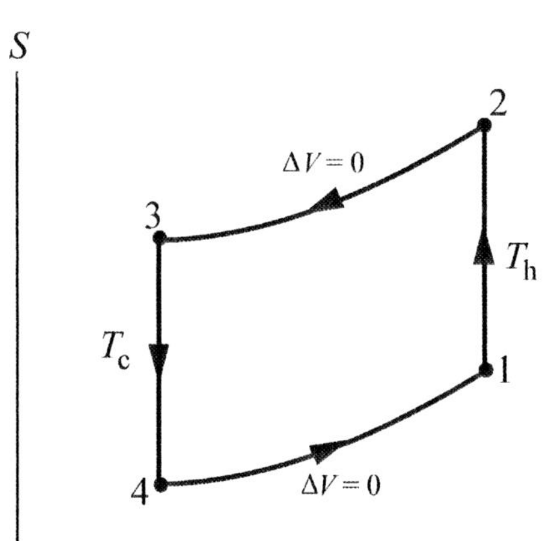

37 (*a*) 5.16%. No contradiction. (*b*) Most warm-blooded animals survive under roughly the same conditions as humans. To make a heat engine work with appreciable efficiency, internal body temperatures would have to be maintained at an unreasonably high level.

38 $\varepsilon = 1 - \dfrac{V_c^\gamma - V_b^\gamma}{\gamma V_a^{\gamma-1}(V_c - V_b)}$

40 The work done by the system is the area enclosed by the cycle, where we assume that we start with the isothermal expansion. It is only in this expansion that heat is extracted from a reservoir. There is no heat transfer in the adiabatic expansion or compression. Thus, we would completely convert heat to mechanical energy, without exhausting any heat to a cold reservoir, in violation of the second law.

41 (*a*) 33.3% (*b*) 33.3 J (*c*) 67 J (*d*) 2.0

42 (*a*) 20.0% (*b*) 33 J

44 If the reversible engine is run as a refrigerator, it will require 100 J of mechanical energy to take 400 J of heat from the cold reservoir and deliver 500 J to the hot reservoir. Now let the second engine, with $\varepsilon_2 > 0.2$, operate between the same two heat reservoirs and use it to drive the refrigerator. Because $\varepsilon_2 > 0.2$, this engine will remove less than 500 J from the hot reservoir in the process of doing 100 J of work. The net result is then that no net work is done by the two systems working together, but a finite amount of heat is transferred from the cold to the hot reservoir, in violation of the refrigerator statement of the second law.

45 (*a*) 33%

46 (*a*) 74.3% (*b*) 74.3 J (*c*) 26 J (*d*) 0.35

47 (*a*) 100°C (*b*) 3.12 kJ, $Q_{2\to3} = 0$, $Q_{3\to1} = -2.91$ kJ (*c*) 6.7% (*d*) 35.5%

48 (*a*) $0.740\varepsilon_{max}$ (*b*) 1.68 GJ

49 (*a*) 6.3 (*b*) 3.2 kW (*c*) 5.3 kW

50 (*a*) 0.30 MJ (*b*) 0.21 MJ

51 (*a*) 0.17 MJ (*b*) 0.12 MJ. Because the temperature difference increases when the room is warmer, the COP decreases.

52 56 s

53 6.05 kJ/K

54 –22.0 J/K

55 $\Delta S_u = 2.40$ J/K and, because $\Delta S_u > 0$, the entropy of the universe increases.

56 (*a*) 11.5 J/K (*b*) 0

57 (*a*) 0 (*b*) 267 K

58 (*a*) 11.5 J/K (*b*) 11.5 J/K

59 (*a*) 244 kJ/K (*b*) −244 kJ/K (*c*) The entropy change of the universe is just slightly greater than zero.

60 (*a*) 10.1°C (*b*) 22 J/K

61 (*a*) −117 J/K (*b*) 138 J/K (*c*) 21 J/K

62 11 J/K

63 (*a*) 0.42 J/K (*b*) 125 J

64 (*a*) 5.76 J/K (*b*) $W_{\text{lost}} = 1.73$ kJ

65 (*a*) $W_{\text{cycle}} = 20.0$ J (*b*) $Q_{\text{h,cycle}} = 67$ J, $Q_{\text{c,cycle}} = 47$ J

66 (*a*) 16.7% (*b*) 0.777

67 (*a*) 51% (*b*) 0.10 MJ (*c*) 98 kJ

68 25 J/K

69 113 W/K

70 (*a*) 0.404 (*b*) 1.48 GW (*c*) 2.48 GW (*d*) 7.1×10^5 L/s

71 (*a*) You should explain to him that, because the efficiency he claims for his invention (83.3%) is greater than the efficiency of a Carnot engine operating between the same two temperatures, his data is not consistent with what is known about the thermodynamics of engines. He must have made a mistake in his analysis of his data–or he is a con man looking for suckers to swindle. (*b*) 135 W

72 60.0%

73 (*a*) Process (2) is more wasteful of ***available*** work. (*b*) $\Delta S_1 = 1.67$ J/K, $\Delta S_2 = 0.833$ J/K

74

(*a*)

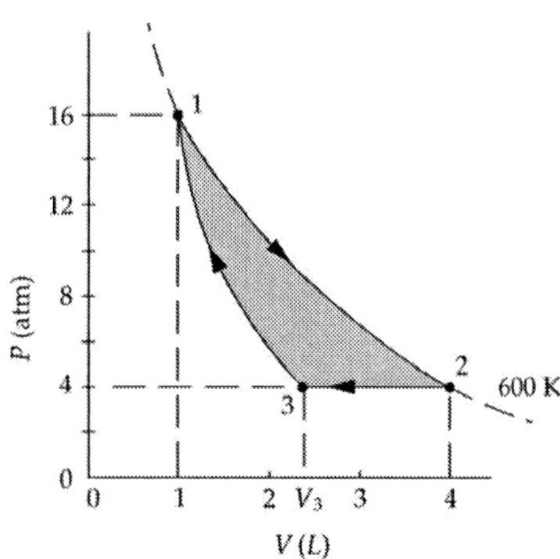

(*b*) 2.3 L, 3.4×10^2 K (*c*) 5 atm·L (*d*) about 20%

75 313 K

77 10 W

78 (*a*) 19.7 L (*b*) 39.4 L, 1200 K (*c*) 600 K (*d*) 223 L (*e*) 9.98 kJ, $W_{B-C} = 24.9$ kJ, $W_{C-A} = -24.2$ kJ (*f*) $Q_{A-B} = 34.9$ kJ, $Q_{B-C} = 0$, $Q_{C-A} = -24.2$ kJ

79 (*a*) 253 kPa (*b*) 462 K (*c*) 6.97 kJ

80 (*a*) 19.7 L (*b*) 39.4 L, 1200 K (*c*) 600 K (*d*) $V_C = 111$ L (*e*) $W_{A-B} = 9.98$ kJ, $W_{on,B-C} = 15.0$ kJ, $W_{C-A} = -17.3$ kJ (*f*) $Q_{in,A-B} = 24.9$ kJ, $Q_{B-C} = 0$, $Q_{C-A} = -17.3$ kJ

81 (*a*) 253 kPa (*b*) 416 K (*c*) 6.59 kJ

82 $\varepsilon_{Carnot} > \varepsilon_{Otto}$

83 (*a*)

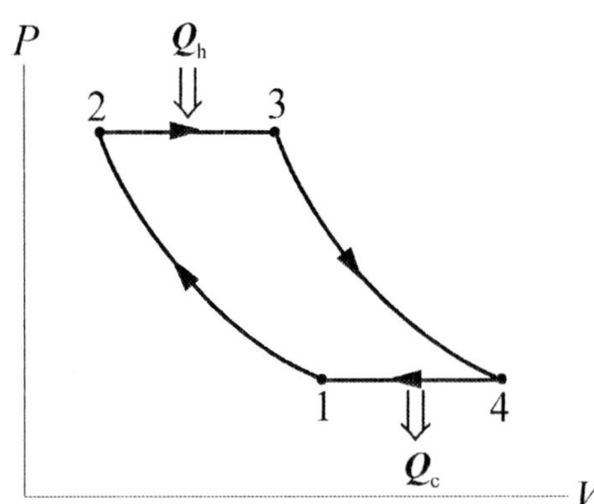

84 (*a*)

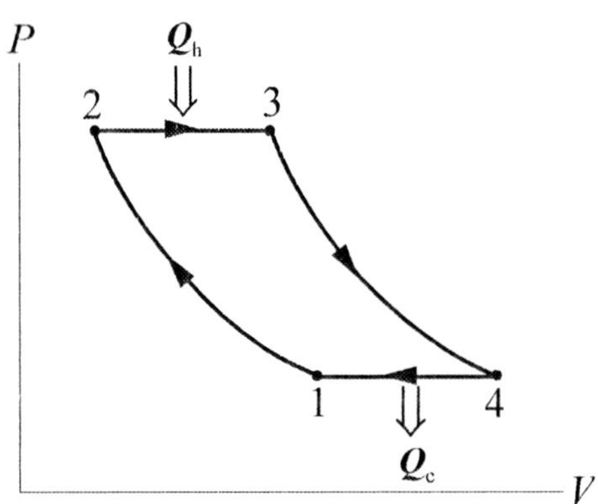

(*c*) 1.1 (*d*) 0.21 kW (*e*) about $4

86 (*c*) The heat-engine and refrigerator statements of the second law only state that *some* heat must be rejected to a cold reservoir and *some* work must be done to transfer heat from the cold to the hot reservoir, but these statements do not specify the minimum amount of heat rejected or work that must be done. The statement $\Delta S_u \geq 0$ is more restrictive. The heat-engine and refrigerator statements in conjunction with the Carnot efficiency are equivalent to $\Delta S_u \geq 0$.

89 $T = 10^{484}\ \text{y}, T \approx 10^{478} T_{\text{Russell}}$

Chapter 20
Thermal Properties and Processes

1 The glass bulb warms and expands first, before the mercury warms and expands.

2 (*b*)

3 Water expands greatly as it freezes. If a sealed glass bottle full of water is placed in a freezer, as the water freezes there will be no room for the expansion to take place. The bottle will be broken.

4 You should use the wooden ruler. Because the coefficient of expansion for wood is about half that for metal, the metal ruler will have shrunk considerably more than will have the wooden ruler.

5 The strip will curl more tightly.

6 (*b*)

7 (*c*)

8 Gases that cannot be liquefied by applying pressure at 20°C are those for which $T_c < 293$ K. These are He, Ar, Ne, H_2, O_2, NO.

9 (*a*) With increasing altitude, decreases; from curve OC, the temperature of the liquid-gas interface decreases as the pressure decreases, so the boiling temperature decreases. Likewise, from curve OB, the melting temperature increases with increasing altitude.
(*b*) Boiling at a lower temperature means that the cooking time will have to be increased.

10

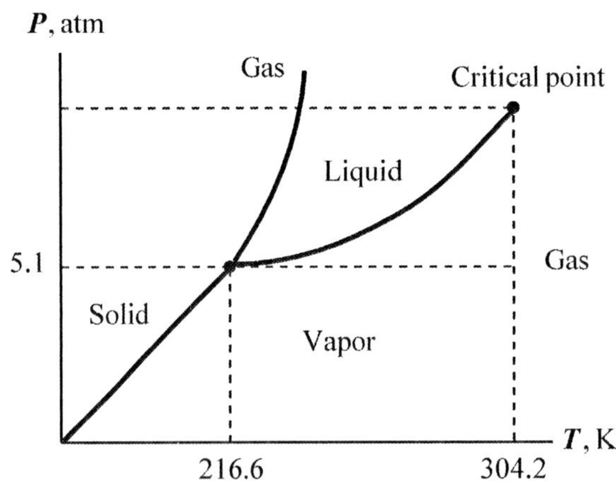

11 At very low pressures and temperatures, carbon dioxide can exist only as a solid or gas (or vapor above the gas). The atmosphere of Mars is 95 percent carbon dioxide. Mars, on average, is warm enough so that the atmosphere is mostly gaseous carbon dioxide. The polar regions are cold enough to enable solid carbon dioxide (dry ice) to exist, even at the low pressure.

12 The amount of heat lost by the house is proportional to the difference between the temperature inside the house and that of the outside air. Hence, the rate at which the house loses heat (that must be replaced by the furnace) is greater at night when the temperature of the house is kept high than when it is allowed to cool down.

13 (*a*)

14 (*d*)

15

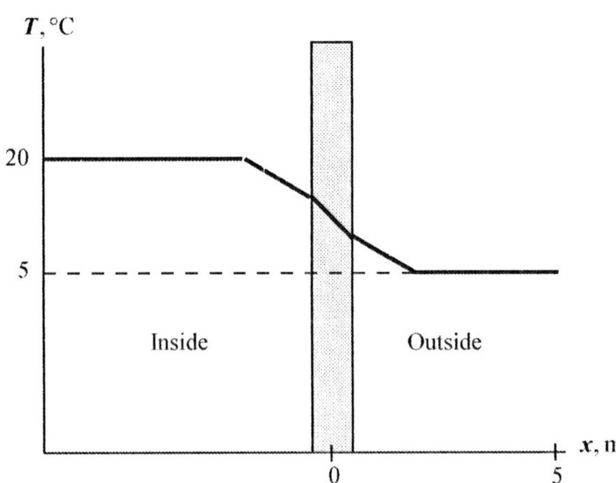

16 The tradeoff is the reduction of convection cells between the walls by putting in the solid insulation, versus a slight increase in conductivity. The net reduction in convection results in a higher *R* value.

17 Your assumption was not correct and 56 mL of water overflowed.

18 3.12 × 10–6 W/m·K

19 17 mW/ m·K

20 450 W. This result is almost four times greater than the basal metabolic rate of 120 W. We can understand the difference in terms of the temperature of your skin when you first step out of the sauna and the fact that radiation loses are dependent on the fourth power of the absolute temperature.

21 0.28 kW, 5.0, 0.14 K/W

22 0.61

23 2.9 nm

24 24%

25 $8\dfrac{\text{F}^\circ\cdot\text{h}\cdot\text{ft}^2}{\text{Btu}}$

26 (*a*) Because $T_\text{P} \propto \sqrt{L}$ and L is temperature dependent, the clock runs slow. (*b*) 8.2 s

27 220°C

28 580°C

29 $15 \times 10^{-6}\ \text{K}^{-1}$

30 0.8 L

31 $3.7 \times 10^{-12}\ \text{N/m}^2$

32 (*a*) 30.6 L (*b*) 375 K

33 (*a*) 90°C (*b*) 78°C (*c*) 127 kPa

34 $3.94 \times 10^{-23}\ \text{cm}^3$/atom, 0.211 nm

35 2.1 kBtu/h

36 (*a*) $R_{Cu} =$ 0.0831 K/W, $R_{Al} = 0.141$ K/W (*b*) 0.224 K/W (*c*) 0.36 kW (*d*) 70°C

37 (*a*) $I_{Cu} =$ 0.96 kW, $I_{Al} = 0.57$ kW (*b*) 1.53 kW(*c*) 0.052 K/W

40 9.47 μm

41 1.3 mm

42 4140 K $\leq T \leq$ 7250 K

43 93.5 cm^2

44 2.2×10^{-3} K/s

45 1598°C

46 97 g/h

47 2.1 km

49 5800 K

50 $0.39 \frac{\text{K} \cdot \text{m}^2}{\text{W}} = 2.2 \frac{\text{F}° \cdot \text{ft}^2 \cdot \text{h}}{\text{Btu}}$

51 (*b*) The values agree to within 0.3%

52 (*b*) 430 cm

53 1.3×10^{10} kW, The ratio of I/A to the solar constant is less than 0.002%.

54 101°C

55 142 W

56 $R = \dfrac{4L}{\pi k d_0^2 (1 + aL)}$

57 $L_2 = L_1$, $\omega_2 \approx (1 - 2\alpha\Delta T)\omega_1$, $E_2 = E_1(1 - 2\alpha\Delta T)$

58

Cell	Formula/Content	Algebraic Form
B1	255	
B4	0.4	e
B5	B4+0.01	$e + 0.1$
C4	\$B\$1/(B4^0.25)	$(255\,\mathrm{K})e^{-1/4}$

	A	B	C	D
1	$T=$	255	K	
2				
3		e	T	
4		0.40	321	
5		0.41	319	
6		0.42	317	
7		0.43	315	
23		0.59	291	
24		0.60	290	
25		0.61	289	
26		0.62	287	

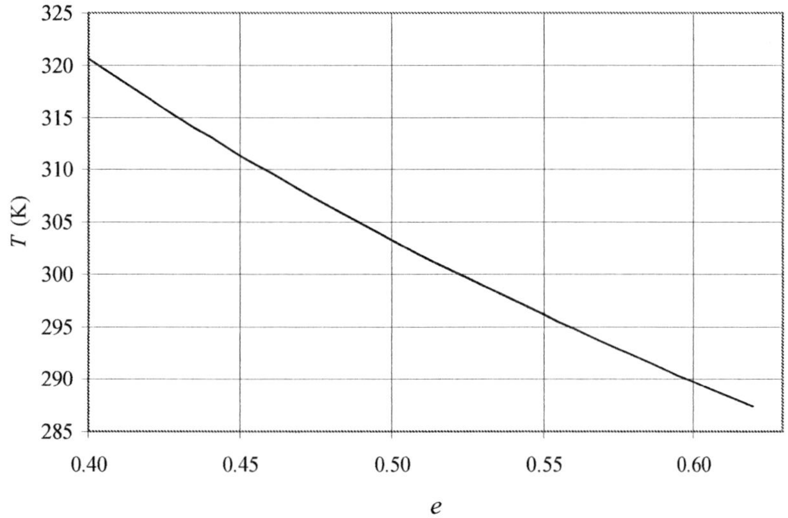

$\frac{\Delta e}{e} = -0.014$ or about a 1.4% change.

59 (*a*) 0.70 cm/h (*b*) 12 d

60

(*b*)

Cell	Formula/Content	Algebraic Form
B1	5.67×10^{-8}	σ
B2	6.00×10^{-4}	A
B3	3.45	C
B4	273	T_0
B5	10	Δt
A9	A8+$B$5	$t+\Delta t$
B9	B8-($B$1*$B$2/$B$3) *(B8^4–$B$4^4)*$B$5	$T_n - \frac{e\sigma A}{C}\left(T_n^4 - T_0^4\right)\Delta t$

	A	B	C
1	σ=	5.67E–08	$W/m^2{\cdot}K^4$
2	A=	6.00E–04	m^2
3	C=	3.45	J/K
4	T_0=	273	K
5	Δt=	10	s
6			
7	t (s)	T (K)	
8	0	573.00	
9	10	562.92	
10	20	553.56	
11	30	544.85	
248	2400	288.22	
249	2410	288.08	
250	2420	287.95	
251	2430	287.82	

From the spreadsheet solution, the time to cool to 15°C (288 K) is about 2420 s or 40.5 min.

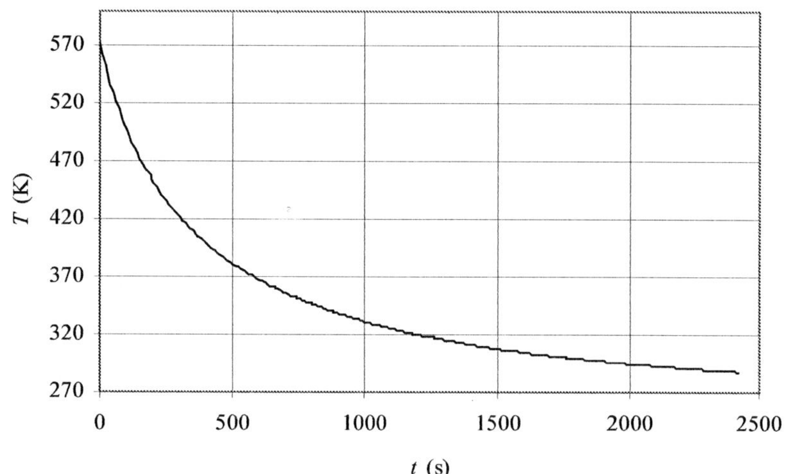
570
520
470
420
370
320
270
T (K)
0
500
1000
1500
2000
2500
t (s)